Philos: A Designation for the Jesus-Disciple Relationship
An Exegetico-Theological Investigation of the Term in the Fourth Gospel

European University Studies

Europäische Hochschulschriften
Publications Universitaires Européennes

Series XXIII

Theology

Reihe XXIII   Série XXIII
Theologie
Théologie

Vol./Bd. 475

PETER LANG

Frankfurt am Main · Berlin · Bern · New York · Paris · Wien

Eldho Puthenkandathil

Philos: A Designation for the Jesus-Disciple Relationship

An Exegetico-Theological Investigation of the Term in the Fourth Gospel

PETER LANG

Frankfurt am Main · Berlin · Bern · New York · Paris · Wien

Die Deutsche Bibliothek - CIP-Einheitsaufnahme

Puthenkandathil, Eldho:

Philos : a designation for the Jesus-disciple relationship ; an
exegetico-theological investigation of the term in the fourth
gospel / Eldho Puthenkandathil. - Frankfurt am Main ; Berlin ;
Bern ; New York ; Paris ; Wien : Lang, 1993
    (European university studies : Ser. 23, Theology ; Vol. 475)
    Zugl.: Rom, Univ., Gregoriana, Diss., 1992
    ISBN 3-631-45841-X

NE: Europäische Hochschulschriften / 23

ISSN 0721-3409
ISBN 3-631-45841-X

© Verlag Peter Lang GmbH, Frankfurt am Main 1993
All rights reserved.

Printed in Germany 1 2 3 4 5 6 7

This Dissertation is Dedicated

To The Loving Memory of

Most Rev. Zacharias Mar Athanasios

The Late Bishop of Tiruvalla

(1908-1977)

PREFACE

There are many who in one way or other have assisted or encouraged me in the completion of this dissertation. To all concerned I would like to express my profound feelings of gratitude.

First and foremost, I am indebted and grateful to Prof. José Caba S.J., the director of my dissertation, for his scholarly and exegetical excellence, critical and constructive advice, and friendly and continuous encouragement. I appreciate most his spirit of dedication and availability. My thanks go also to Prof. Edmond Farahian S.J., the relator of the dissertation for his critical and valuable observations.

I sincerely thank my Bishop, Most Rev. Dr. Cyril Mar Baselios, for giving me the opportunity to pursue my higher studies in Rome and for his scholarly advice and personal interest at every phase of my studies. My gartitude is due in a special way to the Congregation for the Oriental Churches for providing me with a scholarship for studies in Sacred Scriptures.

My sincere thanks go to all my Professors in the Paurastya Vidyāpīṭham, Kottayam, India and the Pontifical Biblical Institute, Rome for the biblical formation I have received from them and to the Library Staff for the facilities made available to me. I express my heartfelt gratitude also to Rev. Dr. Eugene J. Hayes, O. Praem, who helped me to improve the language and style of this work by patiently going through the manuscript. In a special way I wish to thank Rev. Fr. Peter M. Slors for his invaluable assistance and willingness to share his linguistical and patristic expertise. Sincere thanks to Collegio Damasceno and Collegio Olandese, where I could experience the spirit of love and the atmosphere of study. I am grateful to all my near and dear ones, who were near to me all through the years of preparation of this work. I am indebted to *Verlag Peter Lang* for their readiness to publish this dissertation in the "European University Studies" series.

TABLE OF CONTENTS

CHAPTER THREE
THE FRIENDSHIP BETWEEN JESUS
AND THE BETHANY FAMILY (Jn 11,1-46)

CHAPTER FOUR
YOU ARE MY FRIENDS AND I CALL YOU FRIENDS
(Jn 15, 1-17)

CHAPTER FIVE
THE BELOVED DISCIPLE AND PETER:
TWO MODELS OF TRUE FRIENDSHIP WITH JESUS
(Jn 13,21-30; 19,25-27; 20,1-10;
21,1-14; 21,20-24; 21,15-19)

CHAPTER SIX
FRIENDSHIP: JESUS - DISCIPLE RELATIONSHIP
(Synthetical Conclusions)

LIST OF ABBREVIATIONS

For the books of the Bible, we have followed the abbreviations of *the Holy Bible: Revised Standard Version - Catholic Edition* (London 1966) xi-xii. For the periodicals, reference works and series, the list of abbreviations given in the "Instructions for Contributors", *Biblica*, Vol 70 - Fasc.4 -1989 is followed as a guideline.

AJA	*American Journal of Archeology* (Princeton NJ)
AnBib	Analecta Biblica (Roma)
AndNewtQuart	*Andover Newton Quarterly* (Massachusetts)
AnGre	Analecta Gregoriana (Roma)
Anton	*Antonianum* (Roma)
AssembSeign	*Assemblées du Seigneur* (Bruges, Paris)
ATANT	Abhandlungen zur Theologie des Alten und Neuen Testaments (Zürich)
AusBR	*Australian Biblical Review* (Melbourne)
BBB	Bonner biblische Beiträge (Königstein)
BeO	*Bibbia e oriente* (Brescia)
Bib	*Biblica* (Roma)
BibLeb	*Bibel und Leben* (Düsseldorf)
BibOr	Biblica et orientalia (Roma)
BiTod	*The Bible Today* (Collegeville, Minnesota)
BK	*Bibel und Kirche* (Stuttgart)
BLit	*Bibel und Liturgie* (Wien-Klosterneuburg)
BT	*The Bible Translator* (Stuttgart)
BTB	*Biblical Theology Bulletin* (St. Bonaventure, New York)
BulBezanClub	Bulletin of the Bezan Club (Leiden)
BVC	*Bible et vie chrétienne* (Paris)
BWANT	*Beiträge zur Wissenschaft vom Alten und Neuen Testament* (Stuttgart)

BZ	*Biblische Zeitschrift* (Paderborn)
CahBib	*Cahiers bibliques* (Paris)
CB	*Cultura Bíblica* (Madrid-Segovia)
CBQ	*Catholic Biblical Quarterly* (Washington, D.C.)
CiTom	*Ciencia Tomista* (Salamanca)
CJT	*Canadian Journal of Theology* (Toronto)
ColctMech	Collectanea Mechlinensia (Mechlinae/Louvain)
CollBrug	*Collationes Brugenses* (Bruges)
CQR	*Church Quarterly Review* (London)
CristStor	*Cristianesimo nella Storia* (Bologna)
DeltBiblMelet	*Deltío Biblikôn Meletôn* (Athenai)
DNTT	*The New International Dictionary of New Testament Theology* (Michigan)
DownRev	*Downside Review* (Exeter)
EB	*Etudes bibliques* (Paris)
ErJb	*Eranos Jahrbuch* (Frankfut/M)
EstBíb	*Estudios bíblicos* (Madrid)
ETL	*Ephemerides theologicae Lovanienses* (Louvain)
ÉTR	*Etudes théologiques et religieuses* (Montpellier)
EvQ	*Evangelical Quarterly* (London)
ExpTim	*Expository Times* (Edinburgh)
FoiVie	*Foi et Vie* (Paris)
FRLANT	Forschungen zur Religion und Literatur des Alten und Neuen Testaments (Göttingen)
GCS	Griechische Christliche Schriftsteller (Leipzig)
GeistLeb	*Geist und Leben* (Würzburg)
HNT	Handbuch zum Neuen Testament (Tübingen)
ICC	International Critical Commentary (Edinburgh)
Int	*Interpretation* (Richmond, Virginia)
JB	*Jerusalem Bible*
JBL	*Journal of Biblical Literature* (Philadelphia)

JETS	*Journal of the Evangelical Theological Society* (Wheaton IL)
JNES	*Journal of Near Eastern Studies* (Chicago)
JSNT	*Journal for the Study of the New Testament* (Sheffield)
JSOR	*Journal of the Society of Oriental Research* (Chicago)
JTS	*Journal of Theological Studies* (Oxford, London)
LavThéolPhil	*Laval Théologique et Philosophique* (Québec)
LifeSpir	*Life of the Spirit* (Oxford)
LumVie	*Lumière et Vie* (Lyon)
LXX	The Septuagint
NEB	*The New English Bible*
Neot	*Neotestamentica* (Pretoria, NTWerk)
NGG	*Nachrichten der Gesselschaft der Wissenschaften in Göttingen* (Göttingen)
NT	The New Testament
NT	*Novum Testamentum* (Leiden)
NTD	Das Neue Testament Deutsch (Göttingen)
NTS	*New Testament Studies* (Cambridge)
OT	The Old Testament
PG	J. Migne, *Patrologia Graeca* (1857-1866)
PL	J. Migne, *Patrologia Latina* (1878-1890)
PSV	*Parola Spirito e Vita* (Bologna)
RB	*Revue biblique* (Jerusalem, Paris)
RéAug	*Revue des Études Augustiniennes* (Paris)
RechScienRel	*Recherches de Science Religieuse* (Paris)
RivB	*Rivista biblica* (Bologna)
RoczTK	Roczniki Teologiczno-Kanoniczne (Lublin)
RR	Review of Religion (London, Washington)
RSV	*The Revised Standard Version Catholic Edition*
RThPhil	*Revue de Théologie et de Philosophie* (Lausanne)

SANT	Studien zum Alten und Neuen Testament (München)
SBB	Stuttgarter biblische Beiträge (Stuttgart)
SBLDS	Society of Biblical Literature Dissertation Series (Chico, CA)
SBT	Studies in Biblical Theology (London)
Scr	*Scripture* (London)
SE	*Studia Evangelica I, II, III (=TU 73 [1959], 87 [1964], 88 [1964],* etc) (Oxford, Berlin)
SJT	*Scottish Journal of Theology* (Edinburgh)
SR	*Studies in Religion* (Waterloo)
SUNT	Studien zur Umwelt des Neuen Testaments (Göttingen)
TDNT	G. Kittel and G. Friedrich (eds.), *Theological Dictionary of the New Testament* (Michigan)
ThSt [B]	Theologische Studien [hrgs. Karl Barth] (Zollikon-Zürich)
ThR	*Theologische Rundschau* (Freiburg i.B.)
ThV	*Theologia Viatorum* (Berlin)
TLond	*Theology* (London)
TLZ	*Theologische Literaturzeitung* (Berlin)
TS	*Theological Studies* (Baltimore)
TTZ	*Trierer theologische Zeitschrift* (Trier)
TU	Text und Untersuchungen (Berlin)
VD	Verbum Domini (Roma)
VS	Verbum salutis (Paris)
ZKG	*Zeitschrift für Kirchengeschichte* (Stuttgart)
ZKT	*Zeitschrift für katholische Theologie* (Wien)
ZNW	*Zeitschrift für die neutestamentliche Wissenschaft* (Berlin)
ZTK	*Zeitschrift für Theologie und Kirche* (Tübingen)

GENERAL INTRODUCTION

The origin of the concept of "friend of God" is rooted in ancient Greek literature and in the OT.[1] History proves that divine-human friendship is not a utopian but rather a realistic idea which entails responsibility and privilege for both partners. The Biblical understanding of friendship between God and man is based on divine initiative and man's active co-operation with God. Only just men are called friends of God according to the doctrine of the Council of Trent.[2] Catholic theologians are unanimous on the idea that friendship with God is some way rooted in the gift of sanctifying grace.[3] The establishment of such Biblical and Catholic teaching concerning the intimate relationship between God and man serves as a corrective for the modern trend of reducing the relationship between Jesus and Christians to the level of pure human friendship. In such a context lies the relevance of the exegetico-theological study of the term φίλος in the Fourth Gospel as a designation for the Jesus-disciple relationship.

In the Fourth Gospel the Greek term φίλος (φίλοι) is found only six times (Jn 3,29; 11,11; 15,13.14.15;19,12). In majority of the cases the Evangelist uses it to express the theme of the friendship between Jesus and others. Such a friendship is the expression of Christian unity, a theme which is the kernel of Johannine thought. Unlike the other Evangelists, St. John presents Jesus as the friend of His own followers, rather than of sinners and tax-collectors. In

---

[1] Cf. G. STÄHLIN, φιλέω, *TDNT* IX, 146ff.; E. PETERSON, "Der Gottesfreund. Beiträge zur Geschichte eines religiösen Terminus", *ZKG* 42 (NF V) 2 (1923) 161ff.

[2] Cc Trident: Sess. VI: Decr. de iustificatione, Cap.7: Cf. H. DENZINGER & C. BANNWART (eds.), *Enchiridion Symbolorum, definitionum et declarationum de rebus fidei et morum* (Freiburg 1928³¹) 1528 (799). cf. 1535 (803).

[3] Cf. J.F. DEDEK, "Friendship with God", in: *New Catholic Encyclopedia*, Vol VI (Washington 1967) 207.

other words, according to John, only authentic Christian disciples can enter into a friendship with Him. By "disciples" he means not only the "Twelve", but all genuine Christian followers as well. The term φίλος is deeply theological in the Johannine presentation since it is employed by the Evangelist to depict the friendship between Jesus and the disciples. The revelation and faith, the central themes of the Fourth Gospel, solidify the interpersonal relationship between Jesus and the disciples. Since revelation and faith are intrinsically connected with the theological meaning of the term φίλος, our attempt to study the meaning of φίλος in the Fourth Gospel appears particularly relevant for the field of Johannine scholarship.

Field of Study and its Limits

As it is clear from the title of the study, the research will concentrate mainly on the term φίλος as the designation for the friendship between Jesus and the disciples (cf. Jn 3,29; 11,11; 15,13.14.15). Since our study is thematic, while making an investigation of the friendship between Jesus and the disciples in the Fourth Gospel, we consider also the Beloved-Disciple texts (Jn 13,21-30; 19,25-27; 20,1-10; 21,1-14; 21,20-24) and the one Petrine text (Jn 21,15-19), in which the Beloved Disciple and Peter are presented in intimate relationship to Jesus. Likewise the verbs ἀγαπᾶν and φιλεῖν, in so far as they are used in the context of the theme of the friendship between Jesus and the disciples, will be analyzed. However a detailed study of these verbs does not come within the scope of our research. Finally, and as has been stated above, even though the term φίλος is used in 19,12 it is not an object of this study since it is not connected with the theme under consideration. [4]

Methodology of the Thesis

The methodology followed will be the *Redaction Critical Method*, that is to say, an analysis of the individual texts in their context and in the context of the whole Gospel by emphasizing the theology of the Evangelist (final redactor) so as to give a detailed and total picture of the theme. Each text will be analyzed in its particular context, with great attention to literary style and historical

---

[4] The Fourth Evangelist adopts the term φίλος in Jn 19,12 not in the same sense as he uses it in other instances. Connected with the name of the king it acquires a nuance different from all other usages in the Fourth Gospel. In later Roman usage the expression " φίλος τοῦ Καίσαρος " (friend of Caesar) is generally understood as a honorific title bestowed in recognition of service. Even though J.H. Bernard (cf. *A Critical and Exegetical Commentary on the Gospel according to St. John* (ICC), A.H. McNEILE (ed.) Vol II (Edinburgh 1985) 621) says that the official title is not found before the time of Vespasian (A.D. 69-79) other authors (cf. E. BAMMEL, " Φίλος τοῦ Καίσαρος ", *TLZ* 77 (1952) 205-210; A. DEISSMANN (rev. ed.), *Light from the Ancient East* (New York 1927) 378) argue for a much earlier use of the title. Hence the term φίλος in 19,12 can be understood as an official title. Moreover, in Hellenistic times the "friends of the king" were a special group of people honored by the king for loyalty and entrusted by him with authority (cf. 1 Mac 2,18; 3,38; 10,65; 2 Mac 6,22-23; Josephus, *Antiquitates Judaicae*, XII. vii. 3, 298). The coins of Herod Agrepa I (A.D. 37-44) frequently bear the inscription PHILOKAISAR, "friend of Caesar" (cf. Philo, *In Flaccum*, VI, 40). R.E. Brown (cf. *The Gospel according to John*, Vol II (New York 1970) 879-880) gives further arguments in favor of considering φίλος in Jn 19,12 as an imperial title. In the light of all the above mentioned arguments we see this Johannine usage as the honorary traditional title of Pilate. Therefore, a study of φίλος to establish the nature of Jesus-disciple relationship need not include an analysis of Jn 19,12. Since φίλος in 19,12 is an official title, its exclusion in the context of the present research seems appropriate and will not in any way lessen the value of the theological conclusions which are presented.

background. Then there will follow a synthesis in so far as it helps to bring out the theological implications of the theme.

Division and Contents of the Work

The study will be divided into **six chapters**. The **first chapter** deals with the etymological and historical development of the term φίλος outside the Fourth Gospel. Since this chapter serves only as an introduction and background to the study of the term φίλος in the Fourth Gospel, no particular text is analyzed here. The origin and meaning of the term φίλος in non-biblical antiquity will be treated as a preliminary to the study of the OT use of the term φίλος as it refers both to human friendship and divine-human friendship. The figures of Abraham and Moses particularly will be considered as the exemplary figures who enjoyed a true friendship with God. As an important background to the study, the use of the term φίλος in other NT texts which refer to the friendship between Jesus and the disciples will also be considered.

Chapter two initiates the study of the term φίλος in the Fourth Gospel. Since the term occurs first in Jn 3,29, there will be an exegetico-theological study of the entire pericope that extends from 3,22 to 3,36. Because the expression ὁ φίλος τοῦ νυμφίου is a historically and theologically rich one, we shall explain it rather fully in its historical and theological background.

Chapter three deals with the friendship between Jesus and the Bethany family. We study Jn 11,1-46 as a unit in which the interpersonal relationship of friendship is illustrated. It is in Jn 11,11 that the second Johannine use of the term φίλος, applied to Lazarus, is found. However the study is not limited only to this expression, but rather considers all the expressions of friendship on the part of Jesus towards the members of the Bethany family and their reciprocal responses to that friendship with Jesus. Such an analysis will illustrate the theological depth of the friendship between Jesus and the Bethany family.

Chapter four considers Jn 15,1-17, the well known Johannine text on the theme of unity and friendship. It is specifically in Jn 15,13.14.15 we see the repeated use of the term φίλος in its reciprocal sense, a usage which is a key to the development of a Johannine theology of the friendship between Jesus and the disciples. Jesus calls His disciples "friends" on the basis of His revelation to them and he invites them to experience that friendship by keeping His commandments especially the commandment of fraternal love. In the Johannine presentation the teaching of Jesus on friendship is illustrated best by consideration of the background of the *mashal*[5] of the vine and branches, an imagery of interpersonal relationship. Accordingly, this chapter then establishes the textual unity of the pericope, Jn 15,1-17. After treating the textual problems and literary genre the historical and theological background of the imagery of the vine and branches will be traced. Then we shall proceed to the analysis of the *mashal* of the vine and branches as an imagery of inter-personal relationship on two levels: that of the *mashal* itself and then its application.

In **chapter five** we introduce the Beloved Disciple and Peter as two models of true friendship with Jesus. As a support for this assertion there will be an exegesis of the "Beloved disciple texts" (Jn 13,21-30; 19,25-27; 20,1-14; 21,20-24) and the one "Petrine text" (Jn

---

[5] *Mashal* is a literary term applied to Jn 15,1-17 to explain its literary genre. The features of this literary term and its relevance in the context of Jn 15 will be treated later when we deal with that text itself.

21,15-19), in which the intimacy of this true friendship is well depicted by use of the verbs φιλεῖν and ἀγαπᾶν. Each pericope will be studied in its context, giving due attention to the expressions of friendship between Jesus and these two representative figures, which in one sense provides the foundation for the Johannine theology of Jesus-disciple friendship.

The concluding chapter of the study, **chapter six**, presents a theological synthesis based on conclusions presented in the preceding chapters. As a synthesis of the entire study it will propose systematically the Johannine theology which forms the basis for the use of the term φίλος in the Fourth Gospel. There will be a comparison with and contrast between the Fourth Gospel and other Biblical texts regarding the use of the term φίλος. In this concluding chapter, in the light of our exegesis the essential nature of the friendship between Jesus and the disciples as envisaged by St. John will be presented.

Originality of the Thesis

Even though many studies had already been done on the Greek verbs φιλεῖν and ἀγαπᾶν, no scientific doctoral study has ever been done on the substantive form φίλος in the Fourth Gospel in its theological perspective as designating the friendship between Jesus and the disciples.[6] Since this work is thematic and theological in nature it is not limited to the use of the term φίλος, but rather goes further to include its verbal forms as far as they illustrate a close

---

[6] We do not ignore the studies done on certain individual Johannine texts which are within the scope of our present research. For example, the doctoral dissertation of L. INFANTE, *L'amico dello Sposo, Figura del Ministero di Giovanni Battista nel Vangelo di Giovanni* (Roma 1982) is an exegetico-theological study of Jn 3,22-4,2.

relationship with Jesus. In the selection of the texts herein we claim an originality since they include all the key texts which present the depth of the Johannine theology concerning Jesus-disciple relationship as friendship. We claim also a certain novelty in the process of exegesis as we follow a thematic approach rather than a mere philological or verse-by-verse analysis. Thus, both in the presentation and development of the theme there are elements which are original. Finally it is our intention, that this study will be a genuine contribution to the understanding of the Johannine theology on the friendship between Jesus and the disciples, a theme which is especially relevant even in modern times.

CHAPTER ONE

THE UNDERSTANDING OF THE TERM ΦΙΛΟΣ
AND THE THEME OF FRIENDSHIP
OUTSIDE THE FOURTH GOSPEL

Introduction

A general idea of the pre-Johannine understanding of the term φίλος facilitates the exegetico-theological study of the term in the Fourth Gospel which is the scope of the present dissertation. Hence, as a preliminary to the investigation of the term φίλος in the Gospel of John one has to examine its etymological and historical development. Accordingly, the origin and development of φίλος in non-biblical antiquity, its diverse usage in the OT, in the inter-testamental literature, and in the NT other than the Fourth Gospel will be briefly treated in the present chapter.

I. The Term φίλος in Non-Biblical Antiquity
A. The Etymological Meaning

The term φίλος finds its origin in the context of non-biblical antiquity. It is used both in ancient Greek and Roman literature to denote the interpersonal relationship among the human beings and between God and man. The etymological origin of φίλος is from the root ΦΙΛ . It is used first as an adjective in ancient Greek literature, especially in the writings of Homer [1] where it means "intrinsic", "proper to", "beloved", "dear" etc. As a noun φίλος originally means "his own", "relatives" etc. and later it acquires the

---

[1] Cf. HOMER, *Iliad*, 20, 347f.

meaning "friend"[2] in its various nuances.[3] The term ἑταῖρος was used in antiquity as corresponding to φίλος.[4] But some distinction was made when they were used in pairs. Terms such as ἴδιος, οἰκεῖος, γνώριμος and γνωστός were used identically with φίλος. So also συγγενής is a term connected with φίλος from early time onwards.

---

[2] Cf. M. LANDFESTER, *Das griechische Nomen "philos"und seine Ableitungen* (Spudasmata 11) (Hildesheim 1966) 71ff.

[3] The various nuances according to the relationship are depicted as follows: "personal friend" (cf. Sophocles, *Philoctetes*, 421; Aristotle, *Ethica Nicomachea*, IX, 11, p. 1171b, 2), the "loved one" in a homo-erotic sense (cf. Xenophon, *Respublica Lacedaemoniorum*, 2, 13), "the lover" (cf. Plato, *Phaedrus*, 255b), the "favorite", especially of Gods (cf. Aeschylus, *Promethus Vinctus*, 304), "ally" (cf. Xenophon, *Historia Graeca*, VI, 5, 48), "followers" of a political leader [cf. Plutarch, *Apophthegmata Pisistratus*, 1(II, 189b)], "friends" ("clients") who cluster around a prominent and wealthy man; in contrast to the equal relation in personal friendship. The most characteristic development of such use is in φίλοι τοῦ βασιλέως (cf. W. Dittenberger, *Orientis Graecae Inscriptiones*, I, 100, 1f.). Usually φίλοι is used as a self-designation for a philosophical or religious fellowship (cf. Pythagoreans, Epicureans etc.): Cf. G. STÄHLIN, φίλος κτλ., *TDNT* IX, 147; M. PAESLACK, "Zur Bedeutungsgeschichte der Wörter φιλεῖν, φιλία, φίλος in der LXX und im Neuen Testament unter Brücksichtigung ihrer Beziehungen zu ἀγαπᾶν, ἀγάπη, ἀγαπητός", *ThV* 5 (1953-54) 53-56.

[4] The noun ἑταῖρος was understood in antiquity as "one who is linked to another" which has different nuances according to the context. Plutarch (*Convivalium Disputationum*, I, 4 [II, 622b]) and Philo (*De Somniis*, II, 245) used it corresponding to φίλος in the sense of friend or companion. In the LXX ἑταῖρος translates Heb. רֵעַ (friend, fellow) whereas in other Greek translations of the OT it occasionally replaces the terms πλησίον, φίλος and ἀδελφός found in the LXX. In the NT ἑταῖρος is found only three times in the Gospel of Mathew. In all the three cases it is in vocative case and the person speaking is addressing an inferior who has insulted him in some way. Hence, in the NT there is no correspondence between φίλος and ἑταῖρος. Cf. D.A. CARSON, ἑταῖρος, *DNTT* I, 259-260.

B. The Term φίλος and the Theme of Friendship

Since the term φίλος etymologically means "friend", it was used in the ancient Greek and Roman literature in the context of the theme of relationship and friendship. The ancient Greek naturalists employed the term φίλος and its derivatives to explain the principle of attraction in nature. With Socrates the Greek thought began to restrict the use of the term to explain the relationship between persons who are related on the basis of certain psychological aspects.[5] The friendship between older and younger man was practiced and praised by Socrates.[6]

After Socrates both Plato and Aristotle used φίλος as a designation for their disciples. Aristotle portrayed the concept of friendship in classical antiquity by way of a series of maxims and proverbs (cf. *Ethica Nicomachea*, IX, 8. p.1168b, 6-8). Different from his predecessors he restricts friendship (φιλία) to a type of accord among human persons and distinguishes it from the love (φίλησις).[7] For him friendship thrives only when there is a community of living, characterized by a perfect association and communication between the partners.[8] The communication aspect in friendship is explained by the Greek philosophers differently. For example, Pythagoreans saw it as a community of resources while Aristotle considered it as a community of likes and interests.

---

[5] Cf. W.A. WALLACE, "Friendship", *New Catholic Encyclopedia*, Vol VI (Washington 1967) 203.

[6] Stählin considers this relationship as one corresponding to the relationship between the teacher and a student. Cf. STÄHLIN, φίλος, *TDNT*, Vol IX, 152.

[7] Cf. WALLACE, *Friendship*, 203.

[8] Cf. *Ibid.*, 204.

Epicureans and Stoics viewed it as a community of philosophical
beliefs. The idea of personal friends is important among the Greeks
and for them real friendship is possible only with a few.[9]

In Roman society the idea of friendship was well respected.
Cicero based his notion of friendship on the instinct for sociability
which is found in man, defining it as a perfect agreement of wills,
tastes, and thoughts accompanied by benevolence and affection.[10]
Friendship is really enduring since it is based on virtue. A true
friend must be another self and therefore if one desires to find
friends, he must become good himself and then seek out someone
similar.[11]

The concept of the "friend of God" developed already in pre-
christian literature.[12] In the *Vita Homeri*, 143 attributed to Plutarch
one reads: οἱ Στωικοὶ φίλους θεῶν τοὺς ἀγαθοὺς ἄνδρας
ἀποφαίνοντες παρ᾽ Ὁμήρου καὶ τοῦτο ἔλαβον.[13] The concept of
"friend of God" is much more evident in the writings of Xenophon
where he explicated the idea of man's friendship with God (cf.
Symposium, IV, 46ff.). For him virtue (ἀρετή) makes men friends of
God (cf. *Memorabilia*, II, 1.33). Plato's idea of divine-human
friendship is noteworthy. According to him friendship originates on

---

[9] Cf. STÄHLIN, φίλος, *TDNT* IX, 152.

[10] Cicero writes: "...id in quo omnis vis est amicitiae, voluntatum studiorum
sententiarum summa consensio" (*De Amicitia*, IV, 15). He continues, "Est enim
amicitia nihil aliud nisi omnium divinarum humanarumque rerum cum benevolentia
et caritate consensio" (*De Amicitia*, VI, 20).

[11] Cf. WALLACE, *Friendship*, 204.

[12] Cf. PETERSON, *Gottesfreund*, 161-172.

[13] Cf. *Ibid.*, 161.

the part of God (cf. *Leges*, IV, 716 CD).[14] Aristotle also wrote about the human friendship with God (cf. *Ethica Nicomachea*, VIII, 7,4f.).

II. The Term φίλος in the OT

The Greek OT (LXX) employs the term φίλος 70 times as the translation of different Hebrew terms: רֵעַ (רִיעַ), מֵרֵעַ, אָהַב, חָבֵר, אַלּוּף. In more than 30 instances φίλος translates the Hebrew term רֵעַ[15] and 27 times it is the translation for אָהַב. In the LXX φίλος is used in its various nuances, viz. the very intimate personal friend (Deut 13,6(7); the friend of the house (Prov 27,10); friend of the bridegroom or "best man" (1 Mac 9,39); the client or political supporter (Est 6,13), as a title "friend of the king" (1 Chron 27,33) etc.[16] The term φίλος is also used with certain synonymous terms such as ἀδελφός, ἑταῖρος, οἰκεῖος, σύμβουλος, γνωστοί, γείτων.

The OT gives excellent examples of human friendship and divine-human friendship. Even though the term φίλος is not directly employed in all such cases one can consider a few examples of

---

[14] Cf. *Ibid.*, 164.

[15] At the conceptual level the terms רֵעַ and φίλος are not used in the same sense. When the LXX authors translated רֵעַ with φίλος they had the Greek concept of friendship in mind. Hence, the Alexandrian translators, who thought of friendship in Hellenistic categories employed φίλος for רֵעַ.

[16] Cf. STÄHLIN, φίλος, *TDNT* IX, 154. The expression φίλος τοῦ καίσαρι in Jn 19,12 is generally understood as the title for the king's officer as a friend and originated already in antiquity.

intimate friendship in the OT which will help to portray the sense of friendship between Jesus and His disciples illustrated in the Fourth Gospel by using the term φίλος.

A. The Term φίλος Referring to Human Friendship

In the OT there are some of the finest instances of friendship designated by the term φίλος at least in its etymological nuances. Accordingly Jonathan and David were considered as intimate friends (2 Sam 1,26; cf. also 1 Sam 18,1.3; 19,1; 20,17)[17] and their friendship can be seen in the light of the ancient Greek concept of friendship where idea of the "pair of friends" is evident.[18] The real nature of their friendship is clear in 1 Sam 19,1-7 where one notices the "sharing of knowledge" (revelation) as one of the main expressions of friendship (cf. v.3). The love of friendship between Jonathan and David is compared to one's love of his own soul (1 Sam 18,1-2).[19] So also the ancient idea of sealing the friendship with a solemn pact is an evident expression of their friendship (cf. 1 Sam 18,3ff.). Their friendship is sealed with a symbolic act of handing over the cloak and weapons to David and thereby David is made the *alter ego* of his

---

[17] Since φίλος has the nuance of "beloved", a relationship between Jonathan and David designated through the expression "loved as his own soul" refers to a friendship which is same as that expressed through φίλος.

[18] Cf. STÄHLIN, φίλος, *TDNT* IX, 156.

[19] There is supreme love among intimate friends and a friend is depicted as one's own soul (Deut 13, 6(7). It is true when one considers the etymological meaning of the term φίλος as a part of body in the sense of "intrinsic", "proper to" etc. Cf. supra, pp. 9-10.

friend Jonathan. [20] This ceremony usually involved an oath before Yahweh, expressly mentioned here in 1 Sam 20,16ff. The oath includes a responsibility, a reciprocal response to the love and friendship.

B. The Term φίλος Referring to Divine-Human Friendship

In the OT the term φίλος is used also to express the relationship between God and man. There are certain texts which present the divine-human relationship in terms of friendship. [21] In order to understand better the nature of such a friendship one has to consider the figures of Abraham and Moses who are presented as friends of God.

1. Abraham as Friend of God

There are certain OT texts which directly or indirectly present Abraham as a friend of God. It is a fact that the LXX does not use the term φίλος as a designation for Abraham's relationship with God. However, certain ancient versions of the OT and Hellenist writings present Abraham as a friend of God also by employing the term φίλος. For example, Gen 18,17 is translated by Philo with the

---

[20] Cf. STÄHLIN, φίλος, *TDNT* IX, 156.

[21] In the OT the divine-human relationship is depicted in the covenant relationship between Yahweh and His people. The covenant relationship can be understood mainly under the aspect of friendship. According to Barrosse, "Covenant-partners can certainly be called friends": T. BARROSSE, *Christianity: Mystery of Love: An Essay in Biblical Theology* (Notre Dame, Indiana 1964) 11.

expression φίλος Θεοῦ μου as a designation for Abraham (cf. *De Sobrietate*, M. I, 401). Is 41,8 is translated by LXX with the expression σπέρμα Αβρααμ, ὅν ἠγάπησα which has another reading with φίλος.[22] So also 2 Chron 20,7 in the LXX utilizes the expression σπέρματι Αβρααμ τῷ ἠγαπημένῳ σου which is translated in the Vulgata as "semini Abraham amici tui". Against the background of the above mentioned OT texts St. James considers Abraham as a friend of God (cf. Jas 2,23). Hence, one can say that Abraham enjoys a close personal relationship with God and he is given the accolade "friend of God".[23] The reciprocity of the friendship is evident in the case of Abraham's friendship with God. The complete revelation on the part of God and Abraham's reciprocal response through faith and obedience are the main elements of their friendship.

a. The Complete Divine Revelation to Abraham

From the very beginning of Abraham's divine call God appeared as one who constantly revealed His plan to Abraham (cf. Gen 12,1ff.). God's constant and complete revelation to Abraham is expressly mentioned in Gen 18,17 where God's decision to communicate to Abraham what He had in mind dressed in the form of a question. The basis of the divine decision to communicate

---

[22] Cf. FIELD, *Hexapla*, Vol II, 513, where it reads: σπέρμα ʿΑβρᾶαμ τοῦ φίλου μου (Symmachus); cf. also Vol I, 744.

[23] Cf. B.W. ANDERSON, "Abraham , the friend of God", *Int* 42 (1988) 363. Even today the Muslims call Abraham in Arabic language as *'al-Chalîl* which means "the friend (of God)". The city of Abraham, Hebron is also known after this denomination as *'al-Chalîl*: Cf. L. BAUER, *Wörterbuch des palästinischen Arabisch. Deutsch-Arabisch* (Leipzig/Jerusalem 1933) 419.

everything to Abraham is nothing but the promise which he received from God (v.18) and the divine choice and commission connected with it (v.19). V.17 manifests God's reflection which seems to be a preparation for the divine communication depicted in the following verses of the pericope. [24] The "promise made long ago" raises Abraham to the level of friendship with God and makes him worthy to share God's plan. In the particular context of the text God communicates to His friend His decision to destroy the city (vv.17-19). The expression "what I am about to do" sheds light on the divine plan explained in the following verses. God's revelation to Abraham can be considered as an expression of their close relationship. [25] The divine revelation presupposed a relationship of trust which is qualified as friendship between God and Abraham (cf. 2 Chron 20,7; Is 41,8).

b. The Exemplary Faith and Obedience of Abraham

Abraham's response to the divine friendship based on revelation is verified in his exemplary faith and obedience. Both the OT and the NT present Abraham as the Father of faith due to his complete surrender to the divine will by way of his faith and obedience (cf. Gen 12,4; 15,6; Rom 4,1ff.; Gal 3,6; Jas 2,21-23). The faith of

---

[24] Cf. C. WESTERMANN, *Genesis 12-36:A Commentary*, J.J. SCULLION (trs.) (Minneapolis 1985) 288.

[25] Cf. *Ibid.*, 290. About God's reflection he writes: "because Abraham enjoys such esteem, I will make him privy to my plans". According to Von Rad God's act in history which otherwise was hidden from man, was revealed to Abraham who was called into "a relationship of trust" with God. Cf. G. VON RAD, *Genesis: A Commentary* (Old Testament Library) (London 1985) 210.

Abraham primarily means faithful obedience to the will of God.[26]
Faith is a venture which one undertakes without any proof and since
Abraham responded positively to God's call by believing the promise
of God (Gen 15,1) he will be called the Father of faith.[27] The
positive response of Abraham is evident in different phases of his
life, viz. when he undertakes the mission which God entrusted to
him together with a promise (Gen 12,1-4); when he believes God's
promise concerning the conception of Sarah (Gen 17,15ff.);when he
shows his readiness to sacrifice his only son Isaac in accordance with
the command of God (Gen 22,2ff.) etc. It is Abraham's privileged
position as one who was in intimate relationship with God which
gave him courage to stand before God and discuss with Him the way
of His justice.[28]

In the light of the OT texts referring to Abraham St. James
presents Abraham as φίλος Θεοῦ (friend of God) (Jas 2,23).[29] Here
he connects the title φίλος θεοῦ with Abraham's faith and
righteousness (obedience). St. James seems to intend that Abraham,
because of his works (eg. the sacrifice of Isaac) and his faith, was
called "friend of God".[30] In this context the patristic interpretation

---

[26] The faith of Abraham was expressed through his obedience to the divine will.
Obedience and listening are the same. The Hebrew verb שׁמע (to hear, to listen)
is the great creedal affirmation of Judaism (cf. Deut 6,4-5). Cf. ANDERSON,
Abraham, 358ff.; PETERSON, *Gottesfreund*, 188; STÄHLIN, φίλος, *TDNT* IX,
254; W. BAIRD, "Abraham in the New Testament, Tradition and the New Identity",
Int 42 (1988) 368ff.

[27] Cf. ANDERSON, *Abraham*, 360-362.

[28] Cf. *Ibid.*, 363.

[29] Since Jas 2,23 is directly connected with the OT portrayal of Abraham, we
discuss it here in connection with the OT understanding of φίλος.

[30] Cf. PETERSON, *Gottesfreund*, 173.

on Jas 2,23 is noteworthy.[31] For example, St. Basil comments on the text as follows: φίλος θεοῦ ὁ μακάριος ᾿Αβραὰμ καὶ εἴρηται καὶ ἔστι· Φίλος διὰ πίστιν, Φίλος δὶ ὑπακοὴν θεοῦ.[32] Here ὑπακοὴν (obedience) is used instead of ἔργα (works). So also Clement of Alexandria writes that Abraham διὰ πίστιν καὶ φιλοξενίαν (through faith and hospitality) became the friend of God.[33] Considering the interpretation of the Fathers, one can conclude that St. James affirms the OT title of Abraham, "the friend of God" on the basis of Abraham's deep faith and obedience (obedient works).

2. Moses as Friend of God

Besides Abraham, Moses was also portrayed in the OT as a friend of God (cf. Ex 33,11; Num 12,8; Deut 34,10). The designation "friend of God" is applied to Moses by considering the intimate relationship between God and Moses mainly in terms of revelation.[34] The Fathers of the Church in general present the figure of Moses as a friend of God when they comment on the above mentioned OT texts.[35] The reciprocal nature of friendship between God and Moses

---

[31] *Ibid.*, 174.

[32] Cf. *Adversus Eunomium*, V, 2, 33, in: *PG* 29, 752. Basil's authorship of *Adversus Eunomium*, IV-V, however, is contested: Cf. E. CAVALCANTI, *Studi Eunomiani* (Roma 1976) 55-66.

[33] Cf. CLEMENS ALEXANDRINUS, *Stromateis* IV, 17, 105,3, in: O. STÄHLIN (ed.), *GCS* 2 (Leipzig 1909).

[34] Cf. PETERSON, *Gottesfreund*, 172.

[35] Peterson refers to the patristic witnesses regarding the title of Moses as "friend of God": Cf. PETERSON, *Gottesfreund*, 176-177.

is well depicted in the OT where God's full and direct revelation to
Moses and Moses' life of obedience, faith and trust are duly
considered.

a. The Complete Divine Revelation to Moses

Direct communication and a total sharing are characteristics of
friendship also verified in the case of God's relationship with Moses.
God revealed Himself to Moses in the theophany of the burning
bush at Horeb (Ex 3,1-22). In Ex 33,11 the term φίλος is used to
depict the depth of relationship between God and Moses where the
co-relationship between revelation and friendship is highlighted. The
Hebrew expressions פָּנִים אֶל פָּנִים (Ex 33,11; Deut 34,10) and אֶל פֶּה
פֶּה (Num 12,8) usually denote the equality of rank and a complete
transparency. Connected with the verb of saying they denote the
immediacy and a total revelation. As a partner in friendship God
revealed Himself directly to Moses.[36] In the context of the OT
presentation God's direct and complete revelation to Moses is an
expression of God's friendship with Moses.

b. The Obedience, Faith and Trust on the Part of Moses

The OT portrays Moses as one closely related to God and
functioning as a mediator between God and the people of Israel.
Moses believed God's words with great trust and in faith followed

---

[36] According to Gray, even 'friendship' is an acceptable image for the relationship
between God and Moses. Cf. G.B. GRAY, *A Critical and Exegetical Commentary
on Numbers* (I.C.C.) (Edinburgh 1903) 137.

God's paths as revealed to him. So also, Moses obeyed the command of God to deliver the people of Israel from the Egyptian captivity. Even in despair he reproached God for the impossible task and received the renewed promise of God's help (Ex 6,1-7,7). Moses showed deep faith and trust in the power of God who called him for the task of liberating Israel. God's direct and full revelation of His salvific plans to Moses as to an intimate friend does not take away his responsibility, rather it requires from him a trustful attitude of fulfilling the divine will. Hence, the friendship between God and Moses was highly theological since it involves reciprocity in relationship based on divine revelation and Moses' faith and obedience.

3. "Friends of God" in the Wisdom Literature

The Wisdom literature, especially Proverbs and Sirach, adopt the term φίλος and its derivatives to denote "friends" and "friendship". They mainly speak of dubious friends (cf. Sir 6,15-17) and warn against unreliable friends (cf. Sir 37,2; 5,15). The idea of unreliable friends and friendship in the Wisdom literature seems to be a development from the concept of friendship in Greek philosophy.[37] The Wisdom literature connects friendship with wisdom (Wis 8,18). The OT idea of "friends of God" is also expressly mentioned in the book of Wisdom (Wis 7,27; 7,14). The statement that "she (Wisdom) passes into holy souls and makes them friends of God,

---

[37] Many statements in both the Greek wisdom and in the OT Wisdom literature refer to bad experiences with unreliable friends. According to them most friends are egoists and therefore only the fortunate (cf. Sir 12,9) and the rich (cf. Prov 14,20) have many friends. Cf. STÄHLIN, φίλος, *TDNT* IX, 157.

and prophets" (Wis 7,27) illustrates the divine initiative and human response in the divine-human friendship.[38] Hence, the reciprocity in divine-human friendship is evident here since wisdom represents divine revelation and holiness of souls presupposes human response to the divine will.

III. Friendship in the Inter-Testamental Literature

In Palestinian Judaism there existed certain forms of friendship which were different from Greek understanding of friendship.[39] In Rabbinic Judaism the relationship between the students and the teachers of the Law (Torah) was characterized as friendship.[40] In the Judaism of the NT times the idea of friendship as close and comprehensive fellowship is found in the Qumran community. But, since there existed a separation and gradation among the members and novices in the Qumran community the concept of friendship cannot be applied to them in its strict sense.[41]

Philo developed the idea of friendship, especially divine-human friendship, in the line of the OT (cf. *De Fuga et Inventione*, 58; *De Plantatione*, 90). He presents Moses and Abraham as friends of God in the light of their intimate relationship with God as found in the

---

[38] Commenting on Wis 7,14.27 Dedek writes that those who perfectly observe God's law are called friends of God. Cf. DEDEK, *Friendship with God*, 207.

[39] Cf. STÄHLIN, φίλος, *TDNT* IX, 157.

[40] Cf. *Ibid.*, 157. The Rabbinic teachers speak of the Jews as friends of God: Cf. H.L. STRACK & P. BILLERBECK, *Kommentar zum Neuen Testament aus Talmud und Midrasch*, Vol II (München 1924) 564f.

[41] Cf. STÄHLIN, φίλος, *TDNT* IX, 158.

OT (cf. *De Sobrietate*, 56; *De Abrahamo*, 273; *De Vita Mosis*, I, 156; *De Sacrificiis Abelis et Caini*, 130; *De Migratione Abrahami*, 45).[42] For Philo all the righteous can be called "friends of God" (cf. *De Fuga*, 58; *De Ebrietate*, 94).

IV. The Term φίλος in the NT

The term φίλος occurs 29 times in the NT, while φίλη and φιλία only once each.[43] As in the OT this terminology is found in those NT books which were supposed to be under strong Hellenistic influence.[44] Among the Synoptics, Mark does not use the term φίλος at all. There is a single occurrence of the term in Mt 11,19 where he presents Jesus as the friend of sinners and tax-collectors. A majority of its occurrences are in Lucan (Gospel and Acts) and Johannine (Gospel and Epistle) writings.[45] St. James employs the term φίλος twice and φιλία once in his Epistle (Jas 2,23; 4,4). A brief treatment of the use of φίλος in Luke's writings and in the

---

[42] Cf. *Ibid.*, 158-159, where Stählin gives a number of examples from Philo's writings regarding friendship.

[43] Cf. *Ibid.*, 159; R. MORGENTHALER, *Statistik des Neutestamentlichen Wortschatzes* (Zürich 1982) 153.

[44] Cf. STÄHLIN, φίλος, *TDNT* IX, 159 where he presents Lucan and Johannine writings as the books which were under Hellenistic influence.

[45] John in his letter uses the term φίλοι as a self-designation for Christians (3 Jn 15). The Christians have become friends by their relationship with Jesus and as "fellow-believers"they greet each other as friends. Cf. STÄHLIN, φίλος, *TDNT* IX, 166; W. GÜNTHER, φιλέω, *DNTT* II, 549. John adopts also the similar expressions ἀγαπητός, ἀγαπητοί (beloved) to depict his intimate relationship to those whom he addresses his letters.

letter of St. James will help us to illustrate the specific usage of the
term in the Fourth Gospel.

A. φίλος/φίλη in Luke's Writings

Out of the 29 NT occurrences of φίλος 17 are in the writings of
Luke and also the single instance of φίλη. In majority of the cases,
unlike the parallel tradition, Luke, being a Hellenist, uses φίλοι (Lk
7,6 with Mt 8,8; Lk 12,4 with Mt 10,28; Lk 15,6 with Mt 18,3; Lk
21,16 with Mk 13,12 and par.). He attributes the term φίλος only
once to Jesus in 7,34 to denote Jesus' relationship with the sinners
and the tax-collectors, a reference, which he takes from the Q
source.[46] It is noteworthy that only in 12,4 Luke employs φίλοι as
a designation for the Jesus-disciple relationship which is closer to Jn
15,15.[47] Almost all other Lucan usages of φίλος are in the context
of profane speech.

Luke employs the term φίλος for a "close personal friend" (Lk
11,5.8; 23,12), "guest" (Lk 11,6) and member of a circle of friends
gathered around a leader (Lk 7,6; Acts 10,24; 16,39). It is only Luke
who combines φίλος with συγγενής and γείτων as found in

---

[46] Cf. STÄHLIN, φίλος, *TDNT* IX, 159. Unlike in the Fourth Gospel, the
synoptic presentation of Jesus as the friend of sinners and tax-collectors seems to be
based on a different theological stress. John's presentation of Jesus as the friend of
"his own" is not an exclusion of Jesus' universal salvific mission. It goes well with
Johannine theology of discipleship as friendship.

[47] The idea of revelation, sharing of knowledge and martyrdom are connected
with φίλος in both the Johannine and Lucan texts. But, in the parallel text, in Mt
10,26ff. the term is omitted. Unlike Luke, in Mathew the warning begins with μὴ
φοβηθῆτε. Peterson gives the reason behind the difference in expression between
the Mathean and Lucan texts: Cf. PETERSON, *Gottesfreund*, 180-181.

antiquity.[48] At the same time in 14,12 the Evangelist adopts the term in an open antithesis to the conventions of antiquity to invite friends for a festal meal.[49] Luke explicates the co-relationship between friendship and table fellowship which is a very early expression of hospitality (Lk 14,12). The idea of reciprocity at the level of natural friendship is evident in Lk 11,5-13 which is a Lucan parable of prayer. A mutual availability is also stressed in Luke's presentation of friendship.[50]

Friendship and joy are intrinsically interrelated (Lk 15,6.9.29). So also, real friendship demands a sharing in the lot of a friend even in hardships (Lk 12,4). For Luke friendship demands service, concern and sacrifice even up to the point of life itself (Lk 11,5-8). In Acts 27,3 Luke speaks of Christians as φίλοι (friends) of Paul.[51] In Luke the idea of friendship between God and men is developed at least in an implied way in the context of parabolic sayings (cf. Lk 11,5-8; 14,10; 16,9).[52] In sum, one can say that generally Luke employs the term φίλος as a designation for the human relationship with the exception of 12,4 where it expresses Jesus-disciple relationship. But in line with the ancient thought his usage of the

---

[48] Cf. STÄHLIN, φίλος, *TDNT* IX, 159.

[49] Cf. *Ibid.*, 160.

[50] Cf. *Ibid.*, 161.

[51] Luke refers also to the μαθηταί of Paul in Acts 9,25 which probably alludes to the "friends". But Paul never uses the terms φίλος and μαθητής; instead he uses ἀδελφός and τέκνον. In Lucan presentation Paul was the head of a large circle of friends who gathered around him.

[52] Cf. STÄHLIN, φίλος, *TDNT* IX, 163.

term explicates the different aspects of friendship common to human and divine-human friendship.

B. φίλος/φιλία in James

In Jas 2,23 and 4,4 one finds the two occurrences of φίλος and the single instance of φιλία related to the concept of "friendship with God".[53] As we have already seen the term φίλος in Jas 2,23 refers to Abraham's traditional title "friend of God".[54] Abraham is the only OT figure to whom the NT grants the honorary title -φίλος θεοῦ. St. James explains this title in the light of Abraham's faith and obedience. By using the theological passive ἐκλήθη he illustrates the divine initiative of Abraham's friendship with God.[55] The use of the aorist here sheds light on certain events in Abraham's life expressing his deep faith in, trust of and obedience to God which made him worthy to be called "friend of God" (cf. Gen 15,1-6; 22,9ff; Jas 2,21f.).[56] Thus the reciprocity of divine-human friendship is evident also in James' usage of the term φίλος.

---

[53] In Jas 4,4 φίλος and φιλία are used to express one's relationship with the world as an antithesis of his enmity with God. In the particular context it denotes one's expected relationship with God.

[54] Cf. supra, pp.18-19.

[55] Cf. STÄHLIN, φίλος, TDNT IX, 169. The divine initiative is an important aspect in the divine-human friendship.

[56] Cf. Ibid., 169, n.186, where Stählin gives other reasons too for the designation of Abraham as φίλος θεοῦ.

Conclusion

This introductory chapter has treated briefly the origin and development of the term φίλος and the theme of friendship in the course of history from the time of non-biblical antiquity. Its primary uses and various nuances are found already in ancient Greek philosophers. The concept of the "friend of God" had originated among the Greeks, a concept expressed through φίλος and certain other similar terms. The Greek OT also employed the term φίλος and its derivatives with various nuances to depict both the human friendship and the divine-human friendship. In the inter-testamental literature also the term φίλος is used with its different ranges of meaning.

With regard to the NT occurrences it is noteworthy that φίλος is mainly employed by those NT authors who were under a strong Hellenistic influence. Accordingly, the majority of occurrences are found in Lucan writings, both the Gospel and Acts. Luke uses the term φίλος mainly in profane speech to depict a natural human relationship with the exception of 12,4 where it denotes Jesus-disciple relationship. The single occurrence of the term in Mt 11,19 presents Jesus as the friend of sinners and tax-collectors. The letter of St. James employs φίλος mainly to explain divine-human friendship, whereas the two usages of the term in the third letter of St. John have the sense of a self-designation for the Christians. Against the background of the above mentioned usages of the term φίλος, the exegetico-theological investigation of the term in the Fourth Gospel found in the following chapters will be dedicated to a detailed analysis of φίλος in its theological perspective.

CHAPTER TWO

THE FRIEND OF THE BRIDEGROOM (Jn 3, 22-36)

Introduction

In the Fourth Gospel the first occurrence of the term φίλος (friend) is in 3,29, where the Evangelist uses the term to designate John the Baptist as the friend of the bridegroom, Jesus. At the beginning of the investigation concerning the theological content of the term φίλος in Jn 3,29 one can ask the following questions: What is the nature of the relationship between the bridegroom and the friend of the bridegroom? What are the characteristics of the relationship between Jesus, the bridegroom and John the Baptist, the friend? What is the significance of the term φίλος in Jn 3,29 in the Johannine theology of Jesus-disciple relationship?

The scope of this chapter is to discover the answers to the above mentioned questions through an exegetico-theological study of Jn 3,22-36, wherein occurs the theologically rich term φίλος. As the steps preliminary to exegesis the textual unity of Jn 3,22-36 will be established, its textual problems will be discussed and the literary genre will be considered. The analysis of the text will be based on the structure and style of the pericope while the theological conclusions will be drawn on the basis of the analysis. Since the expression "ὁ φίλος τοῦ νυμφίου" (the friend of the bridegroom) is a historically and theologically evolved one, consideration of the historical and theological background of the expression is appropriate in the exegesis of the pericope.

I. Delimitation of the Text

In the process of exegesis, the primary step is to discover the literary and theological unity of the text under consideration. Of course, one cannot deny the text's position in the context of the *whole* with theological, thematic, stylistic and literary affinities. In the development of Biblical narratives the Evangelists use certain literary criteria, dramatic techniques and structural patterns, which mark the independent literary unity of an individual text.[1] Considering these elements, we will try to mark out the *limits* of the pericope before any detailed treatment of the text.

Regarding the delimitation of the text under consideration there is no agreement among scholars. Exegetes like Bernard, Bultmann, Schnackenburg find it difficult to accept the textual unity of Jn 3,22-36 since they do not consider vv. 31-36 as a continuation of the last testimony of the Baptist which ends in Jn 3,30. According to them, Jesus is the one speaking in vv. 31-36 and accordingly it should follow v.21.[2] Barrett, Hoskyns, Bauer and Lindars maintain the unity of vv.22-36, holding that there is no change of the speaker from v.30 to v.31. Explaining that a shift in tone is usual in the Fourth Gospel, these scholars consider that it is still John the Baptist contrasting himself with Jesus in vv.31-36.[3] Brown and Dodd, while

---

[1] Cf. G. MLAKUZHYIL, *The Christocentric Literary Structure of the Fourth Gospel* (AnBib 117) (Roma 1987) 87-135.

[2] Cf. BERNARD, *St. John*, Vol I, XXIII-XXIV; R. BULTMANN, *The Gospel of John. A Commentary*, G.R. BEASLEY-MURRAY (trs.) (Philadelphia 1971) 160, n.2; R. SCHNACKENBURG, *The Gospel according to St. John*, Vol I, K. SMYTH (trs.) (London 1980) 380-392.

[3] Cf. C.K. BARRETT, *The Gospel according to St. John* (London 1987) 219; E.C. HOSKYNS, *The Fourth Gospel*, F.N. DAVEY (ed.), (London 1947) 229-231; W. BAUER, *Das Johannesevangelium* (HNT 6) (Leipzig 1933) 62-65; B. LINDARS,

maintaining the unity of the text, hold another position. Brown argues that the discourse in vv.31-36 resembles closely the style of speech attributed to Jesus in the rest of the Gospel (3,11-21; 12,44-50) with particularly close parallels to Jesus' words addressed to Nicodemus. [4] Dodd for his part considers vv.31-36 as a recapitulation of the preceding section with immediate reference to the themes developed in vv.11-14. Refuting the argument of those who prefer a transposition of vv.31-36 to immediately after v.21 basing on thematic connection he says: "Such a recapitulation of its leading ideas, with some additional points, is quite in accord with our author's technique, but there is no ground for insisting that such a recapitulation must follow immediately upon the passage which it recapitulates: it may so follow, or it may not".[5] According to Dodd it is possible to consider vv.25-30 as an effective introduction for the recapitulatory passage. The contrast between Jesus and John the Baptist is well depicted in vv.28-30, a contrast continued in the following section. Seeing the thematic connection between vv.31-36 and the Nicodemus incident, Dodd considers vv.31-36 as an explanatory appendix to the dialogue with Nicodemus and the following discourse, without ignoring the place of vv.22-30 as an introduction for this appendix. [6]

In the light of the above mentioned argument of Dodd one can at least arrive at the conclusion that the present sequence of the text

---

The Gospel of John (New Century Bible) (London 1972) 162.

[4] Cf. R.E. BROWN, *The Gospel according to John*, Vol I (New York 1970) 159; Cf. also W. KLAIBER, "Der irdische und der himmlische Zeuge: Eine Auslegung von Joh 3.22-36", *NTS* 36, 2 (1990) 207-209.

[5] C.H. DODD, *The Interpretation of the Fourth Gospel* (Cambridge 1953) 309.

[6] Cf. *Ibid.*, 311.

has its logic in the mental frame of the Evangelist. In spite of the similarities of vv.31-36 with the Nicodemus incident, we need not consider the whole chapter 3 as one literary unity nor vv.31-36 as a theological recapitulation of the Nicodemus-episode. Nevertheless, one can argue for the independent literary unity of the last testimony of the Baptist starting with 3,22 and ending with the theological reflection in vv.31-36.[7] In the attempt to ascertain the textual unity of the pericope we consider also the literary criteria, dramatic techniques and structural patterns which the Evangelist himself uses.[8]

V.22 shows a clear beginning of a new section with temporal, geographic, thematic and personnel changes from those of the preceding section. As for the *temporal transition* μετὰ ταῦτα[9] (v.22) is a temporal particle which indicates the initial section of a pericope. This expression connects the following section with the preceding one and at the same time it disconnects the following verse from the preceding section. Likewise there is a *change of place* in v.22. The previous action took place in Jerusalem and now the action shifts to the Ἰουδαία γῆ, understood as the Judean country side.[10] So also there is a *change of the characters* in this section. In

---

[7] Cf. M.J. LAGRANGE, *Évangile selon saint Jean* (EB) (Paris 1948) 96, where he says that vv.31-36 represent the Evangelist's commentary on the scene involving John the Baptist (22-30), just as vv.16-21 represent the commentary on Nicodemus scene.

[8] Cf. supra, p. 30.

[9] Μετὰ ταῦτα appears in the Fourth Gospel as a general formula of transition: Cf. Jn 3,22; 5,1; 6,1; 7,1; 19,38; 21,1.

[10] Γῆ is used here in the sense of Χώρα. According to Panimolle the first part of this pericope (vv.22-26) gives a geographical description of the last testimony of the Baptist. The verb ἦλθεν (v.22) indicates a shift of place and a change of the circumstances to the region of Judea: Cf. S.A. PANIMOLLE, *Lettura Pastorale del*

the previous scene Jesus and Nicodemus are the characters, whereas here Jesus and His disciples are the focus along with the Baptist, his disciples and a certain Jew. One can notice also a *change of action* when the Evangelist presents Jesus and His disciples in v.22 as baptizing which was not at all attributed to them in the preceding verses.

After this introductory setting, a scene opens characterized by a dialogue in which the main speaker is John the Baptist, a dialogue which ends in a monologue.[11] The *theme* of the dialogue is continued in the monologue. Vv.31-36 seem to be the Evangelist's reflection on the person of Christ in relation to humanity represented by John the Baptist who is a main character in the preceding section. The theme of the distribution of the Spirit through Christ (v.34b) can be better explained if we consider the unity of the text which begins in v.22 with a baptismal setting (cf. Jn 1,33). The idea of the wrath of God (ὀργή), according to the Christian tradition, is connected with the preaching of the Baptist (cf. Mt. 3,1-12; MK 1,2 ff.; Lk 3,1ff.). The theme of testimony (Μαρτυρεῖν, λαλεῖν) runs throughout the pericope (vv.26.28.31.32.33),and so there is no thematic break in between vv.30 and 31.

Regarding the *conclusion* of the pericope there are difference of opinions. Seeing the cross reference between 3,22-23 and 4,1-3 some authors consider 4,1-3 as the conclusion of the text[12] or a historical

---

Vangelo di Giovanni, Vol I (Bologna 1988) 336.

[11] Cf. DODD, *Interpretation*, 308.

[12] Cf. INFANTE, *L'amico dello Sposo*, 29-31. Infante illustrates here the literary unity of Jn 3,22-4,3 on the basis of geographical unity (3,22=4,3), temporal unity (3,22=4,1), unity of the characters (3,22.23=4,1) and the unity of the activity (3,22.23=4,2-3). Cf. also MLAKUZHYIL, *The Christocentric Structure*, 192.

summary of the Baptist-episode. [13] But on the basis of the following
reasons the present study considers a text that concludes with v.36.
Just as the Nicodemus-episode is ended with a monologue, the
monologue section in vv.31-36 can be considered as the conclusion
of the Baptist-episode in vv.22-30.[14] Moreover one can find a true
anticipation of the general conclusion of the Gospel (Jn 20,30-31) in
the final verse of this monologue (v.36). The theme of faith and
eternal life to which the whole Gospel is orientated is clearly
mentioned in v.36. In short we can find a clear-cut conclusion
already in v.36 and take 4,1-3 as a recapitulation of the preceding
section, which serves to facilitate the narrative flow. With this said,
we arrive at the conclusion of the delimitation of the text to be
considered, Jn 3,22-36 as a unit.

II. Textual Problems

The second step in Biblical exegesis is to deal with the variant
readings of the text under question and arrive at conclusions that are
conducive to the translation and understanding of that pericope. In
the light of the external and internal evidence one can arrive at
certain conclusions regarding the correct reading of the text. As for
the pericope in question there are instances of variant readings that
are not so problematic. Here however we are not interested in all
existing variant readings, but only with those which have the support

---

According to him Jn 4,1-3 serve as 'bridge verses' that can be seen as a conclusion
to the preceding section and as an introduction to the following, thus serving a
transitory function.

[13] Cf. G. SEGALLA, *Giovanni* (Roma 1976) 133.

[14] Cf. supra, p. 32, n.7.

of considerable and important witnesses. Accordingly we will treat the following textual problems.

V.25: - Μετὰ Ἰουδαίου (singular): P[75], א[c], A, B, K, L, W[supp], Δ, Π, Z, Ψ and many other minuscoli.

- Μετὰ Ἰουδαίων (Plural): P[66], א[*], Θ, f[1], f[13] and many other minuscoli.

Both the singular and the plural readings are ancient and external support is rather evenly divided. According to Brown the plural may be on the analogy of Mk 2,18 and parallels which associate the Pharisees with the disciples of John the Baptist concerning the legality of fasting. He is of opinion that if we read the singular, then its connection with the following verse is not clear.[15] Boismard argues for the plural, suggesting that the singular Ἰουδαίου is by analogy with Ἰωάννου.[16] There are also some authors who hold for a totally different reading, i.e. "Jesus".[17] Even though such a reading makes sense in the context there is no external evidence for it. In spite of the difference of opinion among the scholars[18], it is likely to read it as singular because the external evidence is in favour of that

---

[15] Cf. BROWN, *John*, Vol I, 152.

[16] Cf. M.E. BOISMARD, "Les traditions johanniques concernant le Baptiste", *RB* 70 (1963) 25, n.24.

[17] Cf. A. LOISY, *Le Quatrième Évangile* (Paris 1921) 171. Loisy, along with others (Bauer, Goguel) holds the view that the text originally read "Jesus" or "disciples of Jesus", but due to pious reasons the ancient writers changed it in order to avoid a dispute between the disciples of John the Baptist and of Jesus.

[18] Cf. BARRETT, *St.John*, 221; SCHNACKENBURG, *St. John*, Vol I, 414, n.11; SEGALLA, *Giovanni*, 183; B.M. METZGER, *A Textual Commentary on the Greek New Testament* (London 1975) 205.

and because the singular, just as the plural, does not make any difference in the understanding of the text.

V.28: - Μοι : P⁶⁰, A, B, D, K, L, W^supp, Δ, Θ, Π, Z, f¹³, Vg...
     - Ἐμοί : f¹, 565, 1365, 1⁵⁴⁷...
     - Omitted : P⁷⁵, א, 28, 1009, 1195 ...

There is much external evidence in favour of μοι than of ἐμοί. The omission from the important codices like P⁷⁵, א etc. may be accidental, perhaps due to the succession of the syllables that begin with the same letter. [19] So, one can accept the first reading as original.

Vv. 31-32: - Ἐρχόμενος ἐπάνω πάντων ἐστίν· ὅ ἑώρακεν καὶ ἤκουσεν τοῦτο μαρτυρεῖ: P⁵ ^vid (P⁶⁶* omit ἐρχόμενος), P⁶⁶ᶜ (אᶜ omit τοῦτο) B, L, W^supp, Z, al...

- Ἐρχόμενος ἐπάνω πάντων ἐστίν· καὶ ὅ ἑώρακεν καὶ ἤκουσεν τοῦτο μαρτυρεῖ : A, K, Δ, Θ, Π, 063, f¹³,al...

- Ἐρχόμενος ὅ ἑώρακεν καὶ ἤκουσεν τοῦτο μαρτυρεῖ : P⁷⁵, Cop^sa, Origen.

- Ἐρχόμενος ὅ ἑώρακεν καὶ ἤκουσεν μαρτυρεῖ : D, f¹, 565, al...

Since each of the above mentioned readings has some omission or addition in particular and is supported by equally important witnesses, it is difficult to arrive at a definite conclusion. The omission of the second ἐπάνω πάντων ἐστίν in many manuscripts is

---

[19] Cf. METZGER, *Textual Commentary*, 205.

noteworthy. This can be explained as a scribal deletion of the words (seen as redundant after the opening part of v.31). The addition of the second ἐπάνω πάντων ἐστίν can be understood as a mechanical addition, after the second instance of ἐρχόμενος, by an inattentive scribe.[20] Seeing the repetition and inclusion as characteristic of Johannine style many exegetes argue for the long reading.[21] Brown and Segalla leave the question open since there are favourable reasons for both readings.[22] Accordingly, in many of the critical editions it is preserved and put in parenthesis.

V.34 : - οὐ γὰρ ἐκ μέτρου δίδωσιν τὸ πνεῦμα : $P^{66.75}$, א, B^2, C^*, L, W^s, 083, f^1, 33. 565. 1241...

- οὐ γὰρ ἐκ μέτρου δίδωσιν ὁ Θεὸς τὸ πνεῦμα : A, C^2, D, Θ, Z, 086, f^{13}, μ, lat.$sy^{p.h}$, Co., Or...

- οὐ γὰρ ἐκ μέτρου δίδωσιν : B, Pc...

In the case of v.34 we see three different readings. Even though there are some important witnesses which support each of the above mentioned readings, it is the first reading that is supported by many of the major codices. The addition of Θεὸς as the subject of the verb δίδωσιν is due to a preoccupation to give clarity, thereby avoiding theological disputes and it can be considered as

---

[20] Cf. *Ibid.*, 205.

[21] Cf. BARRETT, *St. John*, 224; SCHNACKENBURG, *St. John*, Vol I, 383, n.104; B.F. WESTCOTT, *The Gospel according to St. John* (London 1958) 65.

[22] Cf. BROWN, *John*, Vol I, 158; SEGALLA, *Giovanni*, 185.

secondary.[23] In the third reading the term Πνεῦμα is omitted, an omission supported by the main witness **B** and some other minor uncials. This can be considered as negligence.[24] In the Fourth Gospel theologically speaking, it is the Son who receives the Spirit from the Father in fullness and pours out the same Spirit to the humanity (cf. Jn 7,38-39; 15,26). Accordingly, to establish the Johannine theological position regarding the distribution of the Spirit one need not look for a reading with an addition of Θέος in v.34. Therefore, in the light of both external and internal evidence we prefer the first reading.

III. The Literary Genre

For a correct exegesis of a Biblical text it is essential to know the literary genre of that text. One cannot attribute a single literary genre to the pericope (Jn 3,22-36). The text is formulated in a dialogue-monologue style, viz. Jn 3,22-30 in the form of a dialogue with a clear introduction (vv.22-24) and vv.31-36 as a monologue formulated in the theological frame work of the Fourth Evangelist which serves also as a conclusion or summary of the dialogue section. In v.29 we see a specific literary style concerning which there is no common agreement among the exegetes. For some it is

---

[23] Cf. BROWN, *John*, Vol I, 158; D. MOLLAT, *La révélation de l'Esprit-Saint chez saint Jean* (Roma 1971) 95f.

[24] Cf. BARRETT, *St. John*, 226; BROWN, *John*, Vol I, 158. Bultmann, however, has a different opinion. Cf. BULTMANN, *John*, 164, n.1.

a metaphor or a small parable, where as for others it is a comparison, allegory or an analogy.[25]

While admitting the metaphorical traits of Jn 3,29 based on the matrimonial metaphors of Judaism and the OT, we, together with a group of exegetes, consider Jn 3,29 as a small parable.[26] An OT metaphor is adopted by the Evangelist, who puts it into the mouth of John the Baptist, thereby explaining the relationship of Jesus and the New Israel in the historical context of a mass-movement of people, with Jesus as the head. It is to be noted that such a matrimonial metaphor is used often in the prophetic literature and also in Judaism in general to illustrate the close relationship between Yahweh and His people. In this small parable of John, Jesus is compared to the bridegroom and John the Baptist to the friend of the bridegroom.[27] These two figures (the bridegroom and the friend of the bridegroom) are familiar and concrete figures in history and in the present *Sitz im Leben* of the text under consideration.

The mutual relationship between Jesus and the Baptist is theologically presented in the second part of the text (vv.31-36). The depth of the metaphorical presentation of the relationship between

---

[25] According to Bultmann it is not an allegory but a true metaphor. Cf. BULTMANN, *John*, 173, n.11. But Hoskyns calls it an analogy. Cf. HOSKYNS, *Fourth Gospel*, 222-231. Aristotle did not find much difference between metaphor and comparison. For him ὡς indicates a comparison while its absence indicates a metaphor. A parable, for its part, is longer and more efficacious. Cf. ARISTOTLE, *Ars Rhetorica*, 1406 b, 20.

[26] Cf. G. ZEVINI, "Gesù lo Sposo della communità messianica (Jn 3,29)", *PSV* 13 (1986) 109; INFANTE, *L' amico dello Sposo*, 69f.; BARRETT, *St. John*, 222; B. LINDARS, "Two Parables in John", *NTS* 16 (1969-70) 329; SCHNACKENBURG, *St. John*, Vol I, 416, where he says: "in its form it is a short parable with allegorical traits, a type often found in the jewish mashal".

[27] It is to be noted that there is no explicit comparison here since no ὡς is used. But in the light of the OT metaphor and in the present context Jesus and the Baptist are compared to the concrete figures of a jewish marriage.

those two figures can be understood only in the light of the theological reflection of the Evangelist. With such a consideration of the literary genre of the pericope, one finds a further reason to delimit the text with a terminal point of v.36.

IV. The Structure and Style of the Text

For any meaningful exegesis it is always essential to see the text in its literary structure. It is a universally accepted fact that the structure and style of the text convey its message in a more profound way. The idea of the author is well communicated through the structural pattern which he employs. The stylistic elements of a text in question help us to ascertain its structure. Structure is to be found on both holistic and unitary level. In other words there are macro and micro structures. [28] Since the unity of the text (vv.22-36) presupposes a macro structure it is of interest to illustrate its micro structure which is based on the subunits of the pericope. In the light of thematic and literary characteristics the text can be divided into three units.

A. Introductory Section (Jn 3,22-26)

This section serves as the background for the last testimony of the Baptist which is apparent in the following section. The

---

[28] By macro structure we mean the literary unity of the whole pericope in a particular pattern, i.e. with an introduction, body and conclusion. In the case of our text, it follows a structure and style of other Johannine pericopes. In the *delimitation of the text* we have already mentioned the textual unity and its parallelism with the Nicodemus-episode. In both these episodes there is a short narrative followed by a dialogue and a theological discourse. Thus its macro structure is well patterned.

introduction sets the scene by means of geographical notes, side-by-side presentation of the characters involved in the episode and the parallel ministry in contrast, which is conducive in communicating the superiority of Jesus over all human witnesses. The introductory section uses two important verbs, viz. μαρτυρέω (to bear witness) and βαπτίζω (to baptize) which play an important role in the establishment of the superiority of Jesus in the following section of the pericope.

There is a thematic inclusion between v.22 and v.26 established by the use of the verb βαπτίζω in reference to Jesus. It is only in the verses of this subsection that this verb refers to Jesus. In the rest of this the verb is attributed to John the Baptist. The introductory section is structured as follows:

A
Μετὰ ταῦτα ἦλθεν Ὁ ἸΗΣΟΥΣ ... Ἰουδαίαν γῆν (v.22a)

καὶ ἐκεῖ διέτριβεν μετ' αὐτῶν καὶ ἘΒΑΠΤΙΨΕΝ. (v.22b)

B
a ῏Ην δὲ καὶ Ὁ ἸΩΑΝΝΗΣ (v.23a)

b ΒΑΠΤΙΨΩΝ ἐν Αἰνὼν ἐγγὺς τοῦ Σαλείμ..εκεῖ (v.23b)

b¹ καὶ παρεγίνοντο καὶ ἘΒΑΠΤΙΨΟΝΤΟ· (v.23c)

a¹ οὔπω γὰρ ἦν βεβλημένος... Ὁ ἸΩΑΝΝΗΣ (v.24)

A¹
Ἐγένετο οὖν ζήτησις...περὶ καθαρισμοῦ. (v.25)

καὶ ἦλθον πρὸς τὸν Ἰωάννην...῟ΟΣ ...τοῦ Ἰορδάνου (v.26a)

ᾧ σὺ μεμαρτύρηκας, ἴδε ΟΥΤΟΣ ΒΑΠΤΙΨΕΙ (v.26b)

καὶ πάντες ἔρχονται πρὸς ΑΥΤΟΝ· (v.26c)

In these verses one finds a perfect correspondence between the baptism of Jesus mentioned at the beginning (v.22) and at the end (v.26), which is clearly depicted in the schema (A - A^1). In the schema, the letter **B** refers to the baptismal ministry of the Baptist which is chiastically arranged, viz. **a** and **a**^{1} refer to the person of John whereas **b** and **b**^{1} deal with his baptismal activity. While both Jesus and the Baptist share the same ministry but there is a great difference in terms of the result of their respective ministry. It is worth noting that the final expression in these verses: καὶ πάντες ἔπχονται πρὸς αὐτόν ("and all are going to him") provides the immediate context for the Baptist's proclamation of the superiority of Jesus and His divine transcendence. [29]

B. The Last Testimony of the Baptist (Jn 3,27-30)

Since this section consists of the words of the Baptist, it forms an obvious literary unity. The beginning is marked by verbs indicating speech: ἀπεκρίθη and εἶπεν. The testimony of the Baptist highlights the superiority of Jesus. In v.27 a general divine principle is presented, i.e. "no one receives anything unless it is given to him from heaven". The power of the divine will is mentioned in this statement. The last words of the Baptist (v.30) also admit the power of the divine will by use of the particle δεῖ (must). Moreover this section of the pericope is considered as containing the words of the Baptist, words he utters in view of showing the superiority of Jesus as well as his own important yet subordinate role in relation to Jesus. Such a concept of the Jesus-Baptist relationship is depicted well through a literary style, which can be schematized as follows:

---

[29] Cf. PANIMOLLE, *Giovanni*, Vol I, 334.

A   ἀπεκρίθη Ἰάννης καὶ εἶπεν· οὐ δύναται ˝ΑΝΘΡΩΠΟΣ
    λαμβάνειν οὐδὲ ἓν ἐὰν μὴ ..ἐκ τοῦ οὐρανοῦ. (v.27)

B   αὐτοὶ ὑμεῖς ...ὅτι οὐκ εἰμὶ ἐγὼ ὁ χριστός,
    ἀλλ᾽ ὅτι ἀπεσταλμένος εἰμὶ ἔμπροσθεν ἐκείνου.(v.28)

A¹ ὁ ἔχων τὴν νύμφην ΝΥΜΦΙΟΣ ἐστίν· (v.29a)

B¹ ὁ δὲ φίλος τοῦ νυμφίου ὁ ἑστηκὼς... πεπλήρωται (v.29b)

A²   a. ἐκεῖνον δεῖ
               b. αὐξάνειν (v.30a)

B²   a¹. ἐμὲ δὲ
               b¹. ἐλαττοῦσθαι. (v.30b)

In the above schema the terms of the pairs, **A** and **B**, **A¹** and **B¹**, **A²** and **B²** are contrast to each other. **A**, **A¹** and **A²** refer to Jesus whereas **B**, **B¹** and **B²** pertain to the Baptist. While in **A¹-B¹** and **A²-B²** the contrast is quite vivid, in **A-B** it is not so clear. In the schema **A** refers to Jesus[30] as one who receives the divine gifts in their fullness. **B** refers to the Baptist, who, denying the Messianic title for himself, professes that he is the one who is sent before the Messiah. **A¹** refers to Jesus, the bridegroom, already in possession of the bride, the Messianic community. **B¹** denotes the role of the Baptist as the friend of the bridegroom, a secondary role which is at the same time uniquely important since the friend stands nearby the bridegroom, listening to him and rejoicing in his words.   The

[30] Cf. C. PANACKEL, *ΙΔΟΥ Ο ΑΝΘΡΩΠΟΣ (Jn 19,5b): An Exegetico-Theological Study of the Text in the Light of the Use of the Term ΑΝΘΡΩΠΟΣ Designating Jesus in the Fourth Gospel* (AnGre 251) (Roma 1988) 63-69.

reason for the fullness of his joy is that the bridegroom now possesses the bride, the reality to which every action of the *friend of the bridegroom* aims at.[31] A^2 and B^2 are also in perfect contrast, viz. Jesus must increase but the Baptist must decrease which is theologically explained in the following verses.

C. Jesus, the Unique Revealer of the Father (Jn 3,31-36)

The treatment of these verses represents an obvious continuation of the preceding section. As seen above the testimony of the Baptist (vv.27-30) affirms the superiority of Jesus and his intimate role in relation to Jesus. This last subsection is the Evangelist's theological reflection regarding the superiority of Jesus, which presents him as the unique revealer of the Father. Just as the dialogue between Jesus and Nicodemus develops into a monologue, so also the dialogue between the Baptist and his disciples (vv.26-30) leads into a monologue (vv.31-36).[32] In this subsection the various statements are situated in close parallelism, which can be viewed as follows:

---

[31] Black finds a number of *plays on words* in the aramaic origin of vv.29-30 such as כלתא (bride), קלא (voice), כלל (to be completed) קלל (decrease): Cf. M. BLACK, *An Aramaic Approach to the Gospels and Acts* (2.ed.) (Oxford 1954) 109.

[32] Cf. PANIMOLLE, *Giovanni*, Vol I, 340; DODD, *Interpretation*, 384.

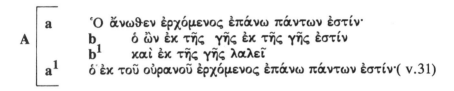

A   a   Ὁ ἄνωθεν ἐρχόμενος ἐπάνω πάντων ἐστίν·
     b   ὁ ὢν ἐκ τῆς γῆς ἐκ τῆς γῆς ἐστίν
     b^1 καὶ ἐκ τῆς γῆς λαλεῖ
     a^1 ὁ ἐκ τοῦ οὐρανοῦ ἐρχόμενος ἐπάνω πάντων ἐστίν·(v.31)

B   ὃ ἑώρακεν... καὶ ΤΗΝ ΜΑΡΤΥΡΙΑΝ αὐτοῦ ΟΥΔΕΙΣ
   ΛΑΜΒΑΝΕΙ (v.32)

B^1 Ὁ ΛΑΒΩΝ ΑΥΤΟΥ ΤΗΝ ΜΑΡΤΥΡΙΑΝ... (v.33)

C   ὃ γὰρ ἀπέστειλεν Ὁ ΘΕΟΣ ...ΔΙΔΩΣΙΝ τὸ πνεῦμα (v.34)

C^1 Ὁ ΠΑΤΗΡ ἀγαπᾳ ...καὶ πάντα ΔΕΔΩΚΕΝ ἐν τῇ χειρὶ αὐτοῦ
   (v.35)

D   Ὁ ΠΙΣΤΕΥΩΝ εἰς τὸν υἱὸν ΕΧΕΙ ΖΩΗΝ αἰώνιον· (v.36a)

D1   Ὁ ΔΕ ΑΠΕΙΘΩΝ τῷ υἱῷ ΟΥΚ ΟΨΕΤΑΙ ΖΩΗΝ... (v.36b)

In the above schema **A** (v.31) is in chiastic structure. Thematically, one finds vivid contrast between the one who comes from heaven (Jesus) and all those who are of earth (represented by the Baptist). The theological reason for the superiority of Jesus is further explained by parallelism in v.34 and v.35 (**C** + **C^1**). Both the negative and the positive response to this authentic revelation and its after-effects are also expressed in a parallel way, as seen in the schema (**B. B^1** + **D. D^1**). This subsection terminates in an obvious conclusion which expresses also the motive of the whole gospel.

It is to be noted that all these micro-structures are well placed in the macro-structure (3,22-36). There is a clear flow from one part of the pericope to the other.[33] Moreover the introduction exposes a problem in the form of an accusation, viz. "all are going to him", the solution of which is theologically explained in the following sections by means of a statement expressing the necessity of believing in the Son (v.36).[34]

V. Exegesis of the Text

Rather than a detailed verse by verse analysis, a thematic consideration now will be done in so far as possible in order to highlight the theological meaning of the pericope. The key interest of the exegesis in the particular context of present study aims at a clear understanding of the nuance of the metaphorical title φίλος τοῦ νυμφίου designating Jesus-Baptist relationship. The meaning of this expression will be explained in the context of the entire pericope, and so, the text will be treated on the basis of literary and stylistic structure [35] under three headings: the setting of the scene; the last testimony of the Baptist; Jesus as the unique revealer.

---

[33] As we have already mentioned above, the first section ends with the expression *"all are going to him"*, that serves as the immediate context of the testimony of the Baptist (vv.27-30). So also, the last expression *"he must increase"* needs a theological explanation which is clearly proposed in the last sub-section.

[34] For the Fourth Evangelist "going" or "coming to Jesus" means "believing in Jesus". It can be seen therefore, that the entire section is characterized by a thematic unity.

[35] Cf. supra, pp. 40-46.

A. The Setting of the Scene (vv.22-26)

The entire introductory part (Jn 3,22-26) comes under this heading. Unlike the synoptic tradition the Fourth Evangelist presents the beginning of Jesus' public ministry even before the imprisonment of John the Baptist. W.Wink's observation supports the authenticity of the Johannine presentation of Jesus and the Baptist together on the scene, engaged in their ministry.[36] For Bultmann the introductory section (vv.22-26) gives the impression of being the Evangelist's own composition.[37] In spite of these opinions one can say that the introductory verses of the pericope may be a mixing up of the ancient oral tradition (v.23) and the Evangelist's own invention (v.22). Whatever the case the Evangelist establishes a background for the presentation of the last testimony of the Baptist concerning the superiority of Jesus and the Baptist's relationship with Him.

1. Geographical Description

The events described in the preceding section took place in Jerusalem (Jn 2,23). The pericope under consideration opens with the description of a shift of place in connection with the baptismal ministry of Jesus. The geographical expression "Judean land" in v.22

---

[36] W. WINK, *John the Baptist in the Gospel Tradition* (Cambridge 1968) 94, where he says: "Jesus' work does not follow the Baptist's, but parallels it. Jesus is not simply John's successor".

[37] Cf. BULTMANN, *John*, 167.

can be understood as the country districts of Judea, outside the city
of Jerusalem. [38]

In v.23 the Evangelist gives also a clear geographical note
regarding the Baptist's baptismal activity. But for a modern reader
the places *Aenon* and *Salim* cannot be easily and certainly identified
since there are differences of opinion among the scholars. [39] Besides
these opinions based on archaeological findings there is also an
allegoric or symbolic interpretation of these two geographical names,
viz. *Aenon* as fictional springs and *Salim* as salvation. In this context
John the Baptist is depicted as being near Salim, i.e. near
salvation. [40] According to Bultmann these names are real, but for
the Evangelist they have a symbolic meaning also. [41] In spite of the
actual situation, Jesus and John were presented by the Evangelist as
carrying out their ministry in different places. A clear, but distinct

---

[38] Cf. F.F. BRUCE, *The Gospel of John* (Michigan 1984) 93. According to
Bultmann the Evangelist assumes that either some events have taken place in Galilee
between the Nicodemus-episode and the Baptist-episode, or the Evangelist is not
interested in the geographical precision. Cf. BULTMANN, *John*, 220. For Brown,
γῆ originally meant (אֶרֶץ) and not country district. He points out that many
consider it as Jordan valley. Cf. BROWN, *John*, Vol I, 150-151.

[39] The archaeological findings propose three possible opinions: a) In Perea, the
Transjordan, where John was active in his ministry (Jn 1,28). The 6th century
Madaba mosaic map indicates an Aenon just northeast of the Dead sea, opposite of
Bethabara. b) In the northern Jordan valley, about 8 miles south of Bethshan, where
there is a remarkable group of seven springs, that can explain the description:
ὕδατα πολλά, and the local description in v.26.c) In Samaria, four miles east-
southeast of Shechem there is a town called Salim, known from ancient times and
8 miles northeast of Salim lies the modern Ainun. The nearby sources of the Wadi
Far'ah are extremely well provided with water. Cf. EUSEBIUS, *Onomasticon*, in: E.
KLOSTERMANN & H. GRESSMANN (eds.), *GCS* 11^i, p.40,1-4; p.153,6-7;
BERNARD, *St. John*, Vol 1, 128; W.F. ALBRIGHT, *The Archaeology of Palestine*
(London 1960) 247.

[40] Cf. N. KRIEGER, "Fiktive Orte der Johannestaufe", *ZNW* 45 (1954) 122.

[41] Cf. BULTMANN, *John*, 170, n.9.

geographical description concerning their ministry will help one to understand the general tone of the entire pericope, a tone of distinction between Jesus and the Baptist.

2. Characters Involved

The scene opens with the juxtaposition of many characters. On one side Jesus appears with His disciples. At the same time John the Baptist is also actively present on the stage. As demonstrated above in the treatment of the structure of the introductory section, [42] both Jesus and John are involved in a baptismal ministry which presupposes the presence of a great number of people. Once more, the great success in Jesus' ministry is clear from the accusation that *all are going to Him* (v.26). [43] The disciples of John the Baptist are actively involved in this episode. They appeared on the scene, discussing with a Jew over purificatory rites. All the characters are actively involved in one way or other. The presence of these characters in various levels of involvement help to set the context appropriate for the testimony of John concerning the superiority of Jesus.

---

[42] Cf. supra, p. 41.

[43] In connection with John's baptism one reads the expression "people came" (v.23) whereas with Jesus' baptism the Evangelist writes that "all are going to him" (v.26). The success of Jesus' ministry compared to that of John is evident in those expressions.

3. Actions Narrated

In the introductory verses one finds two main actions described:
a) The ministry of baptism; b) a discussion concerning purification
resulting in a complaint against Jesus' success in baptism.

a. Ministry of Baptism

At the beginning of the pericope the Evangelist gives an account
of a baptismal ministry attributed to Jesus (vv.22.26).[44] Actually
there is no synoptic account regarding such a ministry of Jesus.
Since there is a correction in Jn 4,2 that Jesus did not baptize, one
can consider the above statement, that Jesus baptized, in a general
way, i.e. as a baptism administered by His disciples.[45] Obviously the
baptism attributed to Jesus was not sacramental because at that
stage the Spirit had not been given (Jn 7,39).[46] Some scholars
consider it as merely a preparatory baptism meant to initiate the

---

[44] The verb in its imperfect (ἐβάπτιζεν) and present (βαπτίζει) tenses
indicate a continuity of action.

[45] Cf. G. GANDER, "Jean III,22 á IV,3 Parle-t-il d'un baptême administré par
Jésus?", *RThPhil N.S.* (1948) 133-137. On the basis of two Syriac manuscripts he
argues that Jn 3,22 does not speak of a baptism administered by Jesus. Cf. also
HOSKYNS, *The Fourth Gospel*, 227, where he says that the disciples of Jesus
baptized by His authority and in their action Jesus acted. According to this view the
Pharisees would not be wrong in supposing that Jesus was baptizing, eliminating the
contradiction between 3,22 and 4,2.

[46] Cf. PANIMOLLE, *Giovanni*, Vol I, 337; SCHNACKENBURG, *St. John*, Vol
I, 411.

followers to listen His preaching. [47] It is neither the same baptism administered by John nor the Christian sacrament of Baptism. [48]

Already in the patristic writings the Johannine account of baptism administered by Jesus (Jn 3,22.26) had been a matter of discussion. For example, John Chrysostom considered this baptism as a practice continued by the former disciples of John, who had already become Jesus' disciples. They might have tried to gain more followers to Jesus (4,1), and when they practised it, it remained as a baptism of repentance, but it admitted those who wished to join Jesus. The words of Chrysostom runs as follows:

> If anyone should inquire, "in what was the baptism of the disciples better than that of John?" we will reply, "in nothing"; both were alike without the gift of the Spirit, both parties had one reason for baptizing, and that was to lead the baptized to Christ. [49]

Against such a background, the baptismal ministry attributed to Jesus is best considered as a preparatory rite administered by the first disciples of Jesus, i.e. as a ritual purification for those who want

---

[47] In Hendriksen's opinion, the baptism attributed to Jesus can be considered as a transition between Johannine and Christian baptism: Cf. W. HENDRIKSEN, *The Gospel of John* (London 1969) 146. Infante considers it as a preparatory rite for the Christian baptism, something for a mere internal conversion: Cf. INFANTE, *L' amico dello Sposo*, 39.

[48] SCHNACKENBURG, *St. John*, Vol I, 411, where he writes "it cannot be equivalent to the baptism of John, and either can it be connected with the later Christian baptism. To the mind of the evangelist, it cannot yet be the baptism in the Spirit (cf.7,39);and Jesus hardly have practised a mere baptism of penance like John, since all our other sources are silent on the point. It would also have been contrary to the preaching of John, as understood by John (cf.1,26.33). From the way it is mentioned, however no particular importance is attached to this baptism. It merely serves to introduce a dispute between a Jew and John's disciples".

[49] JOHANNES CHRYSOSTOMUS, "Homilae in Ioannem" in J.P. Migne, *PG* 59, col 167; Cf. also BERNARD, *St. John*, Vol l, 128; G.R. BEASLEY-MURRAY, *Baptism in the New Testament* (London 1962) 72.

to follow Jesus. More than establishing the theological nature of the baptism attributed to Jesus, in the context of the present study one has to see the Evangelist's intention of presenting Jesus and the Baptist in juxtaposition engaged in the same ministry with apparent difference in their success. The difference and contrast which are obvious in the ministry of baptism will help one to explain the nature of their relationship as friendship explained in the following verses of the pericope.

In v.23 John the Baptist appears within the context of the ministry of baptism. One notices the vocational similarity between Jesus and the Baptist concerning this baptismal ministry.[50] While in the synoptic accounts John the Baptist disappears from the ministry when Jesus appears, in the Fourth Gospel John's activity continues until his arrest, an idea supported by v.24. The Johannine presentation of the simultaneous ministry of Jesus and the Baptist corrects a possible misunderstanding [51] by showing that there was a considerable period of time during which Jesus and the Baptist were engaged in a parallel ministry between Christ's temptation and the arrest of John the Baptist.[52]

The baptism administered by the Baptist was not equal to that of Jesus (Jn 1,31.33). John's baptism was always understood as preparatory and designed to introduce the people to a true baptism in the Holy Spirit. By presenting Jesus and the Baptist side-by-side in the same ministry with noticeably varying results the Evangelist

---

[50] Cf. E. LINNEMANN, "Jesus und der Täufer", in: G. EBELING, E. JÜNGEL & G. SCHUNACK (eds.), *Festschrift für Ernst Fuchs* (Tübingen 1973) 220-221.

[51] One notes that in the parallel places in the synoptic gospels, there is no ministry presented between the temptation of Christ and the imprisonment of the Baptist (cf. Mt 4,11.12;Mk 1,13.14;Lk 4,13.14).

[52] Cf. HENDRIKSEN, *John*, 147.

aims to underline the superiority of Jesus to the Baptist, as the one increases and as the one decreases respectively.[53] In this context the presentation identifies the proper elements of a divine friendship, with Jesus as superior and John the Baptist not as inferior, but as one who accomplishes in himself the basic qualities of a true Christian disciple such as witnessing and humility. It can be said then that the baptismal ministry serves as the background for the intimate relationship between Jesus and the Baptist.[54]

b. Discussion Concerning Purification

The discussion[55] between the disciples of John and a Jew regarding purification is the immediate context for the final testimony of the Baptist which proclaims the superiority of Jesus and John's own unique position in the salvific ministry. The subject matter of discussion as one of purification is so general and there arise exegetical disputes among scholars in their attempts to explain it, since besides Johannine baptism and traditional jewish

---

[53] Cf. SCHNACKENBURG, *St. John*, Vol I, 451; LAGRANGE, *Saint Jean*, 93; WINK, *John the Baptist*, 96.

[54] BARRETT, *St. John*, 221, where he says: "...it seems probable that John's aim is not to furnish an interesting piece of historical information but to provide a background for v.30".

[55] The verbal noun ζήτησις is to be understood best in the sense of a discussion or argument rather than a dispute. The preposition ἐκ is not partitive, but it indicates the origin of the discussion on the part of the disciples of the Baptist. This has the value of the preposition ἀπό: Cf. A. BLASS & F.-DEBRUNNER, *A Greek Grammar of the New Testament*, R.W. FUNK (trs. & ed.) (Chicago 1961) § 209; N. TURNER, "Syntax", in: J.H. MOULTON, *A Grammar of New Testament Greek*, III (Edinburgh 1963) 259; M. ZERWICK, *Biblical Greek*, J. SMITH (trs. & ed.) (Rome 1963) § 87f.

purification there existed many purificatory rites in the Qumran
community. The term καθαρισμός refers to ritual or ceremonial
purification in general. The Fourth Evangelist uses the same term
to designate the jewish ritual purification (Jn 2,6) and also to denote
cleansing, clean etc., seen in its overtone as the effect of Christian
baptism (Jn 13, 10; 15,3; 1 Jn 1,7.9). One notes that the Evangelist
does not use the term βαπτισμός. Rather he uses καθαρισμός in
v.25 without the article (general sense), a word well known in the
early Church conveying the effects of different baptisms by which
intrinsic purity and absolution of sins etc. are conferred (cf. Heb 1,3;
9,14.22f.;10,2; 2 Pet 1,9; 2 Cor 7,1; Eph 5,26; Tit 2,14). Against this
background there is no difficulty to consider the usage of the word
as indicative of baptismal purification. [56]

In the light of these elements it can be asserted that the
accusation of the Baptist's disciples against Jesus (v.26) took place
in the context of a discussion concerning the comparative value of
Johannine baptism in relation to that of Jesus (His disciples). [57]
According to the synoptic tradition the baptism administered by the
Baptist was for repentance and the remission of the sins (Mk 1,4; Lk
3,3). According to the Johannine theology however it is only Jesus
who can take away the sins of the world (Jn 1,29). So, there may

---

[56] Cf. SCHNACKENBURG, *St. John*, Vol I, 414; Cf. also THOMAS
AQUINATIS, *Super Evangelium S. Ioannis Lectura*, P. RAPHAELIS CAI (ed.)
(Roma 1952) 507, where St. Thomas considers καθαρισμός as baptism itself.

[57] There are authors who consider this discussion on purification as centred on
the comparative value of the Johannine baptism and the Jewish purificatory rite. In
the course of the discussion the Jew might have been referring to the successful
baptism, which Jesus was giving simultaneously with the Baptist: Cf. H. VAN DEN
BUSSCHE, *Jean* (Bruges 1967) 176-177; Cf. also INFANTE, *L' amico dello Sposo*,
43.

probably have been a question from this person[58] regarding the value of the baptism administered by John, a question perceived as a challenge to the disciples of the Baptist. John's disciples actually wanted to know the reason for the speciality of Jesus' successful baptism.

The discussion about purifying resulted in a complaint of the Baptist's disciples regarding the incomprehensible success of Jesus' baptism as expressed in an exaggerated expression: πάντες ἔρχονται πρὸς αὐτόν (v.26).[59] For John's disciples it is a matter of jealousy and irritation. The key-expression "all are going to him" shows the superiority of Jesus, the content of the last testimony of the Baptist. Thus, through the stylistic expression πάντες ἔρχονται πρὸς αὐτόν, puts into the mouth of the Baptist's disciples in the form of an accusation, the Evangelist establishes the immediate context for the last testimony of the Baptist regarding the interpersonal relationship between Jesus and the faithful and Jesus and the Baptist.[60]

---

[58] This individual may be one who was baptized already or going to be baptized by Jesus (his disciples). Cf. M.E. BOISMARD, "L'ami de l' époux (Jo 3,29)", in: A. BARUCQ, -J. DUPLACY et al. (ed.), *A la rencontre de Dieu - Mémorial A. Gelin* (Paris 1961) 289. Regarding this Bultmann writes: "the only way of making sense of it in the context would be to suppose that the disciples of John have met up with a Jew, who has been or wants to be baptized by Jesus". BULTMANN, *John*, 169.

[59] The term πάντες in this context is not so absolute, since the speakers are not included. It can be a *hyperbole*, which by means of contrast shows the seriousness of the matter (all are going to him, i.e. soon you will be without any follower). According to Barrett this πάντες is a "historical exaggeration": Cf. BARRETT, *St. John*, 222; But for Marsh it is more likely to be a means by which the Evangelist tells his readers that a new people of God was being gathered rather than a number of individual converts. Cf. J. MARSH, *The Gospel of St. John* (London 1968) 199.

[60] Cf. BARRETT, *St. John*, 219-221. He finds the whole introductory section (vv.22-26)as an occasion to introduce the renewed testimony of the Baptist on Jesus.

To sum up the entire introductory section one can rightly
ascertain that the Evangelist stylistically and theologically cuts the
figure of Jesus as superior to that of the Baptist. This assertion will
help one to establish the nature of the relationship between Jesus
and the Baptist as one of friendship which is verified in v.29 when
the Evangelist adopts the the term φίλος.

B. The Last Testimony of the Baptist (vv.27-30)

The last testimony of the Baptist is presented as an answer to
the accusation of his disciples concerning the great success of Jesus.
In the process of clarification, John first of all establishes a general
principle regarding the great success and superiority of Jesus. Then
by rejecting any personal claim to be the Messiah and presenting
himself as the forerunner of Christ, he extols the position of Christ.
Thirdly John uses the metaphor of the bride-bridegroom
relationship, which has a social and biblical background. Finally,
John identifies himself with the friend of the bridegroom, i.e. the
one who prepares and leads the bride, stands and hears (obeys),
rejoices greatly in the success of the bridegroom and who then
diminishes at the appearance of the bridegroom, Jesus.

1. The General Principle (v.27)

In v.27 John brings the general principle that God has assigned
to everyone a place in his eternal plan.[61] Whatever one has, is truly
a gift of God (cf. 1 Cor 4,7) and without the power of God one can

---

[61] Cf. HENDRIKSEN, *John*, 148.

do nothing (cf. Jn 15,4). There are some particularly semitic expressions in this verse.[62] In the Baptist's answer it is clear that the success of Jesus was due to the Divine will (from heaven). In the general sense this principle is valid for all including Jesus and John the Baptist. In the context it refers particularly to Jesus[63] since it is the Divine will that Jesus gain more followers. It is also the Divine will that Jesus must (δεῖ) increase and John must decrease (v.30). Thus one sees a thematic inclusion between v.27 and v.30.

In the light of Johannine theology v.27 can be understood in two ways, viz. Jesus as the receiver of all Divine gifts (cf. Jn 3,35; 6,37.39; 10,29; 12,32; 17,2.9.11.24) or the faithful as the receivers of the Divine gifts (Cf. Jn 6,44.65). The first understanding (Christological) goes hand in hand with the context. This general principle is an explanation for the mass-movement of the people towards Jesus. It is the fulfilment of the Divine will that "all are going to him".[64]

---

[62] Cf. SCHNACKENBURG, *St. John*, Vol I, 415, ns.13.14.15, where he says that term ἄνθρωπος (man) referring to τίς (someone), though occurs in classical Greek, is a frequent semitic expression. Cf. also PANACKEL, *ΙΔΟΥ Ο ΑΝΘΡΩΠΟΣ*, 66. The expression δίδοσθαι ἐκ (given from) is semitic as Niphal or Hophal of נתן with מן. So also οὐρανός (heaven) is a well known circumlocution for God in semitism. In the OT this substitutes for the name of God and furnishes a reverential way of saying "from God": Cf. G. VON RAD, οὐρανός, *TDNT* V, 504-507.

[63] Cf. PANACKEL, *ΙΔΟΥ Ο ΑΝΘΡΩΠΟΣ*, 66.

[64] Cf. PANIMOLLE, *Giovanni*, Vol I, 339; BOISMARD, *L' ami de l'epoux*, 290; BROWN, *John*, Vol I, 155.

2. John, a Witness and Forerunner of Christ (v.28)

In answering the disciples John again refers back to his former testimony once again (cf. 1,20.27.30). Through a negative expression the Baptist affirms the supreme position of Jesus as well as his important role in relation to Jesus. He presents himself as precursor and herald of the Messiah (1,6.15.23) since he was the one sent (ἀπεσταλμένος)[65] before Him (ἐκείνου).[66] This sending is with a particular mission to prepare and to lead the people of God to Christ. John indirectly indicates that the mass-movement of the people to Jesus represents the fulfilment of his own mission. As a result of his first testimony (1,19-34) two of his disciples followed Jesus (1,35-51). Later at the marriage of Cana, Jesus' disciples, representing the Church (bride), were present along with the bridegroom, Jesus. The expression "all are going to him" here represents the real result of John's testimony precisely in his role as *the friend of the bridegroom*.[67] While the forerunner has the preparatory role to announce the coming of his master, he is not the master and deserves no honour. It is worth noting that the general tone of the personal testimonies of the Baptist are expressed in

---

[65] ἀπεσταλμένος εἰμὶ in 3,28 is a timeless present that shows a continuous witnessing, a role proper to a Christian disciple. By using this verb in this particular context the Evangelist highlights one of the main characteristics of the Baptist which makes him worth to be considered as a genuine Christian disciple.

[66] ἐκεῖνος is a typical Johannine usage and referring to Christ in the present context the Evangelist shows the importance of Christ. Cf. E. RUCKSTUHL, *Die Literarische Einheit des Johannesevangelium* (Freiburg 1987) 194.204, n. 17; W. BAUER, *A Greek-English Lexicon of the New Testament and Other Early Christian Literature*, ARNDT, F. & GINGRICH, F.W. (trs.) (Chicago 1979) 239, where the author proposes its special usage to denote well-known people like Jesus.

[67] Cf. I. DE LA POTTERIE, "Le nozze messianiche e il matrimonio Cristiano", *PSV* 13 (1986) 88-90.

negative formulae (Jn 1,19-34; 3,27-30).[68] By presenting himself as the one sent before Christ and by asserting once again that he is not Christ, John acknowledges and announces the superiority and the unique role of the Messiah.

Apart from polemic and apologetic interests the Fourth Evangelist desires to portray John as the ideal witness to Christ. Regarding this witnessing role of the Baptist Wink writes, "the Evangelist has interpreted the figure of John completely under the perspective of his relationship to Christ as a witness".[69] This continuous witnessing, an inevitable characteristic of any disciple, identifies John the Baptist as a true Christian disciple and a "confessing Christian".[70]

3. The Metaphor of the Bride-Bridegroom Relationship (v.29a)

In v.29 the theme of the spiritual marriage between Christ and the people of God appears. This metaphor, one deeply rooted in the OT imagery of marriage between Yahweh and Israel (cf. Ex 34,15; Ps 73,27; Hos 2,19; Jer 2,2; Is 54,5; 61,10), is used to depict the covenant relationship of God to His people, His covenant faithfulness and His forgiving patience. However in the OT it is not intended for the relationship between the Messiah and the Messianic community.[71] Likewise in later Judaism, especially in the Song of

---

[68] Cf. X. LÉON-DUFOUR, *Lecture de l'évangile selon Jean*, Vol I (Paris 1988) 324. Of course, there are also positive expressions: Cf. Jn 1,23.26.

[69] WINK, *John the Baptist*, 89.

[70] *Ibid.*, 90.

[71] Cf. J. JEREMIAS, νύμφη νυμφίος, *TDNT* IV, 1099.

songs, this imagery is clearly presented, but without any application to Messiah.

The NT and the early Church for their part do attribute this relationship to Christ and the New Israel (cf. Mk 2,19f.;Mt 9,15;Lk 5,34f;Mt 25,1-13;2 Cor 11,2;Eph 5,22f;Rev 19,7.9;21,2.9;22,17).[72] When John the Baptist declares that "he who has the bride is the bridegroom"(v.29a), he presupposes an OT understanding of the Yahweh-Israel matrimonial relationship, but with a more immediate application, i.e. to the Christ-Church relationship. [73] Just as Israel is the legitimate bride of Yahweh in the OT, so also the Church is the legitimate bride of Jesus. What John announced in 3,29 was already accomplished in the miracle at Cana (Jn 2,1-11) when Jesus, as the bridegroom, serves the wine at the messianic banquet. [74] In almost all the above mentioned NT texts, including Jn 3,29, the idea of Jesus-bridegroom is situated in the eschatological setting of a nuptial banquet. [75]

4. The Figure of the Friend of the Bridegroom (v.29b)

In the small parable of Jn 3,29 the Evangelist introduces the figure: ὁ φίλος τοῦ νυμφίου (the friend of the bridegroom). Since

---

[72] Cf. F.M. BRAUN, *Jean le Théologien*, III (Paris 1966) 100; BARRETT, *St. John*, 222-223.

[73] Bauer finds some connection between this metaphor and the gnostic idea of heavenly bridegroom and ἐρὸς γάμος : Cf. BAUER, *Johannesevangelium*, 63.

[74] Cf. BOISMARD, *Les Traditions*, 34.

[75] While the themes such as the 'going of all to Christ' (v.26), the fullness of joy (v.29), the divine judgement (v.36) etc. have an eschatological tone, for John they represent a realized and final eschatology.

the concept of the *friend of the bridegroom* is developed over several places and era of history, this historical process must be traced to highlight the meaning of the metaphor used in the present context.

a. In Extra-Biblical Literature

The figure of *the friend of the bridegroom* has its origin in Babylon, where it was expressed by the term *Susapînu (Susabinu)*. [76] For a long time this term was used for an official title [77] in spite of its unique significance of "the bridal attendant". [78] Babylonian matrimonial law explicitly refers to the companion of the bridegroom, stating:

> If a man has caused to bring a present to the house of his father-in-law and has paid the betrothal gift and his *companion* has acted against him, and his father-in-law has said to the husband; "you will not take my daughter!", he shall double and render everything which was brought unto him, and *his companion must not take his wife.*[79]

So also in the Sumerian law we see similar legislation, to the effect that:

---

[76] Cf. B. MEISSNER, *Akkadisches Handwörterbuch*, (on Susapînu) (Weisbaden 1965).

[77] Cf. F. DELITZCH, *Assyrisches Handwörterbuch*, (on Susapînu) (Leipzig 1896).

[78] Cf. A. VAN SELMS, "The Best Man and the Bride. From Sumer to St.John", *JNES* 9 (1950) 72-75, where Van Selms explains the role of *susapînu*. According to him this term refers to a piece of cloth used to wipe the virginal blood of the bride during the first night. It can also be a garland or crown used to decorate the bride.

[79] Code of Hammurabi: § 161, cf. VAN SELMS, *The Best Man*, 68-69 (Italics mine).

If a son-in-law has entered the house of his father-in-law
and has performed the betrothal gift, and afterwards they
have made him go out and have given his wife to his
companion, they shall present to him the betrothal gift which
he has brought and *that wife may not marry his companion.* [80]

In both these codes the word *companion* [81] is used in a restricted
sense in contrast with its wider meaning as friends or playmates. In
both cases we see the word companion in its singular form. This
companion is someone who could be compared to the *best man* in
the western marriages whose relation to the groom is of such a
nature that, when the marriage is cancelled, he may not take the girl
as a wife for himself. [82] The reason why the companion dare not
marry the girl is not explicitly mentioned. Probably it may be due
to the fact that the best man, as *the most intimate friend of the
bridegroom,* must show himself as one with the bridegroom in every
respect. [83]

---

[80] Code of Lipit-Ishtar: § 29, Cf. F.R. STEELE, "The Code of Lipit-Ishtar", *AJA*
(1948) 425-450 (Italics mine).

[81] For the term companion the code of Hammurabi used the term *ibru*, whereas
the code of Lipit-Ishtar used *kuli*. There is no substantial difference, but close
identity between these terms: Cf. A. DEIMEL, *Sumerisches Lexikon*, II, 4 (1933) 977;
Cf. also VAN SELMS, *The Best Man*, 70.

[82] Cf. *Ibid.*, 68.

[83] Such a close friendship is envisaged between Jesus and the Baptist in our
pericope. In the bride-bridegroom relationship between the Church and Jesus, John
has the role of the best man, who cannot marry the bride.

b. In the Old Testament

In the OT there are only a few texts which deal with Israelite marriage. The marriage ceremony had three main phases:[84] i) The reception of the bride in the house of the bridegroom; ii) the banquet; iii) the consummation of the marriage. In each of these three moments the *best man* played an important role.

For the reception ceremony the bridegroom was accompanied by a group of friends, one of whom had a special position (Judg 14-15). In Judg 14,11 one reads of thirty *companions*, brought to Samson by the men of Timnath on the occasion of Samson's marriage. To be noted is the word *friend* used in the singular in Judg 14,20 and rendered by the Hebrew word מרע which is very rare in the Masoretic text. During the bridal festivities, when Samson rejected his wife, she is given in marriage to his *companion* (מרעהו) who had fulfilled the duty of a *best man* (אשר רעה לו). This text of Judg 14,20 is translated differently in the LXX of the Vatican Codex as well as in Alexandrian manuscripts. LXX - B renders it as: ... ἑνὶ τῶν φίλων αὐτοῦ, ὧν ἐφιλίασεν; but LXX A reads: τῷ νυμφαγωγῷ αὐτοῦ, ὅς ἦν ἑταῖρος αὐτοῦ.[85] Here there is the mention of a best man. As for the Syriac version the equivalent expression *Pranympho ipsius* is used. From these texts it becomes

---

[84] Cf. INFANTE, *L' amico dello Sposo*, 98f.

[85] The use of the noun ἑταῖρος (friend) is noteworthy in this context, because it is not an acceptable action in the presence of the bridegroom. It is in fact against the existing law. The early translators probably wanted to show this unfavourable act of the so-called friend by using the Greek noun ἑταῖρος with its negative connotation.

clear that early translators underlined the role of Samson's friend, a role different from his other friends. [86]

During the banquet, which usually lasted for seven days and sometimes more (Tob 8,20; 10,8), and before the consummation of marriage there was a custom of appointing a certain number of youths as companions to the bridegroom. This practice is one clarified in the modern folklore of the Arabic-speaking population of the East. Throughout this one week the bridegroom and the bride were referred to as king and queen while the leader of the groom's companions was called *Wazir (Vizir)* of the bridegroom, who is the מרע in the strict sense of the word. [87]

The consummation of the marriage occurred in the first night of the matrimonial week in a specially prepared room. Even though there is no direct reference in the OT, it is supposed to have been the duty of the bridegroom's special friend to verify the virginity of the bride by examining the piece of the cloth stained with the blood, indicating the bride's virginity. [88] In short, the friend of the bridegroom enjoyed a close and intimate relationship with the bridegroom.

c. In Jewish Marriage Custom

The Johannine expression "*the friend of the bridegroom*" has an exact parallel in Mishnah, Sanhedrin iii,5, with its clear reference to

---

[86] Cf. INFANTE, *L' amico dello Sposo*, 94.

[87] Cf. VAN SELMS, *The Best Man*, 71. It is supposed that this *best man* in the wedding of the kings in Israel and Egypt is called later as *the friend of the king*

[88] Cf. INFANTE, *L'amico dello Sposo*, 92.

the bridegroom's best man - אַרהב זה שׁוֹשביני[89]. Regarding the practice of having a שׁוֹשבין for a bride and bridegroom, one notes the difference between Galilean and Judean marriage. According to the Talmud there was no such custom in Galilee. In Judea however one finds the practice of having two *friends* (Brautführer), one of the bride and the other of the bridegroom. According to the Judean custom these friends were to sleep near the couple to testify to the virginity of the bride.[90]

In the context of the tradition it was this *best man* who was in charge of arranging and celebrating the marriage. About his role Derrett writes:

> Since it was not usual for marriages to be arranged by the parties in person, the prospective bridegroom's parents employed a man to act as their agent in effecting the betrothal of their son. The interests of the bridegroom were represented by this independent *go-between* and the selected bride's family saw to it that they too were represented by what may not improperly be described as an agent. When it came to the actual ceremony of the marriage the bridegroom's representative saw his work come to fruition and assisted at the critical moment.[91]

This individual, therefore, had an economic, ceremonial and social role to play. According to Jewish custom the friends of the bride and bridegroom were present at the betrothal ceremony. Since

---

[89] Cf. I. ABRAHAMS, *Studies in Pharisaism and the Gospel* (New York 1967) 213. Etymologically the expression is connected with שׁבב and חבר = one who stands nearby, who is related; Cf. also J. LEVY, *Wörterbuch über die Talmudim und Midraschim*, Vol IV (Berlin 1924) 526; J. LEVY, *Chaldäisches Wörterbuch über die Targumim*, Vol II (Leipzig 1881) 464-465.

[90] Cf. STRACK & BILLERBECK, *Talmud und Midrasch*, Vol I, 46; Cf. also INFANTE, *L'amico dello Sposo*, 11f.;ABRAHAMS, *Pharisaism and the Gospel*, 213.

[91] J.D.M. DERRETT, "Water into Wine", *BZ* 7 (1963) 81.

he took the place of the bridegroom the friend was eligible to present gifts to the bride.[92] Likewise, for the marriage ceremony, the friend or "the best man" (along with other friends) accompanied the bridegroom as the bridegroom went to meet the bride and lead her to his house. It is the one friend who took the lead in arranging for the marriage ceremonies.[93] He officially presents the bride to the bridegroom, stands (ἵστημι) outside the nuptial room and listens for the voice of the bridegroom.[94] Thus this individual is called *the friend of the bridegroom*, because his role is superior to that of all other friends and guests.[95]

d. In The NT Matrimonial Texts

In the light of the NT matrimonial texts one can distinguish two moments of the ceremony: the betrothal and the wedding itself. After the betrothal there was an interval of about one year and during this period there was no cohabitation by the partners (Mt 1,19). The wedding included two distinct moments of celebration: the reception ceremony (Mt 25,1-13) and the wedding lunch (Jn 2,1-10; Mt 22,1-10; Lk 14,15-24).

---

[92] Cf. E. NEUFELD, *Ancient Hebrew Marriage Laws* (London 1944) 143.

[93] Talmud (Keth. 12a) attests that in Galilee it was only one, while in Judea two ie. one each from the side of both the bride and the bridegroom.

[94] Cf. V. DELLAGIACOMA, "Il Matrimonio presso gli Ebrei", *RivB* 7 (1959) 235.

[95] Cf. W. DE BOOR, *Das Evangelium des Johannes*, Vol I (Wuppertal 1971) 122-123; J. NEUBAUER, *Beiträge zur Geschichte des Biblisch-Talmudische Eheschliessungsrechts* (Mitteilungen der Vorderasiastischen Gesselschaft) (Leipzig 1920) 61-62; JEREMIAS, νύμφη, *TDNT* IV, 1101; PANIMOLLE, *Giovanni*, Vol I, 339; H.H. SCOBIE, *John the Baptist* (London 1964) 152.

In some NT texts we see the mentioning of the wedding guests - υἱοὶ τοῦ νυμφῶνος (Mk 2,19-20; Mt 9,15; Lk 5,34-35). Besides these guests there is also the individual identified as ὁ φίλος τοῦ νυμφίου (Jn 3,29). In the immediate context of this text, the friend of the bridegroom is presented as one who has already led the bride (the people of God) to the bridegroom (Jesus). Being identified with the traditional figure, the friend of the bridegroom, as the one who is in charge of the wedding celebrations, he presents himself earnestly executing his responsibilities by standing nearby the bridegroom and listens to his voice.[96] There is also a reference to his great joy at the voice of the bridegroom in the fulfilment of the wedding ceremony for which he was appointed. [97] In considering the above mentioned duties, the friend of the bridegroom referred in Jn 3,29 is closer to the figure of the best man (שׁוֹשׁבִין) in the Judaistic matrimonial rites, mentioned in Talmud and Mishna. [98]

Allusion to the friend of the bridegroom is also found in the writing of St. Paul. In 2 Cor 11,2 he attributes to himself the role of the friend of the bridegroom at least in a symbolic way. Describing his apostolic office, he compares the community with a bride, Christ with the bridegroom, and himself with the best man,

---

[96] The verb ἵστημι denotes the attitude of a servant (cf. 1 Kg 17,1) and ἀκούειν (שׁמע) means an obedient listening: Cf. BARRETT, St. John, 223.

[97] There are difference of opinion among the scholars concerning the voice of the bridegroom. Some consider it as the call of the bridegroom from the bridal chamber for the friend who customarily fetches the signum virginitatis: Cf. JEREMIAS, νύμφη, TDNT IV, 1001f.; PANIMOLLE, Giovanni, Vol I, 339. Others consider this voice as the solemn prayer of seven blessings uttered by the bridegroom as the concluding words of the feast (Jer 33,11): Cf. ZEVINI, Gesù lo Sposo, 110; H. SCHNEID, Marriage (Jerusalem 1973) 32; INFANTE, L' amico dello Sposo, 13; R.P. VAN KASTEREN, "Jo 3,29: Vox Sponsi", RB 3 (1894) 64.

[98] Cf. C. SPICQ, Agapè dans le Nouveau Testament. Analyse des Textes, Vol III (Paris 1959) 238-239.

who obtained the bride, watches over her virginity, and who will lead her to the bridegroom at the wedding.[99] It appears that Paul has the idea of שׁוֹשׁבִין in mind when he writes 2 Cor 11,2.[100]

In short, we can say that in the NT times, especially in St. John and also in St.Paul there is highlighted the figure of *the friend of the bridegroom*, who enjoys a very important role in the matrimonial relationship between Jesus and the Church. This figure is closely connected with the figure of שׁוֹשׁבִין in the jewish marriage custom. Therefore, in the first level of interpretation one must consider the historical development of this figure. Beyond this, when John the Baptist identifies himself with this figure by calling himself *the friend of the bridegroom*, many theological considerations also emerge. Therefore the reference to the figure of the friend of the bridegroom merits not only a historical analysis done above but also a theological interpretation which follows.

5. John the Baptist as the Friend of the Bridegroom (vv.29c-30)

Having traced the historical and cultural development we begin to investigate the theological implications of the figure of the *friend of the bridegroom* as a metaphor applied to John the Baptist. The immediate application is vivid in the expression of the Baptist, αὕτη οὖν ἡ χαρὰ ἡ ἐμὴ πεπλήρωται, by which he identifies his joy with the joy of the *friend of the bridegroom*. Moreover he thereby identifies his person with the figure of the ὁ φίλος τοῦ νυμφίου since

---

[99] Cf. JEREMIAS, νύμφη, *TDNT* IV, 1104; Cf. also BOISMARD, *L' ami de l'époux*, 292.

[100] Cf. VAN SELMS, *The Best Man*, 75.

it conveys both the Baptist's mission as well as his spiritual relationship to Christ. [101]

In the introductory part of the pericope Jesus is presented giving baptism with great success (v.26). In Johannine theology the great success of Jesus can be considered as the fruit of the mission, with which John is entrusted by God. The Fourth Evangelist presented John as an envoy, sent from God with a special mission (cf. Jn 1,6.33; 3,28). John as the witness of Jesus was the voice who called the bride (the people of God) for the spiritual marriage with the bridegroom (Jesus). As the friend of the bridegroom he prepared and presented the bride to the bridegroom. The fulfilment of the duty of the Baptist as herald of Jesus solidify their interpersonal relationship.

Against the background of the metaphor John presented himself as the friend who stands and hears the voice of the bridegroom and rejoices greatly at the success of the bridegroom. By affirming that his joy is now full, John expresses his wish to be no more than a friend of the bridegroom, who leads the bride to the bridegroom and fulfils all his responsibilities connected with that. [102] By the fulfilment of the spiritual wedding of Jesus with the New Israel the Baptist's role of the friend of the bridegroom is accomplished. John the Baptist's role can be compared to that of Moses in the OT, who concluded the alliance between Yahweh and His people in mount Sinai. [103]

---

[101] Cf. G. GAETA, "Battesimo come Testimonianza. Le Pericopi sul Battista nell' evangelo di Giovanni", *Crist Stor* I (1980) 304.

[102] Cf. SCHNACKENBURG, *St. John*, Vol I, 416-417; VAN SELMS, *The Best Man*, 75; DE LA POTTERIE, *Le nozze Messianiche*, 91; KLAIBER, *Joh 3.22-36*, 225, esp.n.56.

[103] Cf. STRACK & BILLERBECK, *Talmud und Midrasch*, Vol I, 501-502.

Just as the friend of the bridegroom disappears from the scene when his duty is fulfilled, so also John the Baptist disappeared from the scene by giving place to Jesus and saying: "he must increase, but I must decrease" (v.30).[104] As his true friend, John the Baptist was not an obstacle to the progress of the bridegroom, Jesus. The increasing of Jesus is a **must** in the salvation history. Once all people are going to Jesus, then the mission of the Baptist is completed. By hiding himself from the scene John the Baptist draws all attention to Jesus. In this respect the expression in v.30 is the culmination of the witnessing role of the Baptist. Because all the work of the friend of the bridegroom is directed towards the successful matrimony of the bridegroom, John the Baptist proves himself worthy to be identified with this figure. He does all so that Jesus may successfully enter a covenant relationship to his people.

C. Jesus, the Unique Revealer (vv.31-36)

In the final subsection of the pericope the Evangelist presents Jesus as the unique and supreme revealer and thereby inspires all to believe in Him. In the preceding section the great success of Jesus is reported by the disciples of the Baptist with jealousy. John the Baptist by means of a metaphor explains the secret of Jesus' success as well as His superiority in all humility. These final verses of the pericope (vv.31-36) recapitulate and further explain the superiority of Jesus in the form of a monologue. The Evangelist does this by making use of the scattered sermons of Jesus and arranging them

---

[104] Bultmann considers the verbs αὐξάνειν and ἐλαττοῦσθαι in the solar sense: Cf. BULTMANN, *John*, 174-175; Dodd considers this verse as an *aphorism* (wise saying): Cf. C.H. DODD, *Historical Tradition in the Fourth Gospel* (Cambridge 1963) 279.

properly within his scheme along with theological and personal notes. Such a presentation of the Evangelist has also some historical relevance and it refers to his own relation with the Jewish religion.[105] In the section the Evangelist speaks of faith in three aspects: the obligation to believe because Jesus is the unique revealer, the scarcity of those who believe, the reward for belief and unbelief.[106]

The main theme of this subsection (vv.31-36) is the superiority of Jesus, which obliges the hearers to believe. Jesus is presented here as the unique and supreme revealer. The reasons for this uniqueness are brought out stylistically and systematically in this subsection. The divine origin of Jesus is the first principle of his superiority. The expressions such as "the one who comes from above" (ὁ ἄνωθεν) and "he who comes from heaven" (ἐκ τοῦ οὐρανοῦ) refer to Jesus (cf.Jn 3,13.31). He is above all who are earthly, including John the Baptist. The expression "he who is of earth" (γῆς)[107] refers to all those who prepare for the definitive revelation. Since Πάντων stands for humanity in general, so also the one who comes from earth could be taken generically. Yet in this context it refers to John the Baptist who represents the natural

---

[105] One sees here the polemic motive of the Fourth Gospel. Contemporary Jewish society (represented by Nicodemus in ch.3) and the disciples of the Baptist try to project only the human nature of Jesus. But here the Evangelist tries to prove the contrary.

[106] Cf. THOMAS, *Evangelium S. Ioannis*, 535.

[107] In the Fourth Gospel heaven and earth are theological terms rather than concrete, physical entities. Earth (γῆ) has no negative connotation as world (κόσμος) does. It refers to natural existence. Nor earth is to be seen as subordinated to heaven: Cf. SCHNACKENBURG, *St. John*, Vol I, 382; BROWN, *John*, Vol I, 156-158; BARRETT, *St. John*, 224; BRUCE, *The Gospel of John*, 96; BERNARD, *St. John*, Vol 1, 124.

reality. This presentation of the Baptist is consistent both with the Johannine presentation of the Baptist and with the polemic against the sectarians of the Baptist. John the Baptist is not equal to Jesus (cf. Jn 3,5.13; 1 Jn 5,6), but was the man *sent* from God (Jn 1,6; 3,28) while Jesus is He who *came down* from heaven (Jn 3,31; 6,41.51). The contrast is made to show the supreme nature of the unique heavenly revealer.

The difference between Jesus and the Baptist then is that the Baptist has only mediate access to God (i.e through depending on Jesus), while Jesus as one who has seen and heard God has an immediate relation to God.[108] Because of His divine origin, Jesus is the unique, authentic and eschatological revealer of the heavenly realities (v.32). Jesus' testimony is authentic, since He bears witness to what He has seen (ἑωράκεν)[109] and heard (ἤκουσεν).[110]

God's truthfulness guarantees the truth of Christ's testimony (v.34). Thus the truth of Jesus' words is God Himself, a truth which therefore is supreme and unique. In this section the Evangelist connects faith with the trinitarian mystery (vv.33-34). Belief in Christ's testimony is an attestation (σφραγίζειν) that He speaks the words of God. The same idea is expressed in 1 Jn 5,10 negatively.

---

[108] Cf. J. MATEOS & J. BARRETO, *Il Vangelo di Giovanni* (Asissi 1982) 203-204.

[109] Greater stress is given to the *seeing* by using the perfect tense, which shows a continued action, continuing reaches until the present moment: Cf. BLASS - DEBRUNNER, *Greek Grammar*, § 342, 2.

[110] In Jn 15,15 one finds the use of the same verb as the basis of Jesus' calling His disciples friends.

Another reason for the uniqueness of Jesus' testimony is that Jesus is one who is sent[111] by God. God Himself speaks in the words of the God-sent Revealer. As the one "speaking the words of God" Jesus is the supreme prophet, the one who receives the Spirit in its fullness (without measure). [112] It is because (γάρ) God gives[113] His Spirit to Jesus fully that he can be a spokesman of God.

The authenticity of Jesus' witnessing is still attested to by presenting Jesus as the beloved of the Father with whom the Father shares His authority (v.35). It is the nature of the love to give without measure (cf. Jn 3,16; 13,9; 14,31). 'To give something into the hands of another' is a semitic expression, indicating the conferral of power and authority. It is the Johannine way of expressing the *authority* of the revealer and saviour as he is sent into the world.[114] The expression "the Father has given all things into his hand" means that the Father is present in the Son and the Son represents the Father. [115] The "handing over of all things to the Son" is a frequent

---

[111] It is a fact that in the Fourth Gospel both Jesus and John the Baptist have been sent by God (cf. 1,6; 3,28; 3,17; 5,36.38; 6,29.57; 7,29; 8,42; 9,7; 10,36; 11,42; 17,3.8.21.23.25; 20,21). From the context of our text it is clear that 'one who is sent by God' is Jesus.

[112] God's prophets were charged with speaking the words of God, but they enjoyed the Spirit in different measures "as weighed out" or "by measure" (ἐκ μέτρου): Cf. STRACK & BILLERBECK, *Talmud und Midrasch*, Vol II, 431; cf. also THOMAS, *Evangelium S. Ioannis*, 541-543.

[113] Concerning the subject of the verb δίδωσιν (to give) there is a dispute among the exegetes. Some proposes God as the subject (cf. SCHNACKENBURG, *St. John*, Vol I, 386; BERNARD, *St. John*, Vol 1, 125), while others find the Son as the subject (cf. BROWN, *John*, Vol I, 158.161). In our textual context it is the Father who gives the Spirit to His Son. Cf. pp. 35-36.

[114] Cf. SCHNACKENBURG, *St. John*, Vol I, 388.

[115] Cf. BULTMANN, *John*, 165.

theme   in   the   Fourth   Gospel   (5,22.26.27;   6,37;   12,49;
17,2.6.8.11.12.22) and also one present in the Synoptics (cf. Mt
11,27; Lk 10,12).

The second aspect the Evangelist develops in the final section
of the pericope is the scarcity of the believers. He uses an absolute
negative term οὐδεὶς (no one) to express the general tendency of
rejecting the testimony of Jesus (v.32). But such a Johannine
absolute negation always leaves place for exceptions (cf. Jn 1,11&12;
8,15&16; 12,37&42). By means of the absolute negative expression
followed by the positive response from a remnant (v.33) the
Evangelist wants to depict the scarcity of those who believe in Jesus
in spite of His authentic revelation.   Jesus' superiority and
uniqueness are highlighted even in the midst of the tension between
the negative and positive response to His testimony.

V.36 exposes the third aspect of the final section of the
pericope, viz. the reward for belief and unbelief. A concrete
expression of the power of Jesus is His judgment of the world (Jn
3,36; 5,20-30; 17,2) by which He gives eternal life to those who
believe and punishes those who do not believe (disobey). [116] To
accept the supreme revelation of Jesus and thereby to believe in
Him is essential in order to have eternal life (ζωὴ αἰώνιος). The
denial of the unique revelation of Jesus and a consequent
disobedience (unbelief) to His commandments results in a privation
of eternal life, characterized by the permanence of God's wrath (ἡ

---

[116] In v.36 one sees a contrast between believing and disobeying. For John,
believing and obeying are the same. One cannot obey Jesus without believing in
him. Eternal life is God's commandment (12,50) and so, "to believe" is "to obey".
For him faith in the Son involves an obedient submission to the Son and acceptance
of his revelation and commandments (15,14). John always uses the verb form -
πιστεύων - to speak of *faith* which shows the Johannine understanding of faith as
a vital and personal attitude: Cf. SCHNACKENBURG, *St. John*, Vol I, 389.

ὀργὴ τοῦ Θεοῦ).[117] In short the judgment of God will be determined by one's relation with Jesus. The possession of life or denial of life depends on human response (negative or positive) to the revelation of the supreme revealer.

VI. Theological Perspective

The whole pericope (Jn 3,22-36) is focused on the superiority and divinity of Jesus and on the interpersonal relationship between Jesus and John the Baptist. Their relationship, as illustrated here by the Fourth Evangelist, is neither purely psychological nor superficial. The Evangelist introduces Jesus as the bridegroom (ὁ νυμφίος) and John the Baptist as the friend of the bridegroom (ὁ φίλος τοῦ νυμφίου) and thereby he intends to convey a profoundly theological relationship. This relationship is not between equals but between Jesus, the bridegroom and the Baptist, the friend of the bridegroom. Throughout the text the superiority of Jesus is clearly exposed. At the same time the unique and important role of the Baptist is clearly affirmed. John the Baptist possesses the essential characteristics of a true Christian disciple. In the following part of this chapter, we theologically synthesize both the elements that manifest the superiority of Jesus as well as the characteristics of the Baptist which portray him a genuine Christian disciple.

---

[117] The same idea of having life (by being pruned) and eternal punishment (by being cut away and thrown into fire) are clear in Jn 15,2.6. The idea of eschatological punishment for the unbelieving is developed by St. Paul also (cf. Rom 1,18; 2,5.8; Eph 2,3).

A. The Superiority of Jesus
1. Jesus, a Successful Baptizer

Even though, as pointed out earlier, Jesus Himself did not baptize (cf. Jn 4,2) the Fourth Evangelist presents Jesus as a successful baptizer, who appears side-by-side with John the Baptist, [118] in this way showing their closeness even in their mission and activity. It is obvious that Jesus and the Baptist share something in common but in different degree. [119] The great success of Jesus in His ministry is clear from the accusation of the disciples of the Baptist: "all are going to him" (v.26). The movement toward Jesus is deeply theological since it indicates accepting Jesus' superiority and believing in Him (v.36). Likewise the movement toward Jesus is directed toward faith in Him in order to obtain eternal life, for which reason the Fourth Gospel was written (Jn 20,31). John the Baptist proclaims this success of Jesus as an authentic divine gift (v.27).

2. Jesus, the Messiah and Bridegroom

Jesus' messianic role is repeatedly affirmed by the Baptist throughout his testimonies. When John the Baptist affirms that he is not the Christ (Jn 1,20; 3,28), he indirectly proclaims that Jesus is the Christ, the lamb of God who takes away the sins of the world, the one for whom all Israel was waiting. For the Baptist in the Fourth Gospel there was no doubt about the messianic role of Jesus.

---

[118] Cf. supra, pp. 50-53.

[119] Cf. M. DIBELIUS, *Die Urchristliche Überlieferung von Johannes dem Täufer* (FRLANT 15) (Göttingen 1911) 111.

Additionally, in the pericope under consideration John identifies Jesus as the bridegroom of the messianic community. When he presents Jesus as the bridegroom, it is an assertion which presupposes the Yahweh-Israel relationship portrayed in the OT.[120] The people of God are seen as the legitimate bride of the bridegroom, Jesus, while the figure of the bridegroom sheds light on the Jesus' supreme role, i.e. His Messianic role. The supreme transcendental role of Jesus, the bridegroom emphasizes the secondary role of the Baptist, the friend of the bridegroom.[121] Thus the bridegroom, as the chief person in the matrimonial ceremony, takes precedence overall since he must increase in all respects.

3. Jesus, the one who Came from Heaven

Since Jesus came from above and he is above all (v.31) all must follow him. Compared to all earthly realities and humanity in particular, Jesus because of His divine origin is far superior. Therefore the disciples of the Baptist need not become jealous when all are going to Him. Jesus Himself says, "when I am lifted up from the earth I will draw all men to myself" (Jn 12,32). Needless to say, the divine origin of Jesus was an unfashionable mystery for His contemporaries, a mystery of which Jesus Himself spoke (Jn 6,33.38.41.50.58).

---

[120] Cf. BRAUN, *Jean*, Vol III, 99; WESTCOTT, *St. John*, 59; PANIMOLLE, *Giovanni*, Vol I, 344.

[121] PANIMOLLE, *Giovanni*, Vol I, 345, where he writes: "Il quarto evangelista, quando presenta Gesù come lo sposo del nuovo Israele, s'ispira a una tradizione antica, per proclamare la trascendenza divina di Gesù e per sottolineare l'inferiorità del Battista dinanzi a questo personaggio eccezionale".

4. Jesus, an Authentic Divine Witness

As one came from heaven Jesus gives authentic testimony concerning the divine realities.   Jesus is the sole authentic and unique revealer of the Father. [122]   Later, on the basis of His revelatory role Jesus claims to be the friend of the disciples (Jn 15,15). Jesus communicates the word of God (Jn 3,34). He bears witness to the heavenly realities that he has seen (and continues to see) [123] and heard (Jn 3,11.32).   Since Jesus is in continuous communion with the Father He is authentic in His testimony (cf. Jn 1,17.18; 14,6). Jesus came to bear witness to the truth (Jn 18,37), i.e. to reveal and communicate divine life.

5. Jesus, the Beloved of the Father

Jesus is loved by the Father in a special and profound way, as seen in the fact that the Father has entrusted all His power to His Son (Jn 3,35). In this way, the Son can receive the Spirit in fullness from the Father and can impart the same Spirit to the community of the believers abundantly.   He even enjoys the power to establish eternal life for those who believe in Him and punishment for those who disobey Him (v.36). The love of the Father is the rode by which Jesus measures His love for His disciples (cf. Jn 15, 9f.). Additionally Jesus was conscious of His powers He received from the Father (cf. Jn 13,3), a fact which the disciples also acknowledged

---

[122] Cf.   *Ibid.*, 341; J. BEUTLER,   *Martyria: Traditionsgeschichtliche Unter-suchungen zum Zeugnisthema bei Johannes* (Frankfurt 1972) 316f.

[123] Cf. supra, p. 72.

(cf. Jn 17,7). The divine love, specifically manifested in the love of the Father for the Son, also highlights the superiority of Jesus.

B. The Figure of John the Baptist

While the Synoptics present John the Baptist only as a forerunner of Jesus, the Fourth Evangelist presents him as an authentic witness of Jesus (cf. Jn 1,19.32.34;3,26; 5,33). In other words, the Johannine presentation of the figure of the Baptist is to be seen completely from the perspective of his relationship to Christ as a *witness*.[124] One sees this witnessing role clearly in the Baptist's first testimony (Jn 1,19-51). It is again reaffirmed in his last testimony (Jn 3,22-36) and even in the accusation of John's disciples regarding the success of Jesus the Baptist's witnessing role (μαρτυρία) is once again portrayed (v.26). It must be noted how even in his answer John reminds them of his former testimony. The witnessing role is fulfilled finally when John's own disciples follow Jesus as a result of his witnessing (cf. Jn 1,37).

The authentic testimony of the Baptist was the expression of his deep knowledge and faith in the person of Christ. Such a genuine testimony of the Baptist motivated many to come to faith in Jesus, thereby obtaining salvation. Thus, through his witnessing role John the Baptist already became a *genuine Christian* since he possessed faith in and knowledge of Christ and led many to Christ.[125] In the perspective of the Fourth Gospel an authentic Christian disciple is one who opens himself to the divine call (cf. Jn 1,39ff.) and who is

---

[124] WINK, *John the Baptist*, 89; Cf. also DIBELIUS, *Johannes dem Täufer*, 120.

[125] Cf.I. DE LA POTTERIE, *Gesù Verità: Studi di Cristologia Giovannea*, A. MILANOLI et al. (trs.) (Torino 1973) 173.

sent by Jesus to bear witness to Christ both in words and deeds (cf. Jn 13,34-35; 15,16). John the Baptist is sent (ἀποστέλλω) by God to bear witness (μαρτυρέω) to Christ (Jn 3,26.28) just as every Christian disciple is sent by Christ to give testimony to His Gospel of fraternal mutual love (Jn 4,38; 13,34-35). Giving testimony to one's own unique Christ-experience is the real mission of a disciple.[126] This mission is perfectly fulfilled already in the life of John the Baptist since he was the greatest witness to the Messiah.[127] The Evangelist presents him as an ideal witness to Christ, one whose testimony and confession of faith enable others to come to faith in the Johannine Christ.[128] However, in spite of this one cannot consider John the Baptist as a Christian disciple in the strict sense of the term, i.e. as one of the Twelve; but rather in its wider sense as one who remained in Jesus' words and accomplished his kerygmatic and witnessing role regarding Jesus (cf. Jn 8,31).[129] Such a consideration goes well with the Johannine theology of discipleship.

In the pericope under consideration one finds other reasons to establish the Baptist's Christian discipleship. By considering four terms, viz. φίλος (friend), φωνή (voice), ακούω (hear), and χαρά

---

[126] Cf. M. VELLANICKAL, *Studies in the Gospel of John* (Bangalore 1982) 123.

[127] Cf. INFANTE, *L' amico dello Sposo*, 154.

[128] Cf. C. PAJOT, "L'interprétation johannique du ministere de Jean Baptiste (Jean I)", *FoiVie* 63,3 = *CahBib* 7 (1969) 36; WINK, *John the Baptist*, 105f.; PANIMOLLE, *Giovanni*, Vol I, 354; S. GAROFALO, *Con il Battista incontro a Cristo* (Milano 1981) 98.

[129] The Johannine Jesus considers those who believe in Him and remain in His words as His genuine disciples. Without a faith in the person and teaching of Jesus one cannot be real witness of Jesus. When John the Baptist gives testimony to Christ he has already possessed a deep faith in Jesus and thereby fulfilled the essential characteristic of a Christian disciple.

(joy) found in the Baptist's confession (Jn 3,29) one can establish John the Baptist as an authentic Christian disciple.[130] One arrives at such a conclusion through a comparison of those terms as used in this pericope with other usages connected to Christian discipleship found elsewhere in the Fourth Gospel.

With the exception of Jn 19,12 the Fourth Evangelist uses the term φίλος to depict Jesus' relationship with others. In Jn 11,11 φίλος is used to qualify Lazarus. But when the Johannine Jesus addressing His disciples uses the expression "our friend Lazarus has fallen asleep", He thereby includes Lazarus in the circle of His disciples. The other three occurrences of the term φίλος are to be found in Jn 15,13-15, where it explains the interpersonal relationship between Jesus and His disciples. Here the Evangelist uses the term as a designation for those who are asked to keep His commandments and to whom He reveals what He has heard from the Father. Thus in the Johannine presentation generally the term φίλος is closely connected to discipleship. In this context then it is legitimate to conclude that the use of the term in Jn 3,29 designating John the Baptist presupposes a consideration of the Baptist as a genuine Christian disciple.

The terms φωνή (voice) and ἀκούω (hear) are deeply theological. In Jeremiah the voice of the bridegroom is connected with the spiritual status of the people of God. When Israel wandered from God's commandments they were deprived of His voice (cf. Jer 7,34; 16,9; 25,10). Obedience to Yahweh's commandments is a necessary preliminary to listening to the bridegroom's voice. One finds a parallelism between John the Baptist in the present pericope and the friends mentioned in the

---

[130] Cf. BRAUN, *Jean*, Vol III, 99-103.

Canticle of Canticles (cf.8,13).[131] The term φωνή in Jn 3,29 indicates the voice of the bridegroom, Jesus who is sent by the Father. The voice of Jesus represents His authentic testimony, including the Father's precepts. Often the Fourth Evangelist uses the term ἀκούω to denote spiritual hearing and obedience. [132] The listeners of Jesus are true believers; true believers are therefore true disciples and true disciples logically are true friends. In the allegory of the Good Shepherd the voice of the shepherd is heard by the sheep (Jn 10,3), a reference to the Christian's positive response to the revelation of the Good Shepherd as well as attitude of obedience to his commandments. Such an obedient listening is an essential characteristic of a real disciple, one which is verified in the case of John the Baptist (Jn 3,29). By listening to the voice of Jesus, the bridegroom John the Baptist became an authentic Christian disciple.

The fourth term under our consideration is χαρά which literally means joy. Since in its theological consideration χαρά lacks the characteristic of a purely human joy, its meaning is to be found in the context of the Johannine presentation of eschatological joy.[133] This is the same joy which, in all its fullness, Jesus shares to His disciples when he departs from this world (Jn 15,11; 17,13; 1 Jn 1,4). Each disciple is called to experience the same joy of Christ in its fullness through a life of obedience (Jn 15,10-11). The joy referred in Jn 3,29 results from the total obedience of the friend of the bridegroom, which obedience culminates in the successful wedding with its awaited conclusion, viz. the voice of the bridegroom. When

---

[131] Cf. *Ibid.*, 102.

[132] Cf. THOMAS, *Evangelium S. Ioannis*, 520.

[133] Cf. BULTMANN, *John*, 174.

John the Baptist claims that he has already obtained the fullness of joy, he states the fact that he has already become a genuine Christian disciple.[134]

In this rich context one can conclude that the metaphor of the ὁ φίλος τοῦ νυμφίου symbolically presents John the Baptist as a genuine Christian disciple. He is the one who has already undergone the experience of a perfect disciple by denying himself and listening to the voice of Jesus. Thus he became the first participant in eschatological joy and entered into the state of friendship with Jesus, to which all disciples of Jesus are later called (cf. Jn 15,1-17). Accordingly John the Baptist therefore can be considered as a prototype of a perfect disciple.[135]

C. The Friendship Between Jesus and the Baptist

In his final testimony John the Baptist presents himself in the close relationship of friendship with Jesus. It is a friendship with responsibilities, one that presupposes a responsible interpersonal relationship. The nature of the relationship between Jesus and the Baptist is well depicted throughout the pericope both stylistically as well as through the content of the text. Jesus and the Baptist are

---

[134] Cf. BOISMARD, L'ami de l'époux, 291; PANIMOLLE, Giovanni, Vol I, 344.

[135] Braun's words support our position when he writes: Que le Christ doive être identifié avec l'Époux des noches messianiques, le contexte des chapitres II-IV le prouve. Au lieu du paranymphe (שׁוֹשְׁבִין), l'expression ὁ φίλος τοῦ νυμφίου ne fait-elle pas penser dès lors qu'anticipant sur la condition à laquelle les Douze parviendront sur le tard, Jean était déjà passé de la condition de serviteur à celui de l'ami? La voix de l'époux ne serait-elle pas la Parole dont il avait éprouvé la puissance transformante? Jean, enfin, ne nous aurait-il pas été proposé comme prototype des parfaits disciples, parce, que, dans le renoncement le plus complet de lui-même, lui, le tout premier l'avait écoutée?: BRAUN, Jean, Vol III, 103.

presented in contrast but also in a mutual relationship. Jesus appears as a successful baptizer, as Messiah and bridegroom, as beloved of the Father and as the supreme and unique revealer of the Father. The success and superiority of Jesus are accepted by the Baptist, with extreme humility, as the fulfilment of the divine will. The presence and the mission of the Baptist are secondary compared to that of Jesus. He was not Christ but one sent before Christ to bear witness to Him. By assuming the role of the friend of the bridegroom the Baptist fulfilled a most serious responsibility on behalf of the bridegroom, Jesus, seen in his constant readiness to execute his mission, i.e. listening the voice of the bridegroom and denying himself for the sake of his friend (vv.29-30). All the above mentioned duties of the friend of the bridegroom are proper to a genuine Christian disciple in the relationship to his master, Christ.

The role of the Baptist was one of docility and submission to his supreme master. As a real witness of Jesus he first had to live out the teaching of Jesus by giving testimony to the world around in view of preparing a community of believers (bride) for his friend (bridegroom). There is a reciprocal relationship between Jesus and the Baptist since they bear witness to each other. John bears witness to Christ in the beginning (Jn 1,19-36; 3,26-30). Later Jesus Himself bears witness to John the Baptist (Jn 5,31-35). Being the friend of the bridegroom John the Baptist is entitled to listen to his voice and the voice here is understood as the revelation of the Messiah, a revelation proper to the friendship between Jesus and His disciples (cf. Jn 15,15).[136] The joy of the bridegroom which is the ultimate aim of the vigilance of his friend is shared with the friend in its fullness. This symbolic sharing of joy in their bond of friendship is patterned after the eschatological joy which Jesus

---

[136] Cf. supra, p. 81.

shares with His disciples. Therefore the relationship between Jesus and the Baptist as friends can be understood as a master-disciple relationship. [137] In short, in this friendship there is always place for Jesus' superiority and the Baptist's acceptance and openness to such a superiority seen in fulfilment of the essential characteristics of a Christian disciple.

Conclusion

In the light of the exegesis done in the present chapter one may derive certain conclusions regarding the nature of the friendship between Jesus and John the Baptist. Their friendship is based on other than purely psychological aspects and is not accordingly a relationship between two equals. Rather their friendship is theological, a friendship which includes the characteristics of a master-disciple relationship. Those conclusions are helpful to expose the theological depth of the term φίλος in Jn 3,29 since φίλος is used here to designate the relationship between Jesus and an authentic Christian disciple. In the pericope examined Jesus' superiority over the Baptist is well depicted when the Evangelist presents Him as a successful baptizer, the Messiah and bridegroom, one who came from heaven, an authentic divine witness and the beloved of the Father. The important, but secondary, role of John the Baptist is also portrayed when the Evangelist presents him as the

---

[137] The nature of the friendship between John the Baptist and Jesus as a master-disciple relationship is evident in the comments of St. Augustine which can be summed up as follows: I listen; he is the one who speaks (Jn 3,29). I am enlightened; he is the light (Jn 1,6-9). I am the ear; he is the word (Jn 3,29): Cf. AUGUSTINUS HIPPONENSIS, "Tractatus in Evangelium Ioannis", in: J.P. Migne, *PL* 35, 1498.

friend of the bridegroom, Jesus. In the metaphorical presentation of their mutually related roles, i.e. "bridegroom" and "friend of the bridegroom", the nature of their interpersonal relationship is exposed. As the analysis of the text suggests their relationship is equivalent to Jesus-disciple relationship, a relationship which involves mutual responsibility, viz. the responsibility of a master and that of a genuine disciple. In summary we can assert that the term φίλος is reciprocal in its theological content and it is an appropriate designation for the Jesus-disciple relationship.

CHAPTER THREE

THE FRIENDSHIP BETWEEN JESUS AND THE BETHANY FAMILY (Jn 11, 1-46)

Introduction

The investigation of the theological meaning of the term φίλος in the Fourth Gospel draws one's attention to the Lazarus-episode (Jn 11,1-46), wherein one finds the second occurrence of the term in v.11. The Evangelist uses the term φίλος to designate Lazarus' relationship with Jesus and His disciples. The theological content of this designation can be understood only in the context of the entire pericope which portrays the intimate relationship between Jesus and the members of the Bethany family.[1] Immediately from the beginning of the episode the Evangelist also presents the intimate relationship between Jesus and the sisters of Lazarus whose words and deeds illustrate the families attitude although only their brother's relationship is qualified in terms of φίλος (φιλεῖν).

---

[1] It is noteworthy that the Evangelist uses two different terms to depict the love and friendship between Jesus and the members of the Bethany family. He uses the term φιλεῖν (φίλος) to express the affectionate love of Jesus towards Lazarus (vv.3.11.36) whereas ἀγαπᾶν is used to denote Jesus' love towards all three members of the Bethany family (v.5). In Johannine usage the φιλεῖν (φίλος) seems to stress the affectionate aspect of love (cf. Jn 5,20; 11,3.11; 21,15.16.17) while ἀγαπᾶν emphasizes the active aspect of love (cf. Jn 3,16; 13,2.34-35; 15,9.12.17). Therefore they are not two forms of love, one higher than the other, but rather they underline two aspects of love. Cf. MLAKUZHYIL, *The Christocentric Structure*, 285, n.147. In the context of the Lazarus-episode the use of these two verbs is complementary, showing both aspects of Jesus' love. Therefore, although our primary aim is to elucidate the meaning of the term φίλος as a designation of Lazarus, due consideration of the love-relationship between Jesus and the entire Bethany family is also in place since the development of the story depends on the active involvement of Martha and Mary.

The historicity, literary source and the literary unity of the Lazarus-story are points of discussion among the exegetes.[2] The questioning of the historicity and relevance of the episode may be due to the lack of a holistic vision of the Gospel.[3] An overview of the redactional critics reveals the importance and relevance of the Lazarus-story in the Fourth Gospel. By consideration of the Gospel and its meaning in its actual form it becomes apparent that the mode and order of presentation of the episodes indicates a deliberate logical sequence given it by the final redactor (whoever he may be).[4] Thus the sign of the raising of Lazarus stands as the climax of Jesus' public ministry and it paves way for the death and glorification of Jesus.[5]

---

[2] Cf. BULTMANN, *John*, 395-396, n.4; E.SCHWARTZ, "Aporien im vierten Evangelium" *NGG* 3 (1908) 166-171; J. WELLHAUSEN, *Das Evangelium Johannis* (Berlin 1908) 50-53; P. WENDLAND, *Die Urchristlichen Literaturformen* (HNT 1,3) (Tübingen 1912) 305-307; HIRSCH, *Das Vierte Evangelium*, 272f.; E. HÄNCHEN, *John, a Commentary on the Gospel of John*, Vol II, R.W. FUNK (trs.) (Philadelphia 1984) 67-72; LAGRANGE, *Saint Jean*, 309-312; HOSKYNS, *The Fourth Gospel*, 395-396; DODD, *Historical Tradition*, 228-232; R. DUNKERLEY, "Lazarus", *NTS* 5 (1958-59) 321f.; J.N. SANDERS, "Those whom Jesus Loved (Jn XI,5)", *NTS* 1 (1954-55) 29f.; R.T. FORTNA, *The Gospel of Signs* (Cambridge 1970) 75-87; H.M. TEEPLE, *The Literary Origin of the Gospel of John* (Evanston 1974) 207-213; M.E. BOISMARD & A. LAMOUILLE, *L'Évangile de Jean: Synopse des quatre Évangiles en français*, III (Paris 1977) 277-287; PANIMOLLE, *Giovanni*, Vol III, 23-24; K. PEARCE, "The Lucan Origins of the Raising of Lazarus", *ExpTim* 96 (1984-85) 359-361; J. KREMER, "Der arme Lazarus. Lazarus, der Freund Jesu. Beobachtungen zur Beziehungen zwischen Lk 16,19-31und Jn 11,1-46",in: *A Cause de l'Évangile*,FS. J. Dupont (Cerf 1985) 571-584; X. LÉON-DUFOUR, *Lecture de l'évangile selon Jean*, Vol II (Paris 1990) 408-410.

[3] Cf. L.P. TRUDINGER, "The Meaning of 'Life' in St. John. Some further Reflections", *BTB* 6 (1976) 258f.

[4] Cf. C.F.D.MOULE, "The meaning of 'Life' in the Gospels and Epistles of St. John. A Study in the Story of Lazarus, John 11:1-44", *Theology* 78 (1975) 116.

[5] The raising of Lazarus became the immediate cause for Jesus' arrest and crucifixion which leads to His glorification in His resurrection. In Johannine presentation there is a great contrast between the raising of Lazarus and the

In the theological framework of the Fourth Evangelist the story of the raising of Lazarus has a christological and soteriological stress.[6] In this episode Jesus is revealed as the Son of God and the source of Life. Jesus' divinity and humanity are well depicted in the Johannine presentation of the Lazarus-story. It is in Jesus that the believer finds salvation and obtains eternal life, which is both a present and future reality. Only in the context of real friendship with Jesus can the believer experience Him as the source of life and the eternal life as the gift of God.

In this chapter we are concerned not with establishing either the historicity of the story or its literary source, but rather with understanding the nature of the friendship between Jesus and the Bethany family in view of the theological meaning of φίλος within the context of the pericope. The nature of the present study renders a detailed exegesis of the entire pericope superfluous. Rather an exegetico-theological approach to the expressions of friendship between Jesus and the members of the Bethany family will be sufficient to explicate the theological meaning of the term φίλος in Jn 11,11. After delimitation of the text and treatment of its literary genre the different literary units of the pericope will be traced for a better understanding of the story's development. Finally, in view of establishing our argument certain theological conclusions will be drawn on the basis of the analysis.

---

resurrection of Jesus. Cf. L.P. TRUDINGER, "The Raising of Lazarus - A Brief Response", *DownRev* 94 (1976) 288-290; "The Meaning of 'Life' in St. John. Some Further Reflections", *BTB* 6 (1976) 260-263; B. BYRNE, *Lazarus. A Contemporary Reading of John 11:1-46* (Zacchaeus Studies: New Testament) (Collegeville 1991) 16-17.

[6] Cf. PANIMOLLE, *Giovanni*, Vol III, 33f.

I. Delimitation of the Text

Concerning the delimitation of the text under consideration there are difference of opinion among the exegetes.[7] According to Kremer one can establish the textual unity of Jn 11,1-46 on the basis of the following arguments: **a)** In v.1 there is an evident *introduction* with the Greek particle δέ (then), which presents a new incident (cf. 12,20.37; 13,1), viz. the sickness of Lazarus. At the same time there is a definite conclusion in Jn 10,42[8] which thereby facilitates a new unit with Jn 11,1. **b)** There is a *thematic unity* in the pericope (11,1-46). It starts with the announcement of the sickness of Lazarus, moves through his death and ends with his resurrection.[9] The verses immediately following deal with another theme, i.e. the plot against Jesus. **c)** *Unity of the characters* in this episode presents a third reason for the unity of the pericope (11,1-46). In the text under question almost all the characters (Lazarus, Mary, Martha, Jesus, disciples and the Jews) are present actively or

---

[7] Kremer argues for the literary unity of Jn 11,1-46. Cf. J. KREMER, *Lazarus: Die Geschichte einer Auferstehung: Text, Wirkungsgeschichte und Botschaft von Joh 11,1-46* (Stuttgart 1985) 12-13. According to Descamps, the narrative ends with v.44. Cf. A. DESCAMPS, "Une lecture historico-critique", in: *Genese et Structure d' un texte du Nouveau Testament (Jn 11)* (Paris 1981) 35. Suggit considers this pericope as one that extends from 11,1 to 12,11. Cf. J.N. SUGGIT, "The Raising of Lazarus", *ExpTim* 95 (1984) 106-108.

[8] The ultimate aim of the Fourth Gospel is that people believe in the divinity of Jesus for their eternal life (cf. 20,31). In different phases of this Gospel one sees a progress in the faith-response of the people. Each sign of Jesus is visualized to deepen the faith and the Evangelist concludes many pericopes by commenting on the positive and negative response of the people (cf. 2,11; 3,36; 4,39-42; 4,53; 7,31; 8,30; 11,45-46). In 10,42 there is such a comment of the Evangelist in the form of the conclusion of a pericope.

[9] Actually treatment of Lazarus' resurrection ends in v. 44. Vv. 45-46 speak about the effects of this sign, i.e. positive and negative responses of the bystanders, serving as the narrative's conclusion.

passively from the beginning until the end. In the immediately following verses (vv.47-53) they do not appear at all. **d)** While it is a fact that there is no geographical unity throughout the episode, the shift of place within the episode can be explained stylistically. Considering its specifically dramatic style the lack of geographical unity within the episode need not be taken as a hindrance to the textual unity. **e)** There is a definite and clear *conclusion* for this Lazarus-episode in vv.45-46,similar to the Johannine conclusions of the 'sign-narratives'. **f)** Finally, there is also a *thematic inclusion* which maintains the unity of the text, viz. both in the introductory and concluding section of the pericope, one finds mention of the δόξα τοῦ θεοῦ (glory of God). [10] Accordingly the sign of the raising of Lazarus is called the sign of the glory of God. [11] In the light of the above mentioned reasons one can legitimately argue for the textual unity of Jn 11,1-46.

II. The Literary Genre

For a better understanding and interpretation of the pericope a brief discussion on its literary genre is useful. In the episode of the raising of Lazarus there is a combination of narrative and discourse. Schneiders says, "In the Lazarus event the narrative and discourse are so intricately interwoven that they cannot be separated". [12] The

---

[10] Later we will see the subdivisions of the pericope.

[11] Cf. PANIMOLLE, *Giovanni*, Vol III, 20.

[12] S.M. SCHNEIDERS, "Death in the Community of Eternal Life. History, Theology and Spirituality in Jn 11", *Int* 41 (1987) 44; cf. also R.A. CULPEPPER, *Anatomy of the Fourth Gospel: A Study in Literary Design* (Philadelphia: Fortress 1983) 73; DODD, *Interpretation*, 363; DODD, *Historical Tradition*, 228; BYRNE,

episode is highly dramatic with a lively interchange of dialogue, a noteworthy characteristic of the Evangelist's style. The characters are introduced as interlocutors and their words and deeds form an indivisible whole.[13] Regarding the unique literary genre Dodd writes: "Formally the pericope is narrative containing discourse, in substance it might equally well be described as didactic dialogue containing symbolic narrative by way of illustration".[14]

The two crucial pieces of dialogue in the text (vv.7-16; 21-27) contain certain essential theological themes. At the outset, it should be pointed out that this pericope is unique for the usual Johannine style of narrating a sign. Usually, a sign is preceded or followed by a discourse. But here, the discourse is interwoven with the narrative. In other words, one can say that there is a fusion of sign and revelatory discourse in the Lazarus-account. [15] In its formal structure, the narrative resembles a healing pericope, with the introduction of a sickness, the restoration of health, and its effect upon the bystanders. In this narrative one sees much dramatic or picturesque detail to express the particularly Johannine theological themes of faith and life. From the literary point of view the Lazarus-episode is exemplified as "a Musterstück of its writers art".[16] In short, the text under examination can be considered as a recital, both dramatic and didactic, which two qualities determine its form.

Lazarus, 25.

[13] Respecting the pericope's dramatic nature the analysis of the text will be based on the words and deeds of the actors.

[14] DODD, *Interpretation*, 363.

[15] Cf. SEGALLA, *Giovanni*, 320.

[16] DODD, *Historical Tradition*, 228.

And behind the narrative there is a Christian teaching, expressed through the words and deeds of the characters.

III. The Division and Development of the Text (Jn 11, 1-46)

Preliminary to the analysis one can divide the text into five subsections on the basis of the development of the episode considering different categories of criteria.[17] In each subsection there is a thematic unity, concluding with an element of suspense, which leaves room for the introduction of the next subsection. Other literary devices are to be found as well in the pericope and serve as the criteria for such a division. Each segment is well situated and interconnected within the holistic structure.[18] To illustrate this and to attain a better understanding of the entire pericope the main divisions and their contents will be treated here.

A. Vv. 1-6 : The Announcement of the Sickness of Lazarus

The first subsection (vv.1-6) serves as an appropriate introduction for the entire narrative. The development of the story is based upon Lazarus' sickness, a fact repeatedly announced by the Evangelist in the introductory verses (vv.1.2.6), confirmed and related by the sisters (v.3) and positively recognized upon by Jesus

---

[17] It is to be noted that Panimolle divided the pericope (Jn 11,1-44) into four sections: cf. PANIMOLLE, *Giovanni*, Vol III, 21f. Since the present text is highly dramatic, the dramatic techniques help to determine the division and structure of the pericope.

[18] Taking into account the context of the present study, a detailed presentation of structure can be omitted as superfluous.

(v.4). Thus, throughout the introductory section (vv.1-6) sickness
(ἀσθένεια) either in its noun or verb form occurs altogether five
times. Encountered at the beginning and the end , as well as at the
centre, it thus forms a parallelistic concentric structure. In this
subsection the unity of the theme of sickness is expressed in the
repeated use of the term ἀσθένεια. Jesus' friendship with the
Bethany family and the manifestation of divine glory, the principal
themes of the entire pericope, are rightly stressed here.[19] In this
scene only two characters appear on the stage, Jesus and the
messenger. This subsection concludes with the mention of Jesus' two
days delay, in spite of His love towards the Bethany family, thus
adding an element of suspense to the flow of the story.

B. Vv. 7-16 : The Dialogue between Jesus and His Disciples

The second part begins with v.7, where there is a clear temporal
transition from the preceding section indicated by the Greek
expression - μετὰ τοῦτο.[20] This subsection clearly concludes at v.16
with the disciples' apparently positive reaction to Jesus' invitation to
go to Judea. It should be noted that this suggestion is used first by
Jesus to initiate the dialogue and then by the disciples to conclude
it. Thus, there is an evident *inclusion* between vv.7-8 and 15-16

---

[19] In the development of the episode there is a frequent emphasis on the love
and friendship between Jesus and the Bethany family. The symbolic importance of
the miracle is God's glory and Jesus's glorification. These two leading thoughts are
presented in the introductory section itself. Cf. BROWN, *John*, Vol I, 431.

[20] For the function of μετὰ ταῦτα cf. supra, p.32, n.9.

indicated by the verb ἄγωμεν (let us go!)[21] which maintains the unity of this subsection. So also, it is only here beginning with v.7 and ending with v.16 that one sees the disciples' active role. Only Jesus and His disciples appear on the scene. These verses of dialogue between Jesus and His disciples contribute much to the development of the episode. The two phases of the subsection (vv.7-10 & 11-16) are well marked with the temporal expression μετὰ τοῦτο in v.11. The degree of revelation differs between these two phases, viz. in the first phase there is general teaching, whereas in the second there is a concrete revelation given by Jesus.

C. Vv. 17-28a : The Dialogue between Jesus and Martha

This segment opens with an introductory note (vv.17-19) by the Evangelist, which sets a scene appropriate for the dialogue between Jesus and Martha. Such an introduction with its *shift of place and actors* helps one to understand the development of the story.[22] It introduces the relevance of a personal dialogue between Jesus and Martha, thus keeping the unity of these verses (vv.17-28a). Initially one notes the narrative particle οὖν (v.17), which marks a new phase in the narrative and signifies a further step from the preceding section. For vv.20-28a only Jesus and Martha are present on the stage. In the course of this dialogue a progressive revelation by Jesus and a deep expression of faith on Martha's part are well

---

[21] Cf. C.H. GIBLIN, "Suggestion, Negative Response, and Positive Action in St. John's Portrayal of Jesus (Jn ii,1-11;iv,46-54;vii,2-14;xi,1-44)", *NTS* 26 (1980) 209f.

[22] As hinted at above (cf. p.90) since the Lazarus-episode is dramatic in style such a shift of place and actors calls for a change of scene likewise marking the beginning of a new subsection. Cf. MLAKUZHYIL, *The Christocentric Structure*, 112f.

expressed. Both revelation and the faith-response play an important role in the eventual execution of the sign. This subsection has a clear literary structure with the two 'going' of Martha (vv.20.28a) marking the outer frame centred around the faith expression in the resurrection of the dead (v.24). When Martha disappears from the stage the scene changes.

D. Vv. 28b-37 : Jesus' Meeting with Mary

The scene opens with Martha's message regarding Jesus' wish to meet Mary (v.28b). In this subsection there is a *change of actors*. Martha disappears from the scene, [23] while Mary and the Jews appear on the stage besides Jesus. Unlike the preceding scene there is no shift of place and no discourse. Stylistically these verses are structured in two parallel parts. In the first part (vv.28b-31) the three characters (Mary, Jesus, Jews) are presented one after another. As for the second part (vv.32-37) their activity in both words and deeds parallels their appearance, a parallel which concludes with the comments of the Jews. The subsection culminates to the sentiments of the actors, thus paving the way for a further action, i.e. the execution of the sign.

E. Vv. 38-46 : The Raising of Lazarus and its Effects

The final subsection deals with the actual execution of the sign of raising Lazarus with its positive and negative effects. At the

---

[23] The disappearance of Martha from the scene can be considered as the "technique of vanishing characters", since she being an active character of the previous scene is instrumental in introducing the next scene and then practically disappears from the stage: Cf. MLAKUZHYIL, *The Christocentric Structure*, 116.

outset (v.38) there is a *shift of scene* characterized by the second appearance of Martha in v.39. In a usual Johannine pattern the positive and negative effects of the sign serve as the conclusion of this subsection as well as that of the entire pericope. [24] In this final section one finds the actualization of Jesus' words uttered in the introductory section (cf.v.4), viz. the sickness of Lazarus is not for the sake of death, but for the glory of God. In the enactment of the sign the divine glory is manifested and the physically dead Lazarus is bestowed with the fullness of Life (v.44).

IV. The Friendship Between Jesus and the Bethany Family

One who reads the Lazarus-episode in the Fourth Gospel gets the impression that Jesus was a close friend of the Bethany family. Throughout the narrative one can notice many references to their interpersonal relationship. Since the episode is dramatic in its literary style and the central teaching is expressed through the dialogue and action of the actors, one can trace the expressions of friendship between Jesus and the Bethany family by analyzing the words and deeds of the characters and the occasional comments of the Evangelist. The present analysis will deal only with those words and deeds which elucidate the reciprocal friendship between Jesus and the members of the Bethany family. In our treatment of the text we interpret the historical events from the redactional point of view.

---

[24] Cf. p. supra, 90, n.8.

A. In the Words and Deeds of Jesus
1. In Jesus' Words

Jesus' love and friendship towards the Bethany family is well expressed in His words recorded in the pericope. Jesus' comment concerning the sickness of Lazarus (v.4), His consideration of Lazarus as a common friend (ὁ φίλος ἡμῶν) both of Himself and of His disciples (v.11), His decision and invitation to go to Judea in spite of danger (vv.7.11b.15b.),His words of consolation to Martha (vv.23.25.26) and His wish to meet Mary in her painful situation (v.28) etc. are all the sublime expressions of His friendship with the Bethany family verified in His words.

a. Jesus' Comment on Lazarus' Sickness (v.4)

Jesus finds the sickness of Lazarus, His friend, not as an occasion for eternal death. Rather it will be for the glory of God and for His own glorification (ὑπὲρ τῆς δόξης τοῦ θεοῦ, ἵνα δοξασθῇ ὁ υἱὸς τοῦ θεοῦ δι᾽ αὐτῆς). In this statement, Jesus presupposes the sign of the raising of His friend which will serve as a means to express God's glory and His own glorification. In other words, the death of Lazarus would provide Jesus an occasion to perform a sign so that thereby the glory of God might be manifested. [25] Jesus' comment clarifies the fact that He will not

---

[25] All the signs of Jesus in the Fourth Gospel are meant for revelation of the uniqueness of divine work and for the glory of God (cf. 2,11;9,3;11,40). According to Brown the aim of the miracle is the glory of God and the deepening of the faith of the people in Jesus: Cf. BROWN, *John*, Vol I, 431-432; cf. also PANIMOLLE, *Giovanni*, Vol III, 26; HENDRIKSEN, *John*, 139.

allow His friend for an eternal separation. [26] Jesus considers *this sickness* as an occasion to manifest God's glory by imparting life to His friend. In this way Jesus' words in v.4 clearly manifest the nature of their friendship.

The glory of God is revealed in the glorification of the Son (cf. 13,31). For the Fourth Evangelist the glory of God and the glorification of the Son of God go together (cf. 17,1.5;9,3) so closely as to be practically synonymous. [27] The clause ἵνα δοξασθῇ ὁ υἱὸς τοῦ θεοῦ δι' αὐτῆς suggests that the finality of Lazarus' sickness will be the death, resurrection and glorification of Jesus. [28] In the sickness of His friend Jesus foresees His own hour which ultimately leads Him to His glorification. [29] In other words, the raising of Lazarus becomes the immediate cause for the death and resurrection of Jesus Himself. Through this God reveals His glory by glorifying Jesus (cf. 17,5) so that He may be capable of giving eternal life to every believer (cf. 17,2). In this sense one may say that Jesus attains His glorification ultimately through the sickness of His friend.

In Jesus' theological expression (v.4) one sees the reciprocal nature of the friendship between Jesus and Lazarus. It is vivid in its sacrificial dimension. The physical death of Lazarus has a supreme motive, viz. the glory of God and the glorification of the Son of God.

---

[26] Cf. HENDRIKSEN, *John*, 139-140.

[27] Cf. SEGALLA, *Giovanni*, 319; also SCHNACKENBURG, *St. John*, Vol II, 323, where the author recalls: "the mutual 'glorification' of the Father and the Son is a dominant theme in Johannine Christology".

[28] Cf. LÉON-DUFOUR, *Jean*, Vol II, 411, n.21. The expression δι' αὐτῆς (by means of it) probably refers to sickness, but grammatically it can also refer to God's glory.

[29] DE BOOR, *Johannes*, Vol II, 24, where he writes: "Jesus hört in der Erkrankung des Freundes den Schlag der Stunde". Cf. also HOSKYNS, *Fourth Gospel*, 400.

Lazarus must undergo the sacrifice of his physical life for the glorification of his friend, Jesus. So also, the sign of raising Lazarus leads to the sacrificial death of Jesus for His friends, including Lazarus. Therefore, in its double dimension the sickness and death of Lazarus has a sublime sacrificial aspect,[30] an aspect which is envisaged by the Fourth Evangelist as essential for genuine and supreme friendship (cf. Jn 15,13). In short, Jesus' response to the message of Lazarus' sickness expresses the nature and depth of their friendship.

b. Jesus' Expression: "Lazarus our Friend" (v.11a)

Jesus qualifies Lazarus as ὁ φίλος ἡμῶν (our friend), a friend of Himself and of His disciples.[31] The friendship between Lazarus and Jesus extends to encompass a common friendship also with Jesus' disciples. The concept of friendship with Jesus is envisaged here on two levels. On the first level, the friendship between Jesus and His disciples is presupposed and indirectly affirmed. Jesus reminds the disciples of the friendship which He has already established with them (cf. Jn 15,14-15; Lk 12,4).[32] As one expression of this friendship, Jesus shares His knowledge to them by announcing the

---

[30] The Greek particle ὑπέρ in v.4 strengthens this argument. According to Westcott, in every other Johannine passage, where the preposition ὑπέρ (Vulg. pro) is used, it is to mark the notion of "sacrifice in behalf of someone": Cf. WESTCOTT, *St. John*, 165.

[31] Cf. J. LEAL, "De amore Jesu erga amicum Lazarum (Jo 11)", *VD* 21 (1941) 61. Leal sees this expression a means to motivate the disciples to undertake a dangerous journey.

[32] Cf. WESTCOTT, *St. John*, 166. where commenting on Jn 11,11 he says, "the Lord joins His disciples with Himself in one bond of friendship (our friend)".

death of Lazarus (cf. Jn 15,15). On the second level, Jesus considers Lazarus as their common friend.[33] The basis of this consideration is Jesus' love towards Lazarus and also Lazarus' personal qualities of Christian discipleship. Jesus loves Lazarus as He loves other disciples and so Lazarus also belongs to the circle of Jesus' disciples.[34]

In the NT writings the term φίλος (friend/ beloved) is used as a designation for a Christian believer besides the terms ἀδελφός and ἀγαπητός (cf. 3 Jn 15; Lk 12,4; Acts 27,3; esp. Jn 15,13-15). The members of the early Church were friends of Jesus and friends among themselves. This mutual love among the baptized and for Jesus provides them the status of discipleship.[35] Lazarus was a disciple, not in the sense of 'one among the twelve' but as one who was a real believer in Jesus, who closely followed Jesus' teaching and who was beloved of Jesus (cf. vv.3.5.36).[36]

Therefore, Jesus' reference to Lazarus as *our friend* (v.11) is a vivid expression of His friendship with Lazarus as one belongs to the circle of disciples. It is self-evident that Jesus has already established His friendship with Lazarus. This also implies that Lazarus has already responded positively to Jesus by entering into "the circle of genuine Christian disciples". To enter into a friendship with Jesus one has to become first a genuine Christian disciple in

---

[33] According to Bernard, "Lazarus was within the circle of those whom Jesus called His "friends":BERNARD, *St. John*, Vol II, 378.

[34] DE BOOR, *Johannes*, Vol II, 26, where he writes: "Liebt er Lazarus, dann gehört dieser Mann auch den Jüngern als 'unser Freund'". Cf. also MARSH, *St. John*, 422.

[35] Cf. KREMER, *Lazarus*, 353.

[36] John frequently uses the term μαθητής (disciple) mainly to denote a Christian disciple: Cf. MLAKUZHYIL, *The Christocentric Structure*, 279f.

the Johannine sense of the term. Discipleship and friendship with Jesus are verified in the life of Lazarus. In short, the reciprocal dimension of the friendship between Jesus and Lazarus is evident in Jesus' expression: "our friend Lazarus".

c. Jesus' Presentation of Lazarus' Death as a Sleep (v.11)

Jesus considers the physical death of His friend, Lazarus as a sleep when He says, "Our friend Lazarus has fallen asleep (κεκοίμηται)". In the OT the death of a member of the chosen people is often compared to a sleep (cf. Gen 47,30; 2 Sam 7,12; Job 3,13; 14,12).[37] So also, the death of the Christians in the NT is depicted as a sleep (cf. Mt 27,52; Acts 7,60; 1 Cor 7,39; 11,30; 15,6.18.20.51; 1 Thess 4,13-15). Κοιμᾶσθαι is used also in later Christian literature in the sense of death (cf. Ignatius, *Rom* 4,2; 1 Clement 44,2; Hermas, *Sim* IX,xvi,7).[38] According to Johannine Jesus the death of a believer is only sleep and not eternal separation (v.26).[39]

---

[37] Hanson presupposes an OT background for this Lazarus-story based upon of the similarity of context and vocabulary in Jn 11,11 and in Job 14,12-15a. In both cases κοιμᾶσθαι is used to depict the sleep of the death and ἐξυπνίζω is used for the waking up from the sleep in the sense of raising. In Job 14,12 ἀναστῇ is referred to the resurrection rather than a waking from sleep: Cf. A.T. HANSON, "The Old Testament Background to the Raising of Lazarus", *SE* 6 (1973) 252-254. It is noteworthy that the concept of cemetery as a resting place originated from the Greek word κοιμᾶσθαι: Cf. M. BALAGUÉ, "La resurrección de Lázaro (jn 11,1-57). Confirmación solemne del poder de Jesús sobre la vida", *CB* 19 (1962) 19.

[38] Cf. BARRETT, *St. John*, 392.

[39] Cf. PANIMOLLE, *Giovanni*, Vol III, 27.

It is noteworthy that in a comforting manner Scripture treats the death of believers as sleep.[40] Such imagery is appropriate since the believers' death represents not an eternal separation but rather the means to a glorious awakening. In the case of Lazarus, an immediate raising takes place, thus symbolizing hope for all believers. Lazarus, a beloved of Jesus and an authentic Christian disciple, cannot be a victim of eternal separation from Jesus. So it is quite apt and striking to depict his physical death as a sleep.[41] Indirectly Jesus affirms that His friend cannot die eternally. Thus, in His portrayal of Lazarus' death as a sleep, Jesus underlines the nature of Lazarus' state of life in relationship to Him as well as the depth of their interpersonal relationship of friendship.

d. Jesus' Decision to go to Judea (vv.7.11.15)

In v.7 Jesus suggests to His disciples: "let us go to Judea again".[42] There is no mention of the reason of His journey, no reference to the name of Lazarus. Judea, elsewhere in John, represents a place of hostility and unbelief. Here the Evangelist probably wants to present the dangerous situation in Judea which will lead Jesus to His decisive end (cf. 8,59; 10,31.39). The disciples'

---

[40] Cf. BYRNE, *Lazarus*, 45; LÉON-DUFOUR, *Jean*, Vol II, 414.

[41] Cf. HENDRIKSEN, *John*, 142-143. According to some authors, Jesus uses a riddle to explain a truth. This is considered by them as a part of Johannine misunderstanding to make the partner of the dialogue to understand and admit a truth in a better way in the course of the following dialogue: Cf. H. LEROY, *Rätsel und Missverständnis. Ein Beitrag zur Formgeschichte des Johannesevangeliums* (BBB 30) (Bonn 1968) 184; cf. also HOSKYNS, *Fourth Gospel*, 401.

[42] For the former visits: cf. Jn 2,13; 5,1; 7,10. For the Fourth Evangelist Judea stands for Jerusalem, where Jesus' fate will be acted out.

objection to the suggestion of Jesus and His decision to go in spite
of their objection etc. help the reader to understand the value of
Jesus' self-sacrifice for the sake of His friend (cf. 15,13).

As noted above, even though the disciples object, Jesus presents
an incentive to risk the journey for the sake of Lazarus, "their
common friend", who is now dead.[43] In v.11 Jesus repeats His
intention to go to Bethany to wake Lazarus from his sleep. Jesus
personally decides to go to Judea, though the disciples do not wish
to accompany Him. Such a decision expresses the depth of Jesus'
friendship with Lazarus. Not understanding fully, the disciples once
again hinder Jesus' plan to go to Judea by saying that, "if he has
fallen asleep he will recover" (v.12).

The Johannine Jesus clarifies the misunderstanding of His
disciples and invites them again to go to Lazarus (πρὸς αὐτόν)
(v.15). It is no longer an invitation to go to comfort the bereaved
family, but to go to Lazarus as a living person.[44] Jesus draws the
attention of the disciples to their real and present relationship to
Lazarus.[45] Still the response of the disciples in the person of
Thomas (v.16) makes the situation more critical, since it highlights
that the way which they are taking is one of danger, i.e. death.[46]
Even if one considers the words of Thomas as the expression of his
readiness to die with Jesus they recall a dangerous fate for all of
them.

---

[43] Cf. supra, p. 100, n.31.

[44] Cf. HOSKYNS, *Fourth Gospel*, 401.

[45] Cf. WESTCOTT, *St. John*, 167

[46] According to Bultmann the statement of Thomas in v.16 signifies a resignation
to the fate which threatens the disciples and Jesus alike. Cf. BULTMANN, *John*,
400.

Against the background of such a dangerous situation understood as such by the disciples, one sees the merit of Jesus' positive decision to go to Judea to raise Lazarus from death. Jesus is ready to take a bold step for the sake of His friend. More than His own fate Jesus considers the fate of His friend as something more precious. In other words, in spite of the knowledge of approaching danger and constant discouragement from His disciples, Jesus is motivated by friendship with Lazarus to risk going to Judea. [47] Thus, in Jesus' positive decision, made in the face of danger to His life, one sees the nature and depth of their friendship, a friendship that demands the ultimate self-sacrifice (cf. 15,13).

e. Jesus' Words to Martha (vv.23.25.26)

In the third subsection of the pericope (vv.17-28a) the Evangelist gives an account of Jesus' dialogue with Martha. As a response to Martha's great trust in Jesus, He gives a consoling assurance to her by saying that her brother will rise again. It is a usual consolation offered by friends to those in bereavement. [48] The verb ἀνίστημι is used without any time specification (v.23). This could be interpreted either as an immediate raising through a divine sign or as the final resurrection based on Jewish belief (cf. Acts 23,6; Mt 22,23).[49] Since Martha understood the words of Jesus in the sense of a final

---

[47] Cf. B. MCNEIL, "The Raising of Lazarus", *DownRev* 92 (1974) 270.

[48] Cf. BERNARD, *St. John*, Vol II, 386.

[49] The Greek verb ἀνίστημι has a double meaning, viz. 'rise up' or 'return to life'. The Fourth Evangelist uses many such ironical expressions especially in this Lazarus-episode. According to Barrett the use of words of double meaning is a Johannine characteristic: Cf. BARRETT, *St. John*, 395.

resurrection it probably was not an immediate consolation for her. But the words of Jesus provide the background for establishing the Christological basis for the miracle of raising the dead and for the Fourth Evangelist's eschatological view. In contrast to Jewish expectation of a future eschatology John presents salvation here and now in Jesus Christ.[50] By promising an immediate resurrection to Lazarus and making him a pattern of life in Jesus for all Christians, Jesus shows the depth of their friendship.

In the context of Martha's incapability to understand the present eschatology Jesus wants to reveal a fundamental principle of faith, a profound Christological truth, that Jesus is the Resurrection and the Life.[51] Here the Fourth Evangelist presents Jesus' revelatory role by adopting the famous ἐγώ εἰμι (I am) revelatory formula.[52] The term ζωή (life) in v.25a is connected to the following phrases regarding believers who inherit the true life, i.e. Jesus Himself. The resurrection opens the gate to an everlasting life. By believing in Jesus, His beloved can inherit eternal life.[53] Jesus is the "fountain

---

[50] Cf. SCHNACKENBURG, St. John, Vol II, 330.

[51] It is important to note that in v.25 the expression καὶ ἡ ζωή (and the life) is omitted in P[45], some OL, OS[sin] as well as both Origen and Cyprian. The expression may have been omitted for two reasons: a) The Church Fathers quote the well known texts in abbreviated form; b) in the context of Lazarus' death only "resurrection" seems to be sufficient, relevant and important: Cf. HÄNCHEN, John, Vol II, 62. Harris proposes other reasons for this omission in some of the important manuscripts. According to him it might be due to the Christian tradition seen in the inscriptions on an Egyptian lamp of the Greco-Roman period as ἐγώ εἰμι Ἀνάστασις. For him the shorter text may be original: Cf. R. HARRIS, "A note on John xi,25", BulBezanClub 5 (1928) 5-8.

[52] Cf. BULTMANN, John, 225, n.3.

[53] Throughout the Gospel of John life is closely connected with believing in Jesus and believing in Him is made possible through obedience. In the Lazarus-narrative the connection between life and believing in Jesus is of particular importance: Cf.

of the believers' glorious resurrection and of their everlasting life".[54]
To attain such a life one must have a deep faith in Jesus Christ (vv.
25b-26a). Jesus gives an assurance, that since He is the resurrection
and life, the one who lives in relationship to Him (a believer or a
friend) will enjoy the same life. In Jesus' words to Martha it is
affirmed that Lazarus, as a believer in and friend of Jesus, will be
granted life. Lazarus' faith in Jesus is recognized by Him in the
statement that Lazarus will live in spite of his death.

The essential connection between faith and life is stylistically
developed in vv.25b-26 in a structure of concentric parallelism as
follows:

v.25b   a   ὁ πιστεύων εἰς ἐμὲ

         b   κἂν ἀποθάνῃ

         c   ζήσεται

v.26 c^1 καὶ πᾶς ὁ ζῶν
                καὶ πιστεύων εἰς ἐμὲ

        b^1 οὐ μὴ ἀποθάνῃ εἰς τὸν αἰῶνα.

     a^1 πιστεύεις τοῦτο;

In this structure the letters **a** and a^1 refer to faith in Jesus (in His
words); **b** and b^1 speak of physical and spiritual death consecutively
which are put in parallelism; **c** and c^1 deal with spiritual divine life
(**c** as a result of believing in Jesus, whereas c^1 as a cause for not

---

T.E. POLLARD, "The Raising of Lazarus (John XI)", *SE* 6 (T.U.112) (1973) 436.

[54] HENDRIKSEN, *John*, 150.

undergoing eternal death). The one who believes in Jesus, though he undergoes a physical death, will live spiritually (v.25b). The believer who lives in Jesus will not die for ever (v.26a). In both cases faith is fundamental and essential to have eternal life. A believer, though he undergoes a physical death, is still alive within the society of those who love Jesus. In that society he will still live in and through Christ's solidarity with him.[55] Also the present resurrection is possible for a believer. Such a believer in Jesus possesses the power to be raised from the dead. The physical death of a believer is no longer a death.

Jesus' words to Martha clarify the nature and depth of the friendship between Jesus and Lazarus. It is clear from the text, that Lazarus and Jesus were in a relationship based on love and faith (cf. vv.3.5.11.36).Jesus promises life to Lazarus on the basis of his faith in Jesus. In short, through love and faith, the primary characteristics of Christian discipleship, Lazarus can regain physical life which is the prefiguration of eternal life.[56] Moreover, Jesus' words to Martha also are words of consolation and strength for the bereaved Martha and those words express Jesus' close friendship with the whole Bethany family. Jesus' promise has a general character since the reward of life is also possible for the living believer like Martha.[57] The promised life becomes an immediate reality for the Bethany family which is in real friendship with Jesus.

---

[55] Cf. MARSH, St. John, 428.

[56] Cf. K. ROMANIUK, "Je Suis la Résurrection et la Vie (Jean 11,25)", Concilium 60 (1970) 63-70.

[57] Cf. WESTCOTT, St. John, 169.

f. Jesus' Wish to Meet Mary (v. 28)

Only from Martha's words (v.28) does one come to know of Jesus' wish to meet Mary. Martha says to Mary, "the teacher is here and is calling you (καὶ φωνεῖ σε)" (v.28b). But one does not see such a message of Jesus in the preceding section of the narrative, an omission[58] which seems deliberate. It may be to show that even without an explicit command by Jesus Martha could communicate her Christ-experience and desire the same experience for her sister. Whatever the case, Jesus' wish to meet Mary is explicit from Martha's message to her sister.

From the comment of the Evangelist in v.30 it is clear that Jesus expected Mary's arrival at the place where He met Martha. Since Jesus wished to meet Mary, He remained there to have an opportunity for a private talk. His personal and private words of consolation and strength to Martha and Mary show His love and friendship with the Bethany family.[59] Jesus wanted to have a personal talk with His beloved and friends in their difficult and painful situation (cf. Jn 14,1f.). Thus, through the indirect expression of Jesus' wish to meet Mary, the Evangelist depicts the depth of Jesus' real and close friendship with the Bethany family.

---

[58] Cf. *Ibid.*, 169, where Westcott says, "we can not suppose that Martha herself framed the message out of the general tenor of the Lord's words". Jesus might have already expressed His wish to meet Mary in private.

[59] Cf. SCHNACKENBURG, *St. John*, Vol II, 333. He considers Jesus' wish to have a private talk with Martha and Mary as a sign of intimacy with the members of the Bethany family.

2. In Jesus' Deeds

The friendship between Jesus and the Bethany family is also well documented through Jesus' actions. All Jesus does in connection with the Lazarus-episode is with a positive motive. His delay of two days, His eventual coming to Bethany, His sympathy with the bereaved to the point of shedding tears, and above all, the manifestation of His divine power by raising Lazarus, all His deeds are concrete expressions of His friendship with the Bethany family.

a. Jesus' Delay Before Going to Bethany (v.6)

At face value, Jesus' delay for two days can be misunderstood initially as cruelty or lack of love. But one has to interpret it both in the remote context of the entire Gospel of John and in the immediate context of the text under consideration. Jesus' delay in Jn 11,6 can be seen in the Johannine pattern of delay found in other Johannine texts, viz. the miracle of Cana (Jn 2,4), the healing of the Official's son (Jn 4,47-50), the context of the unbelief of Jesus' brothers (Jn 7,1-9). In all these texts the delay of Jesus emphasizes the sovereign independence of Jesus' action[60] and shows the fulfilment of the hour in accordance with the Father's will and plan.[61]

In the context of the present pericope one can trace other motives also for Jesus' delay. In v.5 Jesus' love towards the Bethany

---

[60] Cf. SCHNEIDERS, *Community of Eternal Life*, 47; HÄNCHEN, *John*, Vol II, 58.

[61] Cf. GIBLIN, *Negative Response and Positive Action*, 199; BULTMANN, *John*, 303.

family is well attested to by the Evangelist, so that the reader can imagine the reason for Jesus' delay in a positive sense, i.e. to show a greater love.[62] The literary construction of vv.5-6 offers a paradox[63] and v.6 seems to be contradictory to what is already explained in v.5. It may be the Evangelist's deliberate intention to give the impression that Jesus' behaviour is determined by the will of the Father, rather than human affection. But ultimately it is for the good of the people though this apparently is incomprehensible. The delay of Jesus is presented as the consequence of divine affection and divine knowledge.[64]

There are other theological and apologetical motives too behind Jesus' delay. Jesus waited not for the death of Lazarus, since He knew that Lazarus was already dead (cf. v.17). Probably Jesus stayed two more days to make sure of his death, so that the sign which Jesus was going to do would be convincing to the bystanders, especially to the Jews.[65] By raising the verifiably dead Lazarus, Jesus wanted to reveal Himself, thereby deepening the faith of His

---

[62] Cf. BALAGUÉ, *La resurrección de Lázaro*, 18-19; A. HENDERSON, "Notes on John 11", *ExpTim* 32 (1920-21) 124.

[63] Here the construction is noteworthy: ὡς οὖν ἤκουσεν (when, therefore he heard). The following action seems to be the consequence of the preceding. Through this paradox Jesus tests the faith of the two sisters: Cf. W. WILKENS, "Die Erweckung des Lazarus", *TZ* 15 (1959) 34.

[64] Cf. WESTCOTT, *St. John*, 165.

[65] According to the Jewish belief a person's death can be asserted after three days. According to the belief the soul of the dead lingers three days after the death. On the fourth day one can be considered as really dead: Cf. STRACK & BILLERBECK, *Talmud und Midrasch*, Vol II, 544f.; PANIMOLLE, *Giovanni*, Vol III, 27; BARRETT, *St.John*, 391.

disciples and the bystanders.[66] In Jesus' words to His disciples in v.15 this theological motive of Jesus' delay and absence is made clear. If Jesus were there, Lazarus would be healed (cf. vv.21.32). Raising the dead is a more powerful action than healing the sick in proving the divinity of Jesus and thereby deepening the faith of His followers, among them the Bethany family.

It seems then that Jesus' delay for two days can be considered in its positive sense. It came from the most tender concern for the spiritual welfare of the disciples including the members of the Bethany family.[67] It was for the deepening of the faith[68] of the disciples and of the Bethany family. Jesus' delay was not out of fear or lack of love and affection, but rather it was a genuine expression of His love for and friendship with the Bethany family.[69]

b. Jesus' Coming to Bethany (v.17)

In the dialogue with His disciples Jesus expressed His desire to go to Bethany to raise Lazarus from the death. In v.17 one sees the

---

[66] Cf. HENDERSON, *Notes on John 11*, 124; D. MERLI, "La scopo della risurrezione di Lazaro in Giov. 11,1-44", *BibOr* 12 (1970) 69. According to Merli this idea of the deepening of the faith is the scope of all signs in the Fourth Gospel. But it presupposes a fundamental attitude of faith even for the execution of the signs.

[67] Cf. HENDRIKSEN, *John*, 140.

[68] Cf. *Ibid.*, 140, where Hendriksen says, "the more faith was strengthened, so much more the glory of God would be extolled".

[69] Cf. SCHNEIDERS, *Community of Eternal Life*, 51; J.R. JONES, *Narrative Structures and Meaning in John 11,1-54* (Ann Arbor: University Microfilms 1982) 317.

actualization of His desire and decision.[70] Jesus' love and friendship towards Lazarus and the Bethany family forced Him to take the risk of going to Bethany.[71] Jesus could have done the miracle even without coming to the place. In the case of other signs Jesus appears as one who merely commands (Jn 4,50; 9,7 etc.). But His personal presence and consolation are something valuable in His close relationship with the Bethany family. This also represents a quite human reaction of a personal effort (walking in this case) to visit the bereaved people and show one's love and friendship. Thus, the very act of Jesus' coming to Bethany in such a painful situation is a concrete expression of His friendship with Lazarus and his sisters.

c. Jesus' Internal Reaction and Weeping (vv. 33.35.38)

The redundant expressions of Jesus' feelings upon the death of His friend, Lazarus are made clear in vv. 33.35 & 38 of the text. From the earliest days of patristic exegesis until contemporary times the interpretation of these verses has been diverse and to some extent uncertain.[72] For a better exegesis of these verses (33.35.38) one must consider them in the particular context of the pericope in which they occur. Additionally, they have to be interpreted in the

---

[70] The Greek expression ἐλθὼν οὖν (when he came, more literally "having come") in v. 17 denotes an already actualized act. In the manuscripts D[33] [69], pm, sy etc. there is an addition εἰς Βηθανίαν (to Bethany) to indicate Jesus' arrival more clearly.

[71] Cf. LEAL, *Amicum Lazarum*, 61.

[72] Cf. HOSKYNS, *Fourth Gospel*, 404, where he summarizes the opinions of different exegetes regarding these verses; cf. also LINDARS, *John*, 398-399.

light of the Johannine theology. Likewise the original meaning of
the vocabulary and its particular sense in its usage here and
elsewhere are also to be taken into account.

The verb with two forms ἐνεβριμήσατο (v.33)[73] and
ἐμβριμώμενος (v.38) originally meant anger or indignation (cf. Dan
11,30 (LXX); Lam 2,6; Mk 1,43; 14,5; Mt 9,30; Ps 7,12). By
considering their root meaning and usage in other Biblical texts
many exegetes interpret Jesus' reaction in Jn 11,33 and 38 as an
outburst of anger. According to this line of thought, Jesus was
angered [74] by seeing the heartless hypocritical wailing of the Jews[75]
and the faithless weeping (κλαίοντας)[76] of Mary. The Greek
Fathers also understood their use in John in the sense of an internal
fight against the pain of death, which would be an immediate reality

---

[73] P[45 vid.] [66c] and D uses ὡς ἐμβριμοῦμενος for easy reading and it weakens the
sense of anger.

[74] Cf. SCHNACKENBURG, *St. John*, Vol II, 335f. Schnackenburg confirms
Jesus' internal reaction as an outburst of His anger in spite of the Evangelist's
attempt to interpret it as Jesus' inward emotion by adding τῷ πνεύματι (v.33) and
ἐν ἑαυτῷ (v.38) and further glossed it with his preferred term ταράσσω (v.33).
He says, "any attempt to reinterpret it in terms of an internal emotional upset caused
by grief, pain or sympathy is illegitimate". Cf. also BAUER, *Johannesevangelium*,
152; WESTCOTT, *St. John*, 170-171; BULTMANN, *John*, 406-407; MATEOS &
BARRETO, *Giovanni*, 479. De Boor is of opinion that the anger of Jesus is caused
by the power of death, the faithless cry of Mary and the Jews or by foreseeing His
own death on the cross: DE BOOR, *Johannes*, Vol II,32. For Henderson this
indignant emotion was not due to the horror of death, because he calmly speaks of
the death of Lazarus (v.11) and finds this death with positive attitude (vv.14-15).
Rather it may be the faithless cry of the "wailers" that causes such an indignant
emotion in Jesus: Cf. HENDERSON, *Notes on John 11*, 123-124.

[75] Actually in the Fourth Gospel there is no mention of the hypocrisy of the Jews.

[76] This verb depicts the lamentation on the day of burial (cf. Mt 2,18; Mk 5,38;
Lk 7,13; Jn 20,11-13). The technical term for official and liturgical lament for the
dead is θρῆνος. For details cf. G. STÄHLIN, θρηνέω, θρῆνος, *TDNT* III, 148-
155; K.H. RENGSTORF, κλαίω, κλαυθμός, *TDNT* III, 722-726.

even for Jesus.[77] Some other authors consider the anger of Jesus as a reaction of His encounter with power of death, i.e. satanic power which Lazarus has faced, from which Jesus was going to save him.[78]

In v. 38 Jesus appears once again indignant immediately after the sceptical remark of the Jews in v.37. If one considers τῷ πνεύματι (v.33) and ἐν ἑαυτῷ (v.38) as spheres of Jesus' emotion, then the expressions ἐνεβριμήσατο τῷ πνεύματι (v.33) and ἐμβριμώμενος ἐν ἑαυτῷ (v.38) can be seen as identical. The expression τῷ πνεύματι has nothing to do with the Holy Spirit.[79] However, the use of this verb in v.38 seems to be different from that of v.33. The emotions in v. 38 can be considered as anger due to the explicit expression of the Jews' lack of faith (v.37b). But it is difficult to consider the emotion of Jesus in v.33 as anger[80] since Jesus bursts into tears in v.35 in the absence of any expression of lack of faith in the preceding section.

In the particular context of the Lazarus-episode and in the general context of the Fourth Gospel Jesus' emotion in vv.33.35and 38 suggests sympathy[81] and sorrow rather than anger. It is Jesus'

---

[77] Cf. JOHANNES CHRYSOSTOMUS, "Homiliae in Ioannem", 63,2 in: *PG* 59, 350; ORIGEN, "Joannis", frag.84,in: *GCS* IV, 549; CLEMENS, "Commentariorum in Ioannem", in: *PG* 74, 53 A.

[78] Cf. E. BEVAN, "Note on Mark 1,41 and John 11,33.38", *JTS* 33 (1932) 187-188.

[79] Cf. BARRETT, *St. John*, 398.

[80] If one takes the Greek translation of the Syriac expression 'eth 'azaz bᶜruha, then there is no connotation of anger: Cf. BLACK, *Aramaic Approach*, 174-177.

[81] Cf. HENDRIKSEN, *John*, 154; BERNARD, *St. John*, Vol II, 392-393; LAGRANGE, *Saint Jean*, 304-305.

sympathetic reaction to the sorrow of Mary and others.[82] Here the
verb ἐμβριμᾶσθαι joined to τῷ πνεύματι (v.33) and ἐν ἑαυτῷ (v.38)
expresses internal emotion of a person.[83] In the Fourth Gospel the
verb ἐμβριμάομαι occurs only in the present text and it governs no
personal object. Instead it is presented as an internal emotion of
Jesus specified by the expressions τῷ πνεύματι and ἐν ἑαυτῷ.[84] So
also, the verb ἐτάραξεν (troubled)[85] in v.33 is a manifestation of
Jesus' human sentiments.[86] Such a feeling motivated Jesus to
enquire about the tomb of His beloved friend and resulted in the
shedding of tears. Jesus' intense feeling expressed in v. 38 can only
be understood in the light of the entire preceding section and not of
v.37b alone.[87] The whole context of the preceding section is
characterized by sorrow. In such a context Jesus' emotions in v.38

---

[82] Though the weeping of the mourners can be considered as a traditional ritual
act, we cannot explain the cry of Lazarus' beloved sister of Lazarus as something
hypocritical. Therefore, there is no place for anger on Jesus' part in the context of
the pericope.

[83] By considering the use of this verb in the particular context of the text Segalla
arrives at the conclusion that it shows the interior emotions of Jesus. Cf. SEGALLA,
Giovanni, 329.

[84] But, in the Synoptic Gospels ἐμβριμάομαι is followed by personal objects
where it denotes an emotion directed to somebody else (cf. Mt 9,30; Mk 1,43; 14,5).

[85] The verb ταράσσω is a term preferred by the Fourth Evangelist (Mt 2x, Mk
1x, Lk 2x, Jn 7x) who unlike the Synoptics, uses it mainly to depict the internal
human feelings (cf. Jn 12,27; 13,21; 14,1.27).

[86] The use of the verb ταράσσω together with ἐμβριμάομαι denotes the
manifestation of internal sentiments. It is an expression of feeling which is closer to
"cry"(v.35) or leads to the shedding of tears. Cf. SEGALLA, *Giovanni*, 329; cf. also
HENDRIKSEN, *John*,154.

[87] The particle οὖν is a recapitulation of the preceding section. Even though
some find a connection only with the immediately preceding verse (v.37) it can be
connected with the other preceding verses too.

are sympathy and sorrow at the death of His friend, especially as he approaches Lazarus' tomb.

While the Greek verb ἐδάκρυσεν (burst into tears) in v.35 denotes a cry which is serene and is different from κλαίω (weeping with groaning), it shows the genuine tears of Jesus at the death of His friend.[88] According to some authors the crying of Jesus also is an outburst of His anger.[89] In the context of the pericope the crying of Jesus is interpreted even by the Jews as an expression of genuine love and affection towards His friend (cf.v.36). It can be interpreted as an expression of love also towards Mary, Martha and others.[90] Crying shows Jesus' humanity[91] and emotional warmth.[92] In the context of Jesus' emotions seen in vv.33 and 38 the shedding of tears

---

[88] ἐδάκρυσεν in v.35 is its only occurrence in NT. To express Jesus' crying over Jerusalem Luke uses the verb κλαίω (cf. Lk 19,41). Westcott makes a distinction between these verbs which helps one to understand Jesus' sentiments in the context of John 11,35: Cf. WESTCOTT, St. John, 171.

[89] Cf. POLLARD, Lazarus, 440f.; cf. also HOSKYNS, Fourth Gospel, 403-405. Hoskyns interprets here the tears of Jesus similarly to His weeping over Jerusalem (Lk 19,41). But the expression used in Lk 19,41 is ἔκλαυσεν ἐπ᾽ αὐτήν.

[90] Cf. HENDRIKSEN, John, 155-156. He describes this tears of Jesus "not as the tears of professional mourner, nor those of the sentimentalist, but those of the pure and holy sympathizing High-priest. They proceed from the most genuine love for man found in the entire universe, the love which gave itself".

[91] According to Westcott, Jesus' weeping shows His humanity. The Fourth Evangelist uses similar words like thirst (cf.4,7;19,28), fatigue (cf.4,6), love (cf.20,2) to affirm Jesus' humanity. WESTCOTT, St. John, 171; cf. also HOSKYNS, Fourth Gospel, 403.

[92] Cf. HÄNCHEN, John, Vol II, 66; MATEOS & BARRETO, Giovanni, 479-480; LEAL, Amicum Lazarum, 61-62, where Leal considers Jesus' tears as an outburst of His inner distress at the death of His friend. It is also an expression of Jesus' love and mercy towards Lazarus and also towards the bereaved sisters. Cf. also BERNARD, St. John, Vol II, 394. Bernard considers Jesus' weeping as a human reaction to a painful situation.

in v.35 can be understood as an expression of human sentiments, an intimate human feeling.[93]

In short, apart from the theological motives[94] Jesus' deep emotions which culminated in the bursting into tears express His genuine love and friendship with the Bethany family. Actually, with His painful sentiments Jesus associated Himself to Martha and Mary at the death of their beloved. His cry was not simply like the weeping of the bystanding Jews.[95] The Johannine Jesus can be one with the suffering man.[96] More than merely psychological, His friendship with the Bethany family is theological as evidenced in Jesus' emotional feelings in the particular context of the pericope.

---

[93] WILKENS, *Lazarus*, 36, where he considers the crying of Jesus as "echt menschlichen Empfindens". Cf. also KREMER, *Lazarus*, 364f.; THOMAS, *Evangelium S. Ioannis*, § 1537, where he writes: "Consequenter Dominus affectum suum lacrymis demonstrat; unde subditur **Et lacrymatus est Iesus**: Quae quidem lacrymae non erant ex necessitate, sed ex pietate et causa. Fons enim pietatis erat, et ideo flebat ut ostenderet non esse reprehensible si aliquis ploret ex pietate; Eccli. C. XXXVIII,16: *Fili, super mortuum produc lacrymas*. Flevit ex causa, ut doceret hominem Propter peccatum fletibus indigere, secundum illud Ps. V,7: *Laboravi in gemitu meo, lavabo per singulas noctes lectum meum*".

[94] The tears of Jesus have certain theological motives. They shed light on Jesus' incarnation. Jesus became a human being with human sentiments. Another theological motive is the obscurity of death that has already overcome His friend and that will decide His own fate. Cf. SCHNACKENBURG, *St. John*, Vol II, 336-337. According to Wilkens this cry of Jesus foreshadows his future cross: Cf. WILKENS, *Lazarus*, 36.

[95] Cf. HENDERSON, *Notes on John 11*, 125. He says, "There the disciples saw and were amazed as the silent tears fell from His eyes. How near to them He was - how far off from those miserable wailing comforters!"

[96] Cf. SCHNACKENBURG, *St. John*, Vol II, 337; SCHNEIDERS, *Community of Eternal Life*, 54.

d. Jesus' Performance of the Sign (vv. 39-44)

In the final section of the narrative the Evangelist gives an account of the sign of raising Lazarus. It is the actualization of Jesus' promise of His great gift of life to the believers here and now. This life-giving sign is simultaneously a sublime expression of Jesus' divine power and mission, a supreme manifestation of His love and friendship. Jesus raises Lazarus from death, as he cannot permit death to terminate the relationship into which He and Lazarus had entered. [97] In this section of the episode Jesus takes full command of the story and bestows His friend an unsought and unmerited gift.[98] The nature of the interpersonal relationship between Jesus and the believer is clearly manifested in this subsection of the pericope. The superiority of Jesus due to His divine origin and the obedience of the believer are the two essential elements in the divine-human friendship. In the enactment of the sign Jesus appears as one who exercises His divine authority. [99]

Vv. 39-40 can be seen as the immediate preparation for the execution of the sign which is the supreme expression of the friendship between Jesus and Lazarus. In v. 39 Jesus appears as one who gives a powerful command. [100] Jesus' divine authority is manifested in this command. Even removing the stone from the

---

[97] Cf. MCNEIL, *The Raising of Lazarus*, 273.

[98] Cf. MARSH, *St. John*, 435.

[99] According to John Chrysostom the miracle of the raising testified to Jesus' authoritative power. Cf. JOHANNES CHRYSOSTOMUS, "Homiliae in Ioannem", 62 in: *PG* 59, 341-348.

[100] The verb ἄρατε (take away) is aorist imperative which shows the force of His command.

tomb is interpreted as an occasion to manifest Jesus' close friendship with Lazarus, since thereby He wishes to have a look at His dead friend.[101] The intervention of Martha in v.39 affirms once again the death of Lazarus and at the same time gives a chance to Jesus to teach the bystanders about the necessity of faith to see the divine glory (cf. v.40).

In Jesus' prayer (vv.41-42)[102] His divine origin, mission and constant relation with His Father[103] are made clear. The prayer expresses Jesus' deep faith in the power of His Father. The constant communion with the Father expressed in His prayer is very apt in the context of the life-giving miracle for the sake of His intimate friend. Jesus' prayer includes an unexpressed petition for His friend.[104] The motive of Jesus' prayer is not only the execution of the sign[105] but also the deepening of the faith of the bystanders including Martha and Mary.[106] Thus, Jesus' love and concern towards the Bethany family is vivid even in His prayer.

---

[101] Cf. LINDARS, *John*, 400.

[102] There is a parallelism in Jesus' prayer of thanksgiving in v.41 and Ps 118,21a, where Is 65,24 is quoted. Hanson presupposes the OT background for the Lazarus-episode on the basis of this parallelism and thematic similarity between Jn 11 and Ps 118: Cf. HANSON, *Old Testament Background*, 255. Cf. also supra, p. 102, n.37.

[103] By analyzing the prayer of Jesus in vv. 41-42 Wilcox affirms the presence of the constant relationship between Jesus and the Father. The use of the aorist tense ἤκουσας (v.41b) and the Greek adverb of time πάντοτε (v.42) explain such a constant relationship. Cf. M. WILCOX, "The 'Prayer' of Jesus in John XI.41b-42", *NTS* 24 (1977) 128-132.

[104] According to Barrett: "Jesus is in constant communion with the Father, who always 'hears' even the unspoken thoughts of his heart, and therefore has already 'heard' his petition for Lazarus": BARRETT, *St. John*, 402.

[105] Cf. *Ibid.*, 402-403.

[106] Cf. HENDERSON, *Notes on John 11*, 126.

With an authoritative command Jesus calls back Lazarus to life (v.43). Κραυγάζειν is a Johannine term (1x Mt; 0x Mk; 1x Lk; 6x Jn) which denotes the authority of the saviour.[107] So also, the expression φωνῇ μεγάλη (loud voice) shows Jesus' majesty and power.[108] The powerful voice of Jesus is heard by the dead addressing him personally and becomes an effective instrument of the resurrection (cf. Jn 5,25.28).[109] When Lazarus acquires life he proves himself a true believer and one who is in friendship with Jesus (cf. vv.25-26).[110]

Jesus calls Lazarus by name, a sign of one's personal knowledge, friendship and closeness.[111] Jesus addressed the dead Lazarus as if he were alive.[112] Jesus also gives a command to set Lazarus free, so that he can enjoy the fullness of life. Thus, in the life-giving sign of Jesus one can vividly notice the love and friendship between Him and the Bethany family. Jesus could manifest His genuine friendship with such a beloved family by means of His words and deeds as expressed by the Evangelist in the pericope. The divinity and

---

[107] Cf. SEGALLA, *Giovanni*, 331.

[108] Cf. SCHNACKENBURG, *St. John*, Vol II, 340. We have already discussed the theological aspect of the expression φωνῇ in the previous chapter: Cf. supra, pp. 81-82.

[109] Commenting on Jn 11,43 Hendriksen writes: "Jesus cried out so forcibly in order that everyone in the crowd might be aware of the fact that the dead would respond to his call": HENDRIKSEN, *John*, 159.

[110] According to Jesus' promise of life which He has made clear in vv.25-26, one must be a true believer to inherit His gift. In other words, faith is essentially connected with life. See our detailed treatment above, pp. 105-108.

[111] Cf. H. BIETENHARD, ὄνομα, *DNTT* II, 648-655.

[112] Cf. JOHANNES CHRYSOSTOMUS, "Homiliae in Ioannem", 64 in: *PG* 59, 353-360.

superiority of Jesus, essential elements in the Jesus-disciple relationship, are also evident in the words and deeds of Jesus towards the Bethany family.

B. In the Words and Deeds of Martha and Mary

Since the friendship between Jesus and the Bethany family is reciprocal there are several expressions of intimate friendship in the words and deeds of Martha and Mary. In their message to Jesus concerning Lazarus' sickness, in their personal meetings and dialogue with Jesus etc. they acknowledge Jesus' divinity and superiority which are important elements in His friendship with them.

1. The Message of Martha and Mary (v.3)

The message of the sickness of Lazarus is sent (ἀπέστειλαν) by his sisters, Martha and Mary in their own words (λέγουσαι). Within the message the friendship can be seen on two levels: On the first level, the Bethany family's friendship with Jesus is very evident in the very act of sending such a message. On the second level, Jesus' love and friendship with them, especially with Lazarus, is clear in the words of their message. [113]

Their addressing of Jesus as Κύριε (Lord) in this context is noteworthy. It is a theologically developed and post-resurrectional title, attributed to Jesus by the Christian believers. In the historical context of Lazarus-event it was a title of courtesy. But, by the time

---

[113] Commenting on this message De Boor says, "Wir spüren, dass ein besonderes Band Jesus mit diesem Haus verbindet": DE BOOR, *Johannes*, Vol II, 23.

of the redaction of the Fourth Gospel the title Κύριε had become a theologically developed term. On the redactional level the Evangelist puts such a theologically developed title into the mouth of Martha and Mary in order to present them as genuine Christian believers and intimate friends of Jesus.

In the content of the message Jesus' friendship with Lazarus is explicitly brought out through the expression: "he whom you love is ill" (ὅν φιλεῖς ἀσθενεῖ).[114] Here there is no plea or prayer, even though the prayers of friends are very powerful (cf. Lk 4, 38.39); there is neither mention of blood-relationship, though God does many things in favour of blood relations (cf. 3 Kings 11,13; Gen 18,26) nor mention of the sick man's love for Jesus, though such prayers are always heard (cf. Lk 7,4.5). The sisters consider Jesus' love for their brother so important and great as to get a favour from Jesus. The love of the person who helps is more efficacious than the

---

[114] The New English Bible translated it as "your friend". The use of the verb φιλέω in its participle form in the present context is noteworthy as it denotes the affectionate love of Jesus towards His friend, Lazarus. Even though the Fourth Evangelist seems to use the verbs ἀγαπάω and φιλέω synonymously (cf. BERNARD, St. John, Vol II, 702-704; BARRETT, St. John, 584; BROWN, John, Vol I, 497-499; BULTMANN, John, 711, n.5) there is a theological distinction between these verbs in the strict sense. Φιλέω is the most general word to depict love or regard with affection. It denotes the attraction of people to one another who are close together both inside and outside the family; it includes concern, care and hospitality. So, φίλος is a friend in the sense of affection. Φίλος in the NT is a friend to whom one is under a basic obligation (cf. Lk 7,6;11,5f;14,10.12;15,6.9.29; 23,12;Jn 11,11;Acts 10,24;19,31;27,3). But ἀγαπάω is salvific and active love (cf. supra, p.87,n.1). In the NT it is used to speak of the love of God or the way of life based upon it. Cf. W. GÜNTHER & H.G. LINK, ἀγαπάω, DNTT II, 538-547; cf. also GÜNTHER, φιλέω, DNTT II, 547-549; STÄHLIN, φιλέω, TDNT IX, 113-171.

love of the one in need. [115] From the message it is unquestionably clear that the sisters were fully aware of Jesus' warm and personal affection for Lazarus. [116]

The sisters of Lazarus express no plea, but simply state their situation as in the case of the miracle at Cana (cf. Jn 2,3). [117] They were sure that Jesus as one who was close to them, would not abandon them but would react positively. [118] They leave everything to the discretion of the one who loves, by trusting in Him. From the expression: "he whom you love", one can conclude that Lazarus was already in friendship with Jesus by fulfilling the necessary qualities of a believer and a Christian disciple. [119] Lazarus' sisters were sure enough of Jesus' friendship with their brother as to mention it publically in their message.

Summing up then, one may say that the very act of sending the message and the mode of their addressing Jesus as well as the content of their message etc. testify to the fact of the friendship between Jesus and the Bethany family. It likewise sheds light on Jesus' divine power and on the Christian discipleship of this family as its members express their deep faith and trust in Jesus. [120]

---

[115] Cf. LEAL, *Amicum Lazarum*, 59-60.

[116] Cf. HENDRIKSEN, *John*, 139.

[117] Cf. SEGALLA, *Giovanni*, 323.

[118] AUGUSTINUS, "Tractatus", 49 in: *PL* 35, 1749, where he writes: "sufficit ut noveris: non enim amas et deseris".

[119] Cf. DE BOOR, *Johannes*, Vol II, 23.

[120] Cf. HOSKYNS, *Fourth Gospel*, 339; MARSH, *St. John*, 422.

2. The Words of Martha (vv. 21.22.24.27.28)

In the episode of Lazarus' resurrection there is Martha's first direct utterance in v.21 where she addresses Jesus by the title: Κύριε (Lord!).[121] At the level of the redaction it can be considered as a Christian title, an expression of her faith and confidence in Jesus, though at the level of history one may take it only as a title of courtesy. Martha then expresses her faith and love in the person of Jesus without any words of complaint or criticism (v.21).[122] It is not an utterance of disappointment with Jesus,[123] rather it can be considered as an expression of her deep trust and poignant grief.[124]

From her opening words it is evident that Martha felt Jesus' absence as well as the power of His presence. According to her even the very presence of Jesus could have prevented the death of her brother. Her faith and trust in the person of Jesus is once again highlighted in her following words in v.22. In spite of the death which has conquered her brother in the absence of Jesus, she still[125] acknowledges[126] the power of Jesus. The Evangelist presents her as one who recognizes Jesus as one sent by the Father, the Son of God

---

[121] Κύριε is omitted by the manuscripts B and Sy³.

[122] Cf. SCHNACKENBURG, *St. John*, Vol II, 329.

[123] Cf. R.T. FORTNA, *The Fourth Gospel and its Predecessor* (Edinburgh 1989) 101.

[124] Cf. HENDRIKSEN, *John*, 147.

[125] In v.22 the Greek expression καὶ νῦν is an example of adversative use. It means - *and even now.*

[126] οἶδα (I know) is not simply an intellectual knowledge. In Johannine theology it is a profound knowledge which enters even in the realm of faith.

and the Revealer to whom God gives everything (cf.3,35).[127] Her faith in His power is a faith in the power of His prayer to the heavenly Father as it is later verified at the execution of the sign in vv. 41f. (cf. 9,31; 15,7.16; 16,23). According to Schnackenburg: "Martha is presented as a woman prepared to believe (καὶ νῦν οἶδα), who, in a form deliberately kept general (ὅσα ἂν) and indefinite, indicates a hope and express a request which leaves all possibilities open".[128] Thus, in the words of Martha there is a perceived combination of grief at the death of a brother and an expression of the soul of a Christian disciple filled with reverence and hope. The Fourth Evangelist presents Martha in v.22 as one who expresses her faith and confidence in Jesus admitting His special relationship with God the Father.[129]

Further, in v. 24 Martha expresses her deep faith in the resurrection on the last day, which at the time was a disputed question among the Jews. Such belief in a final resurrection was quite intrinsic to pharisaic Judaism. It represented the faith of the Christians among whom the Fourth Gospel took its shape and so Martha seems to be a true believer. Even in the teaching of Jesus there is a mention of the resurrection of the dead on the last day (cf. Jn 5, 28-29). As a genuine Christian disciple Martha had accepted in faith Jesus' teaching concerning the resurrection on the last

---

[127] Cf. F.F. BRUCE, *The Gospel of John* (Michigan 1984) 243.

[128] SCHNACKENBURG, *St. John*, Vol II, 329; HENDRIKSEN, *John*, 148. Hendriksen says, "in the mind of Martha, the raising of Lazarus is not excluded from this whatever"; cf. also LEAL, *Amicum Lazarum*, 60.

[129] Cf. BERNARD, *St. John*, Vol II, 385. According to him ὁ θεός at the end of the sentence is emphatic which stylistically illustrates the Father's glory as the ultimate aim of the Son's work.

day.[130] By experiencing the raising of Lazarus Martha was able to believe in an anticipation of this final eschatology through the person of Jesus. It seems therefore, that one can argue that before the realization of this present eschatology Martha believed only in Jesus' teaching on a final eschatology. On account of Martha's faith in Jesus' teaching one arrives at the conclusion that she was already an authentic Christian disciple and thus in friendship with Jesus.

The dialogue between Jesus and Martha climaxes in a profound expression of her faith in a confessional formula, where she recognizes Jesus as the Son of God, the saviour of the world and the source of everything (cf. v.27). To Jesus' question about the essence of His person (as resurrection and life) Martha answers also in the form of a solemn confession of faith.[131] Her confession can be identified with the Christian faith, the ultimate aim of the Gospel itself (cf. 20,31). Faith in Christ as the Son of God, is the expression of mature Christian belief in the historical Jesus, already developed by the time of the Evangelist. In this context Martha's words, formed in a liturgical style, represent a genuine Christological confession of faith.[132]

In the confession of Martha, a perfect tense form, πεπίστευκα (I have believed),[133] is noteworthy since it signifies that she had already attained a deep faith in Jesus (cf. vv. 3.21.22.24),a faith in which she still continues. Martha's faith was central to the

---

[130] Cf. HENDRIKSEN, *John*, 149.

[131] Cf. DE BOOR, *Johannes*, Vol II, 30; BRUCE, *John*, 245. Martha's words in v.27 can be considered as a confession of faith at the level of redaction.

[132] Cf. HÄNCHEN, *John*, Vol II, 64.

[133] Such a usage can be seen in the early Church's confession of faith especially in baptismal rite: Cf. G. BORNKAMM, *Geschichte und Glaube*, Vol II (München 1971) 192.

confession formula which, as an answer to the question concerning Jesus' person (I am), is structured stylistically. The concentrated chiastic structure is as follows:

a   ναὶ Κύριε

    b   ἐγὼ

        c   πεπίστευκα

  b^1 σύ

a^1 εἶ ὁ Χριστὸς .....

In the structure the letters **a** and a^1 refer to Jesus in His titles; **b** and b^1 refer to Martha and Jesus respectively. Martha expresses her faith in the person of Jesus. The central point is the dynamic faith which is indicated by **c**.[134]

Martha's confession of faith consists of three elements: a) Jesus' Messianic role (Christ). b) Jesus' divine sonship, i.e. His divine origin as Son of God.[135] c) Jesus as one who is coming into the world from heaven to save the world. Martha's confession of faith can best be summarized thus: "He is the head of the new Israel; he is uniquely related to the Father; and he has a special mission to perform".[136] This confession of Martha is the expression of the

---

[134] Real faith is dynamic or active in nature. It is an active reception of the Revelation of God made manifest in Jesus Christ.

[135] Historically speaking one cannot claim that Martha was already characterized by such a deep faith. But at the redactional level the Evangelist presents her as one believing firmly in the divinity of Jesus.

[136] MARSH, *St. John*, 430.

common faith of the community among whom the Fourth Gospel took its shape.

After this confession of faith Martha goes and calls her sister, by communicating the wish of their Master (v.28). In her summons to Mary she gives a new title to Jesus as ὁ διδάσκαλος (the teacher), a title important in the second part of the Gospel (cf. 13,13f.; 20,16f.).[137] In Martha's use of this title one notices the nature of the relationship as a master-disciple relationship. Thus the title διδάσκαλος sheds further light on the discipleship of the Bethany family.[138] Moreover, Jesus' invitation is expressed as φωνεῖ σε (calling you)[139] which highlights Jesus' revelatory role and the nature of the interpersonal relationship.

In short, Martha's positive and comprehensive confession of faith regarding the person of Jesus, and the titles which she gives to Him etc. are expressions of her intimate relationship as a genuine Christian disciple with Jesus. Martha, through her profession of faith in the person of Christ, becomes the model for all the

---

[137] The title ὁ διδάσκαλος is applied to Jesus against the historical background of the Jewish title רבי. But when the NT adopts it as a title for Jesus, it is in perfect contrast with the Jewish concept of רבי. The title רבי might be applied to any exalted personage with all privileges, whereas διδάσκαλος is reserved unequivocally for the teacher. Applied to Jesus the title gives more importance to Jesus' teaching role admitting His authority and dignity. When Martha uses it, she uses its absolute from ὁ διδάσκαλος which shows their special relation, a relation of reverence and trust as well as their intimacy. For further details: Cf. K.H. RENGSTORF, διδάσκαλος, *TDNT* II, 148-159.

[138] Cf. J.MARSH, *St. John*, 432. Marsh finds this title as one used by the disciples of Jesus. He says, "it may well represent the way in which the disciples of Jesus spoke of him when he was not present".

[139] Cf. supra pp. 81-82 for a detailed treatment of the theological meaning of the term φωνή.

disciples.[140] The words of Martha illustrate the nature of their
friendship as supernatural and theological since she acknowledges
the divinity and superiority of Jesus by believing and trusting in Him.
That is to say, in their interpersonal relationship there was place
both for Jesus' superiority and for Martha's profound faith. Through
faith and trust she became an authentic Christian believer and
thereby a beloved of Jesus.

3. The Deeds of Martha (vv. 20.28)

The Evangelist records as Martha's deeds two acts of going: one
towards Jesus (v.20) and the other towards Mary (v.28). In hearing
of Jesus' arrival at Bethany Martha went to meet Him while Mary
remained at home.[141] As a genuine Christian believer Martha
showed her love and respect to Jesus by approaching Him instead
of waiting for His visit. Thus in Martha's act of going to Jesus the
nature of their friendship, a friendship characterized by Jesus'
superiority, is well expressed.

In Martha's second "going" as depicted in v.28, she executes the
mission entrusted to her by Jesus, viz. to call her sister to Jesus. As
a disciple of Jesus not only is she sent for a mission but she also
wishes her sister to have the same experience of the master which
she already had. Being sent and personal witnessing to Christ are
portrayed as typical characteristics of a disciple in the Fourth Gospel

---

[140] Cf. PANIMOLLE, *Giovanni*, Vol III, 30. He writes: "In tal modo questa
donna si mostra come il modello di tutti i discepoli, i quali dovranno credere che
Gesù è il Cristo e il Figlio di Dio (Gv. 20,31)".

[141] In the synoptic tradition Martha is presented as obliging and active while
Mary is considered as contemplative (Lk 10,38-42). There are many cross references
between the Johannine and Lucan accounts: Cf. BROWN, *John*, 432.

(cf. Jn 1,35-37; 41-42; 45).[142] In this light by the very act of approaching Mary with a message Martha exemplifies the quality of a Christian disciple.

In summary and on the basis of the analysis of Martha's words and deeds one sees that Martha, whom Jesus loved was also an authentic Christian disciple.   Such a conclusion helps one to interpret the love-relationship between Jesus and the Bethany family as a master-disciple relationship.

4. The Words of Mary (v. 32)

In our text Mary utters only one sentence which contains a profound expression of her deep faith in the person of Jesus. She repeats the same words of her sister.[143] In Mary's words there is no added note of confidence as with Martha (cf. v.22). But her deep faith and confidence in the power of Jesus are expressive when she says, "Lord, if you had been here my brother would not have died" (v.32). Mary expresses her trust in Jesus by affirming that where Jesus is present, death has no power. Indirectly she recognizes Jesus as the source of life. In these words of Mary one can find her close relationship with Jesus similar to that of Martha, i.e. one based on love, faith and trust.

---

[142] M. VELLANICKAL, "'Discipleship' according to the Gospel of John", *Jeevadhara* 10 (1980) 131-147. In this article he treats the different characteristics of Christian discipleship, one of which is the witnessing role of a disciple.

[143] It seems that they had repeated the same expression of trust in Jesus even before His arrival: Cf. BRUCE, *John*, 246.

5. The Deeds of Mary (vv.29.32.33a)

When Mary was informed of Jesus' call she responded to that call rapidly.[144] She rose quickly (ἠγέρϑη ταχύ) and went to him (ἤρχετο πρὸς αὐτόν).[145] Mary's hastening to Jesus shows that she still has a hope and trust in Him, at least as a source of consolation. Mary's prompt and positive action expresses her attachment to Jesus.[146] As a true follower and beloved of Jesus Mary wants to be consoled by her Master at the moment of distress and pain. Thus she appears: "as a picture of a disciple in sorrow and loss going out to meet her Lord she is a universal symbol of the distressed disciple".[147] Mary hopes to share her sorrow with a close family friend.

In connection with Mary's deeds, her falling at the feet of Jesus (ἔπεσεν αὐτοῦ πρὸς τοὺς πόδας) elucidates the nature of their relationship, again a relationship which admits Jesus' superiority. There are difference of opinion among the exegetes concerning

---

[144] Mary's reaction to the call of Jesus is similar to that of Levi on the basis of quick response (cf. Mk 2,14 and parallels).

[145] The expression "going to him" or "coming to him" as a movement towards Jesus has a theological meaning in the Fourth Gospel. It is considered as an act of faith in its experiential dimension. The act of *going to Jesus* is to establish a personal relationship with Him and to experience His personal presence and thereby to deepen one's faith in the person and teaching of Jesus. This is connected with Johannine concept of discipleship (cf. Jn 1,39). Cf. VELLANICKAL, *Gospel of John*, 113.

[146] Cf. SCHNACKENBURG, *St. John*, Vol II, 333.

[147] MARSH, *St. John*, 431.

Mary's action described in v.32.[148] Considering the relationship between Jesus and the Bethany family expressed in the pericope, in the redactional level one can rightly interpret the action of the "falling down of Mary at the feet of Jesus" as an act of worship, an act of honour rightly reserved for God.[149] It is an external expression of her internal attitude of faith in a divine person. One can conclude from this gesture of Mary that her relationship with Jesus was not merely human and psychological but it was supernatural and divine. What Martha expressed in a confession of faith, Mary communicated in one action of reverence and worship. In this respect Mary's faith was superior in quality or degree than that of Martha.[150]

After uttering an expression of faith and confidence in Jesus, Mary weeps (cf. v.33), not as an expression of disappointment but one of grief and affection. As often happens in difficult situations, the presence of intimate friends combined with the inability to communicate verbally causes people to weep. Mary's weeping could elicit affectionate feelings in Jesus, culminating in shedding of tears.[151] Thus, even the Mary's tears express the intimate relationship between Jesus and the Bethany family.

---

[148] Lindars considers it as an act of supplication at the painful situation of the death of her brother: Cf. LINDARS, *John*, 397. Taking into account the verb ἔπεσεν Hirsch interprets it as an act of veneration (cf. Mt 4,9; 17,6): Cf. HIRSCH, *Das Vierte Evangelium*, 290. Brown considers it as a typical attitude of Mary of Bethany in the Lucan narrative (cf. Lk 10,39; cf. also Jn 12,3): Cf. BROWN, *John*, Vol I, 435.

[149] Cf. HENDRIKSEN, *John*, 153; MARSH, *St. John*, 431; SCHNACKENBURG, *St. John*, Vol II, 334; HÄNCHEN, *John*, Vol II, 64.

[150] Cf. HENDRIKSEN, *John*, 154.

[151] Cf. supra, pp. 117-118.

From the analysis of the words and deeds of both Martha and
Mary one can understand the nature of their relationship with Jesus,
a relationship based on their genuine love, faith and trust in Jesus.
In their positive response to the expressions of Jesus' friendship with
them they fulfilled the essential qualities of Christian discipleship.
Thus, Martha and Mary are presented as types of Christian disciples
in the Fourth Gospel. [152]

C. In the Response of Lazarus

From the beginning of the narrative Lazarus is introduced as a
sick man and later as one who is physically dead. In the course of
the story's development the Evangelist presents Lazarus the object
of Jesus' love and friendship (cf. vv.3.5.11.36). Such a love and
friendship on Jesus' part presuppose a life of adherence to the word
of God, to His commandments by Lazarus. [153] From this one can
infer that Lazarus was already an authentic Christian disciple before
his sickness and death. Even after his death Lazarus appears as one
who responds positively to the call (φωνῆ) of Jesus. [154] Lazarus'
response at the execution of the sign represents an obedience
manifested in two ways, viz. his exit from the tomb at Jesus' call; and
his coming out with bound hands and feet.

---

[152] Cf. WILKENS, *Lazarus*, 38; HENDRIKSEN, *John*, 147.

[153] Cf. DE BOOR, *Johannes*, Vol II, 36.

[154] Cf. MARSH, *St. John*, 432. Marsh says, "Lazarus has been dead for four days,
but is nevertheless a 'lover of the Lord', a disciple who can still 'hear his voice' and
have power to obey".

1. Lazarus' Response to Jesus' Voice (v. 44aα)

In the Evangelist's presentation Lazarus' raising takes place as an immediate effect of Jesus' authoritative call (φωνῇ μεγάλη). Jesus' voice penetrates even into the ears of the physically dead Lazarus giving him the capacity to respond positively to such a life-giving voice.[155] Obviously the listening capacity of a dead man must be considered as a gift of God, a work accomplished through His life-giving φωνῇ. Merely hearing the voice of the Son of God is not enough. One must show adherence to the divine voice. Since Jesus treats Lazarus as a living person, calling him by name, Lazarus' coming forth from the tomb is to be considered his positive personal response to Jesus' call.[156] Jesus' prediction and promise in Jn 5,28f. is actualized in the case of Lazarus at least in a symbolic way. At the level of redaction Lazarus' obedient response to Jesus' call expresses faith in Him and in His words. For the Fourth Evangelist, obedience is the supreme way of showing faith (cf. Jn 3,36).[157] Thus, Lazarus through faith and obedience became a symbol of genuine Christian disciple and a genuine friend of Jesus as well.

---

[155] DE BOOR, *Johannes*, Vol II, 36, n.26.

[156] Cf. MOULE, *The Meaning of Life*, 117; DE BOOR, *Johannes*, Vol II, 36, where he writes, "Und hier hört und gehorcht der, der überhaupt nicht hören und gehorchen kann, dem das Hören und Gehorchen hindurch. Auch der verwesende Lazarus wird als "Person" geachtet und behandelt; er wird bei seinem Namen "gerufen" und zum eigenen "Herauskommen" gefordert".

[157] Cf. SUGGIT, *Lazarus*, 107.

2. Lazarus' Coming out with Bandage (v. 44)

According to the narrative Lazarus comes out of the tomb with bound hands and feet. For the Fourth Evangelist it has a symbolic meaning of Lazarus' total submission to Jesus' voice and supreme expression of obedience. [158] It expresses Lazarus' powerlessness before his divine Master. Likewise Jesus' power is once again affirmed when He orders the bystanders to unbind Lazarus. The command and response underline that salvation has a communitarian dimension. It depends on the obedience of the community as well as on one's personal response to Christ's call which can be summarized here as: "Jesus calls: Lazarus obeys: others set him free".[159]

Lazarus' response to Jesus' concrete love and friendship is expressed in his obedience and submission, based on his own deep faith in his Master's power. Lazarus is called back to a new life because of his belief in Jesus (cf. vv.25-26). After acquiring this new life Lazarus became an instrument of faith both for the disciples and for the Jews (cf. Jn 11,15.45; 12,11).[160] Through his silent witness of faith and obedience, Lazarus became a "type"of Christian disciple and a beloved of Jesus. Thus the reciprocal nature of the friendship between Jesus and Lazarus is highlighted in the narrative.

---

[158] Cf. HOSKYNS, *Fourth Gospel*, 407.

[159] SUGGIT, *Lazarus*, 118.

[160] Cf. F. GENUYT, "Ressusciter pour apprendre à vivre et à mourir. La résurrection de Lazare selon l'évangile de Jean (11,1-44)", *LumVie* 35 (1986) 71.

D. In the Comments of the Jews

The Jews also play an important role in the Lazarus-episode of the Fourth Gospel. Rather than hostile authorities they appear in the course of the event for the most part as ordinary people of Judea and Jerusalem, consoling the bereaved family at Bethany, [161] and often sympathetic to and believing in Jesus (cf. vv.19.31.33.36.45).In v.8 the disciples refer back to a hostility of the Jews not verified in the present account. Even though there are casual negative reactions on the part of the Jews they are only from a minority (τινές). In their comments, both positive and negative, (vv.36.37)the depth of Jesus' friendship with the Bethany family and especially with Lazarus is likewise verified.

1. Positive Comment (v. 36)

The majority of the Jews interpreted the tears of Jesus as an expression of His love and concern towards His friend, Lazarus. They made their comment in an exclamatory tone: ἴδε πῶς ἐφίλει αὐτόν (see, how he loved him!). [162] In their amazement they refer

---

[161] The consoling of the bereaved was a duty and practice in Judaism: Cf. STRACK & BILLERBECK, *Talmud und Midrasch*, Vol IV, 592-607.

[162] In this expression, πῶς (how) is not an interrogative particle, but an exclamatory one to express the quantity and quality of Jesus' love. The verb φιλέω indicates the affectionate love that unites the friends. It is used here in its imperfect tense (ἐφίλει), denoting that Jesus' attitude of love that began in the past and continues in the present.

to Jesus' tender affection for Lazarus. [163] They do give a rather limited interpretation to the tears of Jesus since they see them as an expression of love only towards Lazarus. In fact His weeping can be seen as Jesus' expression of sympathy in the face of the pain and tears of others especially Mary's. Nonetheless even through the mouth of the usually hostile Jews of the Fourth Gospel the Evangelist testifies to the existence of love and friendship between Lazarus and Jesus.

2. Negative Comment (v. 37)

Jesus' tears were interpreted by some Jews (τινές) as an expression of His inability to save Lazarus from death. [164] This comment appears negative in nature in contrast with the comment made in the preceding verse. [165] Their remark regards not the raising of Lazarus from the dead, but the prevention of death which now appears an impossibility. They do not doubt Jesus' power, manifested in opening the eyes of the blind, but they doubt Jesus' ability to save someone from death.   By referring to an as yet unrealized fact they ridicule Jesus. This comment appears to be spoken in mockery.

---

[163] Cf. LEAL, *Amicum Lazarum*, 62. But in Schnackenburg's opinion the Jews' inference of Jesus' love for His friend is superficial: Cf. SCHNACKENBURG, *St. John*, Vol II, 337.

[164] Cf. LINDARS, *John*, 399.

[165] The negative tone of the comment is clear from the Greek particle δέ (but) (cf. 7,12c.41b;10,20) followed by a negative question, οὐκ ἐδύνατο (could not he) which refers to Jesus' inability: Cf. SCHNACKENBURG, *St. John*, Vol II, 337.

However, here we are not interested in the negative overtone of the comment, but in the skill of the Evangelist, who even by means of such a negative comment testifies to the close friendship between Jesus and Lazarus. Even in their negative comment the Jews found it unnatural on the part of Jesus, who gave sight to a blind man out of sympathy, that He did not prevent His intimate friend from dying. The reality underlying their comment is the deep friendship between Jesus and Lazarus. By their negative question the Jews highlight the relevance of an expected miracle on Jesus' part. If Jesus and Lazarus had not been close friends there would be no place for such a comment. It can then be said that even the Jews' positive and negative comments concerning Jesus' tears give witness to the friendship between Jesus and Lazarus.

E. In the Descriptions and Comments of the Evangelist

The Evangelist, through his stylistic presentation and timely comments, exposes the close relationship which existed between Jesus and the Bethany family. As seen above it is only against the background of such a genuine friendship that one can understand the words and deeds of the characters involved. According to Johannine theology one must remain in Jesus, i.e. be united with Him through faith and love, in order to obtain all spiritual benefits including eternal life. Thus, within the framework of the Fourth Gospel, the Bethany family has a pivotal position, because of its close relationship to Jesus. In the introductory part of the pericope there are certain descriptions and comments of the Evangelist which likewise also illustrate the friendship between Jesus and the Bethany family.

1. The Expression: "Lazarus of Bethany" (v. 1)

The Fourth Evangelist opens the Lazarus-story with his usual simple narrative style, viz. by presenting the characters in a general way (eg. "there was a certain man..." cf. 3,1; 4,46b; 5,5). But he proceeds by giving the person's name together with the place of origin (Λάζαρος ἀπὸ Βηθανίας) according to the Jewish custom (cf. 1,44.45.; 12,21; 19,38; 21,2).[166] In the present episode mention of the names of Martha and Mary is to situate Bethany and not to explain the relationship between Lazarus and the two sisters. The reference to Bethany as the domicile of Lazarus and as the village of Martha and Mary provides a suitable background to present the theme of friendship between Jesus and the Bethany family.

In presenting Lazarus as from Bethany and the brother of Martha and Mary, the Fourth Evangelist identifies Bethany with the village of the two sisters where Jesus was well received and well accepted (cf. Lk 10,38-42).[167] Moreover, in the synoptic tradition Bethany was a place dear to Jesus as His resting place when He came to Jerusalem (cf. Mk 11,11; 14,3; Mt 21,17; 26,6; Lk 21,37). By presenting Lazarus as one from Bethany, the Fourth Evangelist tries to emphasize for the readers, who were already familiar with the synoptic tradition, the relevance and depth of Jesus' friendship with the Bethany family. In the dramatic presentation of the pericope such an expression helps one to understand Jesus' positive reaction towards a family which was dear to Him during His public ministry.

---

[166] Cf. SCHNACKENBURG, *St. John*, Vol II, 318; PANIMOLLE, *Giovanni*, Vol III, 25.

[167] Cf. BULTMANN, *John*, 396, n.2. In Lk 10,38-42 the Evangelist does not identify Bethany with the village of Martha and Mary.

2. The Anointing by Mary (v. 2)

In the introductory part of the text (in v.2) Mary is mentioned in connection with her later activity according to the Johannine tradition (cf. 12,3). V. 2 is considered by some exegetes as a gloss of the ecclesiastical redactor. [168] However, it also appears as a technique of the narrator to make the characters known to the readers by reference to their other deeds (cf. Nicodemus: 7,50; 19,39; Caiaphas: 11,49f.; 18,14; Judas the betrayer: 6,71; 12,4; 13,2; 18,2; 3,5; the beloved disciple: 13,23; 18,15f.; 19,26; 20,2.3.8;21,20).[169] In Jn 12,3 the anointing by Mary is presented as an act of her gratitude towards Jesus for the raising of her brother. [170] So, the anticipatory reference to Mary's anointing in the pericope expresses the nature of the interpersonal relationship between Jesus and Mary. It shows Mary's love and concern to Jesus, expressed in the reverence and thankfulness due to the divine Master. The anointing represents Mary's positive response to the supreme love of Jesus, manifested through His words and deeds. Thus, this anticipated description of the Evangelist serves as an effective device showing the reciprocal nature of the friendship between Jesus and the Bethany family.

---

[168] Cf. *Ibid.*, 395, n.4; SCHNACKENBURG, *St. John*, Vol II, 322. They arrive at such a conclusion by considering the use of ὁ Κύριος (cf. 6,23) and the grammatical construction.

[169] Cf. HÄNCHEN, *John*, Vol II, 57.

[170] Cf. HENDRIKSEN, *John*, 138.

3. "Jesus loved Martha and her sister and Lazarus" (v. 5)

This comment of the Evangelist emphasizes Jesus' love and friendship towards the members of the Bethany family. In v.3 Jesus' friendship with Lazarus is recognized, as expressed by the two sisters. Now, in v.5 it is confirmed by the Evangelist along with Jesus' love towards Lazarus' sisters. In the immediate context of the Lazarus-narrative the Evangelist's comment as it now stands aims to convince the reader that Jesus' delay for two days (cf. v.6) was not due to His lack of love and concern for the Bethany family.[171]

To depict Jesus' love and friendship with the whole Bethany family the Evangelist uses the Greek verb ἀγαπάω,[172] thereby underlining the similarity of this relationship to that of Jesus and His disciples (cf. 13,23; 15,9; 17,23.26; 19,26; 21,20). By using ἀγαπάω the Evangelist expresses the active and spiritual nature of Jesus' friendship with the Bethany family.[173] Jesus' continued profound love towards Martha, Mary and Lazarus is the basis of their intimate

---

[171] Cf. BALAGUÉ, *La Resurrección de Lázaro*, 18-19; BROWN, *John*, Vol I, 423; HÄNCHEN, *John*, Vol II, 57; BRUCE, *John*, 240; DE BOOR, *Johannes*, Vol II, 25.

[172] As a variant reading **D** uses ἐφίλει for the sake of agreement with the φιλέω of v.3. In the text under consideration the Evangelist describes Jesus' love by using the verb ἀγαπάω (v.5), whereas when the sisters and the Jews speak, φιλέω is used (cf. vv.3.36). In the use of the verb φιλέω in vv.3 and 36 there is an emphasis upon Jesus' affectionate love. The sisters move Jesus by reminding Him of His affectionate love towards Lazarus and the Jews refer to it when Jesus weeps. Therefore, one can conclude that ἀγαπάω is a term depicting Jesus' supernatural love, whereas φιλέω denotes one's affectionate love: Cf. J.N. SANDERS, "Those whom Jesus Loved (Jn XI,5)", *NTS* 1 (1954-55) 33. Cf. also supra p. 87, n.1; p. 123, n.114.

[173] Cf. BALAGUÉ, *La Resurrección de Lázaro*, 19; SCHNACKENBURG, *St. John*, Vol II, 323. The imperfect tense of the verb ἠγάπα shows the continued nature of Jesus' love and in Hendriksen's opinion it can be better translated as "holding in loving esteem": Cf. HENDRIKSEN, *John*, 140.

relationship with Jesus. In this sense the Evangelist's comment in v.5 expresses the nature of Jesus' friendship with the Bethany family.[174]

V. Theological Perspective
A. The Nature of Jesus' Friendship with the Bethany Family

The above analysis of the Lazarus-episode, in terms of the love and friendship between Jesus and the Bethany family, illustrated that Jesus was bound to them in a most profound friendship. On the part of Jesus this friendship was highlighted through His own words and deeds. It was recognized and acknowledged as well by the Evangelist and the other characters involved in the story. The detailed investigation of Jesus' words and deeds proved that the friendship established with the Bethany family was not purely psychological or human, but theological and divine also. In other words, the words and deeds of Jesus attested to in the narrative express both divine and human elements of His friendship with the Bethany family.[175]

1. The Human Aspects of Jesus' Friendship

Being truly man Jesus' friendship with others is based on

---

[174] Cf. LEAL, *Amicum Lazarum*, 61.

[175] Cf. PANACKEL, *ΙΔΟΥ Ο ΑΝΘΡΩΠΟΣ*, 189-191.

natural, moral and spiritual values.[176]   At the heart of Jesus'
friendship with the Bethany family there is genuine human love on
His part encompassing all these three aspects.

From a natural point of view the Bethany family was dear to
Jesus. Through their hospitality its members fulfilled the role of
Jesus' relatives and benefactors. [177] The Evangelist uses certain
expressions denoting the natural elements of Jesus' tender and
affectionate friendship with the Bethany family, especially with
Lazarus. The expressions ὅν φιλεῖς (v.3), ὁ φίλος ἡμῶν (v.11), πῶς
ἐφίλει αὐτόν (v.36) etc. all express a certain delicate, tender and
affectionate love between Jesus and Lazarus. [178] The truth and
intensity of Jesus' natural love towards the Bethany family is once
again affirmed by the tears and inner turmoil of Jesus (cf.
vv.33.35.38).[179]   Unlike the verb κλαίω (weep) the verb δακρύω
(burst into tears) with its connotation of affectionate feeling is used
to denote Jesus' crying. So also the verbs ἐμβριμάομαι (to groan)
and ταράσσω (trouble) illustrate Jesus' deep human pain at the
suffering of those related to Him in natural order. [180]

---

[176] Leal distinguishes four types of love in Jesus. Of this four types, one pertains
to His divinity, i.e. His love towards mankind as God loves (salvific); and the other
three pertains to His humanity. Being man Jesus' love is natural (based on natural
relationship), moral (based on moral values) and spiritual (based on God Himself,
i.e. a love of charity). Unlike the divine type these three types of human love are
temporary. Jesus' love and friendship with the Bethany family is perfect in all these
aspects: Cf. LEAL, *Amicum Lazarum*, 62.

[177] Cf. *Ibid.*, 63.

[178] In NT the verb φιλέω is used to denote the relationship among close friends
and relatives and for matters dear to one (cf. Mt 10,37; Jn 5,20; 12,25; 20,2). Cf.
supra p. 123, n. 114; p. 142, n. 172.

[179] Cf. PANIMOLLE, *Giovanni*, Vol III, 35.

[180] Cf. supra, pp. 113-118.

Jesus' friendship with the Bethany family was also based on their virtues, especially those proper to Christian discipleship. Jesus' capacity to read the deep faith, love and obedience of the Bethany family and His readiness to deepen further their faith through dialogue and the enactment of the sign are expressions of a friendship based on moral love.

The spiritual aspect of Jesus' friendship is founded in the principle that God is love. Such love is expressed in real charity. Inspired by this spiritual principle Jesus risks going to Judea to console the bereaved and to execute the sign on their behalf. Such a risk for the sake of His friend resulted as is clear from the following pericope (plot against Jesus) even in His self-sacrifice. Thus, in the light of all the aspects of perfect human love Jesus' friendship with the Bethany family was human, sublime and ideal.

2. The Divine Aspects of Jesus' Friendship

Being true God Jesus expresses His love and friendship towards the Bethany family as God the Father does to mankind. This is a friendship based on lasting love since God is eternal. As true God Jesus loved the Bethany family not with the general love with which God loves sinners, but with that special love, by which He loves the just.[181] Jesus' divinity as Son of God is clearly referred to and affirmed by Jesus Himself (cf. vv.4.25.41.42)as well as by Martha and Mary (cf. vv.3.21.27.32). When the Evangelist uses the verb

---

[181] Cf. LEAL, *Amicum Lazarum*, 63.

ἀγαπάω to denote Jesus' love for the Bethany family as a whole (cf.v.5), he stresses the divine aspect of Jesus' love.[182]

The primary aim of the raising of Lazarus is the revelation of Jesus' divinity. Only God can give life to a dead person. The whole narrative is arranged in a dramatic way to arouse and deepen the faith of both actors and audience in the divinity of Jesus. Jesus, the friend of the Bethany family is also the Son of God, Lord and Master. Throughout the narrative Jesus appears as a supreme revealer whose superiority and divinity are clearly manifested in the enactment of the sign of raising the dead Lazarus. [183] This is at the same time the greatest expression of Jesus' friendship with Lazarus and of His love for the Bethany family. Lazarus' return to life became a clear manifestation of Jesus' divine love. Moreover, Lazarus, being raised from the dead, became a model and hope for all Christian believers. Further, it can be asserted that, "Lazarus, by implication a 'disciple' and most certainly 'beloved', becomes the key symbol of the power and meaning of Christ as the Resurrection and Life".[184] In short, Jesus' divinity is well expressed in the execution of the sign. His divine love and friendship transcends His human love which became eternal and supernatural.

---

[182] According to Leal, the verb ἀγαπάω expresses the love with which God loves and with which man by faith, loves God and each other: Cf. LEAL, *Amicum Lazarum*, 63; cf. also supra, p. 123, n. 114; p. 142, n.172.

[183] Cf. PANIMOLLE, *Giovanni*, Vol III, 19.

[184] PEARCE, *The Lucan Origins*, 359.

B. The Nature of the Bethany Family's Friendship with Jesus

The genuine friendship of Jesus with the Bethany family also is based on the exemplary positive response of its members to the person and teaching of Jesus. In the dramatic presentation of the pericope the Evangelist portrays the dynamic nature of the response of Martha and Mary who are active characters in the episode. Their words and deeds verify certain typical qualities of Christian discipleship [185] by which the love and friendship between Jesus and the Bethany family is established. Faith, hope, love and obedience are all verified in the life of the members of the Bethany family and are expressed through their words and deeds. [186] All these qualities made them genuine Christian disciples as well as real friends of Jesus. The deep trust in Jesus' divine power, the strong faith in the person of Jesus and the selfless obedience to Jesus inspired by a genuine love towards Him are the three basic attitudes of the Bethany family characterizing their friendship with Jesus.

1. A Family, which Trusts and Acknowledges the Divine Power of Jesus

The Jesus of the Fourth Gospel appears also as divine and powerful. The Evangelist presents various signs of Jesus as the manifestation of His divine power. The sign of the raising of

---

[185] Cf. MLAKUZHYIL, *The Christocentric Structure*, 282; ROMANIUK, *Résurrection et la Vie*, 63-70.

[186] In the context of our text one finds Lazarus as sick and dead whose positive response to the friendship of Jesus is verified only through the words of others. Lazarus' friendship with Jesus is well attested to in the pericope, although he is a silent and passive character throughout.

Lazarus within the structure of the Fourth Gospel is the climax of the manifestation of His power as the life-giver.[187] The members of the Bethany family, through their words and deeds, trust in Jesus and acknowledge His divine power. In their message to Jesus regarding the sickness of Lazarus (cf. v.3), Martha and Mary acknowledge Jesus' divine power of healing the sick, a fact which is clear from their own words in vv.21.32.[188] Later in their dialogue with Jesus (esp. vv. 21.22.32) they admit His saving power.[189] Finally, at the moment of the execution of the sign, Lazarus as well, through his positive response of obedience, acknowledges the power of Jesus' divine words. Accordingly the nature of the Bethany family's friendship with Jesus is theological since its members acknowledge Jesus' superiority and divinity.

2. A Family, Which Believes in the Person and Teaching of Jesus

The story of the raising of Lazarus is well situated within the theological framework of the Fourth Gospel. It illustrates the theme of faith as a basic requirement for an intimate relationship with Jesus and for eternal life, a participation in the essence of Jesus Himself (vv.25-26; cf. also 20,31). In the words and deeds of the members of the Bethany family there is shown a deep faith in the

---

[187] Cf. HOSKYNS, *Fourth Gospel*, 395.

[188] About this attitude of trust in Jesus' divine power Marsh writes: "Martha and Mary are both sure that Jesus has power to stop death entering, and recognize that this means ascribing to Jesus absolute divine power and honour, though they are not yet confident what such power can or will do for them in the present situation": MARSH, *St. John*, 431-432.

[189] Cf. supra, pp. 125-126.131.

person and teaching of Jesus. In sending the message and in their dialogue with Jesus one sees concrete expressions of this deep faith. Their faith in Jesus' Messianic role as well as in His divine teaching is expressed even in the titles given to Jesus, i.e. Lord (cf. vv.3.21.27.32.39)[190] and teacher (cf. v.28).

As it is evident from the analysis, Martha and Mary express their faith and trust in Jesus, when they say, "Lord, if you had been here, my brother would not have died" (vv.21.32).[191] Martha, representing the other members of the family, professes her faith in Jesus publicly and solemnly (cf. v.27). Only on the basis of her faith could Martha see the glory of God in the raising of her brother (cf. v.40). In the process of Jesus' dialogue with Martha His revelatory words deepened her faith and through her solemn profession of faith she became a prototype for Christian believers.[192] Lazarus, the friend of Jesus (cf. vv.3.5.11.36) had already entered into the status of believer and Christian disciple.[193] Since life after death was promised only to a believer (cf. vv.25-26) Lazarus, the one raised from the dead, proves himself a believer in Jesus.[194] In short, one

---

[190] As mentioned above the title "Lord" is a post-resurrectional title, used by the early Christian believers out of their faith in the resurrected Christ. The Christian nuance of this title can be justified in the redactional level of the Gospel.

[191] Cf. supra, pp. 125-126.131.

[192] Cf. GENUYT, *La résurrection de Lazare*, 70.

[193] Cf. J.P. MARTIN, "History and Eschatology in the Lazarus Narrative, Joh 11,1-44", *SJT* 17 (1964) 336. The already established friendship of Jesus with Lazarus presupposes a deep faith in Jesus on the part of Lazarus.

[194] About this Schneiders writes: "Jesus in this scene gives eternal life to those who believe in him. Lazarus can be raised because he is one whom Jesus loves, that is, a believer": SCHNEIDERS, *Community of Eternal Life*, 55; cf. also W.H. CADMAN, "The Raising of Lazarus (Jn 10,40-11,53)", *SE* (TU 73, 1959) 430.

can conclude that the Bethany family's faith response to Jesus and
His teaching is the essential element in their friendship with Jesus.

3. A Family, Which Obeys Jesus

Jesus' friendship with the Bethany family, verified in the
Lazarus-episode, demands a response of obedience (keeping of
Jesus' words) on the part of its members (cf. Jn 15,14). Since in the
Fourth Gospel faith and obedience are not two different attitudes
but are interrelated (cf. Jn 3,36), their expressions of faith in Jesus
illustrate their obedience. Martha, in the course of her dialogue
with Jesus, listens to His revelatory teaching and through the
profession of her faith enters into a personal commitment with Him.
Mary shows her obedience by responding quickly to Jesus' call (cf.
v.29) and submitting herself at His feet (cf. v.32). These two modes
of action on the part of Mary depict her obedient character.
Lazarus, though physically dead also shows the genuine expressions
of obedience in the narrative, [195] at least in a symbolic way. He
positively responds to the life-giving and powerful call of Jesus by
spiritually listening to His voice. Even Lazarus' resurrection with the
bandages symbolically illustrates his obedient attitude towards Jesus.
Therefore, in the Bethany family's friendship with Jesus there was
always an attitude of obedience to their supreme Master. Such an
attitude of obedience on the part of Christian disciples is inevitable
for close friendship with Jesus.

---

[195] Cf. SUGGIT, *Lazarus*, 107; cf. also supra, p. 135.

C. Lazarus: Friend of Jesus

The entire pericope under consideration is centred around one person, Lazarus, presented at the beginning as sick, then as dead and finally as one raised from dead. His relationship with Jesus and with his family is depicted only through certain literary devices. The words and deeds of all other characters and the comments and descriptions of the Evangelist also identify him as one who was in real friendship with Jesus. Even though the enactment of the sign of raising takes place as an expression of Jesus' love and concern towards all the members of the Bethany family, in the context of the entire narrative a particular emphasis is given to Jesus' love and friendship with Lazarus.

The expression ὃν φιλεῖς ἀσθενεῖ in the message of Lazarus' sisters is noteworthy. The point of emphasis here is Jesus' love towards Lazarus, a love which could be more efficacious in the context of Lazarus' need. [196] By using the verb φιλεῖν with its nuance of an affectionate love,[197] the Evangelist portrays Jesus as moved to an immediate reaction for the sake of His friend. Lazarus who has already enjoyed the affectionate love of Jesus would have been an authentic Christian disciple, since elsewhere in the Fourth Gospel such an expression denotes one who closely followed Jesus (cf. Jn 20,2; 21,15.16.17).

The second direct expression of Jesus' love towards Lazarus is clear in the Evangelist's comment in v.5. By way of a factual statement the Evangelist stresses Jesus' love for Lazarus and his

---

[196] Cf. supra, pp. 123-124.

[197] Cf. supra, p. 123, n.114; p. 142, 172.

sisters by using the verb ἀγαπᾶν[198] which maintains the flow of the narrative, a narrative interwoven with interpersonal relationship. The divine and active aspect of Jesus' love and friendship with the Bethany family, is verified in the comment of the Evangelist.[199]

In v.11 Lazarus is qualified as a friend of Jesus and His disciples alike through the expression: ὁ φίλος ἡμῶν.[200] This expression vividly expresses Lazarus' friendship in terms of discipleship. Spoken by Jesus it shows His initiative in their friendship and His acknowledgement of Lazarus' status of discipleship which permits him to be called: φίλος. By introducing Lazarus as a friend also of His disciples Jesus includes Lazarus in the circle of His disciples. Thus, the designation "our friend" sheds light on Lazarus' discipleship, a discipleship which involves a responsible way of life (cf. Jn 15,14).

Finally, Jesus' affectionate love towards Lazarus is once again expressed by means of the comments of the bystanders.[201] They interpret Jesus' tears at the tomb of Lazarus as an expression of His affectionate love for His friend, and possibly towards the entire Bethany family. Here the Evangelist's interest seems to be to highlight the close friendship between Jesus and Lazarus, the central point of consideration in the pericope.

All the expressions of love and friendship in the words and deeds of Jesus and the members of the Bethany family are focused on the special relationship which existed between Jesus and Lazarus.

---

[198] The verb ἀγαπᾶν in John is not synonymous with φιλεῖν, since they show two different aspects of Jesus' love. Cf. supra, p. 123, n.114; p.142, n. 172.

[199] Cf. supra, pp. 142-143.

[200] Cf. supra, pp. 100-102.

[201] Cf. pp. supra, 137-139.

By repeated and distinctive use of the term φιλεῖν (φίλος) the Evangelist stresses the special character of interpersonal relationship between Jesus and Lazarus. In the light of the Johannine use of this term elsewhere in the Fourth Gospel its use in the context of the Lazarus-episode categorizes the friendship between Jesus and Lazarus as a master-disciple relationship. Accordingly, Jesus' divinity and superiority as well as Lazarus' qualities of discipleship are implied in this designation.

Conclusion

In this chapter the explication of the term φίλος, the designation given to Lazarus by Jesus, required a detailed analysis of the interpersonal relationship between Jesus and the three members of the Bethany family expressed through their words and deeds. In the narrative Lazarus is presented as an intimate friend of Jesus (vv.3.5.11.36) a relationship involving certain characteristics of friendship in their interpersonal relationship. The Evangelist also presents Martha and Mary as objects of Jesus' salvific and active love (v.5). In the course of the development of the story their intimate relationship with Jesus is clearly expressed and identified as the incentive for Jesus to perform the sign.

The reciprocity of the friendship between Jesus and the Bethany family is well expressed in the narrative. Jesus, being perfect man and God, expressed His perfect friendship, both affectionate (φιλέω) and active (ἀγαπάω)[202] for the Bethany family. Besides a natural

---

[202] Cf. STÄHLIN, φιλέω, *TDNT* IX, 134, n.195; cf. also supra, p. 87, n.1; p. 123, n.114; p. 142, n.172.

love Jesus' love was moral, spiritual, divine and theological.[203] The
members of the Bethany family as evident from their words and
deeds expressed their positive response to such a supreme love. By
fulfilling all the essential characteristics of true Christian believers
in their friendship with Jesus they became prototypes of Christian
disciples and genuine models for all believers.[204] In short, the
friendship between Jesus and the Bethany family was a master-
disciple relationship encompassing the divine and human aspects of
Jesus' love. It likewise entailed an active response of obedience,
trust, faith and love on the part of the members of the Bethany
family including Lazarus, distinctly named by Jesus as His friend.
Thus, the interpersonal relationship between Jesus and Lazarus
characterized by the word φίλος exemplified to an outstanding
degree the master-disciple relationship.

---

[203] Cf. supra, pp. 143-146.

[204] Wilkens considers them as "types" of Christian believers: Cf. WILKENS,
Lazarus, 38.

CHAPTER FOUR

YOU ARE MY FRIENDS AND I CALL YOU FRIENDS
(Jn 15,1-17)

Introduction

The theme of Divine-human immanence based on love and friendship is well depicted in a well known Johannine text: Jn 15,1-17. In the process of the investigation of the term φίλος as a designation for the Jesus-disciple relationship one can treat this text as the climax of the Johannine teaching on this theme, since the Evangelist uses the term φίλος consecutively in vv.13-15 in its different nuances. The main theme of the pericope is the communion among the Father, Son and the believers [1] which explains better the Evangelist's teaching on the Jesus-disciple relationship expressed through the term φίλος. St. John presents here the concept of union and friendship against the background of the vine and branches imagery.[2] Therefore, the theological meaning of the

---

[1] Commenting on this Johannine text Barrett writes: "Only in Christ the Christians live. In him there is fruitfulness of the true service of God, of answered prayer, of obedience in love. All who are in him are his friends, and they are necessarily united with each other in love": BARRETT, *St. John*, 470. Mealand considers this idea of unity and communion as the central theme of the Fourth Gospel itself: Cf. D.L. MEALAND, "The Language of Mystical Union in the Johannine Writings", *DownRev* 95 (1977) 21.

[2] St. Paul speaks of a lively union of a disciple with Christ which corresponds to a "state of being in Christ" or "a living of believers in Christ" (cf. 2 Cor 5,17; Rom 8,1-10; Gal 2,20). He illustrates this lively relationship through the figure of the believers as members of the body of Christ (cf. 1 Cor 12,12.27; Rom 12,5; Col 3,15; Eph 4,15f; 5,29). In the vine and branches imagery of the Fourth Gospel we see a parallelism with the Pauline thought of the mystical body of Christ. Regarding this parallelism the Council of Trent says: "Cui enim ille ipse Christus Iesus tanquam *caput in membra* [Eph 4,15] et tanquam *vitis in palmites* [Io 15,5] in ipsos iustificatos iugiter virtutem influat, quae virtus bona eorum semper antecedit...": Cc. Trident.: sess. VI: Decr. de iustificatione: Cf. DENZINGER & BANNWART, *Enchiridion*,

term φίλος in vv.13-15can be traced only in the context of the entire pericope.

In the treatment of the text in question we take a perspective conducive to disclosing the theme of friendship between Jesus and the faithful. As the primary step in the exegesis one has to establish the literary unity of the text under consideration. For a better understanding of the text we deal with the textual problems, literary genre, historical and theological background and the division of the text. Since the approach is thematic, we consider the vine and branches imagery as one of interpersonal relationship explaining the role of the Father, Jesus and His disciples. Against the background of the imagery the friendship between Jesus and the disciples as an expression of the term φίλοι will be treated. Finally, we derive certain conclusions out of the analysis in view of explicating the theological content of the term φίλος in the Fourth Gospel.

I. Delimitation of the Text

The farewell discourse in the Fourth Gospel comprises many fragments [3] and independent literary units since they are not the account of a single discourse of Jesus done after the Last Supper. There is no unanimous opinion among the exegetes regarding the delimitation of the text. Even though there are thematic and stylistic affinities among the various units of the farewell discourse of Jesus,

---

Nr. 1546 (809). More than in Paul, John presents this Divine-human immanence in terms of a mutual remaining of the disciples and Christ (cf. 6,56; 1 Jn 2,5.24;3,6.24).

[3] Cf. A. GEORGE, "Gesù la Vite Vera : Giov.15,1-17", *BibOr* 3 (1961) 121-125; R. BORIG, *Der wahre Weinstock, Untersuchungen zu Jo 15,1-10* (SANT 16) (München 1967) 20ff.

one can see a clear literary and thematic unity within Jn 15,1-17.[4] The arguments for such a conclusion can be summed up as follows: a) Since Jn 14,31 calls for a change of place and theme, Jn 15,1 can be considered as the beginning of a new pericope with a clear and abrupt introduction of the imagery of the vine and branches in vv.1-2.[5] b) V.17 is a summary statement which serves as the conclusion of the text under consideration, since v.18 introduces the theme of hatred which is not anticipated in the preceding verses.[6] c) There is also a thematic unity, viz. the interrelated themes of unity and love run throughout the pericope. The theme of unity which is developed through the imagery of the vine and branches in the first part of the text (vv.1-8) is further developed in its second part (vv.9-17) in terms of love which is the concrete expression of bearing fruit. d) There are thematic and stylistic connections and interconnections between certain verses of the entire pericope which keeps the unity

---

[4] For example, Niccacci finds a literary unity in Jn 15-16. But he divides it into three sub-units in which Jn 15,1-17 enjoys a literary and thematic unity: Cf. A. NICCACCI, "Esame Letterario di Gv 15-16", *Anton* 56 (1981) 43. Many exegetes have pointed out the self-contained nature of these verses: Cf. BULTMANN, *John*, 523; BROWN, *John*, Vol II, 665; J. BECKER, *Das Evangelium nach Johannes*, Vol II (Würzburg 1981) 478. But Borig's consideration of this Johannine text stops with v.10. He comes to such a position on the basis on the literary and stylistic elements. For him the repeated use of μένειν ἐν is seen practically only up to v.10. By way of an inclusion between two identical formulas: ταῦτα λελάληκα ὑμῖν and ταῦτα ἐντέλλομαι ὑμῖν in vv.11 and 17 the Evangelist marks the independent literary unity of vv.11-17 apart from the preceding section: Cf. BORIG, *Der wahre Weinstock*, 19ff.

[5] Cf. J. BECKER, "Die Abschiedsreden Jesu in Johannesevangelium", *ZNW* 61 (1970) 229.

[6] Cf. *Ibid.*, 230; R. SCHNACKENBURG, "Aufbau und Sinn von Johannes 15", in: L. ALVAREZ VERDES Y E.J. ALONSO HERNNANDEZ (eds.), *Homenaje a Juan Prado* (Madrid 1975) 405-409. Though here Schnackenburg argues for a textual unity of Jn 15,1-17 he finds its connection with the following pericope in the line of a contrast.

of the text. For example, the expression καρπόν φέρον (fruit
bearing) in vv.2 and 16 can be seen as a stylistic and thematic
inclusion. Likewise the term μένειν is used throughout the text and
makes an inclusion between v.4 and v.16. In the same way the
mention of the Father, the answering of the prayer etc. spread out
in the verses maintain the unity of the entire section.

It is a well accepted fact that the first part of the text deals with
the *mashal* (משל)[7] of the vine and branches and the second part
deals with the application of the same.[8] The theme of love and
friendship developed in the second part of the pericope can be
better explained against the background of the imagery which is
portrayed in the first part. This also motivates us to see the unity of
the text, Jn 15,1-17.

II. The Textual Problems

With regard to the textual problems of pericope under
consideration we would like to discuss only the major issues which
cause problems in the translation and understanding of the text. The
solutions suggested or the texts stabilized by our attempts are not
conclusive, but they are the possible ways of considering the text on
the basis of the external and internal evidences. Accordingly there
arises 4 following problems which draw one's attention.

---

[7] *Mashal* is the technical semitic term which comprises varied imagery pattern
such as parable, allegory, proverb, maxim, simile, metaphor etc. According to Ralph,
"A Hebrew *mashal* could be a short pithy saying or a long, developed allegory": M.
RALPH, *"And God Said What?"* (New York 1986) 153. When we analyze the
literary genre of the text we will show the reason why we call it *mashal*.

[8] Cf. BROWN, *John*, Vol II, 665.

V.6a ἐὰν μή τις μένῃ ...(אּ* A B D)

There are various manuscripts which prefer a variant reading, viz. ἐὰν μή τις μείνῃ ... (אּ² L Ψ f¹·¹³). They use the aorist subjunctive μείνῃ to make it agree with the following aorist tenses. Since those aorists are considered as gnomic aorists [9] indicating habitual happenings, it is not necessary to use an aorist subjunctive in the opening clause. It is a fact that ἐὰν μή with the present subjunctive is rare in the NT, but we have it three times in vv. 4 and 6. Since the use of the present subjunctive is supported by many of the well known manuscripts and it keeps the internal coherence of the text we prefer the reading with μένῃ. [10]

V.6b. καὶ συνάγουσιν αὐτά......(AB Γ Θ 28 700 ...)

Here "they" (the servants of the Lord of the vineyard is the subject which is understood) collect the branches (αὐτά). The plural subject agrees with the plural object. [11] There is also a different reading: καὶ συνάγουσιν αὐτό ...(אּ D L Δ f¹ f¹³ 33 565 1071 0141 ...) which is considered to be an alteration by the copyists in order to make it agree grammatically with τὸ κλῆμα. [12] Since the use of αὐτά is supported by certain well known manuscripts and it explains

---

[9] Cf. G.R. BEASLEY-MURRAY, The Word Biblical Commentary: John vol 36 (Waco, Texas 1987) 268. Gnomic aorist is the one used classically in axioms and proverbs: Cf. ZERWICK, Biblical Greek, § 256.

[10] Cf. N.R. NICOLL, The Expositor's Greek Testament, Vol I (London 1907) 829.

[11] Cf. BERNARD, St. John, Vol II, 481.

[12] Cf. NICOLL, Greek Testament, Vol I, 829; METZGER, Textual Commentary, 246.

better the internal coherence of the text, the reading with αὐτά can be considered as the original.

V.7 ὅ ἐὰν θέλητε αἰτήσασθε (B L f^{13} 1 28 565 1010 ...)

The αἰτήσασθε here is aorist, imperative, middle voice whereas the variant reading is with αἰτησέσθε (א Θ Ψ 0250 ...) which is future. In the context of an exhortation the future usage does not have the same force of the imperative. Therefore on the basis of the support of important manuscripts and due to the exhortatory nature of the pericope the reading with the aorist imperative form αἰτήσασθε is preferable. [13]

V.8 καὶ γένησθε ἐμοὶ μαθηταί (P^{66} ^{vid} B D L Θ 0250. f^1...)

γένησθε agrees with the preceding φέρητε since both verbs are connected with the same ἵνα clause. Here γένησθε is subjunctive and can be translated as: "and become my disciples". The other reading is with γενήσεσθε (א A K Δ Ψ Syr ^{m} ^{ss} etc.) which must probably be understood as an independent clause or sentence. [14] γενήσεσθε is future and accordingly the translation is: "and you will be (become) my disciples". Since both readings have important manuscript support and make sense in the context of the text the choice is very difficult. Therefore there remains serious doubts

---

[13] Cf. NICOLL, *Greek Testament*, Vol I, 830.

[14] Cf. METZGER, *Textual Commentary*, 246. Yet on rare occasions the future indicative occurs with ἵνα: Cf. BLASS-DEBRUNNER, *Greek Grammar*, § 369 (2).

regarding the original text[15]. Still considering the external evidence and the above said internal coherence the reading with γένησθε is taken probably as the original.

III. The Literary Genre

With regard to the literary genre of the text there is no common agreement among the exegetes. It may be due to the different literary elements (styles) which one finds in Jn 15,1-17. For the whole section one cannot attribute a single literary genre. But a discussion on the various literary elements present in the text will help one to understand the development of the entire pericope and the meaning of the individual units.

The text in question is traditionally and generally considered as an "allegory".[16] From the literary point of view an allegory enjoys two levels of meaning: literal and implied. The union of the vine and branches and the fruitfulness can be understood at the literal level of the allegory, whereas the application of the imagery, viz. the vine to Jesus, the vinedresser to God the Father, the branches to the disciples and the natural fruits of the vine to the spiritual fruits of Christ's followers, are to be understood at the implied level. Moreover, the moral teaching of the allegory is evident in the text, i.e. Jesus' teaching on love and friendship. However, one cannot simply reduce the literary genre of the pericope to "allegory", since

---

[15] The UBS committee rates its decision a "D" choice, indicating the doubt: Cf. B.M. NEWMAN & E.A. NIDA, *A Translator's Handbook on the Gospel of John* (New York 1979) 484.

[16] For a definition and explanation of an allegory: Cf. M.H. ABRAMS, *A Glossary of Literary Terms* (New York 1981) 4-5; J.T. SHIPLEY (ed.), *Dictionary of the World Literary Terms* (London 1970) 10; RALPH, *God Said*, 155.

there are elements of other literary genres such as parable [17], metaphor [18], discourse [19] etc. are vivid in the text. Schnackenburg uses a very general term "figurative discourse" as the literary style of the first part of the pericope. He prefers this term because, according to him it is neither a pure allegory nor a "literal discourse".[20] Since it is neither an allegory nor a parable [21] Borig prefers the term "Bildrede".[22]

Since the literary genre of the text cannot be limited to any of the above mentioned literary terms one has to find out a more apt terminology which can comprise as far as possible all those elements. In this respect Brown's position is more acceptable when he names

---

[17] For a definition and explanation of a parable: Cf. ABRAMS, *Literary Terms*, 6; SHIPLEY, *World Literary Terms*, 230; RALPH, *God Said*, 155; G.B. CAIRD, *Language and Imagery of the Bible* (london 1980) 163-164. The main characteristic of a parable is a "comparison" which is lacking in the opening verse of the pericope. Still we see a kind of comparison in καθώς (v.4) in the light of which the text can perhaps be considered as half parabolic and half non-parabolic: Cf. B. SANDVIK, "Joh 15 als Abendmahltext", *TZ* 23 (1967) 323.

[18] For a definition of metaphor: Cf. SHIPLEY, *World Literary Terms*, 197. According to him metaphor is the identification of two things from different ranges of thought or it is a "simile without like or as". In the light of this definition the first part of the pericope (vv.1-6) is metaphorical due to the application of the vine to Jesus, the vinedresser to the Father, the branches to the disciples and so on. The term καθαίρειν in its double nuance in v.2, the branches' abiding in the vine as a characteristic expression of the believers' relation to Christ are metaphorical expressions.

[19] As part of the well known farewell discourse Jn 15,1-17 is considered as a discourse. It is a lecture or speech including exhortatory elements: Cf. BROWN, *John*, Vol II, 688. The major themes of the Last Discourse from Jn 13 and 14 are illustrated in a more concrete way in Jn 15,7-17.

[20] Cf. SCHNACKENBURG, *St. John*, Vol III, 96.

[21] Cf. BULTMANN, *John*, 406-407.

[22] Cf. BORIG, *Der wahre Weinstock*, 22.

it as *mashal* (מֹשָׁל)[23] even though he admits the emphasis of the allegorical elements in the first part of the pericope.[24] The *mashal* can be used with a paraenetic emphasis to address the community. Since vv.12-17 are Jesus' exhortatory words to His disciples in the context of the allegory of the vine and branches one can consider the text as a "*Christian mashal*".

However, we also consider Jn 15,1-17 against the background of the seven "ἐγώ εἰμι" ("I am") formulas of the Fourth Gospel, since it appears as the last "I am" saying. In the Fourth Gospel the ἐγώ εἰμι formula appears as a literary device to highlight the theology of the Evangelist. The seven "I am" sayings in John's Gospel are considered as the key expressions of the Divine Revelation and some authors find a perfect rhythm and a close connection among the seven "I am" sayings, seven sacraments and seven signs in the Fourth Gospel.[25] The absolute ἐγώ εἰμι in John is the continuation of the OT idea of self-revelation put into the mouth of Jesus.[26] So, when Jesus utters the absolute form of ἐγώ εἰμι He reveals His Father through Himself.[27] The frequent use of the ἐγώ εἰμι coupled with a predicate is the striking feature of Johannine style (6,35; 8,12; 10,7.9.11.14;11,25; 14,6; 15,1.5). In such instances the predicates are

---

[23] Cf. supra, p. 158, n.7.

[24] Cf. BROWN, *John*, Vol II, 668.

[25] Cf. C. RAU, *Struktur und Rhythmus im Johannesevangelium* (Stuttgart 1972) 67, where he writes: "Die Ich-Bin-Worte im Johannesevangelium sind zuerst als ein siebengliediger Organismus erkannt worden, ebenso ihre Beziehung zu den sieben Sakramenten... die Stellung der sieben Ich-Bin-Worte innerhalb des ganzen Evangeliums näher zu betrachten, vor allem ihr Verhältnis zu den sieben Zeichentaten".

[26] Cf. E. SCHWEIZER, *Ego Eimi* (Göttingen 1939) 31-33.

[27] Bultmann calls it as a "Recognition formula": BULTMANN, *John*, 225, n.3.

metaphorical or symbolic titles. They are used in the context of imageries and parables [28] and usually they serve as the background of a discourse. The Fourth Evangelist uses the predicative ἐγώ εἰμι proclamations to express the true meaning of Jesus. They are not christological titles but are the sayings of Jesus to reveal the relevance of His person for man in their different life situations. [29] In the text in question the mention of the Father really emphasizes the real nature of Jesus as the vine belonging to the heavenly order. [30]

As the conclusion of the analysis of the literary genre of Jn 15,1-17 one can say that it is a *mashal* introduced in the context of a well known Johannine "I am" saying. The Jewish *mashal* has allegorical, parabolic, metaphorical and exhortatory features and the present text has all these characteristics, possible vehicles to depict the Johannine theology of divine-human immanence in terms of friendship based on revelation and obedience (vv.14-15).

IV. The Historical and Theological Background of the Text

There is no common agreement among the scholars with regard to the historical and theological background of the Johannine presentation of the imagery of the vine and the branches. Scholars like Bauer, Bultmann and Schweizer turn to gnostic and mandean

---

[28] Cf. BARRETT, *St. John*, 292; BULTMANN, *John*, 167, n.2. They are of opinion that the formula ἐγώ εἰμι introduces an explanation of a parable.

[29] Cf. W. GRUNDMANN, *Der Zeuge der Wahrheit : Grundzüge der Christologie des Johannesevangeliums* (Berlin 1985) 59-69.

[30] Cf. BORIG, *Der wahre Weinstock*, 36.

sources whereas some other like Brown, Schnackenburg and Borig stress the OT and Jewish writings as the background of this Johannine text because of the similarities of context and meaning. There are also some NT parallels in the Synoptics and in the Revelation dealing with vine, fruits of vine and vineyard. However, the *mashal* of the vine and branches fits also in the Johannine theological framework.

A. The OT Background: Israel as Vine

From ancient time Palestine was famous for vine cultivation (Num 13,23; Gen 14,18; Deut 6,11). This natural significance of vine in Palestine served a great role for the application of the vine imageries in the OT. Moreover the vine was famous for its fruitfulness (Jer 48,32; Is 16,8f.). The brides in the OT were compared to the vine from the point of view of its fruit bearing aspect. [31]

John frequently employs OT ideas and images (typological thinking) and applies them to Jesus. [32] Therefore one can legitimately argue that such thinking and application influenced the statement that Jesus is the real vine. John presents the *mashal* of the vine and branches in opposition to the OT concept of Israel as the vine or vineyard. By adding the adjective ἀληθινὴ (genuine,

---

[31] Cf. *Ibid.*, 82.

[32] Some examples of Johannine usages which have OT parallels : lamb of God, bronze serpent, bread from heaven, source of living water, good shepherd etc.

real) [33] he expresses the genuineness of Jesus as the vine and by
presenting the disciples as the branches he points out the formation
of the 'new people of Israel'.[34] In the OT and NT the vine dresser
(farmer) is the Father who shows His eternal love in His activities.
As the cultivator of the vine the Father became the founder of the
Christian community. [35]

In the OT the vine or vineyard is a frequent symbol of Israel.
The prophets of the OT adopted this symbol to insist God's special
care to His people. Sometimes it is a symbol of fruitfulness which
appears in the apocalyptic vision of hope (Is 27,2-6). Very often the
vine symbolizes the unproductive and desolate nature of Israel which
creates the wrath of God (Jer 5,10; 12,10-11; Hos 10,1; Ezek 15,2).
Ezekiel declares that as the vine branches are fit only for burning,
the vine of Jerusalem must be devoured by fire. According to him
Israel was once a fruitful vine, but she was plucked up and
destroyed. Isaiah says that Israel is the choicest vine, planted in the
vineyard of Yahweh, but it is only brought forth wild grapes (Is 5,1).

---

[33] The Greek adjective ἀληθινός can be more accurately translated as
"genuine" or "real" than "true" for which John employs another adjective ἀληθής:
Cf. D.M. STANLEY, "I am the Genuine Vine (Jn 15,1)", BiTod 1,8 (1963) 485. In
the Fourth Gospel the adjective ἀληθής (3,33; 5,31.32; 7,18; 14,17.26) is
predicatively used, whereas ἀληθινός (1,9;4,23;6,32;5,1;17,3) is attributively used.
In the Old Latin version there was only one translation for these two expressions, viz.
verus. Later, for ἀληθής verax was introduced: Cf. G.D. KILPATRICK, "Some
Notes on Johannine Usage (ἀληθής and ἀληθινός) BT 11 (1960) 174. The
adjective ἀληθινός is used in the Fourth Gospel wherever there is an antithetical
progressive presentation of the Mosaic law through Jesus' eschatological revelation
(cf. 1,9;6,32; 15,1): Cf. PANIMOLLE, Giovanni, Vol III, 263.

[34] Cf. SCHNACKENBURG, St. John, Vol III, 106. He argues that the use of
the attribute ἀληθινός and the mention of the Father both in Jn 6,32 (bread from
heaven) and in Jn 15,1 (genuine vine) illustrate the Johannine way of presenting the
truth in opposition to the OT.

[35] Cf. MATEOS & BARRETO, Giovanni, 614.

According to Jeremiah Israel was planted as a noble vine, but it became degenerate (Jer 2,21). It is noteworthy that in the OT, where Israel is compared to a vine, the comparison always introduces a lament over her degeneracy, or a prophecy of her speedy destruction. [36] Considering the fecundity and excellence of the vine it was used symbolically in the love songs and as an image for celebrating the love. In the Canticle of Canticles such allusions occur frequently (1,2.4.6;2,13.15;4,10; 5,1 etc.).

In Jn 15,1-17 the portrayal of Jesus as the real vine seems to be in contrast with the degenerate Israel who was originally planted as the real vine (Jer 2,21). It goes well with John's idea of presenting Jesus as the fulfilment of the Jewish faith. [37] The theme of bearing fruit and the symbolic allusions to love-relationship in the OT, especially in the Canticle of Canticles are evident in the Johannine text (Jn 15,1-17).

In the OT the vine or vineyard symbolizes a people, Israel while John identifies the vine with an individual, Jesus. "It is a feature of Johannine theology that Jesus applied to himself terms used in the OT for Israel and in other parts of the NT for the christian community". [38] Even the collective element is not totally absent from the Johannine presentation. Jesus is not the stem, but the entire vine, and the branches remain part of the vine. Since John identifies the Christian believer as a genuine Israelite (Jn 1,47), one can easily find the relevance of applying the vine as a symbol of Jesus as well as of the believers who are supposed to remain in close friendship.

---

[36] Cf. BERNARD, *St.John*, Vol II, 478.

[37] Cf. NEWMAN & NIDA, *Translator's Handbook*, 478.

[38] BROWN, *John*, Vol II, 670.

Against the OT background the Johannine idea of identifying Jesus as the vine is also a messianic allusion (cf.Ps 80,8f.; 2 Bar 39,7).[39] Jesus is the eschatological vine because he is the culmination of the remnant of Israel. All that missed among Jesus' predecessors are fulfilled in Him. From the point of view of vocabulary there is some close connection between the vine and branches in Jn 15 and the *mashal* of the vine in Ezek 17. It is Ezekiel, the "son of man" who propounds the *mashal* to the house of Israel. Moreover it is significant to note that the vine imagery of Ezek 17 refers to a king of the house of David which denotes the messianic allusion in the OT vine imagery.[40]

In spite of the many similarities between the OT and the Johannine imagery of the vine there are some differences in stress. None of the OT vine passages stresses the vine as the source of life for the branches. But in post-biblical Judaism the vine was considered as a tree of life. In later Jewish iconography the tree of life was pictured as a vine.[41] In the wisdom literature the life-giving power of wisdom is symbolized by the vine (Sir 24,17-21). The use of the vine as a metaphor for Israel is frequent in the Rabbinic literature.[42] The vine was the national emblem, frequent on coins,

---

[39] Cf. G.M. BEHLER, *Die Abschiedsworte des Herrn* (Wien 1962) 161ff.

[40] Borig writes:, "In the OT the imagery of the vine was already associated not only with the community of Israel but also with the picture of an individual person, so that the Johannine transferal of a collective image to a person is already anticipated in Ezekiel's vine symbolism": BORIG, *Der wahre Weinstock*, 101.

[41] Cf. BROWN, *John*, Vol II, 671.

[42] Hoskyns refers to certain Rabbinic literature when he writes: "As the vine is the least of all trees, and yet is master of all, so the people of Israel appear insignificant in this world, but in the future (Messianic Age) their sovereignty will extend from one end of the world to the other": HOSKYNS, *Fourth Gospel*, 474-475.

ceramics, ossuaries and lamps representing Israel from the Maccabaean time onwards.[43] Josephus gives us evidence that a large golden vine was set at the sanctuary entrance in the temple built by Herod (Ant.15,395).

In the light of the above mentioned observations one can conclude that the Johannine notion of the vine and branches seems to be influenced by the notion of the imagery of Israel as the vine and the imagery of wisdom as the life-giving tree or vine.[44] Even though many of the ancient images and ideas which have been blended together with the Johannine thought in the formation of the *mashal* of the vine and branches in Jn 15,1-17, this text also has a unique orientation, consonant with Johannine Christology. In other words, we assume that the OT and Judaism supplied the raw material from which the *mashal* of the vine and branches was composed under the originality of Johannine thought.[45]

B. The Mandean Influence

Among the scholars it has been always a matter of debate, whether the Johannine *mashal* of vine is influenced by the OT sources or mandean and gnostic sources. E. Schweizer[46] is the principal protagonist of a mandean source, although he changed his views in his later writings. S. Schulz observes many formal similarities between the Johannine and mandean texts, though at the

---

[43] Cf. SCHNACKENBURG, *St. John*, Vol III, 106.

[44] Cf. BROWN, *John*, Vol II, 672.

[45] Cf. *Ibid.*, 672.

[46] Cf. SCHWEIZER, *Ego Eimi*, 40ff.

same time he admits a possible OT influence.[47] Bultmann finds the clear gnostic influence behind John's presentation of the vine and branches. According to him John's imagery reflects the oriental myth of the tree of life.[48] He finds some impressive parallels from the semi-gnostic *Odes of Solomon*, which are closely related to the Johannine discourses, for the association of the themes of love and joy with the vine imagery.

There are many statements in gnostic literature regarding the vine, many phrases which are similar to the Johannine imagery of vine in their wording. There are also a number of texts in which the redeemer calls himself "the vine". For example: "I (Hibil) am a gentle vine; I was planted (created) from the place of glorious splendour and the great (life) was my planter (creator)" (Ginza, 301,11-14).[49] According to the mandean and gnostic thought the redeemer represents the individual man or the soul and the vine is presented as the tree of life: "We are a vine, the vine of life, a tree on which there is no lie, the tree of praise, from the odour of which each man receives life" (Ginza 59,39-60,2).[50] In the mandaen revelatory addresses also one can find parabolic sayings which characterize the Revealer as the good shepherd, the real vine etc.[51] There is a parallelism between the Johannine "I am" saying and the boast of Demiurge in the gnostic creation myths: "I am God and

---

[47] Cf. S. SCHULZ, *Das Evangelium nach Johannes* (NTD 4) (Göttingen 1972) 194.

[48] Cf. BULTMANN, *John*, 407.

[49] Cf. BEASLEY-MURRAY, *John*, 272.

[50] *Ibid.*, 273.

[51] Cf. BULTMANN, *John*, 8.

there is no other".[52] Another possible element of similarity is the dualistic presentation of the ideas seen in the gnostic sources and in the pericope under consideration.

Even though there are certain possible areas of mandean influence in Johannine *mashal* of vine, one cannot be certain about such an influence. Many authors object to a gnostic source behind the Johannine imagery. Borig traces the OT and the Jewish background of the Johannine symbolism of the vine, since the mandean symbolism, he finds, as highly mythical and not concentrated on the branches. The life-giving function of the vine in relation to the branches does not appear in the mandean picture of the vine.[53] The gnostic source presented vine as a tree of life which is not very clear in the Johannine text. So also, when John speaks of the fruitfulness of the vine, the gnostic source totally ignores it. Moreover it is clear that the Johannine discourse on the vine, with its figurative and partly parabolic description, can only be understood in an entirely natural and earthly light. There is no reference at all in the Johannine discourse to the 'odour' of the vine.[54]

Considering the above mentioned dissimilarities between the mandean and Johannine imagery one can arrive at the conclusion that the author of the Fourth Gospel was not directly influenced by the mandean sources in the presentation of the *mashal* of the vine and branches. But, it does not exclude absolutely the possibility of a secondary influence of the gnostic source in the formation of this

---

[52] Cf. G.W. MACRAE, "The Ego Proclamations in Gnostic Sources",in: E. BAMMEL (ed.), *The Trial of Jesus* (SBT ll, 13) (London 1970) 123.

[53] Cf. BORIG, *Der wahre Weinstock*, 172.

[54] Cf. SCHNACKENBURG, *St. John*, Vol III, 105.

Johannine text. The main source of inspiration might have been drawn from the OT, since there are many parallelism between Jn 15,1-17 and the OT images of vine.[55]

C. The NT Background

The *mashal* of the vine and branches is well fit in the Johannine theological framework. The imagery of the vine makes clear the theme of the interiorization in the farewell discourse. The relation between the vine and the branches symbolizes close union and possession of life. The style of applying OT images and ideas to Jesus can be frequently encountered elsewhere in the Gospel of John. Thus the *mashal* of the vine and branches has its place in the Fourth Evangelist's presentation.

One cannot find a direct influence of NT sources in the Johannine *mashal* of vine, but it should be admitted that there are several points of departure already provided by the pre-Johannine tradition (Mk 12,1-12; Lk 13,6-9; Mt 21,43 etc.). Besides, John gives the idea of the true Israel and stresses the Christological dimension in the pericope by concentrating on Jesus Christ Himself.[56] However, there are some NT texts which deal with the vine and present symbolically the ecclesiological and the eschatological dimensions of the life of the believers.

The imagery of the vine and the vineyard used in other NT texts, especially in the Synoptics in their natural and figurative

---

[55] Heise finds an influence of both the OT and the gnostic sources: Cf. J. HEISE, *Bleiben. Μένειν in den Johanneischen Schriften* (Tübingen 1967) 81, n.169.

[56] Cf. SCHNACKENBURG. *St. John*, Vol III, 106.

senses, can also be a possible influence in the formation of the Johannine *mashal* of vine. Of course, the synoptic vine texts are not used to explain the communion between Jesus and the disciples as in Jn 15,1-17. In the Synoptic tradition there are certain texts which recall the OT vineyard symbolism (Mk 12,1-9; Mt 20,1-16; 21,28-32; 21,33-34; Lk 13,6-9; 20,9-16). All these texts deal with some elements of the vine, vineyard or persons connected with it representing Israel or a section of Israel. Most of the texts following the OT (Is 5,1-7) present an eschatological crisis. The aspects of the mystery of the kingdom of God, the divine judgment, human response to the divine call etc. are discussed under the natural and figurative use of the vine (vineyard) imageries.

1. The Vine or Vineyard in Its Natural Sense

In the Synoptics (Mk 14,25; Lk 22,18; Mt 26,29) Jesus offers wine to His disciples in His farewell and reminds them that He will never drink from the fruit of the vine until He will be in the kingdom of God. The mention of natural wine shows also the happiness of eternal life.[57] Also the natural vine or vineyard is used parabolically in 1 Cor 9,7 in the context of Paul's apostolic work. In Lk 13,6 and in Mt 21,28-32 the figure of the vineyard is used without a special connotation in itself, but to serve as the background of a narrative or a parable. Though in Mt 20,1-15 there is a reference to vineyard, the accent lies in the wage-giving and thus it sheds light on God's way of evaluating things. The above mentioned aspects of

---

[57] Cf. BORIG, *Der wahre Weinstock*, 129.

eternal life, apostolic work and parabolic background can be traced
also in the Johannine *mashal* of the vine and branches.

2. Vine and Vineyard in Figurative Expressions

The symbolic presentation of humanity in the image of the
grapes of the earthly vine is seen in Rev 14,14-20. There the vine
and the fruits of the vine symbolize the people of God in its
collective nature and the context referred to is the persecution under
Babylonian captivity. The pressing of the grapes inside the great
vine-press of the wrath of God symbolizes the divine judgment in
allowing the people of God into the afflictions of the captivity
(outside the city). This apocalyptic vision highlights the symbolic use
of the vine.

Figuratively speaking, the vineyard stands for the people of God.
In this connection one must consider two texts from the Synoptic
gospels (Mk 12,1-12; Mt 21,33-43). In Mk 12,1-12 the vineyard is
presented allegorically as the people of Israel, a people expected to
bear fruits. It is to this people of God the prophets and Jesus are
sent to collect the fruits. In Mt 21,43 the Evangelist also underlines
the importance of bearing fruit. There the servants and Jesus are
sent to collect the fruits of the vineyard. The community which
bears fruit represents the New Israel. There is parallelism between
those Synoptic texts and Jn 15 in the aspect of the vine and its
bearing fruit. Moreover, all of those texts together with Jn 15 share
the OT background where vine or vineyard represents the people of
God.

In short, in the treatment of the NT background of the
Johannine *mashal* of the vine and branches we have seen the
relevance of the imagery in the context of the whole Johannine

theology and ecclesiology.[58] There are also certain NT parallel texts where vine, vineyard or fruits of the vine are adopted in their natural and figurative sense. Many of those texts are in tune with the Johannine imagery of the vine and branches. The main distinction between the Johannine *mashal* of the vine and branches and the other "vine-texts" is that John deals with a vine rather than a vineyard.[59] In spite of this distinction one can find certain influence of the NT "vine-texts" on the formation of the imagery of the vine and branches in Jn 15.

V. The Division of the Text

Under the delimitation of the text we have already established the textual unity of the pericope (Jn 15,1-17).[60] Even though there is a thematic and literary unity of the text there is also a place for a consideration of the text as subunits. This will be done on the basis of the thematic development marked by literary devices which will facilitate a better exegesis. The discourse of Jn 15,1-17 comprises mainly two subsections marked by two related themes: the *mashal* of the vine and branches and the theme of love and

---

[58] Cf. J.F. O'GRADY, "Johannine Ecclesiology: A Critical Evaluation", *BTB* 7 (1977) 36-44.

[59] In the OT the imagery sometimes shifts back and forth from the vine to the vineyard: Cf. BROWN, *John*, Vol II, 670.

[60] Cf. supra, pp. 156-158.

friendship. There is no unanimous opinion among the scholars regarding the dividing line between these two related units.[61]

After evaluating the opinion of different authors one can still divide the text into three subunits (vv.1-8; 9-11; 12-17) where vv.9-11 can be considered as "bridge verses".[62] This unit of verses bridges the two other subunits as it serves as the conclusion of the first subunit and the introduction of the second. In vv.1-8 the most important ideas are "abiding in Jesus" and "bearing fruit". The bearing fruit is nothing but a life of love in observing the commandments as clear in vv.9-11. The same theme of love and obedience, the necessary requirements to enter into an intimate friendship with Jesus is the central idea of the last subunit (vv.12-17).

In spite of its division there is an inter-connection between the subunits and an organic development of the entire pericope from v.1

---

[61] According to Schnackenburg the concluding formula ταῦτα λελάληκα in v.11 closes the first subunit and there is an inclusion between the expression ἀγαπᾶτε ἀλλήλους in vv.12 and 17 which forms the second subunit: Cf. SCHNACKENBURG, *St. John*, Vol III, 108. Brown considers vv.1-6 as a *mashal* which is exposed and applied in vv.7-17. According to him there are inclusions between vv.1 and 5 with ἐγώ εἰμι, between vv.7 and 16 with the mention of prayer and its fulfilment and between vv.8 and 16 with the idea of "bearing fruits": Cf. BROWN, *John*, Vol II, 665-666. Moloney adopts a different criteria to divide the text into subunits: Cf. F.J. MOLONEY, "The Structure and Message of John 15,1-16,3", *AusBR* 35 (1987) 35-41. Bultmann and others follow a division of the text mainly into two subunits as vv.1-8 and vv.9-17. The actual presentation of the imagery of the vine and branches ends practically with v.8. However, the theme of "love" and "commandment" begin with v.9 and developed into the theme of the disciples' friendship with Jesus and run throughout the rest of the pericope: Cf. BULTMANN, *John*, 539-540; F.F. SEGOVIA, "The Theology and Provenance of John 15,1-17", *JBL* 101 (1982) 115-128.

[62] Cf. MLAKUZHYIL, *The Christocentric Structure*, 104-105. He defines the "bridge verses" as those which connect two successive units by concluding the first and introducing the second.

to v.17. The development and inter-connection can be sketched as follows:

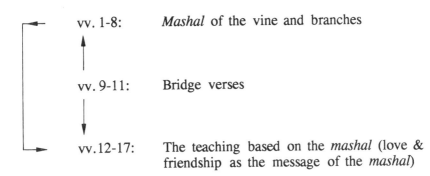

vv. 1-8:   *Mashal* of the vine and branches

vv. 9-11:   Bridge verses

vv.12-17:   The teaching based on the *mashal* (love & friendship as the message of the *mashal*)

In the above diagram one can see a thematic and stylistic development from unit to unit. The *mashal* of the vine and branches in the first subsection finds its application in love and friendship between Jesus and His disciples in the final section. The bridge verses have the linking function between the other subunits. In the entire pericope there is a gradual process of revelation, a characteristic of the Fourth Gospel. For example the exhortation to "abide in me" (v.4) becomes "abide in my words" (v.7). It is further developed into "abide in my love" (vv.9-10) which ends with an invitation to enter into a friendship with Jesus by keeping His commandment of fraternal love (vv.12-17).

VI. The Mashal of the Vine and Branches: An Imagery of Interpersonal Relationship

The mashal of the vine and branches is primarily an imagery of interpersonal relationship. In this section there will be an analysis of the first subunit (vv.1-8) and the bridge verses (vv.9-11) as well, in so far as they are immediately connected with each other. The present consideration will be on two levels, viz. the *mashal* and its application, [63] in the perspective of interpersonal relationship. Such a consideration will help one to explain the reciprocal dimension of friendship between Jesus and the disciples developed in the last part of the pericope (vv.12-17). At the level of the *mashal* the relationship is well expressed in the role of the Father as γεωργός (farmer) [64] who cultivates, cuts off and prunes the vine. It also highlights the role of Jesus as the real vine which holds the branches together and helps them to bear fruit. This also includes the role of the disciples as the vine-branches which remain and grow in the vine (stem) and bear abundant fruits. At the level of application also the interpersonal relationship among God the Father, God the Son and the disciples of Jesus is made clear by the Evangelist. [65] Against the background of such a deep interpersonal relationship brought out by the *mashal* of the vine and branches the Fourth Evangelist highlights the theological depth of the term φιλός (friend) as a term which elucidates the close relationship between Jesus and His disciples. The following analysis will help one to illustrate the nature of the above relationship.

---

[63] In the pericope under consideration, strictly speaking, we cannot compartmentize the mashal and its application on the basis of the already mentioned subsections. From the very beginning of the development of the mashal one finds also its application.

[64] The root meaning of the word γεωργός is farmer or one who tills the soil. But in the context of the mashal of vine it stands for a 'vinedresser'.

[65] The interpersonal relationship which is developed clearly in Jn 17,21ff. is anticipated allegorically in Jn 15,1-17:Cf. B. HINRICHS, *'Ich bin'; die Konsistenz des Johannesevangeliums in der Konzentration auf das Wort Jesu* (SBB 133) (Stuttgart 1988) 80.

A. The Role of the Father

In the pericope in question the Fourth Evangelist presents God the Father in His double role. At the level of the *mashal* He has the role of a farmer, whereas at its application He is presented as the Father of Jesus.

1. Farmer

When the Johannine Jesus narrates the *mashal* of the vine and branches He presents His Father as the farmer (γεωργός). Being a farmer (vinedresser) He has certain functions, viz. cultivating, pruning and cleaning the vine and its branches.

a. One who cultivates (v.1b)

According to the Johannine presentation God the Father is presented as the farmer (γεωργός) who cultivates the vine and takes care of the vineyard. Here one can see the OT allusion to Yahweh as the one who cultivated Israel, the vine (cf. Is 5,2; 60,21; Ps 80,9.16; Jer 2,21).[66] Those who trace a mandaen influence of this Johannine text also base their argument on the idea of presenting the Father as the cultivator (cf. Ginza 301,10f.).[67] This idea of God as cultivator is not alien to the Synoptic tradition (cf. Mt 15,13). It is the Father's interest that the heavenly vineyard should grow (cf. Is 27,3; Jer 4,3; Os 10,12, Mt 20,1ff; 1 Cor 3,9).

---

[66] Cf. supra, pp. 165-169.

[67] Cf. supra, pp. 169-172.

In the Johannine imagery of the vine and branches the Father as the vinedresser is presented in relation to Jesus,[68] the real vine, and in relation to the disciples, the branches of the vine. God the Father, the cultivator of the vine, is interested in the growth and the fruitfulness of the vine together with its branches which are supposed to remain in an organic unity. Jesus presents Himself as the genuine vine tended by His Father and in relationship with the branches, viz. His relationship with His disciples, under the guiding care of the Father. The idea of the Father as the cultivator adds genuineness to the vine and it lays a strong foundation for the branches' remaining on such a genuine vine. The relationship between the Father and the Son motivates the disciples to have a deep faith in Jesus and thereby obtain an encouragement to remain in Him. The farmer's role is not to provide life to the vine, but to give conditions conducive for an organic growth of the vine and branches. Hence, in the imagery of the vine and branches the Johannine idea of interpersonal relationship between the Father and the Son is made clear.

b. One who cuts off the unfruitful branches (vv.2a.6)

The cutting off ($\alpha\iota\rho\epsilon\tilde{\iota}\nu$) of the unfruitful branches of the vine is presented as one of the actions of the Father who is the cultivator of the vine. This taking away or cutting off the unfruitful branches

---

[68] The mention of the Father together with the Son is a characteristic of the Fourth Gospel: Cf. L. MORRIS, *The Gospel According to John* (Michigan 1971) 669. But according to Lindars an over emphasis on the real relationship between the Father and Jesus in this context is not correct: Cf. LINDARS, *John*, 488.

is a common action of the cultivators[69] evident from other texts where the action of γεωργός is mentioned (Cf. Rom 11,16.17; Mt 3,10; Lk 3,9). The cutting off of the unfruitful branches has a purificatory and exhortatory dimension as well. It helps the organic and healthy growth of the vine together with the fruitful branches. At the same time this action, at the level of the application, has an exhortatory value since it warns the already faithful disciples to remain in close organic union with Jesus and to produce abundant fruits.

The expression πᾶν κλῆμα ἐν ἐμοὶ μὴ φέρον καρπὸν (v.2a)[70] illustrates the fact that a branch which remains in the vine, Jesus, can at the same time be unfruitful. In the context of the present pericope, the expression ἐν ἐμοί (v.2a), in contrast with μένειν ἐν (vv.4-7), has a limited meaning in the sense that it denotes an external union. Even though the earliest interpretations of the unfruitful branches were to illustrate the unbelieving Jews, by using ἐν ἐμοί John applies them to the apostate Christians.[71] Every branch, whether fruitful or unfruitful, belongs to the stem and so every disciple belongs to Jesus. An external belonging (ἐν ἐμοί) is not enough to bear fruits. Rather there should be an active abiding (μενεῖν) in Jesus (v.4ff.).

---

[69] The cutting off of the unfruitful branches is a necessary function of the vinedresser, done in the winter, necessary for the organic growth of the vine.

[70] The verb εἶναι (to be) is understood here.

[71] Cf. SCHNACKENBURG, St. John, Vol III, 98; BARRETT, St. John, 473. Some exegetes find an immediate allusion to Judas who had already gone out to betray Jesus: Cf. GEORGE, Vite Vera, 123; BERNARD, St. John, Vol II, 479.

The idea of cutting off of the unfruitful branches (v.2) is
repeated in terms of judgment in v.6 where the Evangelist explains
the tragic fate of the unproductive branches (cf. also Ezek 15,1-5).
The punishment of the Father as the cultivator, carried out through
his servants, [72] is depicted in different terms. One can see here an
eschatological teaching in the context of an imagery. It recalls the
prediction of John the Baptist (cf. Mt 3,10; 7,19; 13,30.40.42)[73] which
can be understood against the background of the eschatological
punishment (cf. Mt 5,22; 18,9; 25,41; Mk 9,43).[74] The continuity of
the divine punishment is clearly expressed in the aorist use of the
verbs ἐβλήθη (thrown out) and ἐξηράνθη (withered). [75] The
unfruitful branches are thrown into the fire (τό πῦρ) which indicates
the eternal judgment of the Father. [76]

The reason for the cutting off (taking away) of the branches is
the absence of their organic union with the stem which results in

---

[72] The verb in the 3rd person plural (συνάγουσιν …καί βάλλουσιν) denotes
the mediation of the divine judgment. The sequence of the aorist passive is
interrupted by two present indicative third person plurals. Probably we have here
the semitic custom of using the active third person plural for the passive: Cf.
BROWN, John, Vol II, 661.

[73] Cf. G. SEGALLA, "La Struttura Chiastica di Giov.15,1-8",BeO 12 (1970) 131.

[74] Lindars does not understand this verse as an eschatological punishment.
According to him Jesus says that a disciple who lives not in a fellowship with Him
is useless: Cf. LINDARS, John, 489.

[75] Barrett considers them as timeless aorists: BARRETT, St. John, 474. In the
light of Johannine usage one can consider them expressing 'a sequence introduced
immediately with absolute certainty': Cf. BULTMANN, John, 537-538;
SCHNACKENBURG, St. John,Vol III, 419.

[76] The use of the definite article with πῦρ supports either the parabolic style of
the text or it refers to the well known fire of eschatological punishment.

their fruitlessness. At the level of application, this role of the vinedresser, expressed in terms of punishment, reminds the believer to have a close union with Jesus.

c. One who prunes the fruitful branches(vv. 2.3)

The pruning (χαθαίρειν)[77] of the fruitful branches is another function of the Father as the vinedresser. Each branch of the vine has to undergo either a extermination or pruning. The actions of the Father as the vinedresser are decisive for the fruitfulness of the vine. Bearing fruit is the function of the branches, but the cultivator can increase their capacity to bear more fruits by pruning them.[78] The pruning is needed only for the branches and not for the stem. Hence, it is done not with a negative intention but for the positive motive of organic growth and fruitfulness.

At the level of application the Father's action of purification fosters the inter-personal relationship between Jesus and His disciples. The action of the Father is directed towards the disciples of Jesus in its wider and strict sense. In the wider sense the Father's

---

[77] Καθαίρειν is not a technical term connected with the pruning of the vine: Cf. DODD, *Interpretation*, 136. In the context of the vine-dressing this Greek verb can be better translated "to prune": Cf. JB & RSV. Καθαίρειν is equally suitable for agricultural processes and for religious purgation: Cf. BARRETT, *St. John*, 473. It is used elsewhere in the NT only in Heb 10,2 (religious cleansing). In ancient Greek literature this terminology is used for the religious ceremony (Cf. Iliad XVI,228) and in a moral sense (Plato, Phaedo 114°). Stylistically, there is perfect parallelism between the two actions of the Father viz. taking away (αἴρει) and pruning (καθαίρει). It is considered as a *paronomasia*, since verbs of the same root are used here in two different senses: Cf. PANIMOLLE, *Giovanni*, Vol III, 264.

[78] In spring-time pruning work is usually done with the already fruitful branches for a better yielding.

purificatory action, meant for every Christian disciple, is not yet completed. But v.3 can be understood in its strict sense which makes clear that the apostles are already made clean[79] by the word of the Father revealed by Jesus, His Divine Son.[80] Here the word of God is the instrument for pruning or cleaning of the disciples of Jesus (cf. also Heb 4,12). The Father's purificatory role is executed by Jesus through His revelation (cf. Jn 15,3; 5,38; 8,37; 17,14). In the pericope under consideration cleaning is attested to as a work of the Father, the cultivator, together with Christ, the revealer. All those who keep the words of Jesus are His disciples and they are made clean through the same words of Jesus. Thus, the purification is connected with the word of God by acceptance of the divine revelation in Jesus Christ through faith (cf. Heb 4,2).[81] The revelation by Jesus of what He has heard from the Father is presented as the basis of Jesus' friendship with His disciples (cf. Jn 15,15). So also the keeping of Jesus' words is a necessary response on the part of the disciples to personalize their friendship with Jesus (cf. 15,14; 14,23). Hence, the pruning action of God the Father

---

[79] Here also the greek verb $\kappa\alpha\vartheta\alpha\dot{\iota}\rho\epsilon\iota\nu$ is used as in v.2,a difference clear only from the context. In v.2 it is used in the sense of an agricultural pruning whereas in v.3 it is used to express a religious purification. By this type of play on words the Evangelist expresses the inner meaning and development of the story: Cf. LINDARS, *John*, 488.

[80] The use of the Greek term $\lambda o\gamma \acute{o}\varsigma$ is noteworthy. It is the revelatory word or teaching of Jesus in its entirety. On the other hand the Greek word $\dot{\rho}\acute{\eta}\mu\alpha\tau\alpha$ is used for the individual teachings or precepts of Jesus. For the distinction between $\lambda \acute{o}\gamma o\varsigma$ and $\dot{\rho}\acute{\eta}\mu\alpha\tau\alpha$: Cf. J. CABA, *La Oración de Petición: Estudio exegético sobre los evangelios sinópticos y los escritos joaneos* (AnBib 62) (Rome 1974) 263, n.11; WESTCOTT, *St. John*, 241; BRUCE, *John*, 309.

[81] Cf. PANIMOLLE, *Giovanni*, Vol III, 264.

through His words (cf.v.3) establishes an organic union among the vine and the branches and ultimately a close friendship between Jesus and the disciples.

2. God the Father

Apart from the role of the vinedresser at the level of the *mashal*, the Father enjoys certain functions proper to His divinity which illustrate the theme of interpersonal relationship.

a. One who answers the prayer (v.7 = v.16c)

In the present pericope the answering of the prayer is presented as a function of the Father [82] whereas in Jn 14,13 it is Jesus Himself who answers prayer. [83] The answering of the prayer by the Father is presented here as an effect of the intimate union between Jesus and His disciples. [84] Since they abide in Jesus their prayers will be

---

[82] In v.7 it is only indirectly mentioned unlike in v.16. The Father's role of answering the prayer is clearly mentioned in v.16, the concluding part of the same pericope.

[83] Actually one need not consider it as a contradictory theological thought of the Fourth Evangelist, since he insists on the theology of mutual indwelling between the Father and the Son. Hence what Jesus does is the Father's own work as well.

[84] Here the abiding of Jesus in the disciples is promised through the abiding of Jesus' words in them. ῥήματα in the Fourth Gospel is used in connection with the revelatory work of Jesus (cf.3,34). It identifies Jesus Himself. Thus the person of Jesus and His words are used alternatively. One's obedience or the acceptance of Jesus' word is the acceptance of Jesus Himself: Cf. BEHLER, *Die Abschiedsworte*, 174; cf. also F.G. UNTERHASSMAIR, *Im Namen Jesu: Der Namensbegriff im*

in fact Jesus' own and such prayers are always answered by the Father (cf. 11,42). The wishes of those who remain in Jesus will not be different from that of Jesus.[85] The disciples' conformity of the will with the Son presupposes the conformity of their will also with the Father. The prayers which are thus in conformity with the will of God will always be answered by the Father.

In the Fourth Gospel usually one is advised to pray in Jesus' name (cf.14,13f.;15,16; 16,23.24.26).[86] In Jn 15,7 it is presupposed because the prayer of the disciples who abide in Jesus can only be in Jesus' name.[87] Those who abide in Jesus can produce abundant fruits and become Jesus' disciples. Such disciples' prayers will always be heard by the Father. They can ask only what Jesus asks, i.e. in conformity to the will of Jesus (cf. 1 Jn 5,14). Hence, prayer in conformity with Jesus' will, rendered in His name, is always heard by the Father. In Jn 15,7 the assurance of hearing the prayer is stated more freely and boldly than anywhere else in the Gospel.[88]

Thus, when the Fourth Evangelist presents God the Father as one who answers prayers, he alludes to a close relationship between Jesus and His disciples and their common relationship also with the Father. In other words, this role of the Father pre-supposes and

---

Johannesevangelium (Stuttgart 1973) 142.

[85] In this respect Unterhassmair writes: "Immanenz zwischen Jesus und seinen Jüngern bedeutet daher Willenskonformität zwischen den Jüngern und Jesus": *Ibid.*, 143.

[86] This idea of praying in Jesus' name will be treated in detail when we deal with the disciples' role of prayer in v.16c.

[87] Cf. BROWN, *John*, Vol II, 679. Interpreting this verse Bernard writes: "A petitioner who 'abides in Christ' asks habitually 'in his name'; i.e. he asks as Christ would ask, and so his satisfaction is sure": BERNARD, *St. John*, Vol II, 482.

[88] Cf. BORIG, *Die wahre Weinstock*, 54.

fosters a close friendship between Jesus and the faithful. In short, the role of the Father as one who answers prayer mentioned in the context of the *mashal* of the vine and branches, an imagery of unity and friendship, goes hand in hand with the Johannine theology of friendship.

b. One who loves the Son (v.9)

The Father's love towards the Son is explicitly mentioned as a source, inspiration and model of the Son's love towards His disciples (cf.v.9). It is the ultimate source and inspiration of Christian love as well while Jesus' love is the immediate source of Christian love. The mutual love of the Father and the Son is not merely a model of the love between Jesus and the disciples and among the disciples, but it is the creative cause from which all Christian love necessarily springs.[89] By using the particle χαθώς[90] in the context of the love-

---

[89] Cf. STANLEY, *Genuine Vine*, 489. Lindars understands it only as a model: Cf. LINDARS, *John*, 490.

[90] χαθώς is used throughout the Fourth Gospel to show the parallelism in the realm of the Father-Son relationship: Cf. M. LATTKE, *Einheit im Wort. Die Spezifische Bedeutung von Agape, Agapan und Philein im Johannesevangelium* (SANT 41) (München 1975) 165. The use of the particle χαθώς in the Fourth Gospel has different nuances according to the context in which it is used. In Jn 15,9.10 χαθώς is used in the context of the love-relationship, where it has the sense of *ground*. Accordingly the Father's love towards Jesus is mentioned as the source and origin of Jesus' love towards His disciples. For a detailed treatment on χαθώς in the Fourth Gospel: Cf. O. DE DINECHIN, "χαθώς: La Similitude dans L'évangile selon Saint Jean", *RechScienRel* 58 (1970) 195-236.

relationship, the Evangelist expresses the origin and intensity of Jesus' love towards His disciples. The use of the aorist ἠγάπησεν gives an absolute dimension to the relation.

At the level of the *mashal* the love of the Father towards the Son is depicted in terms of the farmer's tender care of the vine from the time of cultivation till its bearing fruit. Thus the Father's love towards the Son is an on-going phenomenon. The Father's deep and constant love towards the Son and the acknowledgement of the same by the Son is one of the leading Johannine thoughts.[91] The expected love and friendship between Jesus and His followers is founded on the deep love of the Father towards the Son. Love is not synonymous to friendship, but love is necessary for friendship and love leads to friendship. In this sense the Father's supreme love towards the Son is the primary source of the friendship between Jesus and the believers.

c. One who commands (v.10b)

The Evangelist presents the Father also as one who commands the Son (cf. v.10b). His commandment is not something negative, but positive since it is the expression of the Father's supreme love towards humanity translated into the joyous obedience of the Son in the different phases of salvation history. Even Jesus' self-sacrifice for the salvation of the world is His supreme obedience to the will of the Father (cf. Jn 10,17; 3,16; 1,29; 12,23-28). Jesus' obedience was till the point of His death, an expression of God's love for the

---

[91] In the prologue of the Gospel we read about the intimate union between God the Father and the Son, the Word (cf. 1,1ff.). So also, in 17,24 Jesus makes explicit that the Father loved Him before the creation of the world (cf. also 3,16). Moreover John's Gospel speaks of the Father's love towards the incarnate Son (cf. 3,35; 5,20).

world. The ultimate aim of God's commandment is the salvation of mankind. One can find an intrinsic connection between the love and obedience in v. 10.[92] Hence, the role of the Father as the one who commands the Son and, through the Son, believers, is ultimately an expression of the interpersonal relationship based on love. Jesus insists on the necessity of the disciples' obedience for the establishment of their friendship with Him (v. 14). Jesus' obedience to the Father's commandment is presented as a model and source for the believers' obedience. The keeping of the words is aimed at love and joy within the community of God-head and within the community of the faithful (vv. 9-11).

B. The Role of Jesus

In the context of the present pericope the Evangelist presents Jesus' role on two levels. On the level of the imagery Jesus takes the role of the vine and on the level of its application He has various functions proper to His divine Sonship.

1. The Genuine Vine (vv.1.5)

In the *mashal* of the vine and branches Jesus presents Himself as the genuine (ἀληθινή) vine (vv.1.5). The imagery of Jesus, the real vine can, be better understood against its historical background,

---

[92] Barrett writes: "Love and obedience are mutually dependent. Love arises out of obedience, and obedience out of love": BARRETT, *St. John*, 476.

where Israel is presented as a vine which lost its genuineness. [93] The figure of the vine is an apt symbol of Jesus' relationship to the Father and to His followers. The vine is considered as a tree of life and through such an imagery Jesus presents Himself as the true source of life.[94] As the branches are united with the vine for their organic growth, the followers of Jesus have to unite with Him for their life. The vine has two functions in relation to the branches: holding the branches together for an organic growth and helping them to bear abundant fruits.

a. Holding the branches together

The branches of the vine have no life in themselves unless and until they remain united with the vine (stem). The vine itself by its very nature will always nurture every branch which is organically attached to it. Even the unfruitful branches belong to the vine at least in a limited sense (cf. πᾶν κλῆμα ἐν ἐμοὶ ... in v.2a). If the branch is capable of imbibing the sap from the vine it can properly grow in the vine and produce much fruits. The Evangelist makes no distinction between the stem of the vine and its branches since the branches can be considered as part of the vine just as the believers

---

[93] Cf. supra, pp.165-169. In John the term "genuine" is used to show the contrast with something not genuine (cf. 1,9; 1 Jn 2,8 X Gen 1,3); (6,32 X Ps 77,24-25); (1 Jn 5,20 X Ex 4,23); (Rev 3,14 X 11,3-6). As applied to Jesus Christ, the word "genuine" in the Johannine writings points to Jesus as the prophetic fulfilment of the OT typology: Cf. STANLEY, *Genuine Vine*, 486.

[94] Cf. SCHWEIZER, *Ego Eimi*, 40f. 158; BAUER, *Johannesevangelium*, 189; BULTMANN, *John*, 407.

can be regarded as part of Christ.[95]   It is the function of the vine
to hold the branches together in an organic unity.

b. Helping to bear fruit

The branches cannot bear fruit except by remaining actively
(μένειν) in the vine (v.4). From this statement one can infer that it
is the vine which helps its branches' bearing fruit. Apart from the
vine the branches can do nothing (cf.v.5c). In the Greek text the
expression χωρὶς ἐμοῦ (apart from me) is emphatic and it is
categorically asserted that apart from Jesus the disciples can do
nothing (cf. also 2 Cor 3,5). Even though bearing fruit is presented
as a function of the branches, they cannot actualize it apart from the
vine. Thus, the role of helping the branches to bear fruits is an
essential function of the vine.

2. God the Son

In the application of the *mashal* Jesus presents Himself as God
the Son, in His variety of functions, related to the Father and to His
disciples. His indwelling in the Father and in His disciples, His
obedience to the Father and His love towards the disciples are the
main roles.

a. One who abides in the love of the Father (v.10b)

The relationship between God the Father and Jesus the Son is

---

[95] NEWMAN & NIDA, *Translator's Handbook*, 479.

often described by their mutual love (cf. Jn 3,35; 5,20; 10,17; 15,9; 17,23.26). The Father's love towards Jesus is presented in Jn 15,9 as a source and model of Jesus' love towards the disciples.[96] Jesus' abiding (μένειν)[97] in the supreme love of the Father is through obedience (v.10). The expression 'remaining in the love of the Father' can be understood either as a remaining in Jesus' love towards the Father[98] or as a continued abiding in the Father's love towards Jesus.[99] By doing the will of the Father Jesus expressed His love towards His Father (cf. 4,34; 8,28f.; 14,31). Jesus abides both

---

[96] Cf. supra, pp. 187-188.

[97] μένειν, a Johannine terminology which occurs frequently, has a great theological significance and an added note of permanence: Cf. BROWN, *John*, Vol I, 510; E. MALATESTA, *Interiority and Covenant: A Study of εἶναι ἐν and μένειν ἐν in the First Letter of Saint John* (AnBib 69) (Rome 1978) 25-32. Out of the 118 NT occurrences of this term 68 are in Johannine writings, whereas the Synoptics use it 12 times. In Johannine writings this term expresses the reciprocity of the relationship among the Father, the Son and the Christian believer. It is a term used for mutual indwelling and by using different prepositions the Evangelist makes a clear distinction of the difference of meaning: μένειν παρά ... in the sense of staying with or at the side of ...(cf.Jn 1,39; 4,40; 14,17); μένειν μετά ...also as staying together with...(cf. 11,54); μένειν ἐν ...in the sense of an active remaining in the Lord in the form of a permanent relationship (cf. 6,56; 15,4.5.6.7.9.10). More than in the sense of a mere continuation, μένειν ἐν points to something more tenacious and vigorous. Even though such a dynamic meaning is given to this verb at the level of the *mashal* to explain the relationship between the vine and the branches, in its application it is referring to a permanent relationship between Jesus and His own. The imperative use of this verb denotes a moral union which is clear only at the level of the application, because the branch has no moral power to abide in the vine: Cf. LINDARS, *John*, 489.

[98] Jesus' love for the Father was expressed through a response of obeying the Father's commandments in the spirit of love. Stanley says: "Jesus' love for His Father is proved by His act of obedience to the divine will which desires the salvation of all humanity": STANLEY, *Genuine Vine*, 489.

[99] In v.9 it is clearly mentioned that the Father loves Jesus or in other words Jesus is the beloved of the Father. This state of love continues when Jesus continually obeys the Father.

in His love towards His Father and in the Father's love towards Him through obedience to the Father. Moreover, the Father's entrusting of the salvific work to Jesus, His Son is an expression of the Father's supreme love towards the Son. Jesus' execution of the Father's will is the expression of His love towards His Father. Hence, Jesus' continued remaining in the love of the Father is an expression of a close interpersonal relationship between the Father and the Son.

b. One who abides in the disciples (vv.4.5.7)

The invitation to abide in Jesus and Jesus' assurance of His constant abiding in the believers are well expressed in the first part of the pericope. The mutual indwelling of Jesus and His disciples is clearly developed through an exhortation to abide either in the person of Jesus (cf. vv.4.5.6.7)or in His love (cf. v.9).[100] It is also made clear through Jesus' assurance of His reciprocal abiding on the disciples either personally (v.4.5)[101] or through His words

---

[100] The expressions μείνατε ἐν ἐμοί and μείνατε ἐν τῇ ἀγάπη τῇ ἐμῇ (μου) signify the same, viz. the union of the disciples with Jesus. Jesus' love identifies His person. There is a development in the Johannine thought together with the literary development. While the relation of the vine to the branches is depicted as union, the relation of Jesus to His disciples is portrayed as communion.

[101] In v.4 Jesus advices His disciples to abide in Him and at the same time He promised His continuous abiding in them. The use of καί in v.4 can be explained in three ways: a) As a comparison: As I (abide) in you ...;b) Καί introduces the apodosis of a conditional sentence, the protasis of which is expressed by an imperative: If you abide in me, I will (abide) in you; c) To connect two balanced clauses: Abide in me **and** I (abide) in you. Among these three possibilities, by considering the whole context where there is no comparison or condition for Jesus' initiative, we prefer the third one, where the personal relationship between Jesus and His disciples is stressed.

(v.7).[102] Jesus as the Son of God continuously present in a believer through His divine love. Since Jesus is the incarnated love of the Father, the believers' experience of the divine love manifests Jesus' personal presence in them. Actually there is no substantial difference between Jesus' presence in the disciples either by means of His person or by His words, because Jesus is the Incarnate Word of God. The expression, "my words remain in you" can be understood also as the disciples' keeping of Jesus' words. It can be the disciples' acceptance of Jesus' precepts as a light for their life.[103] The assured reality of Jesus' indwelling in the believer is further developed in terms of friendship in the last section of the pericope.

c. One who loves the disciples (v. 9)

Jesus loved His disciples (cf. vv.9.12; 13,1) in the pattern of (καθώς)[104] the Father's love towards Him (cf.v.9; 3,35; 17,24.26). The specific nature of Jesus' love for His own, manifested in self-sacrifice, is illustrated in the second part of the pericope in the context of Jesus' teaching on friendship. The aorist use of the Greek verb ἠγάπησα (v.9) includes the whole act of Jesus' love up to the point of His death. The disciples are asked to respond positively to the love of Jesus. By observing the stylistic presentation of vv. 9-10

---

[102] Unlike in v.3 here the Greek word ῥήματα is used to denote the words of Jesus. Cf. supra, p. 185, n. 84.

[103] Regarding the interchangeability of the terms "word" and "commandment" Brown writes: "The equivalence of the "word" and "commandment" stems from the OT where the Ten Commandments are referred to as the "words" of God (Exod 20,1; Deut 5,5.22-indeed "word", Heb. dābār, may be a technical term for covenant stipulation)": BROWN, *John*, Vol ll, 642.

[104] Cf. supra, p. 187, n. 90.

Hendriksen comments that Jesus' love towards us precedes our love, accompanies our love, follows our love and in such a process it creates more love in our hearts and thus sublimates our love.[105] Such a supreme love of Jesus motivates His disciples to accept His invitation to enter into a close friendship with Him through a life of obedience.

d. One who obeys the Father (v.10b)

The Fourth Evangelist presents Jesus as one who keeps the commandments of His Father (v.10 b; cf. also Jn 4,34; 6,38; 12,49; 10,18; 14,30-31; Phil 2,8). Jesus' submission to the will of His Father was the aim of His vocation. This submission was not a burden but a free action out of love which provided Him the fullness of joy. The loving obedience of Jesus to the Father's will is put forward as a model (καθώς) for the disciples' keeping of Jesus' commandments. For the keeping of the commandments here the Greek verb τηρεῖν is used and not φυλάσσειν. This usage in the text in question is noteworthy since φυλάσσειν could mean a mere juridical observation of the law, whereas τηρεῖν means an active, docile and prompt obedience to the word with a spirit of charity.[106] Such a usage has a deep meaning in the whole context of the pericope and especially in the context of v.10, where the keeping of the commandment is connected with remaining in love. Observation of the commandment results in remaining in the love of the one who commands. In connection with Jesus' obedience the perfect tense τετήρηκα (I have

---

[105] Cf. HENDRIKSEN, *John*, 303-304.

[106] Cf. VELLANICKAL, *Gospel of John*, 144.

kept) is used which may assert the absolute quality of Christ's love
and obedience. In the second part of the text the keeping of the
commandment is given as a precept necessary for one's friendship
with Jesus (cf.v.14). Accordingly Jesus' obedience to His Father
serves as a model for the believers' obedience to Jesus'
commandments which enables them to enter into a close friendship
with Him.

e. One who shares His joy with His disciples (v.11)

The joy (χαρά) of Jesus in its fullness is promised to His
disciples in the context of Jesus' revelatory words[107] on mutual
indwelling. Jesus shares the fullness of His joy with His disciples as
an effect of revelation. [108] The joy is mentioned as something
immediately following the love and obedience of which Jesus has
spoken in the preceding verses. Jesus' own joy[109] springs from His
union with the Father which finds its expression in obedience and
love (cf. Jn 14,31).[110] Because of the intimate union between Jesus

---

[107] The Greek expression ταῦτα λελάληκα ὑμῖν (v.11) is to be taken into
account as a revelatory formula which recurs like a solemn refrain seven times in the
Last Discourse (cf. 14,25; 15,11; 16,1.4.6.25.33)just as ἐγώ Κύριος λελάληκα
recurs several times in Ezekiel (cf.5,13.15.17etc.): Cf. BERNARD, St. John, Vol
II, 485. The pronoun ταῦτα refers back to the preceding exhortation which cannot
be limited to the immediately preceding words. So also the ἵνα clause connects the
cause of joy with the preceding words.

[108] Cf. PANIMOLLE, Giovanni, Vol III, 266.

[109] The Greek adjective ἐμή shows the intimate sharing among the friends. The
disciples' joy should be same as Jesus' own.

[110] Cf. SANDERS & MASTIN, St. John, 340.

and the disciples, the joy which Jesus enjoys from His unity with His Father, can also be shared by the disciples. For John joy is a fruit of fellowship connected with discipleship since Jesus calls His disciples in pairs. It shows that from the very beginning discipleship is a fellowship and true joy is the after-effect of genuine fellowship.[111] In the context of Jesus' farewell His own joy is promised in its fullness as an eschatological gift (cf. Jn 16,24; 17,13; 1 Jn 1,4; 2 Jn 12). In the OT the joy of the Lord is presented as the source of strength (cf. Neh 8,10). Joy is seen as the sign of Christians as well (cf. Phil 4,4; 2,17 f.; 2 Cor 7,4; 13,11). It is presented also as a salvific gift (Jn 3,29; 4,36; 8,56; 11,15; 14,28) which would reach its fullness at the resurrection of Christ (cf. 20,19-21) and in the disciples' continued life of bearing fruit (cf. v.16). Hence the term χαρά has a Post-Easter connotation.

The fullness (πλήρωμα) of joy is a favourite Johannine expression (cf. Jn 3,29; 1 Jn 1,4; 2 Jn 12) which has an eschatological tone. The reference here is the lasting and spiritual joy, based on peace with God. Jesus' promise of joy to His disciples at the moment of farewell is very apt and necessary. It is the relationship of love which leads to the fullness of joy. Only by walking along the same path of Jesus, a path of suffering unto death through obedience, the disciples enjoy the fullness of joy.[112] In short, Jesus' sharing of His joy in its fullness with His own followers help them

---

[111] Cf. G.S. GIBSON, "Joy", *ExpTim* 94 (1983) 244-245.

[112] Cf. HOSKYNS, *Fourth Gospel*, 477, where he writes: "The delightful divine merriness of the Christians which originates in the Son and deposited in his disciples, is matured and perfected as they love one another, undergo persecution, and readily lay down their lives for the brethren (cf. 1 Jn 3,16)".

to enter into a close interpersonal relationship with Him by means of a loving obedience. [113]

C. The Role of the Disciples

Considering the specific literary style of the pericope one has to trace the role of the disciples on two levels, viz. on the level of the *mashal* and on the level of its application. Accordingly the disciples are portrayed as branches of the vine and as genuine disciples of Jesus. Their functions connected with these two roles illustrate the theme of interpersonal relationship.

1. The Branches

In the context of the *mashal* of the vine and branches the disciples are pictured as branches (κλῆμα).[114] The branches of the vine have no existence in themselves and accordingly they are incapable of bearing fruits as well. The relevance of the branches can be thought of only against the background of their union with the vine (stem). But the union is beyond the capacity of the branches when we consider the union of the vine and the branches in the natural realm. According to the figurative presentation of the

---

[113] The fullness of joy which John the Baptist as the friend of the bridegroom experienced is out of his obedience (listening to the voice) and friendship with Jesus (cf. Jn 3,29): Cf. PANIMOLLE, *Giovanni*, Vol I, 340.

[114] In the NT the term κλῆμα occurs only in Jn 15. But it is used in LXX to denote the shoot of the vine (cf. Num 13,24; Ezek 17,6) as distinct from the branch (κλάδος) of other trees.

text the branches have two attributed roles in relationship with the vine, i.e. remaining in the vine and bearing abundant fruits.

a. Remaining in the vine

The branches of the vine are supposed to remain in the vine for their life and fruitfulness. There can be either a mere external union or an active organic union between the vine and the branches. Even the fruitless branches can externally be united with the vine (cf. ἐν ἐμοὶ in v.2a).[115] The fruitful branches have to remain (μένειν)[116] in the vine for their continuous fruit bearing (cf. vv.4-5). If a branch does not abide in the vine it will be cast forth, withers, to be gathered and thrown into the fire (cf. v.6). By explaining the tragic fate of a branch which does not remain in the vine the Evangelist illustrates the necessity of abiding in the vine. Thus, even through an imagery of the union between the vine and its branches John highlights the necessity of an interpersonal relationship between Jesus and the faithful.

b. Bearing abundant fruits

It is the branches of the vine which bear the fruits. But it is a fact that the branches by their own capacity cannot bear fruits (cf. v.4). They must unite organically with the vine to imbibe its sap and must undergo timely pruning to produce abundant fruits. Hence, the

---

[115] Cf. supra, p. 181.

[116] The branch has no moral power to abide in the vine. The exhortation to abide in the vine has a meaning only at the level of the application of the mashal. For a detailed explanation of Greek verb μένειν cf. supra, p. 192, n. 97.

capacity of the branches to bear abundant fruits is conditioned by outside factors. At the level of the imagery itself the necessity for a union and relationship is vividly pictured. Therefore, under the "bearing fruit" function of the branches the idea of interpersonal relationship also emerges which provides the background for the profound Johannine teaching on friendship in the second part of the pericope.

2. Jesus' Disciples

The pericope under consideration is a part of the last discourse of Jesus addressed to His disciples. The imagery of the vine and branches is used by the Johannine Jesus to explicate the theme of unity and relationship between Himself and His disciples. In the process of the development of the imagery Jesus applies the role of the branches to His disciples. Being authentic disciples they have certain functions to fulfil for the actualization of unity.

a. Who are asked to abide in Jesus (vv.4-7)

At the level of the application of the vine and branches there is direct identification of the disciples with the vine-branches (cf. v.5).[117] Jesus exhorts His disciples to remain (μένειν)[118] in Him to

---

[117] The shift from the third person to the second person in vv. 3ff. shows the identification of the disciples with the vine-branches.

[118] In Jn 15 μένειν is generally used in its imperative form which shows its exhortative nature. It is applied to describe the relation of the believer to Christ: Cf. DODD, *Interpretation*, 136. For a detailed explanation of the verb μένειν cf. supra,

bear much fruits (cf. vv.4-7) while He insures His remaining in them. If the disciples do not remain in Jesus they can do nothing and have to undergo condemnation and judgment (cf. v.6). Only when one remains in Jesus through faith (cf. 1 Tim 2,15; 2 Tim 3,14) and obedience (cf. v.10) will he then be able to produce much fruits. The necessity of depending on Christ for the spiritual works is modelled after Christ's dependence on and unity with God the Father for any work (cf. Jn 5,19.30; 2 Cor 3,5; Phil 2,13). It is noteworthy that the disunity is not reciprocal in the Johannine presentation. It is possible only on the part of the disciples. According to Johannine theology separation from Jesus can be understood as unbelief which calls for God's judgment.[119] In the natural order the branches cannot choose the state of *abiding*, but in the spiritual realm the disciples can willingly and consciously work for *abiding* in Jesus.[120] The disciples' intimate union (μένειν ἐν) with Jesus demands loving obedience on their part to enter into a close friendship with Jesus.

b. Who are asked to abide in Jesus' love (vv.9-10)

Together with the stylistic development of the pericope there is also a thematic development, i.e. from the imagery of vine-branch

---

p. 192, n. 97.

[119] Cf. HEISE, *Bleiben*, 87.

[120] Cf. BERNARD, *St. John*, Vol II, 481.

relationship to the Jesus-disciple relationship.[121] So also, the disciples are asked first to abide in Jesus, and then to abide in Jesus' love (vv.9-10).[122] The Greek expression μείνατε ἐν ἐμοί in vv.1-8 is changed into μείνατε ἐν τῇ ἀγάπῃ τῇ ἐμῇ in vv.9-11 which provides the immediate background for Jesus' teaching on friendship in the following section of the pericope. The expressions *abide in me* and *abide in my love* in this context signify the same, viz. an exhortation for the intimate union of the disciples with Jesus.[123]

The necessity of the disciples' abiding in Jesus' love is expressed through Jesus' exhortation stylistically described in vv.9-10. These verses illustrate the Father's relation to the Son and the Son's to the disciples, and then to the opposite direction, viz. the disciples' relation to the Son and the Son' to the Father. This chain of relations has its beginning and end in the Father's love to the Son, artistically composed in a parallelistic concentric structure as follows:

---

[121] With v.8 the imagery of the vine and branches practically comes to an end, though it reappears in v.16 with the theme of bearing fruit. With v.9 the theme of love is concretely introduced as an application of the *mashal*. In the final section the love develops into a friendship between Jesus and His disciples.

[122] Here an emphasis is given to Jesus' exhortation by using the aorist imperative form of the verb (μείνατε) which means "begin to remain" and "continue to remain". For St. Augustine it was difficult to distinguish the love of which Jesus speaks, whether it is the disciples' love towards Jesus or Jesus' love towards them: Cf. AUGUSTINUS, *Tractatus*, 35, 1844. The Vulgata translated it as *delectio mea* which is confusing. But, in the light of v.10 it is more objective love, i.e. by keeping the commandments one loves Jesus (cf. also Jn 14,15; 1 Jn 5,3). There are many NT references for the objective use of the pronominal adjective (cf. Lk 22,19; 1 Cor 11,24.25; 15,31; Rom 11,31; 15,4).

[123] Ibuki seems to be right in his comment when he writes: "...somit kann gesagt werden, daß die Liebe Jesu zu den Jüngern an die Stelle seiner Person treten kann. "Bleibt in meiner Liebe" in 15,9 kann also an die Stelle des "Bleibt in mir" in 15,4 treten. Die Person Jesu und seine Liebe sind miteinander auswechselbar": Y. IBUKI, *Die Wahrheit im Johannesevangelium* (Bonn 1972) 248.

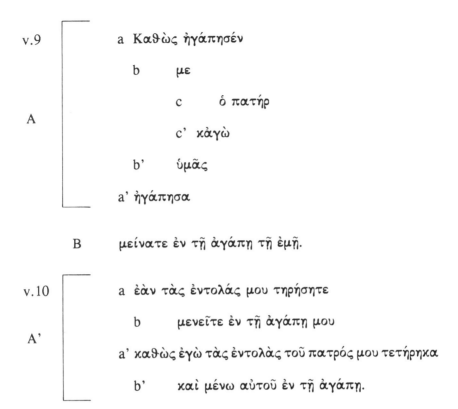

In the above structure A and A' are in parallelism. Both, in A and in A' the interpersonal love-relationship between the Father and the Son and between the Son and the believers are stylistically portrayed. In A itself the Father's love towards the Son and the Son's love towards His disciples are depicted in parallelism. Through the Greek particle καθώς the Father's love is shown as the model and source for Jesus' love towards His disciples. So also, in A' the keeping of the commandments is the means to abide in one's love and Jesus' keeping of His Father's commandment is the model and source of the disciples' observance of Jesus' commandment. In the concentric structure B, being the centre, constitutes the exhortation of Jesus to His disciples to remain in His love.[124]

The central idea of these pair of verses is Jesus' exhortation to His disciples to abide in His love through voluntary obedience. *"Abide in my love"* as a command does not primarily mean a continuation of being loved by Jesus or God, but a positive active obedience on the part of the disciples to remain in Jesus' love.[125] The mutual indwelling of the Father, the Son and the disciples is mutuality of love expressed in obedience which is spontaneous joy and not a painful duty.[126] Since the abiding in Jesus' love is possible only through obedience this relationship is deeply theological as it accepts the superiority of Jesus in one's life of obedience. [127]

---

[124] About this stylistic construction of vv. 9-10 Schnackenburg writes: "Its point of departure, to which it returns, is the love of the Father and two καθώς clauses are arranged chiastically, with the admonition 'to abide in Jesus' love' in the middle": SCHNACKENBURG, *St. John*, Vol III, 103.

[125] Cf. J. DUBLIN, "Continue Ye in my love (Jn 15,9)",*ExpTim* 47 (1935-36) 91.

[126] Cf. BRUCE, *John*, 310.

[127] Cf. PANIMOLLE, *Giovanni*, Vol III, 275; IBUKI, *Die Wahrheit*, 254, where Ibuki writes: "Die Jünger empfangen das Vom-Vater-Geliebtsein Jesu; und das geschieht im Bewahren der Gebote Jesu, d.h. es geschieht, in dem die Jünger diese Gebote, die als das Wort das Geschehen der Liebe selber sind, hören und solches gerade ist das Bleiben der Jünger in der Liebe Jesu".

c. Who are asked to pray with confidence (v.7b)

If one abides in Jesus and if he follows Jesus' words in his life, then he can ask whatever he wishes and that will surely be answered by the Father (cf.v.7). In the context of union with Jesus, a disciple wishes only what Jesus wishes.[128] It is same as praying in Jesus' name (cf. v.16). The interpersonal relationship between Jesus and a disciple makes the disciple's prayer infallibly effective.[129] Just as the "bearing fruit" is the function of the disciples possible only in their constant and deep relationship with Jesus, so also, offering of genuine prayer is an effect of the disciples' abiding in Jesus.[130] In short, fruit bearing and prayer are two effects of the disciples' union with Jesus. An authentic disciple of Jesus who prays in accordance with Jesus' will and spirit can have a close relationship with the Father. Hence, through prayer a disciple keeps a personal relationship with the Father and the Son.

d. Who are asked to render glory to God (v.8)

In the context of the imagery of the vine and branches one can understand that the fruitfulness of the vine is the ground for the joy and honour of the vinedresser. At the level of its application all the good fruits which the disciples bear in union with Jesus bring glory to the Father (cf. v.8; Mt 5,16). In other Johannine texts it is Jesus'

---

[128] Cf. supra, pp. 185-186.

[129] Cf. STANLEY, *Genuine Vine*, 489; NICCACCI, *Esame Letterario*, 47.

[130] Cf. CABA, *La Oración de Petición*, 257-264, where the author presents the prayer as a result of the disciples' unity with Jesus by analyzing Jn 15,7 in the context of the *mashal* of the vine and branches.

own redemptive work which brings the Father's glory (cf. Jn 12,28;
13,31; 14,13; 17,4). By remaining in Jesus the disciples can
participate in the glorifying actions of Jesus which shows the identity
existing between the disciples' work and that of Jesus. [131] In v.8 the
believer's bearing fruit and the becoming a disciple are juxtaposed
with the Greek conjunction καί[132] in a ἵνα[133] clause as the means
of glorifying the Father. Bearing fruit results in the glory of the
Father and in Christian discipleship of the believers. Being united
with Jesus one produces abundant fruits and by producing spiritual
fruits one becomes [134] a Christian disciple, the means of the Father's
glorification. In other words, one's fruitfulness of life as Christ's
disciple glorifies the Father. [135] Hence, the glorification of the
Father presupposes an intimate relationship between the Son and
the believer which develops into a close friendship.

e. Who are asked to keep the commandments (v. 10)

The necessary requirement for abiding in Jesus' love is keeping

---

[131] Cf. STANLEY, *Genuine Vine*, 489.

[132] Here the conjunction καί is explicative.

[133] The ἵνα here is epexegetic or explanatory: ZERWICK, *Biblical Greek*, 139-140, § 410.

[134] No one can be a disciple of Christ in its totality and perfection. Discipleship is a process. It is a growth in Jesus and in that sense it is dynamic: Cf. BEHLER, *Die Abschiedsworte*, 176.

[135] Cf. SANDERS & MASTIN, *St. John*, 338-339.

(τηρεῖν)[136] His commandments. The commandments are summarized and specified as the commandment of fraternal mutual love (cf. vv.12.17).[137] The model and source of the disciples' obedience is Jesus' own obedience to His Father clear in the use of the Greek particle καθώς (cf. v.10). The measure of the disciples' obedience to Jesus' commandments must be the same as His own obedience to the Father's commandments.[138] The keeping of the commandments pre-supposes a deep faith and love in the one who commands. Thus, the disciples are expected to express their love and faith towards Jesus by keeping His commandments (cf. Jn 10,27-28). The love and faith on the part of the disciples are necessary conditions for entering into a close friendship with Jesus. In this sense, Jesus' exhortation to keep His commandments serves as a background for His teaching on the friendship between Himself and His disciples.

VII. The Friendship Between Jesus and His Disciples

In the second part of the pericope (vv.12-17) the theme of friendship between Jesus and the faithful is treated clearly. It is their mutual abiding and love-relationship that culminates in friendship. Against the background of the *mashal* of the vine and branches, the teaching of Jesus on friendship is formulated by the

---

[136] The use of the Greek verb τηρεῖν in this context is noteworthy. It is not merely juridical as the verb φυλάσσειν denotes. For details cf. supra, pp. 195-196.

[137] We will deal with the commandment of fraternal love in detail in the analysis of the last section of the pericope.

[138] Cf. LIGHTFOOT, *St. John's Gospel*, 283.

Fourth Evangelist by consecutively adopting the Greek term φίλος in its plural form in vv.13-15.[139] The theme of friendship between Jesus and the faithful is developed in the context of fraternal mutual love, which serves stylistically as a frame work (cf. vv.12.17).[140] By practising mutual brotherly love which is the sole commandment of Jesus, the disciples can respond positively to the friendship which Jesus has already established with them through His self-sacrifice, revelation, apostolic choice and appointment. The friendship is essentially reciprocal even though in the present text the term φίλος is applied only to the disciples. It is noteworthy that in the pericope in question the expression of friendship on the part of Jesus presented as *already* established, while on the part of the disciples is a *not yet* realized one. The friendship between Jesus and His disciples in its reciprocity and in the light of the present text will be treated in the following section.

A. On the Part of Jesus

Since friendship is reciprocal it must be realized from both sides. As we have mentioned above the friendship on Jesus' part is an already established fact which finds its expression in different ways.

---

[139] According to Dibelius vv.13-15 do not fit well into the context of the entire pericope. He considers vv.14-15 as a kind of "midrashic degression" prompted by the proverb of v.13 and suggests that v.16 is a later gloss: Cf. M. DIBELIUS, "Joh 15,13.eine Studie zum Traditionsproblem des Johannesevangeliums", in *Festgabe für Adolf Deissmann zum 60. Geburtstag* (Tübingen: Mohr 1927) 168-186. Reprinted in DIBELIUS', *Botschaft und Geschichte* 1 (Tübingen: Mohr 1953) 205, n.3; 206.

[140] Stylistically there is an inclusion between vv.12 and 17 which marks a subunit in the pericope: Cf. supra, p. 177.

An analysis of those expressions helps one to understand the theological depth of the term φίλος.

1. Expressed in self-sacrifice (cf. v.13)

In Jn 15,13 love and friendship are connected with self-sacrifice. Here the *laying down of one's life* is presented as a general norm for expressing friendship, [141] not as something immediately connected with Jesus' death. [142] But, since such self-sacrifice was encouraged in pre-Johannine time the Evangelist could understand and interpret Jesus' death in the light of this norm as the greatest expression of His love towards "His own". In the Fourth Gospel the expression of love finds its culmination in a heroic self-sacrifice (cf. Jn 3,16; 10,11;

---

[141] Already in Plato's writings one sees this idea of self-sacrifice for the sake of love: Cf. PLATO, *Symposium*, 179 B.

[142] Cf. DIBELIUS, *Traditionsproblem*, 208-216. According to Dibelius v.13 represents a "heroic" view of love. It is not otherwise characteristic of this Gospel which considers love not in an "ethical" but in a "metaphysical" perspective - as constituting the Father's unity with his Son and the Son's unity with His own. Moreover, except in 10,11; 11,50 and 3,16 the Fourth Evangelist does not interpret Jesus' death as a sacrifice for others. There is no explicit mention of Jesus' death in connection with 15,13. Hence the meaning here is quite a general one. But Furnish criticises this position of Dibelius by saying that he has undervalued the references in 3,16; 10,11; 11,50 to Jesus' death for others. One should not regard these verses as exceptions, since in these texts there is a clear emphasis on the death of Jesus as a life-giving event for his people (cf. 3,14-15.17-21; 10,10.12-18; 11,1-44). Moreover, Dibelius' sharp distinction between the "ethical" and "metaphysical" views of love cannot be attributed to Johannine thought, as ch.13 shows well. In the Fourth Gospel there is a concern that the meaning of the love which unites the Father to the Son and the Son to His followers finds expression in very concrete ways (13, 12-26). The relation between the ethical and metaphysical sides of love is further illustrated in 15,1-11 where abiding in love (metaphysical) and bearing the fruits of love (ethical) are vitally inter-related. Cf. V.P. FURNISH, *The Love Commandment in the New Testament* (London 1973) 141.

11,50).[143] Now, the Evangelist indirectly interprets Jn 15,13 as Jesus'
sacrificial death, an expression of His love for His own. Moreover,
the immediate context of the Johannine teaching the self-sacrifice in
v.13 is the friendship between Jesus and His disciples (cf. vv.14-15).
Hence, in v.13, though the self-sacrifice is depicted in general terms
it is of course a self-portrait of Jesus Himself as the model for the
mutual love of the disciples.[144] Furnish writes:

> It is inevitable, then, that the reader (ancient or modern) of
> this Gospel would interpret the saying of 15,13 in the light
> of the evangelist's conviction that Jesus' own death was the
> culmination ("It has been accomplished", 19,30) of his whole
> mission of love (3,16)".[145]

It is noteworthy that, the Johannine use of the term φίλοι in
v.13 has a very general application. It is not directly applied to
Jesus' disciples as in vv.14 and 15. But the interconnection between
vv.12 and 13 calls for the Christological interpretation of v.13, viz.
Jesus' self-sacrifice for His own disciples (ὑπέρ τῶν φίλων αὐτοῦ).
The expression of Jesus' exemplary love (καθώς ἠγάπησα ὑμᾶς) in
v.12a and Jesus' immediate reference to his disciples as friends
(ὑμεῖς φίλοι μού ἐστε) in v.14a affirm that the general norm of
greatest love mentioned in v.13 is verified in Jesus' sacrificial love

---

[143] Jn 15,13 can be better understood in the light of the Lazarus-story. Lazarus,
one whom Jesus loved, was considered as Jesus' friend (cf. 11,3.11). It was the
greatest expression of Jesus' friendship with Lazarus which motivated Him to go to
Judea in spite of the foretold danger in life. In the Johannine presentation it is the
miracle of the raising of Lazarus which became the immediate cause for Jesus'
death. The expression of sacrificial love for Jesus' friend, Lazarus is already treated
in the third chapter of our dissertation.

[144] Cf. LINDARS, John, 491.

[145] Cf. FURNISH, Love Command, 141.

towards His friends. [146] In the context of the *mashal* of the vine and branches the term φίλοι in v.13 must be understood as another designation for the "branches" already identified with Jesus' disciples (cf. v.8).

a. Self-sacrifice as an expression of greater love towards the friends

Jn 15,13 interprets and expresses the implications in v.12, i.e. the mode of Jesus' love for His disciples. The laying down of one's life for his friends is considered the greatest and most sublime expression of love. "The highest revelation of love is made in the death of Jesus". [147] In the self-sacrifice of Jesus His friendship with His own is made manifest in its perfection. [148] The supreme form of Jesus' love, expressed in self-sacrifice, is an example for the disciples (Rom 5,8; Eph 5,2; 1 Jn 3,16). By foretelling His sacrificial death in terms of a general norm Jesus teaches His disciples the greatest expression of one's love for his friends.

In the light of the Synoptic and Pauline teaching on Jesus' sacrificial love in which enemies and sinners are also included in the love of Jesus (cf. Mt 5,43ff.; Lk 6,27ff.; Rom 5,8-10), it is difficult to explain this Johannine maxim of love, where the self-sacrifice is depicted as the expression of the greatest love towards one's

---

[146] The verb ἠγάπησα (aorist) in v.12 can be understood in the time perspective of the author of the Gospel: Cf. NEWMAN & NIDA, *Translator's Handbook*, 487.

[147] J. DENNEY, *The death of Christ* (London 1956) 262.

[148] Cf. IBUKI, *Die Wahrheit*, 250. Van den Bussche writes: "La mort du Seigneur est la marque suprême de sa fidélité à la mission que Père lui a remise. Elle est aussi la preuve la plus manifeste de son amour pour le siens": VAN DEN BUSSCHE, *Jean*, 426.

friends.[149] But, in the context of the Last Discourse, Jesus is in the midst of His friends and He is speaking only of friends, for whom He is about to give up His life. In Jn 13,1 Jesus' sacrificial love for *His own* is clearly mentioned as an introduction to the whole farewell discourse addressed to Jesus' own disciples. Jesus, the good shepherd, was ready to give up His life for His own sheep (cf.Jn 10,11.15.17). It does not exclude or devaluate Jesus' love for His enemies since John does not exclude the universal dimension of Jesus' salvific death (cf. Jn 1,29; 6,51; 3,14-16). Moreover, the love relationship between the Father and the Son is one of the basic themes of the Fourth Gospel. One's love is patterned after the love between the Father and the Son which is different from the love of an enemy. John's presentation of one's self-sacrifice for his friends as the greatest love can be explained against such a background. [150] Jesus' sacrificial death is presented in v.12 as an example which His disciples must follow. The fact that the disciples are Jesus' friends and He has loved them even to the point of death is an encouragement for the disciples to practise the same love among themselves and towards Jesus, their friend.

The phrase τις τὴν ψυχὴν αὐτοῦ θῇ should be interpreted in the light of the motif-diction, viz. ὑπὲρ τῶν φίλων αὐτοῦ. Since we understand it as Christ's laying down of life, it has a soteriological connotation which shows the communion of Jesus' love. The Greek preposition ὑπέρ expresses the soteriological dimension of Jesus' self-sacrifice (cf. also Jn 6,51). Hence, the interpretation of Jn 15,13 as a mere ideal of human heroism or of his *love* simply as sentimental

---

[149] Cf. W. POPKES, *Christus Traditus* (Zürich/Stuttgart 1967) 284.

[150] Cf. IBUKI, *Die Wahrheit*, 255.

or emotional is not Johannine. Rather it is deeply theological as it expresses the nature of Jesus' friendship with His disciples.

b. Self-sacrifice as an expression of obedience to the Divine Will

Jesus' laying down of His life for His friends is not motivated by personal interest. It is an expression of His love and obedience to the salvific divine will of His Father (cf. Jn 3,16). Jesus' obedience to the Father's commandments is given as a model and source of the disciples' obedience to His commandments (cf.v.10). The new commandment corresponds with the commandment which Jesus Himself has received from the Father (cf. 10,18), according to which He should lay down His life; and it is this commandment which includes all the commandments Jesus has to give (cf. 14,15; 15,20).[151] If love is presented as the greatest commandment (cf. Jn 15,12.17), then the supreme expression of it in the laying down of life has a covenantal connotation which involves the execution of the Divine will.[152]

The gift of Jesus' life "for his friends" is the prefiguration of His death and resurrection. Through His glorified humanity, offered for all men upon Calvary, the risen Lord communicates His life to the Christians. It is not merely Jesus' human love which motivated Him to lay down His life for His friends, but His divine love as Son of God, revealed in perfect obedience to His Father's command. [153] In

---

[151] Cf. W.D. DAVIES, *The Sermon on the Mount* (Cambridge 1966) 124.

[152] *Ibid.*, 125. In the light of the covenantal and sacrificial aspect of love, evident in the pericope Davies finds a Eucharistic connotation.

[153] Cf. STANLEY, *Genuine Vine*, 489.

short, Jesus' laying down of His life according to His Father's will is
the greatest expression of His friendship with His disciples. Hence,
the friendship which Jesus expressed through His self-sacrifice is not
sentimental and psychological but deeply theological.

2. Expressed in Revelation

Jesus establishes a genuine friendship with His disciples by
sharing all His divine knowledge with them (cf. v.15).[154] The inter-
connection between friendship and revelation is also a gnostic
doctrine and one who finds a gnostic influence in the formation of
this Johannine text explains it as a gnostic idea. One can find a
relationship between friendship and revelation in the OT also.
Moses, a revelatory mediator, is presented as a friend of God with
whom God spoke face to face (cf. Ex 33,11; Num 12,8; Deut 34,10).
Abraham, who was named as the friend of God (cf. 2 Chr 20,7; Is
41,8) was privileged by God's revelation (cf. Gen 18,17-18).
Commenting on Jn 15,15 Stanley writes: "Their relationship to Jesus
thus parallels that of Abraham to Yahweh, who had remarked à
propos of the great Patriarch, "Am I to hide from Abraham what I
am about to do ?" (Gen 18,17-18)".[155] There are also similar
expressions in Wis 7,27 and in Jn 15,14f.[156] The friendship is
expressed either in speaking and hearing or communication and
acceptance of the same. By executing His revelatory role among His

[154] Cf. BEHLER, *Die Abschiedsworte*, 187.

[155] STANLEY, *Genuine Vine*, 491.

[156] Cf. PANIMOLLE, *Giovanni*, Vol III, 288; BROWN, *John*, Vol II, 683;
SCHNACKENBURG, *St. John*, Vol III, 111.

disciples Jesus establishes His friendship with them. To understand
the nuances of the inter-connection between friendship and
revelation one has to examine the distinction between a servant and
a friend in the light of v.15, where the sharing of knowledge is
mentioned as a criterion.

a. The contrast between the titles: "servants" and "friends"

In order to express the theological meaning of the title φίλοι
(friends) the Evangelist introduces with contrast the figure of δοῦλος
(slave/servant) (v.15). The juxtaposition of 'servant' and 'friend' is
clear in Is 41,8. In Isaiah's view there is no antithesis between
Israel, the servant, and Abraham, the friend of God, because for the
Jews there is no distinction between servant and free man with
respect to their relation with God. [157]   On the basis of their
mediatory role and sharing of divine knowledge Abraham, Moses
and others were called "friends of God". [158]   On the contrary among
the Greeks the term 'bond-servant' was used antithetically to 'friend'.
For John it may not be antithetical but still there is a contrast
between φίλοι and δοῦλοι on the basis of revelation. [159]   In the OT
δοῦλος Κυρίου (עבד יהוה) was always an honourary title (cf. Josh
24,29; Deut 34,5; Ps 89,20 etc.). The prophets of the OT call
themselves "the servants of God" (cf. Amos 3,7). So also in other
NT writings it is a title of honour since the apostles and the

---

[157] Cf. E.A. ABBOTT, *Johannine Vocabulary* (Diatessarica V) (London 1905)
§ 1789.1791.

[158] Cf. supra, p. 214.

[159] Cf. ABBOTT, *Johannine Vocabulary*, § 1778.

Christians were considered themselves as slaves of God (cf. Lk 2,29; Rom 1,1; Gal 1,10; Phil 1,1; 2 Pet 1,1; Jas 1,1; Rev 1,1). In Gal 4,7 there is a development from slavery to sonship (cf. Mt 17,26). In the light of the above mentioned texts one can conclude that from the view point of service the believers are called servants, but from the viewpoint of sharing of knowledge and intimacy with God they are no more servants but beloved ones. The contrast between φίλοι and δοῦλοι in Jn 15,15 must be understood in the perspective of intimacy between Jesus and the believers evident in the context of the *mashal* of the vine and branches.

In the Fourth Gospel contrast is made not between φίλοι (friends) and ἐχθροί (enemies) but between φίλοι (friends) and δοῦλοι (slaves). The term ἐχθρός never occurs in the Fourth Gospel. In Jn 8,31-36 there is a distinction between sons and slaves on the basis of freedom and sharing of knowledge, parallel to the distinction between slaves and friends. The contrast between a slave and a friend is based on freedom; the freedom to share knowledge and listen to it.[160] Jesus' addressing the disciples as "friends" and not "servants" shows the gratuitous nature of the disciples' friendship with Jesus.[161] Johannine understanding of discipleship is based on friendship with Jesus (cf. 15,12-17) and is different from the traditional Christian understanding of discipleship as διακονία (cf. Rom 1,1; Phil 1,1; Gal 1,10; 2 Cor 4,5; Lk 12,37.43-47; 17,10). In John the relation between friendship and discipleship is clear in the

---

[160] Regarding the distinction between φίλος and δοῦλος based on revelation there is a parallelism between John and Philo (cf. Jn 15,15; Philo 1,104).

[161] Cf. SCHNACKENBURG, *St. John*, Vol III, 110.

use of the perfect tense εἴρηκα[162] together with the title φίλοι (cf. v.15b). This means that here it is only a reaffirmation and continuation of the friendship which Jesus has already established from the very moment of the choice of His disciples (cf.Jn 6,70). V.16 is a reminder of their special choice to experience the friendship in a moment of His sacrificial death which is the highest expression of His revelation. So also, the particle οὐκέτι in v.15 does not have a narrow and purely temporal meaning, but it is a basic introduction to the new relationship which Jesus has created.[163]

In v.15 the contrast between the titles δοῦλοι and φίλοι is made on the basis of revelation, viz. the lack of knowledge and revelation for the slaves and the fullness of revelation and its reception in the case of friends. The basis of this contrast is stylistically portrayed in perfect parallelism through two ὅτι clauses as follows:

v.15 a οὐκέτι λέγω ὑμᾶς **δούλους**
        b ὅτι ὁ δοῦλος **οὐκ οἶδεν** τί ποιεῖ αὐτοῦ ὁ κύριος·
     a' ὑμᾶς δὲ εἴρηκα **φίλους**
        b' ὅτι πάντα ἃ ἤκουσα παρὰ τοῦ πατρός μου
            ἐγνώρισα ὑμῖν

As it is clear in the above schema the distinction of the title is purely based on the communication of knowledge and its

---

[162] Only in the manuscript P[66] we read λέγω which is probably an assimilation with the first λέγω in v.15a.

[163] Cf. SCHNACKENBURG, *St. John*, Vol III, 111.

comprehension. [164] The criterion for the distinction between servants
and friends is the sharing of knowledge. In the case of the slaves
there is a lack of sharing the knowledge whereas in the case of the
friends the sharing is in its fullness.

b. The lack of revelation to the servants

In John's view the distinction between the slaves and friends lies
not in the obligation of obedience to God, but in the gift of
revelation and its comprehension. [165] Usually slaves are not in a
position to know what their master does. For John knowledge
depends also on the person who imparts that knowledge. Therefore,
the expression that the slaves do not know what the master does
means they do not know the master himself. The slave is no more
than an instrument since he is one who carries out the order of the
master. There is an official relationship between slaves and master
since there is no sharing of knowledge between them. They obey
their master out of fear without asking the reason why they have to
obey, unlike the friends who share hopes and plans among
themselves. Between a master and a slave there is a lack of
confidence and therefore no sharing of hopes and plans. In Jesus'
relationship with His disciples there were moments when they did
not know the significance of Jesus' salvific actions and then they
were indirectly called as slaves (cf. Jn 13,7.12). But in the process

---

[164] The distinction of the two verbs of knowledge οἶδα and γινώσκω in the
realm of revelation will be treated in the next chapter of the dissertation.

[165] Cf. STANLEY, *Genuine Vine*, 491. Barrett writes: "According to John, the
difference between a δοῦλος and a φίλος lies in doing or not doing the will
of God, but in understanding or not understanding it": BARRETT, *St. John*, 477.

of revelation there comes a time when Jesus reveals everything to them and brings them from the status of servants into the status of friends (cf. Jn 15,15).[166]

c. The fullness of revelation to friends

In Jn 15,15 the distinction is made between slaves and friends on the basis of the degree of sharing the knowledge of the other partner with whom they are in inter-action. Jesus calls the disciples friends on the basis of the fullness of His divine revelation to them. Friends have a mutual intimacy and confidence on equal terms.[167] Revelation of Jesus to His disciples is a sign of His confidence in them. In v.15 "friends" as a contrast to "servants" means "confidants", those initiated into the principles of the divine life and into the realities which the Father has communicated to Him.[168] Jesus has shared with His disciples the full message of salvation from the Father and calls them into the status of friendship. The disciples, being Jesus' friends, share Jesus' knowledge which He shares with His Father. They also know what their master, Jesus, does. What Jesus does is not His own actions but the actions of the Father (cf. 5,19). By words and deeds Jesus has made known to His disciples whatever ($\pi\acute{\alpha}\nu\tau\alpha$) He has heard (as revelatory knowledge) from His Father. The sharing of the revelatory knowledge in v.15 refers to the Wisdom literature where the divine Sophia is said to inhabit

---

[166] Cf. LIGHTFOOT, *St. John's Gospel*, 283.

[167] Cf. LINDARS, *John*, 491-492.

[168] Cf. SPICQ, *Agapè*, III, 164.

men and make them God's friends.[169] As friends of Jesus who
share divine knowledge [170] disciples are in a position to understand
God's will.[171]

It was only to the chosen disciples that Jesus has made known
the ὄνομα (name) of the Father (Jn 17,26).[172] The verb γνωρίζειν
in the sense of revelation occurs in John only in 15,15 and in 17,26
where Jesus is the subject as Revealer. [173] Also in the Synoptics this
idea of disciples as Jesus' friends is established on the basis of the
revelation of the mysteries of the kingdom of God (Lk 12,4; Mk
4,11).

The relationship between the Father and the Son is once again
made clear with the object of revelation in v.15. It is the Father's
words which Jesus has heard and what Jesus has heard He has
revealed to His friends.[174] The already existing relationship between
the Father and the Son is manifested in the friendship between
Jesus and His disciples. The friendship is made concrete in the

---

[169] Cf. BROWN, *John*, Vol II, 682-683.

[170] About the sharing of knowledge in friendship in v.15 St. Thomas writes:
"Verum enim amicitiae signum est quod amicus amico suo cordis secreta revelet.
Cum enim amicorum sit cor unum et anima una, non videtur amicus extra cor suum
ponere quod amico revelat": THOMAS, *Evangelium S. Ioannis*, 2016.

[171] Cf. BARRETT, *St. John*, 477.

[172] The name of the Father stands for the Person and the salvific work of the
Father itself. Jesus, as the Son of God has the ability to make known the name of
the Father to the believers. For the significance of the revelation of God's name: Cf.
H. BIETENHARD, ὄνομα ..., *TDNT* V, 272ff.

[173] R. BULTMANN, γινώσκω κτλ, *TDNT* I, 718.

[174] Jesus has made known all that he has heard which refers to all past
revelations. It creates a problem: whether there is no more revelations? If one
considers the verbs as "timeless aorists" then this problem can be solved: Cf.
SANDERS & MASTIN, *St. John*, 341, n.1.

context of revelation and the acceptance of the same (announcing and hearing).[175] The object of revelation is divine love and it is that love the disciples are asked to practice through the observance of Jesus' commandment of love. Reciprocity in friendship involves their obedience to Jesus' words which is clear from the positive response of the disciples.[176] "Knowledge" in v.15 is related to discipleship and obedience, not to the mystic apprehension of God's nature and plans.[177] "To be "friends", "sons", "disciples" means to know to whom one belongs and thus to be free -not just from ignorance of God's Will, but from the thraldom of world's darkness. To dispel this darkness and to bring light and life to men (to make "slaves" into "friends") is the whole point of the Son's mission".[178]

3. Expressed in Free Choice and Appointment

In v.16 the Evangelist connects the theme of friendship with the theme of discipleship. Our argument that, according to the Johannine thought, only a true disciple can become a genuine friend of Jesus is clear in this text. Divine election and authentic appointment are necessary aspects of the genuine discipleship. In other words, Christian discipleship consists of a divine choice and appointment on the part of Jesus. In the gospel narrative (both in Synoptics and in John) it is Jesus who chooses, calls and appoints His disciples (cf. Mt 4,18-22; Mk 1,16-20; 3,13-19; Lk 5,1-11; Jn 1,43).

---

[175] Cf. IBUKI, *Die Wahrheit*, 244f.

[176] This reciprocal aspect of friendship will be treated later in this chapter.

[177] Cf. FURNISH, *Love Commandment*, 141, n.31.

[178] Cf. *Ibid.*, 142.

a. Jesus' initiative in the disciples' choice

Since the call to friendship is based on Jesus' initiative, discipleship as a response is also based on Jesus' free choice. The initiative of the disciples' choice is entirely on Jesus' part, a notable difference from the Rabbinic precept [179] according to which the disciples chose their own teachers. The Greek expression οὐχ ... ἀλλά ...(not...but ...)in v.16 emphasizes the second clause, viz. the choice of the disciples as something purely based on Jesus' initiative. [180] The concept of personal relationship is emphasized by the expression: ἐγώ ἐξελεξάμην ὑμᾶς (v.16b). [181] The same aorist form of the verb ἐξελεξάμην is already used in the context referring to the election of the Twelve (cf. Jn 6,70; 13,18). In the Fourth Gospel it is always God's love that precedes man's. "The privilege bestowed on the disciple was not on account of their worth but through electing grace". [182] Discipleship is ultimately a divine choice rather than a personal decision. It emphasizes the free, independent and spontaneous character of Christ's love and the origin of the call to discipleship. This election or choice to discipleship need not be limited only to the Twelve, but it has a wider application to all Christians (cf. Rom 8,33; Col 3,12; 1 Pet 2,4). [183] In the light of

---

[179] Cf. the Rabbinic precept in *Pirqe 'Abot* i.6, 'Get thyself a teacher', in: STRACK & BILLERBECK, *Talmud und Midrasch*, Vol II, 565.

[180] In disjunctive prepositions, it is a Semitic peculiarity to express something negatively to give more stress to the other. In Greek it is expressed by the οὐχ ... ἀλλά ...construction: Cf. ZERWICK, *Biblical Greek*, § 445.

[181] Cf. CABA, *La Oración de Petición*, 229, n.3.

[182] BEASLEY-MURRAY, *John*, 275.

[183] Cf. BROWN, *John*, Vol II, 683; CABA, *La Oración de Petición*, 229.

Johannine teaching election to discipleship is the same as election to friendship, since only the genuine Christian disciples are called friends of Jesus in the Fourth Gospel. [184] The state of friendship to which the disciples are called is not their choice but it is a gift and grace. [185] However, Jesus' initiative in the call to discipleship or friendship does not reduce human freedom and response. "In such a context, "election" to friendship must be regarded as the bestowal of freedom, not the withdrawal of it. Moreover, it is an election to an active life of obedience, a call to bear love's fruit".[186]

The initiative of the election or choice on the part of Jesus in the form of a revelation shows the intimacy and friendship between Him and His disciples.

b. Jesus' initiative in the disciples' appointment

The divine choice of the disciples as friends is followed by an apostolic appointment. The Greek verb $\tau \acute{\iota} \vartheta \eta \mu \iota$[187] is used here to

---

[184] In the preceding chapters of our thesis we have already brought out the connection between discipleship and friendship. John the Baptist and the members of the Bethany family fulfil the qualities of genuine Christian disciples in their lives so that they are considered as friends or beloved of Jesus.

[185] Cf. PANIMOLLE, *Giovanni*, Vol III, 283.

[186] FURNISH, *Love Command*, 143.

[187] The verb $\tau \acute{\iota} \vartheta \eta \mu \iota$ (to put, to place, to lay, to ordain, to appoint) is a technical term for the consecration for an apostolic ministry in the Church tradition (cf. Acts 20,28; 1 Cor 12,28; 2 Tim 1,11). In the OT נתן (give) and סמך (to lay hand upon, to ordain) are the verbs used to express the meaning of the apostolic appointment and even the ordination of a scholar or a Rabbi: Cf. BARRETT, *St. John*, 478. In the Biblical tradition the election is always accompanied by an ordination or an appointment for a mission which is clearly depicted by the verb $\tau \acute{\iota} \vartheta \eta \mu \iota$ and its derivatives (cf. Num 8,10; 27,18; Acts 13,47; 1 Tim 1,12).

depict Jesus' appointment of His disciples. In spite of its
philological nuances the term must be understood in the particular
context of the pericope, which is one of a close union between Jesus
and His disciples, made clear through the *mashal* of the vine and
branches. Here the stress is not on the disciples' missionary role,
but the new status of close union with their master, Jesus, by
organically remaining in Him. In the present context τίθημι must
be understood in its literary construction together with a ἵνα clause,
where the conjunction ἵνα has a consecutive value. The actions
'going', 'bearing fruits' and 'hearing of the prayers' are the
consequences of this appointment (τίθημι) of Jesus.[188] The verb
τίθημι, applied to persons, has the meaning of being uplifted to a
certain dignity. In the context of the present text this dignity can be
understood as the status of friendship towards which Jesus calls His
disciples.[189] In the Fourth Gospel the verb τίθημι is used 18 times
(cf. 2,10; 10,11.15.17.18;13,4.37f.; 15,13.16; 19,9.42; 20,2.13.15)and
among these usages in Jn 15,16 it has a unique meaning which is
made clear through the ἵνα clause. Accordingly the chosen disciple
is supposed to bear fruit in his life by remaining united with Jesus
as His friend.

In the context of Jn 15 the same verb τίθημι is used in v.13 in
the sense of laying down one's life for his friends or beloved (cf. also
Jn 10,11-18). It indirectly emphasizes the Lord's redemptive death
for "His own" which encourages the disciples to remain in union with

---

[188] The ἵνα in v.16 has neither an epexegetic value nor a final value, but it has
an internal consecutive value in the sense that the preceding antecedents enclose
such a dynamism. In such a consecutive value it emphasizes Jesus' election and
designation of the disciples as "friends":Cf. CABA, *La Oración de Petición*, 230.

[189] Cf.*Ibid.*, 230.

Jesus and to follow His path of self-sacrifice.[190] By this the future Christian disciples are reminded of Jesus' love which culminated in His salvific death. Such an understanding helps them to be genuine disciples of Jesus by responding soundly to Jesus' supreme love, by living an authentic life and by carrying out their apostolate among their brethren for which they are chosen and appointed by Jesus Himself. Jesus' initiative in the disciples' apostolic appointment can be considered an expression of His intimacy and friendship with His disciples established through His self-sacrifice and revelation.

B. On the Part of the Disciples

The disciples are expected to respond positively to the friendship which Jesus has already initiated with them. In the form of an exhortation Jesus Himself has given the guidelines for their authentic response. In the context of the present text those expected expressions of friendship show the nature of the friendship between Jesus and the disciples.

1. Keeping the commandments of Jesus (v.14)

The disciples are worthy of carrying the title "the friends of Jesus" only if they do what Jesus commands them (cf. v.14; 14,15ff.). This is true also in the case of certain OT figures who were considered as friends of God, viz. Abraham (Is 41,8; 2 Chr 20,7; Jas 2,23), Moses (Ex 33,11) etc. Since the term φίλος in the Fourth Gospel is reciprocal the disciples' obedience which Jesus expects

---

[190] Cf. STANLEY, *Genuine Vine*, 489; LIGHTFOOT, *St. John's Gospel*, 291.

from them can be understood as their response to the already
established friendship on Jesus' part. When somebody obeys Jesus'
commandment of fraternal mutual love he is responding positively
to the friendship which Jesus initiated with him. In other words,
friendship is initiated by Jesus, but to continue in that friendship the
disciples have to obey His words, the sum total of which is His
commandment of fraternal mutual love (cf. vv.12.17; 13,34; 1 Jn
3,11.23; 4,7.11f.; 2 Jn 5).

In the context of the pericope under consideration it is the
commandment (ἐντολή) of fraternal mutual love which comprises all
other commandments (ἐντολαί) (cf. vv. 12.17).[191] By way of an
inclusion between vv. 12 and 17 the object of Jesus' command in
v.14 is highlighted as fraternal love.[192] In a context of the theme of
friendship the Evangelist presents the commandment of mutual love
as the hallmark of the *friends of Jesus*.[193] The Father's love for His
Son is the model and source of the Son's love for His disciples. As
Jesus remained in His Father's love by keeping His commandments
the disciples are asked to keep Jesus' commandments and remain in

---

[191] The singular use of ἡ ἐντολή in contrast to its plural usage in the preceding
verses summarizes all commandments. Heise considers the plural usage in v.10
which includes faith and love together: Cf. HEISE, *Bleiben*, 90. But for Schrenk the
alternation between singular ἐντολή (13,34; 15,12) and ἐντολαί in the Fourth
Gospel (cf. 14,15.21;15,10) has little significance. The singular use may not be a
summing up of the Jewish multiplicity of ordinances, but the radiating of the one
ἐντολή of love into the manifoldness of the obedient life: Cf. G. SCHRENK,
ἐντέλλομαι, ἐντολή, *TDNT* II, 554. The idea of loving one's fellow Christian
or brother within the community (cf. also Jn 13,34) is shared by John and Qumran,
while the Synoptic Gospels stress the Christian's duty to love all men: Cf. BROWN,
John, Vol I, LXIII. Bernard writes: "A christian disciple must love a christian
because of their common discipleship": BERNARD, *St. John*, Vol II, 486.

[192] The inclusion between vv.12 and 17 maintains the thematic unity of the
subsection.

[193] LATTKE, *Einheit*, 177.

His love (cf. v.10). The same idea is developed in the culminating section of the pericope by using concrete and precise terms. The disciples are asked to become Jesus' friends by doing (ποιεῖν)[194] what Jesus commands (ἐντέλλομαι) them (cf. v.14)[195] which is nothing but the commandments of fraternal mutual love (cf. vv.12.17).

In the context of friendship when a disciple does what Jesus commands, then there is the convergence of their will. A real friendship presupposes the same orientation of the will of the partners. The disciples' obedience to Jesus' commandment in v.14 expresses the unity of their Wills since obedience is demanded as an expression of friendship. Keppler writes:

> Dauerhafte Freundschaft besteht in der Übereinstimmung des Willens der beiden Partner. Ständig auf das vollkommenen Beispiel ihres Meisters schauend, sollen die Jünger nur darauf bedacht sein, daß keiner ihrer Schritte die Bahn seiner Gebote verlasse; dann wird auch keiner ihrer Schritte sie aus der Sonnennähe seiner Liebe entfernen. [196]

The words of Keppler highlights the inter-connection between obedience and friendship. Hence, when a disciple out of his love towards Jesus does what Jesus commands him, then there is the convergence of their will which deepens their friendship.

---

[194] The use of the verb ποιεῖν in v.14 is noteworthy. It does not mean a mere juridical fulfilment of the commandments of Jesus. The use of this verb in the Fourth Gospel referring to the action of man consists mainly in accepting the truth revealed through Jesus Christ. It can be understood as the faith-expression of the people: Cf. S. HEMRAJ, "The Verb 'To Do' in St. John", *SE* 7 (1982) 242f.

[195] In the immediate context of the final subsection of the pericope (vv.12-17) the expression "what I command you" in v.14 refers to the commandment of fraternal mutual love.

[196] P.W. KEPPLER, *Unseres Herrn Trost* 2-3 (Freiburg 1914) 172.

The general application of the term φίλοι (cf. v.13) is restricted
when the expression ὑμεῖς φίλοι μού ἐστε is applied to the disciples
as friends of Jesus (cf. v.14). The conditional clause in v.14 shows
the inter-connection between obedience and friendship, i.e. the
disciples' capacity to become Jesus' friends by keeping His
commandments. But this does not mean that friendship is
something conditional. It is an already established fact by Jesus, yet
one must respond to it by obedience. [197] Love is still not friendship,
but it should grow into friendship through reciprocal concrete
expressions. [198] The disciple's concrete expression of friendship with
Jesus is obedience. Friendship reaches its realization only through
the co-operation of its partners through positive efforts. [199] Keeping
of the commandment is a sign of one's friendship with Jesus, one's
expression of love as a response to Jesus' love towards him. [200]
Hence, obedience and friendship are closely related.

---

[197] About the unconditional nature of friendship Furnish writes: "Friendship is not
conditional upon obedience, however, but upon the Father's prior love: by abiding
in his love one is both sustained and commanded. That has been the whole point
of 15,1ff. The reciprocity of God's action and man's response is presumed":
FURNISH, *Love Command*, 141.

[198] BEHLER, *Die Abschiedsworte*, 185, where Behler writes: "...aber Liebe ist
noch keine Freundschaft. Letztere Gegenseitigkeit der Liebe und Gemeinsamkeit
der Gesinnung und des Strebens voraus".

[199] Cf. IBUKI, *Die Wahrheit*, 244.

[200] Behler writes: "Freundschaft und Gehorsam schließen einander nicht aus, im
Gegenteil: wahre Freundschaft spornt zu immer größerer Treue an, zu immer
größerer Aufmerksamkeit und Bereitwilligkeit gegenüber den leisesten Wünschen
des Freundes": BEHLER, *Die Abschiedsworte*, 185.

Obedience is also a characteristic of true discipleship.[201] According to Morris, "obedience is the test of discipleship".[202] Therefore, the argument that only a genuine Christian disciple can be a real friend of Jesus is verified in the exhortation of Jesus to keep His commandments in order to enter into a friendship with Him. In short, doing what Jesus commands them, viz. practising fraternal mutual love, is the concrete expression of the disciples' friendship with Jesus.[203]

2. Undergoing martyrdom (v.13)

We have already seen that Jesus' teaching on self-sacrifice has the primary application to Jesus' salvific death for His own. Still it has an added implication of the disciples' expression of greatest love towards Jesus in martyrdom. In the general context of the teaching on love and friendship the Evangelist puts forward the connection between friendship and the keeping of the commandment (cf.v.14), i.e. fraternal love itself (cf. vv.12.17). The greatest expression of such fraternal love is self-sacrifice (cf. v.13). Since the disciples can become Jesus' friends by keeping His commandment of mutual love, which can culminate even in self-sacrifice, they are always exhorted to express their greatest love towards Jesus, their friend by laying down their own lives for Him through martyrdom.

---

[201] This idea is already made clear in the former chapters of this dissertation.

[202] MORRIS, *John*, 675.

[203] Cf. SPICQ, *Agapè*, III, 166.

3. Carrying out the duty of bearing fruit (v.16b)

Another expected expression of friendship by the disciples is the bearing fruit. Bearing fruit in the context of the *mashal* of the vine and branches does not have a primary application to the result of one's missionary work. The imperatives ὑπάγητε (go) and καρπόν φέρητε (bear fruit) are presented through a ἵνα clause as the after-effect of divine choice and appointment which is ultimately based on one's friendship with Jesus.[204]   While the divine choice and appointment of the disciples are expressions of Jesus' friendship with them, the execution of the divine mandate of bearing abiding fruits is the reciprocal response of the disciples. In the context the exhortation to go and bear fruits can be understood as one's growth in Jesus and his experience of the results of friendship with Jesus in his own life and in his immediate life situation. The verb ὑπάγειν in other contexts refers to the future mission of the disciples to the world.[205] It is used in Lk 10,3 in the context of the going forth of the seventy on their mission. But, the verb ὑπάγειν in the context of the imagery of vine and branches can be understood as the disciples' gradual growth in the new status of union with Jesus which can be compared to the coming forth of the new buds in the vine-stem.[206] The actions ὑπάγητε and καρπὸν φέρητε must be understood as the effects of Jesus' appointment (τίθημι) which is

---

[204] Cf. PANIMOLLE, *Giovanni*, Vol III, 265.

[205] Cf. BARRETT, *St. John*, 478.

[206] Cf. F. ENGEL, "The Ways of Vines Jn 15,1", *ExpTim* 60 (1949) 84, where he writes: "...the Christian is one whose life springs from Christ, as the branch springs from the stem and draws all its strength and nourishment from it".

clear in the ἵνα consecutive clause.[207] Hence, it is not primarily an appointment for a "mission" outside but it is the effect of one's union with Christ. Of course, one cannot totally deny its missionary dimension since one's union with Christ helps him to produce fruits in the world. By referring to the disciples' role of bearing fruit as an effect of their friendship with Jesus, purely based on His choice, the Evangelist highlights the relation between authentic discipleship and friendship with Jesus.[208]

The expression καρπόν φέρητε (v.16) recalls the *mashal* of the vine and the branches which expects from us an interpretation of v.16 in the same context interpersonal relationship. Accordingly, bearing fruit can be considered as the result of one's friendship with Jesus.[209] The "fruits" in the context of the application of the *mashal* stand for good works with an ethical connotation. St. Paul understands bearing fruit in the context of missions, which is not the background of this Johannine text. In the context of the imagery of

---

[207] Cf. UNTERHASSMAIR, *Im Namen Jesu*, 133.

[208] Cf. STRATHMANN, *Giovanni*, 365.

[209] Niccacci makes a distinction of nuances for the expression "bear fruit" in different verses of the pericope. In v.2 "bear fruit" signifies faith in Jesus as a necessary condition for passing from the OT vine to the NT vine. In vv. 4.5-7 it is used as the effect of remaining in Jesus as the consequence of evangelisation. In v.16 this expression is considered as the effect of going out of the disciples: Cf. NICCACCI, *Esame letterario*, 50, n.18. But such a distinction is too narrow when we consider the unity of the whole text. In the light of the *mashal* and its application bearing fruit in v.16 is also an effect of one's intimate union with Christ. Cf. also CABA, *La Oración de Petición*, 231.

the vine and branches the fruits are not presented as the effect of mission work but are the fruits on the branches themselves. It can be better understood as an effect of being united with Christ (abiding in Him).[210]

The positive act by the disciples is their remaining in Jesus through mutual love. In the context of the text in question "fruits" metaphorically stand for fraternal love.[211] For John bearing fruit and becoming a disciple are the same (cf. 15,8).[212] A disciple, actively abiding in Jesus, can produce much fruits in his own life and also in the community in terms of fraternal love. This mutual love becomes a means for the mission, viz. through their mutual love the world will know that they are Jesus' disciples (cf. Jn 13,35). Thus, according to Johannine understanding bearing fruit has a missionary connotation only in its secondary level.

In the present pericope with the exception of v.16 the subject of the verb μένειν is either Jesus or His disciples. But in v.16 it is the fruit, the result of the intimate relationship between Jesus and His

---

[210] About this Lattke writes: "Von Bild des Lebensweinstocks her heißt καρπὸν φέρειν nicht mehr und nicht weniger als: lebendiger Zweig sein am Lebensbaum Jesus. Die Betonung liegt darauf, daß dies nur möglich ist in der Einheit mit Jesus. μένειν ἐν unterstreicht die Bedeutung dieser reziproken Einheit, die einzig ermöglicht ist durch Jesu Erwählung durchs Wort (Jn 15,3.7.16)"LATTKE, *Einheit*, 186; Cf. also BORIG, *Der wahre Weinstock*, 50; UNTERHASSMAIR, *Im Namen Jesu*, 133.

[211] Cf. LATTKE, *Einheit*, 187, where he writes: "Sicherlich gehört zum "fruchtbringen" das johanninsch verstandene ἀγαπᾶν ἀλλήλους, das aber weder von seinem Inhalt her noch durch seine Setzung als ἐντολή primär ethisch interpretiert werden kann ...".

[212] Cf. *Ibid.*, 186, n.1. Lattke does not accept the popular interpretation of the "fruits" as good works. In the particular context of the text Lattke's position is acceptable.

disciples, which is supposed to remain (μένειν).[213] In v.16 μένειν is used without any adverbs and thus it stands for a continuity of the result of union even after death (cf. 6,27; 12,34; 1 Jn 2,17).[214] The abiding fruits in the life of the disciples provide them a ζωὴ αἰώνιος (cf. Jn 4,36)[215] which is the ultimate aim of the Fourth Gospel itself (cf. 20,31). Bearing fruit is presented as a capacity of the disciples as long as they are in friendship with Jesus. Such a friendship is the result of Jesus' revelation of the Father's words. In this sense a disciple who is in friendship with Jesus is one who remains in relation also with the Father and with his brethren. The fruits which an authentic Christian disciple bears have an abiding nature. When the believers bear much fruits then the will of the Father is being fulfilled. Bearing fruit in v.16 means that the disciples exist in faith by the strength of love which is the result of the intimate union between Jesus and the disciples. Such an existence is realized in availability, sharing and even in self-sacrifice (cf. v.13).[216] In short, by bearing fruits of faith and love, which are conducive for eternal life and which emerges out of their intimate union with Christ, the disciples can express their reciprocal response to the friendship which Jesus has already established with them.

---

[213] Cf. HEISE, *Bleiben*, 91.

[214] Cf. *Ibid.*, 91, n.27. However, Huby understands the "fruits that abides" as the fruits which continue through out life is in contrast with the natural fruits of the vine produced only in one season. Cf. P.J. HUBY, *Le discours de Jésus après la Cène* (Paris 1942) 73.

[215] Cf. HEISE, *Bleiben*, 92; BEHLER, *Die Abschiedsworte*, 188f.

[216] Cf. HEISE, *Bleiben*, 91; E. SCHWEIZER, *Gemeinde nach dem Neuen Testament* (TheSt [B] 26) (Zürich 1949) 105-109. Schweizer considers the organic union between Jesus and His disciples and also among the disciples themselves expressed in love and even in self-sacrifice as the core of the Johannine ecclesiology.

4. Praying in Jesus' name (v.16c)

The possibility of praying in Jesus' name and the promise of hearing such prayers are once again stressed in the pericope. [217] In Jn 15 prayer is presented as a spontaneous and natural effect of the disciples' union and friendship with Jesus. Jesus assures the answering of such prayers by His Father. In the context of the present text the union between Jesus and the disciples is pictured first through the *mashal* of the vine and branches and later through the theme of friendship and discipleship. The mutual abiding of Jesus and His disciples helps one to understand the relevance of the disciples' prayer in Jesus' name (cf. v.16).[218]

The immediate context of prayer in Jesus' name is Jesus' choice and appointment of the disciples as friends with their definite role of living out a fruitful life based on fraternal love. Here one has to consider the function of the two ἵνα clauses in v.16 as ἵνα consecutive [219] and co-ordinated. [220] The consecutive and co-

---

[217] We have already treated prayer and its hearing as a consequence of one's union with Christ in the light of v.7: Cf. supra, pp. 185-187.

[218] Cf. UNTERHASSMAIR, *Im Namen Jesu*, 130; CABA, *La Oración de Petición*, 227ff.

[219] Caba considers this ἵνα as consecutive: Cf. p. 224, n. 188. However, there are authors who consider it as final which causes difficulty in understanding the text: Cf. BLASS-DEBRUNNER, *Greek Grammar*, § 388; W. THUESING, *Die Erhöhung und Verherrlichung Jesu im Johannesevangelium* (Münster 1970) 114.

[220] Many authors consider the second ἵνα as sub-ordinated to the first ἵνα clause and the promise of the hearing of prayers as an after-effect of the disciples' bearing of lasting fruits: Cf. NEWMAN & NIDA, *Translator's Handbook*, 489; NICCACCI, *Esame letterario*, 51; BEHLER, *Die Abschiedsworte*, 188f. For more witnesses cf. CABA, *La Oración de Petición*, 231, n.15. But we consider the two ἵνα clauses as co-ordinated and inter-related. One does not happen without the other: Cf. UNTERHASSMAIR, *Im Namen Jesu*, 138; CABA, *La Oración de Petición*, 232,

ordinating function of the ἵνα clauses in v.16 can be sketched out in the following structure: [221]

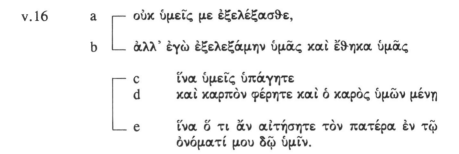

v.16   a   οὐκ ὑμεῖς με ἐξελέξασθε,

       b   ἀλλ' ἐγὼ ἐξελεξάμην ὑμᾶς καὶ ἔθηκα ὑμᾶς

         c   ἵνα ὑμεῖς ὑπάγητε

         d   καὶ καρπὸν φέρητε καὶ ὁ καρὸς ὑμῶν μένῃ

         e   ἵνα ὅ τι ἂν αἰτήσητε τὸν πατέρα ἐν τῷ ὀνόματί μου δῷ ὑμῖν.

As the schema shows, the first and the second ἵνα clauses are directly and evenly connected with ἐξελεξάμην and ἔθηκα[222] which are to be understood in the immediate context of friendship. Hence, the rendering of genuine prayer, which has the assurance of the Father's hearing, is the result of Jesus' revelation, gratuitous election and appointment which are the expressions of His union and friendship with His disciples.[223]

Prayer presupposes one's own limitations and helplessness and at the same time one's confidence in Him to whom the prayer is addressed. In v.16 the disciples are asked to pray to the Father [224]

---

n.16.

[221] Cf. *Ibid.*, 228.

[222] Cf. UNTERHASSMAIR, *Im Namen Jesu*, 136.

[223] Cf. *Ibid.*, 136, n.84. Unterhassmair considers hearing of prayers as the result of one's "abiding in Jesus".

[224] Through the expression τόν Πατέρα the prayer of petition is contextualised against the background of the vine and branches where the Father is introduced in relation with the Son and His disciples.

in Jesus' name.[225] In the Johannine writings the expression "in Jesus' name" presents Jesus as Son of God, the object of revelation and faith (cf. 2,23; 3,18; 16,23-27; 20,31; 1 Jn 3,23; 5,13). Connected with prayer this ὄνομα of Jesus is a means of glorification of the Father (cf. 14,13-14). In this sense the Johannine formula of petition "in the name of Jesus" expresses a spiritual atmosphere of union with Jesus, the Son of God, based on faith.[226] Since the beloved and chosen of Jesus are commissioned by Jesus Himself they can make their petitions in His name. The prayer of petition in v.16 must be understood also in the context of the literary unity of the pericope (esp. its immediate context: vv.12-17) where unity and friendship, connected with faith and revelation, are explicated. By using the Greek preposition ἐν together with ὄνομα abiding in Jesus (vv.4.7.9-10)is once again strongly stressed even in the context of prayer.[227]

---

[225] The expression pray in Jesus' name is a typically Johannine idea (cf. 14,13.14; 15,16; 16,24.26). In Jn 15,16 the prayer is to be made in Jesus' name which goes together with the context of the text where the union between Jesus and the disciples is stressed. In such a case their prayers will be as that of Jesus. Here the name represents His person. In the light of the Johannine theology ὄνομα has a revelatory nuance. ὄνομα applied to the Father has the nuance of the revelation of paternity (cf. 5,43; 10,25; 12,28; 17,6.11-12.26) Likewise, applied to Jesus, it has the nuance of Jesus' Divine Sonship (cf. 2,23; 3,18; 14,13.26;15,16;16,23.26;20,31). But, in Jn 16,23 it is the *granting of the petition* which is in Jesus' name. There are also variant readings for this text referring to Jesus' name connected with the petitions. However, the unity of the petitioner and Jesus is stressed. For a detailed analysis of the prayer of petition in those texts: Cf. Caba, *La Oración de petición*, 227ff.

[226] Cf. *Ibid.*, 236.

[227] Bernard says: "To pray in the name of Christ is not any magical invocation of the name, nor is it enough to add 'per Jesum Christum Dominum nostrum', but it is to pray as one who is in Christ": BERNARD, *St. John*, Vol II, 490.

Prayer in Jesus' name is prayer in conformity to the will of Jesus. It is the prayer of a genuine disciple of Christ, one in constant friendship with Jesus.[228] Such prayer of the disciples glorifies both the Father and the Son and will always be heard by the Father. Thus, the disciples' genuine prayer is a symbol of unity between the Father and the Son and their unity with the Father through the Son. When prayer is in conformity with the will of the Son it will also be in conformity with the will of the Father. Conformity of the will makes one an authentic disciple of Christ and a real friend.[229] Therefore, the prayer of someone to the Father in Jesus' name is an expression of discipleship and friendship with Jesus.

VIII. Theological Perspective

After the thematic analysis of the pericope, we now arrive at certain theological conclusions regarding the nature of the friendship between Jesus and the believer. One can sum up the conclusions under two headings, viz. friendship between Jesus and disciples: a reciprocal relationship, friendship between Jesus and disciples: a master-disciple relationship.

---

[228] Cf. UNTERHASSMAIR, *Im Namen Jesu*, 158-59. He arrives at such a conclusion after analyzing the opinions of different authors regarding the nuance of the prayer "in Jesus' name".

[229] Cf. *Ibid.*, 160-161.

A.   Friendship Between Jesus and Disciples: A Reciprocal Relationship

The analysis of the text clearly brings out the reciprocity of interpersonal relationship in the development of the *mashal* of the vine and branches. In a metaphorical sense the mutual abiding of the vine and branches is stressed for an abundant bearing fruit.[230] At the level of the application of the *mashal* the mutual indwelling of Jesus and His disciples also is clearly depicted through repeated use of the term μένειν in its reciprocal sense.[231] Jesus' abiding in the disciples is categorically assured and asserted demanding a reciprocal response on the part of the disciples through obedience, prayer, bearing fruit and authentic discipleship (cf. vv.7-8). Jesus exhorts His disciples to remain in His love by keeping His commandments.   For such a way of life Jesus' abiding in His Father's love through His obedience is given as a model and source (cf. vv.9-10).

The reciprocity of relationship between Jesus and His disciples is further developed and stressed in His teaching on friendship. Jesus calls them φίλοι on the basis of His self-sacrifice and revelation and invites them to enter into a friendship with Him through their positive responses (cf. vv.12-17). Jesus' friendship with His disciples is an already established fact, clear from the use of the aorist and perfect tenses of the different Greek verbs referring to

---

[230] In the natural order there is no place for active abiding between the vine and branches.   But metaphorically it is presented to communicate the reciprocal relationship between Jesus and the believer.

[231] By using the term μένειν in the sense of a promise and exhortation the reciprocity is well depicted.   Such a double dimensional usage of μένειν in the text is illustrated by Becker: Cf. BECKER, *Johannes*, Vol II, 481.

His relationship with them (ἠγάπησα in v.12; εἴρηκα, ἤκουσα, ἐγνώρισα in v.15; ἐξελεξάμην, ἔθηκα in v.16). The exhorted positive response on the part of the disciples is conveyed through imperatives and conditional clauses (cf. vv.12.14.16.17). The disciples are asked to do what Jesus commands in order to become His friends. So also, as a reciprocal response they have to understand by active listening the message of the Father's words which Jesus graciously revealed to them as a sign of His friendship. Moreover the disciples have to respond positively to the gratuitous choice and appointment by Jesus through abundant fruits and by uniting with the Father through prayer in Jesus' name.[232]

The intimacy between Jesus and the believer is an intimacy honoured by the term φίλοι; but this "friendship" must be carefully understood.[233] It is to be noted that the disciples are Jesus' friends, but Jesus is not called their friend. It seems to be a deliberate attempt of the Evangelist to show that friendship is an offer on the part of Jesus to His disciples. They must still enjoy certain qualities in themselves to reach a status to call Jesus their real friend. By keeping Jesus' commandment of fraternal love and bearing fruit the disciples can establish a friendship with Him. Hence, the reciprocity of the term φίλος can be seen in the theological content of the term rather than in its literal usage.

---

[232] About the reciprocity of relationship Grundmann writes: "Sie verdanken ihre Stellung als Freunde Jesu nicht ihrer eigenen, sondern seiner Wahl; er hat sie zu seinen Freunden bestimt, und also dies sind sie von ihm gesetzt, bleibende Frucht zu bringen und unmittelbaren Zugang zum Vater zu haben": W. GRUNDMANN, "Das Wort von Jesu Freunden (Jn 15,13-16) und des Herrenmahl", NT 3 (1959) 68.

[233] Cf. D.A. CARSON, Jesus and His Friends: His Farewell Message and Prayer in Jn 14-17 (Living Word) (Leicester 1986) 102.

B. Friendship between Jesus and Disciples: A Master-Disciple Relationship

The theme of friendship between Jesus and believer which the Fourth Evangelist develops in the pericope (15,1-17) is neither a relationship of equals nor a friendship based on purely psychological aspects. It is highly theological, rooted in the Johannine theology of divine-human immanence. It is based on Jesus' sacrificial love (vv.12-13), patterned after the Father-Son relationship (vv.9-10) and demands the disciples' dynamic relationship with the Father through the Son (vv.1-2.8.15-16). The friendship between Jesus and the believer is basically a master-disciple relationship. In other words, only by fulfilling the necessary qualities of genuine Christian discipleship can a believer enjoy friendship with Jesus, his master.

The relationship between Jesus and the disciples is patterned after a relationship between the vine and its branches and not between two branches. The branches grow in the vine and without organically remaining in the vine they cannot bear fruits (cf. v.4). This imagery is very apt to bring out the friendship between Jesus and believer as a master-disciple relationship. [234] The disciples are asked to "abide"[235] in the master (cf. vv.4-7) or in his words (cf. Jn 8,31) or in his love (cf. v.9-10) by admitting his superiority. In v.8 the fruit bearing function of the faithful as an effect of his union is

---

[234] This abiding of the believer in Jesus for his fruitfulness is considered by Furnish as a sign of true discipleship. He writes: "Apart from Jesus his followers can do nothing (vv.4-5). But when they "abide" they are fruitful, and this is the sign of true discipleship (v.8)":FURNISH, *Love Command*, 139.

[235] The use of the term μένειν denoting the disciples' relationship with Jesus, seen elsewhere in the Fourth Gospel, is in the context of the call of the first disciples. (cf. Jn 1,38-39).

presented in connection with discipleship.[236] Keeping the commandment of Jesus, a necessary requirement for remaining in His love, is an expression of one's genuine discipleship.[237] Obedience is once again presented as the inevitable condition on the part of the disciples to enter into friendship with Jesus (v.14). It is possible by keeping the commandment of fraternal mutual love, the distinguishing mark of Christian discipleship (cf. Jn 13,35). Hence, discipleship and friendship are closely connected.[238]

In this friendship as the master-disciple relationship Jesus has always priority and superiority. The disciples' friendship with Him is purely an offer on Jesus' initiative. In v.15 the friendship is presented as a master-disciple relationship, based on revelation, in contrast with a servant-Lord relationship, characterized by a lack of shared knowledge. Jesus' superiority is clear also in His initiative of choice and appointment of disciples as friends.[239] The use of the title φίλος only for the disciples and not for Jesus seems to show the distinction or inequality between Jesus and the disciples as master and disciples in their interpersonal relationship.[240] The inequality in their interpersonal relationship is evident also when they are

---

[236] Cf. supra, pp. 230-233.

[237] Furnish writes: "Jesus has remained faithful to his mission to the world by keeping the Father's commandments and remaining in his love, and in like manner his disciples are to remain *faithful in their discipleship* by keeping the Son's commandments and remaining in his love (vs. 10; cf.14,15.21.23-24)":FURNISH, *Love Command*, 140 (Italics mine).

[238] Cf. supra, pp. 230-233.

[239] The subject of the verbs ἐξελεξάμην and ἔθηκα is ἐγώ and in its particular construction it gives emphasis to Jesus' choice.

[240] According to Carson it may be to preserve the fundamental distinction between Jesus and those whom he redeems. Cf. CARSON, *Jesus and His Friends*, 104.

asked to pray in Jesus' name (cf.v.16c). In short, the friendship between Jesus and His disciples is not a relationship between equals and also not in same degree on both sides.[241] It is fundamentally a friendship expressed in a master-disciple relationship.

Conclusion

The Johannine teaching on friendship between Jesus and disciples reaches its climax when Jesus calls them φίλοι (friends). In the narrative of Jesus' earthly ministry the Fourth Evangelist traces the progressive intimacy between Jesus and His disciples (cf. Jn 13,13-16 ---> 15,13-15). This narrative climax on the theme of friendship is formulated against the background of the *mashal* of the vine and branches, an imagery of unity and interpersonal relationship. The "already" but "not yet" friendship between Jesus and the believer is patterned after the Father-Son immanence (cf. vv.10-11). The intimacy between the believer and Christ is an intimacy which, far from being individualistic, is shared within the warmth of love for fellow believers -a love that imitates Christ's love for us (cf. vv. 12-13). In this sense the friendship between Jesus and the believer is not "an exclusivistic, manoeuvring, or selfish relationship. It is a shared intimacy, shared with brothers and sisters in faith, shared within the warmth of love that looks to Christ's love for its standard".[242]

---

[241] Cf. BECKER, *Johannes*, Vol II, 485, where he writes: "Es ist keine Freundschaft, aufgebaut auf gegenseitiger Gleichrangigkeit; insofern ist das hellenistische Freundschaftsideal nicht verwirklicht".

[242] CARSON, *Jesus and His Friends*, 101.

As we have already seen, the friendship between Jesus and the disciples is basically reciprocal. It is reciprocal since it demands a positive response on the part of the believers through an active obedience based on love and faith to Jesus' already established friendship through His self-sacrifice, revelation and personal choice. Thus, more than on its literary level, the use of the term φίλοι in the pericope examined is reciprocal at the level of its theological depth with its variant nuances. In other words, according to John the friendship between Jesus and believer is a master-disciple relationship. The qualities of discipleship such as obedience, love, bearing fruit and genuine prayer are the believers' necessary response to the master's friendship established through His sacrificial love, revelation and gratuitous choice. In short, the term φίλοι is used in Jn 15 as a designation for the Jesus-disciple relationship. Moreover, the Johannine teaching on friendship between Jesus and disciples is an invitation and encouragement to all Christians to enter into close friendship with Jesus.

CHAPTER FIVE

THE BELOVED DISCIPLE AND PETER: TWO MODELS OF TRUE FRIENDSHIP WITH JESUS
(Jn 13,21-30; 19,25-27; 20,1-10; 21,1-14; 21,20-24; 21,15-19)

Introduction

The thesis that the term φίλος in the Fourth Gospel is a designation for the relationship between Jesus and a genuine Christian disciple calls for a close consideration of the two Johannine typological figures, who were in close intimacy with Jesus. These figures are *the disciple whom Jesus loved* [ὁ μαθητής ὃν ἠγάπα (ἐφίλει) ὁ Ἰησοῦς][1] and *Peter*, whose love and intimacy with Jesus are depicted in concrete expressions in the Fourth Gospel.[2] Their friendship with Jesus is not expressed in the same way. Such a diversity in presentation of the two complementary characters is based on theological reasons. Their response to Jesus' call to a deep friendship with Him (cf. Jn 15,14) are diverse but positive. They can be considered as two different models of true friendship with Jesus.

The Beloved Disciple is presented as an ideal disciple who remains always faithful to and in close relationship with Jesus and who follows Jesus in all important moments of His paschal mystery,

---

[1] Hereafter *the disciple whom Jesus loved* will be referred to as *the Beloved Disciple*.

[2] The intimacy between Jesus and these typological figures is expressed in the Fourth Gospel by employing the verbs φιλεῖν and ἀγαπᾶν. Since these verbs are philologically and theologically connected with φίλος and they are also used here to depict the Jesus-disciple relationship, a sufficient treatment of the Beloved Disciple texts and the one Petrine text is necessary in the present context.

even up to the end.[3] More than one among the representative figures, the Beloved Disciple is the *representative figure*[4] in Johannine tradition. He appears as a true believer, an authentic disciple, beloved, and as one who bore witness to Jesus' message. All such ideal characteristics enable him to be in constant friendship with Jesus. In the Fourth Gospel for an unfailing friendship with Jesus the Beloved Disciple appears as a model.

In the theological framework of the Fourth Gospel Peter has also an important role to play.[5] He appears as another possible model of Jesus-disciple friendship. From the very moment of his call (cf. Jn 1,40-41) Peter is a typical disciple who represents the Twelve in his confession of faith (cf. 6,68-69). He follows Jesus with an ardent love (ch.13; 18,10.15.),but with human failure (18,17.25-27). Through a process of rehabilitation [6] Jesus approves his genuineness and makes him a model of discipleship by conferring upon him a pastoral ministry which demands even martyrdom (21,15-19) as verified in his future life. Being an authentic disciple, Peter becomes

---

[3] Cf. S. AGOURIDES, "Peter and John in the Fourth Gospel", in: F. L. CROSS (ed.), *SE* 4 (Berlin 1968) 5.

[4] Cf. R.F. COLLINS, "The Representative Figures of the Fourth Gospel", *DownRev* 94 (1976) 132. Culpepper writes, "The beloved disciple appears close to Jesus in the gospel's climactic scenes, and the evangelist carefully defines his relationship with Jesus... he is unlike the other Johannine characters only in that he is the ideal disciple, the paradigm of discipleship": CULPEPPER, *An Anatomy of the Fourth Gospel*, 121.

[5] Cf. COLLINS, *The Representative Figures*, 126ff.

[6] Brown considers the threefold question of Jesus and the consecutive answer of Peter concerning his love to Jesus in Jn 21,15-17 as Peter's rehabilitation to discipleship after his threefold denial: Cf. BROWN, *John*, Vol II, 1110-1112;cf. also BULTMANN, *John*, 712.

a real friend of Jesus, "a friend by choice (cf. 15,13-16) with responsibility for those entrusted to him".[7] Thus, Peter is presented as another model of friendship with Jesus.

In this chapter we will try to understand the real nature of the Jesus-disciple friendship by analyzing the explicit *Beloved Disciple texts* (Jn 13,21-30; 19,25-27; 20,1-10; 21,1-14; 21,20-24)[8] and the one *Petrine text* (Jn 21,15-19) where the interpersonal relationship between Jesus and these disciples are clearly depicted. The analysis, done in the light of the whole Johannine theology of friendship, will be based mainly on the expressions of friendship in each pericope. As a brief introduction to the Beloved Disciple texts we will discuss the problem regarding the identity, historicity and significance of the Beloved Disciple in the Gospel of John.

I. The Beloved Disciple: a Model of True Friendship with Jesus

From the beginning of Biblical exegesis numerous attempts have been made to establish the identity and significance of the Beloved Disciple in the Fourth Gospel's presentation. [9] Until the 19th century, Biblical scholarship had identified him with John, son of

---

[7] COLLINS, *The Representative Figures*, 129.

[8] There are other implicit *Beloved Disciple texts* such as Jn 1,35-40; 18,15-18; 19,34b-35. Some authors consider the unnamed disciple in these texts as the same disciple whom Jesus loved.

[9] Brown, Lorenzen, Kügler and Segalla put forward the different positions held by different authors: Cf. BROWN, *John*, Vol I, xcii-xcvii; T. LORENZEN, *Der Lieblingsjünger im Johannesevangelium* (Stuttgart 1971) 74-76; J. KÜGLER, *Der Jünger, den Jesus liebte* (SBB 16) (Stuttgart 1988) 439-448; G. SEGALLA, "Il discepolo che Gesù amava e la tradizione Giovannea", *Teologia* 14 (1989) 222ff.

Zebedee. [10] By the dawn of literal and historical-critical exegesis the identity and historicity of the Beloved Disciple became still a matter of discussion among the exegetes. They tried to identify him with different historical Biblical characters, e.g. Lazarus [11], Matthias [12], John Mark [13] or with some indefinite historical persons like one gentile [14], one of the Twelve [15], one of the many disciples of Jesus but not as one of the Twelve [16].

---

[10] The early Church-Fathers in General identified the Beloved Disciple with John, son of Zebedee. Even now there are authors who hold this position: Cf. D. MUÑOZ LEÓN, "¿Es el Apostol Juan el discípulo amado?", EstBíb 45 (1987) 403-492; BARRETT, St. John, 446f.; BROWN, John, Vol I, xcviii. But later he modified this position in his book: The Community of the Beloved Disciple (New York 1979) 33.

[11] Cf. F.W. LEWIS, "The Disciple whom Jesus Loved", ExpTim 33 (1921-22) 42; F.V. FILSON, "Who was the Beloved Disciple?", JBL 68 (1949) 84ff.; B.G. GRIFFITH, "The Disciple whom Jesus Loved", ExpTim 32 (1920-21) 379-381; R. EISLER, "Der Jünger, den Jesus liebte", ErJb 3 (1935) 371-390; V. ELLER, The Beloved Disciple, his Name, his Story, his Thought. Two Studies from the Gospel of John (Grand Rapids 1987) 53-73.

[12] Cf. E.L. TITUS, "The Identity of the Beloved Disciple", JBL 69 (1950) 323-325. According to Titus Matthias fulfils many of the descriptions regarding the Beloved Disciple (cf. Acts 1,21ff. = Jn 20,8; 1,35-40).

[13] Brown puts forward the arguments of Parker, Sanders and Welhausen who hold this position: Cf. BROWN, John, Vol I, xcv-xcvi.

[14] Cf. M. PAMMENT, "The Fourth Gospel's Beloved Disciple", ExpTim 94 (1983) 367.

[15] Cf. LINDARS, John, 34.

[16] Cf. O. CULLMANN, The Johannine Circle. A Study in the Origin of the Gospel of John, J. BOWDEN (trs.) (London 1976) 78; H.B. SWETE, "The Disciple whom Jesus Loved", JTS 17 (1916) 371-374; BROWN, The Beloved Disciple, 34; SCHNACKENBURG, St. John, Vol III, 383-387.

Some authors deny the historicity of the Beloved Disciple and reduce him only to a symbolic figure, an ideal figure ("Idealgestalt") of a true Christian disciple.[17] It is a fact that the Beloved Disciple in the Fourth Gospel has symbolic significance in the sense that he is presented as a model of a faithful Christian disciple called to be in constant relationship with Jesus.[18] But it does not mean that he was not a historical person. Historicity and symbolic significance are not contradictory. In other words, the Beloved Disciple is a historical person with symbolic significance.[19] He is presented as a historical figure with other historical figures like Peter and other disciples of Jesus in certain indisputable historic moments.[20]

---

[17] Cf. BULTMANN, *John*, 483ff.; LOISY, *Quatrième évangile*, 395f.; A. KRAGERUD, *Der Lieblingsjünger im Johannesevangelium. Ein exegetischer Versuch* (Oslo 1959) 45, n.4; E. KÄSEMANN, "Ketzer und Zeuge: Zum johannieischen Verfasserproblem" *ZTK* 48 (1951) 304; E.F. SCOTT, *The Fourth Gospel: Its Purpose and Theology* (Edinburgh 1906) 144.

[18] Cf. BOISMARD & LAMOUILLE, *Jean*, Vol III, 343f.; J.A. GRASSI, *The Secret Identity of the Beloved Disciple* (New York/Mahwah 1992) 81-90.

[19] In this regard Lorenzen writes, "Denn es soll ja nicht behauptet werden, daß der Lieblingsjünger nur eine historische Gestalt ist; sicher trägt er auch ideale und symbolische Züge, die aber eben seine wichtige Position in der Geschichte der johanneischen Gemeinde, seine bedeutende Rolle für die typisch johanneische theologie und auch die theologische Situation der Gemeinde selbst wiedersiegeln": LORENZEN, *Der Lieblingsjünger*, 80-81.

[20] Cf. PANIMOLLE, *Giovanni*, Vol III, 191; BECKER, *Johannes*, Vol II, 436; A. STIMPFLE, *Blinde Sehen: Die Eschatologie im Traditiongeschichtlichen Prozess des Johannesevangeliums* (Berlin 1990) 258; LORENZEN, *Der Lieblingsjünger*, 77-79; K. QUAST, *Peter and the Beloved Disciple* (Sheffield 1989) 12ff.; J.J. GUNTHER, "The Relation of the Beloved Disciple to the Twelve", *TZ* 37 (1981) 135; R. MAHONEY, *Two Disciples at the Tomb. The Background and Message of John 20,1-10* (Theologie und Wirklichkeit 6) (Bern 1974) 80; J. BOGART, *Orthodox and Heretical Perfectionism in the Johannine Community* (Missoula, Mont. 1977) 166, n.40; P. ARENILLAS, "El discípulo amado, modelo perfecto del discípulo de Jesús, según el IV Evangelio", *CiTom* 89 (1962) 3-68.

Now there arises a question: Why such a historical person is
always presented in the Gospel as an anonymous character? There
are some literary [21] and theological [22] motives behind the anonymous
presentation of certain characters [23] in the Fourth Gospel. These
anonymous characters have a representative and symbolic role. For
the Evangelist the descriptive epithets are more effective means of
conveying the symbolism than definite names. [24] One can also find
a close parallelism between the functions of the anonymous "teacher
of justice" in the Qumran community and that of the anonymous
Beloved Disciple of the Fourth Gospel. [25] This approach can be
justified since the Fourth Gospel took shape in the *Sitz im Leben* of
the Qumran community. [26] Minear finds a parallelism between the

---

[21] Cf. GUNTHER, *The Beloved Disciple*, 129.141.

[22] Cf. BROWN, *John*, Vol I, xciv; J. ROLOFF, "Der Johanninsche
'Lieblingsjünger' und der Lehrer der Gerechtikeit", *NTS* 15 (1968) 150; COLLINS,
The Representative Figures, 130.

[23] The name of the mother of Jesus is not mentioned in the Fourth Gospel (cf.
2,1ff. 19,25). So also, some disciples are not named together with the named
disciples (cf. 21,2).

[24] Cf. P.S. MINEAR, "The Beloved Disciple in the Gospel of John, Some Clues
and Conjectures", *NT* 19 (1977) 105-106; KÜGLER, *Der Jünger, den Jesus liebte*,
449; PAMMENT, *Beloved Disciple*, 363.

[25] Cf. ROLOFF, *Lieblingsjünger*, 144-150; COLLINS, *The representative Figures*,
130; KÜGLER, *Der Jünger, den Jesus liebte*, 449.

[26] Cf. S. SCHULZ, *Komposition und Herkunft der Johannischen Reden* (BWANT
LXXXI) (Stuttgart 1960) 182-187. Many authors find a close parallelism between
John and Qumran, especially in theological thought and vocabulary. The idea of
dualism as opposing factors, the ideal of love of one's brother within the community
are some aspects common to both. On the basis of such a parallelism some authors
even find a close dependence of the Fourth Evangelist on Qumran literature. For
details cf. BROWN, *John*, Vol I, LXIII; "The Qumran Scrolls and the Johannine
Gospel and Epistles", *CBQ* 17 (1955) 403-419,559-574. Reprinted in K. STENDAHL
(ed.), *The Scrolls and the New Testament* (New York 1957) 183-207; H. BRAUN,
"Qumran und das Neue Testament", *ThR* 28 (1962) esp.192-234; H.M. TEEPLE,

Deuteronomic and Johannine traditions. Accordingly Jesus is the type of Moses and the Beloved Disciple the type of Benjamin. [27]

All these studies support a symbolic and representative character of the Beloved Disciple, based on the Fourth Evangelist's theological outlook. Following the redaction critical method of exegesis, rather than being pre-occupied with establishing the identity of the Beloved Disciple, we concentrate on the theological content of the interpersonal relationship between Jesus and a model disciple. The analysis of the following *Beloved Disciple texts* of the Fourth Gospel will highlight the nature of their intimate relationship.

A. Jn 13,21-30

In Jn 13,21-30 one sees the first explicit introduction of the Beloved Disciple where the Evangelist dramatically pictures the relationship between Jesus and the Beloved Disciple. The scope of this text is not the presentation of the theme of betrayal, but the intimate friendship of the beloved one. [28] The author of the Gospel in his presentation of the Last Supper traditions seems to be pre-occupied with the problem of true and false discipleship. [29] By presenting the Beloved Disciple in this context the Evangelist provides a sharp antithesis between an ideal disciple and an infidel,

---

"Qumran and the Origin of the Fourth Gospel", *NT* 4 (1960) 6-25.

[27] Cf. MINEAR, *The Beloved Disciple*, 107f.

[28] Cf. SEGALLA, *Il discepolo che Gesù amava*, 225.

[29] Cf. LINDARS, *John*, 457; BARRETT, *St. John*, 438.

between betrayal and love.[30] The Beloved disciple in the text under consideration seems superior to Peter due to the exceptional closeness and intimacy which he enjoys with Jesus. But more than contradictory their roles are complementary if understood respectively.[31] In this short treatment of the present pericope we will concentrate on the expressions of friendship between Jesus and the Beloved Disciple as far as they contribute to the understanding of the true nature of the Jesus-disciple friendship.

1. Delimitation of the Text

With regard to the delimitation of the text in question one cannot ignore its wide context with the remote opening in 13, 1-3, where there is the introduction of the characters (Jesus, "His own" and Judas), and their interaction till v. 30, where Judas disappears from the scene.[32] The consideration of vv.1-30 as a unit can be

---

[30] Cf. PANIMOLLE, *Giovanni*, Vol III, 192. According to Quast, "the Evangelist has purposely refrained from presenting the Beloved Disciple before in order to contrast noticeably the Beloved Disciple with Judas": QUAST, *Beloved Disciple*, 57. According to Lindars the Beloved Disciple in our text is "all that Judas is not": LINDARS, *John*, 458; cf. also BROWN, *John*, Vol II, 577.

[31] Cf. QUAST, *Beloved Disciple*, 69, where he writes: "They do reflect different and supplementary roles used in harmony to be supporting roles in the greater drama of the unfolding hour of Jesus". According to Brown the Beloved Disciple is presented by giving due emphasis on his closeness to Jesus and on his friendship with Peter: Cf. BROWN, *John*, Vol II, 577.

[32] The unity of persons is one of the criteria which determines the literary unity of the pericope. Cf. MLAKUZHYIL, *The Christocentric Structure*, 114. Kügler considers this disappearance of Judas in v.30 as the concluding-mark of the pericope. Cf. KÜGLER, *Der Jünger, den Jesus liebte*, 87; SCHNACKENBURG, *St. John*, Vol III, 6. For a detailed consideration of the unity of the section 13,1-30 cf. G. RICHTER, *Die Fusswaschung im Johannesevangelium. Geschichte ihrer Deutung* (Regensburg 1967) 285-320.

justified on the basis of the *unity of time*, viz. the context of the feast of passover and the special reference to the meal in v.2 which extends till v.30.[33]

In spite of the above said wide context one can see the opening of a new scene within the pericope (13,1-30) in v.21 especially with the taking the meals and the betrayal-theme. [34] The Greek expression ταῦτα εἰπὼν in v.21 marks the opening of the scene (cf. also 9,6; 11,43; 18,1). So also in the new scene there is a *thematic change* from foot-washing to the betrayal of Judas. The pericope ends with v.30[35] because in the following verses there is an explicit literary change with a small hymn (vv.31-32) and the introduction of the new commandment of love (vv.33-35). In this subsection of the pericope (vv.21-30) are certain concrete expressions of friendship between Jesus and the Beloved Disciple which will be taken into consideration in the context of the present study.

---

[33] The following section of the last discourse of Jesus need not be in the context of a meal. After v.30 there is no mention of the meal.

[34] Cf. KÜGLER, *Der Jünger, den Jesus liebte*, 163, where he writes: "Mit v.21 beginnt eine neue Szene, die freilich durch die Mahlsituation und die Verratsthematik mit dem Vorhergehenden Verbunden ist".

[35] With regard to the concluding line of the pericope there are difference of opinion among the scholars. For instance Segalla argues for a pericope that extends from v.1 to v.35 and his arguments are mainly based on the inclusions between 13,1 and 13,34-35 (ἀγαπάω/ ἀγάπη) and between 13,3 and 13,33 (ὑπάγω): Cf. SEGALLA, *Giovanni*, 362-363.

2. The Literary Genre

This subsection of the Fourth Gospel (13,21-30) is very dramatic [36] in style and different from the preceding and following subsections, where one sees a different literary genre, i.e. direct discourse. [37] The pericope in question can be considered a *narrative interwoven with dialogue and actions.* [38] As the literary style suggests there are mainly words and deeds of Jesus and the Beloved Disciple which express their interpersonal relationship. In the attempt to analyze the real nature of the friendship between Jesus and the Beloved disciple one has to consider the expressions of friendship in their words and deeds in the light of the Evangelist's presentation.

---

[36] According to Segalla this pericope is "dialogo drammatico": SEGALLA, *Il discepolo che Gesù amava*, 225.

[37] In the Fourth Gospel chapters 13-16 in general have a special literary genre including *narratives ,dialogues and discourses*: Cf. MLAKUZHYIL, *The Christocentric Structure*, 221.

[38] Dialogue and actions can be understood as words and deeds which are effective means of expressing interpersonal relationship. We have already analyzed the close friendship between Jesus and the Bethany family in the light of their words and deeds.

3. The Expressions of Friendship Between Jesus and the Beloved Disciple

a. The disciple, whom Jesus loved

εἷς ἐκ τῶν μαθητῶν αὐτοῦ, ὃν ἠγάπα ὁ Ἰησοῦς (v.23)

In the Fourth Gospel one of Jesus' disciples[39] is presented anonymously, but always with an attribute which expresses the special intimacy and relationship between them. In the present text he is unnamed but characterized as ὃν ἠγάπα ὁ Ἰησοῦς (whom Jesus loved), a title elsewhere in the Fourth Gospel and hence having representative and symbolic nature.[40] This title seems to be a characteristic one which expresses the particular feature of that disciple. The terminology employed here can be understood as the same used elsewhere in the Fourth Gospel to illustrate the close relationship between Jesus and the Father (cf. Jn 3,35; 10,17; 15,9;

---

[39] The term μαθητής (disciple) has a wider meaning in the Fourth Gospel as it need not be necessarily limited to one of the Twelve. But in the light of the internal evidences and by considering the Synoptic references (cf. Mk 14,17; Lk 22,14) Bernard understands the expression "one of his disciples" as one of the Twelve: Cf. BERNARD, *St. John*, Vol II, 470-471.

[40] Cf. QUAST, *Beloved Disciple*, 57. In Jn 13,1 Jesus' love towards His disciples is clearly mentioned. Against such a background the title, "the disciple whom Jesus loved" has a representative value: Cf. I. DE LA POTTERIE, "Il discepolo che Gesù amava", in: L. PADOVESE (ed.), *Atti del I Simposio di Efeso su S. Giovanni Apostolo* (Roma 1991) 47-48.

17,23-24.26).[41] So, the relationship between Jesus and the Beloved Disciple is of the same grade as that of the relationship between Jesus and the Father.[42]

Jesus' definite expression of love towards the Beloved Disciple is something deeper than the general expression of His love towards "His own" (13,1). In the light of the expression, "whom Jesus loved", one can conclude that the Beloved Disciple enjoyed a special place among other disciples in the aspect of relationship with Jesus.[43] True discipleship is based on love; and the Beloved Disciple who enjoys the primacy of love becomes the ideal of every disciple.[44] Moreover the expression sheds light on Jesus' initiative in their love-relationship. In short, the attribute of the particular disciple as *one whom Jesus loved* brings out the reality and possibility of a genuine friendship between Jesus and an authentic Christian disciple.

---

[41] Cf. GUNTHER, *The Beloved Disciple*, 129. He considers the ideal relationship between Jesus and the Beloved Disciple a model for the other disciples' relationship with the Father and the Son.

[42] Kragerud writes: "As Christ is the one whom God loves par excellence (3:35; 5,20; 10,17; cf. 17,23.24.26),... the beloved disciple stands in the same relation to Christ as Christ to God; as Christ in a special sense the ἀγαπητός of God, so the beloved disciple is portrayed as the ἀγαπητός of Christ in a special way": KRAGERUD, *Der Lieblingsjünger*, 72 (translation by GUNTHER, *The Beloved Disciple*, 129); cf. also LORENZEN, *Der Lieblingsjünger*, 86; A. DAUER, *die Passionsgeshichte im Johannesevangelium. Eine traditionsgeschichtliche und theologische Untersuchung zu Joh 18,1-19,30* (München 1972) 319.

[43] Cf. KÜGLER, *Der Jünger, den Jesus liebte*, 146.

[44] Cf. P.J. HARTIN, "The Role of Peter in the Fourth Gospel", *Neot* 24,1 (1990) 53.

b. The disciple, who is physically close to Jesus
... ἦν ἀνακείμενος ἐν τῷ κόλπῳ τοῦ Ἰησοῦ (v.23)

The Evangelist, by using certain theologically rich terminology, describes the Beloved Disciple's physical closeness with Jesus showing the proximity and intimacy between Jesus and the Beloved Disciple.[45] The expression ἀνακείμενος ἐν τῷ κόλπῳ (lying on the breast)[46] in the particular context of the last supper can be understood in the light of the Hellenistic custom of a formal meal, especially of the Passover meal. Lindars refers to the passover Haggadah which states: 'On all other nights we eat and drink either sitting or reclining, but on this night we all recline'.[47] In the Passover meal there is a practice of lying on the left elbow. If we consider the last supper as a passover meal we see the relevance of

---

[45] Cf. QUAST, *Beloved Disciple*, 57; LINDARS, *John*, 458.

[46] Κόλπος literally means *bosom* (cf.Jn 1,18). The expression, ἦν ἀνακείμενος ἐν τῷ κόλπῳ does not necessarily mean a physical touching on the chest. It can be better explained by the positions of the participants in a festive meal. According to this arrangement the head of the one who sits at the left of the middle man (Jesus) was about chest high: Cf. HÄNCHEN, *John*, 110; It can even mean a part of the tunic and not a part of the body (cf. Lk 6,38). In the context of a meal in the religious context κόλπος designates 'the place of the guest of honour' and can be understood figuratively as an expression of an interior relationship. Meyer writes: " κόλπος (bosom) symbolizes the love and fellowship in a family or religious community or at the feast of the blessed": R. MEYER, κόλπος, *TDNT* III, 824. But this cannot be merely taken as a symbolic expression of their relationship, since there is a second reference of this physical position providing an occasion to the Beloved Disciple to ask Jesus of his betrayer (cf.v.25). Thus it can have a secondary semantic meaning: Cf.KÜGLER, *Der Jünger, den Jesus liebte*, 146.

[47] Cf. LINDARS, *John*, 458.

such a position, viz. the Beloved Disciple, as a favoured person would be at Jesus' right[48] and could bend his head back close to Jesus' breast.[49]

The Greek verb ἀνάκειμαι literally means "lie"or "recline". In a meal context it means "sitting at table" (cf. Lk 22,27). Together with ἐν τῷ κόλπῳ it alludes to the physical closeness of two persons. Therefore, in the context of the meal as narrated in the pericope in question the expression "reclining on Jesus' bosom" can be understood as "close to Jesus at table". Even though the expression literally alludes to a physical closeness between Jesus and the Beloved Disciple at the table, it can also be understood especially against the background of the symbolic presentation of the Fourth Gospel.[50] Hence, the expression ἐν τῷ κόλπῳ τοῦ Ἰησοῦ in 13,23 seems to be a deliberate allusion to Jn 1,18 where Jesus' relation to

---

[48] Why he occupied such a place of honour is a disputable question: Cf. BERNARD, St. John, Vol II, 471; According to some authors this position of the Beloved Disciple was no honourary position in the tradition: Cf. HÄNCHEN, John, 461; BARRETT, St. John, 446. However, Barrett considers the place occupied by the Beloved Disciple was one of a trusted friend.

[49] Cf. LINDARS, John, 458.

[50] Cf. BROWN, John, Vol II, 573f.;DE LA POTTERIE, Il discepolo che Gesù amava, 44.

the Father is described as εἰς τὸν κόλπον τοῦ πατρὸς (in the bosom of the Father).[51] In both cases an intimate communion is depicted by the use of κόλπος.[52]

In this context one can assume some sort of parallelism between the intimacy and relationship of the Father and the Son and that of the Beloved Disciple and Jesus.[53] Such an assumption is based on two reasons: Jesus was the beloved of the Father and Jesus came from the bosom of the Father. Such a spiritual and physical relationship is evident also in the relationship between Jesus and the Beloved Disciple. The parallelism can be seen also in the aspect of the revelatory role. In the context of Johannine usage κόλπος

---

[51] Cf. KÜGLER, *Der Jünger, den Jesus liebte*, 145-146; DE LA POTTERIE, *Il discepolo che Gesù amava*, 48; D.L. BARTLETT, "John 13:21-30", *Int* 43 (1989) 394; HARTIN, *The Role of Peter*, 53. By analyzing the term κόλπος and the use of the particle εἰς Moloney translates this expression in Jn 1,18 as 'turned towards the Father'. On the basis of the different prepositions (εἰς and ἐν) used with κόλπος in 1,18 and 13,23 consecutively he distinguishes the mode of relationship between the Father and Son, and Jesus and the Beloved Disciple. In 1,18 the relationship between the Father and the Son is dynamic, whereas in 13,28 this dynamic relationship is not evident. But he admits a parallelism between these texts since both texts express the idea of closeness: Cf. F.J. MOLONEY, "Jn 1,18: 'In the Bosom of' or 'Turned towards' the Father ?", *AusBR* 31 (1983) 64-66.

[52] About this Gunther writes: "As a close confidant he was more spiritually akin to Jesus rather than any other. As the only begotten Son was in the bosom of the Father (1,18, cf.14), so the beloved disciple lay on the bosom of the Son": GUNTHER, *The Beloved Disciple*, 129.

[53] Cf. QUAST, *Beloved Disciple*, 58; BROWN, *John*, Vol II, 577; BARRETT, *St. John*, 446; KRAGERUD, *Der Lieblingsjünger*, 73; A. DAUER, "Das Wort des Gekreuzigten an seine Mutter und den 'Jünger, den Jesus liebte' : Eine Traditionsgeschichte und theologische Untersuchung zu Joh. 19,25-27", *BZ* 11 (Teil I) 237; KÜGLER, *Der Jünger, den Jesus liebte*, 147, where Kügler proposes the following arguments to accept this analogy between the relation of Jesus and the Beloved Disciple and that of the Father and the Son: a) The term κόλπος is used by the Fourth Evangelist only in 1,18 and 13,23. b) The first occurrence is in the prologue section which sheds light on certain texts in the following section of the Gospel. c) The term κόλπος is used in both texts to explain the love-relationship.

denotes Jesus' revelatory role explicitly $(1,18)^{54}$ and the Beloved Disciple's implicitly $(13, 23-25)$.[55] Thus the relationship between Jesus and the Beloved Disciple is analogous to the relationship between the Father and the Son.

The physical proximity of the Beloved Disciple to Jesus as described in the pericope shows the closest relationship between them.[56] The terms κόλπος and στῆθος in three Johannine usages $(13,23.25; 21,20)^{57}$ connote "closeness to Jesus..., affection, familiarity, trust, intimacy of shared knowledge and intention, permanent friendship."[58] In short, the Johannine presentation of the

---

[54] John Calvin writes, "Men are said to admit to their bosom those to whom they communicate all their secrets. The breast is the seat of counsel. He therefore teaches that the Son knows the most hidden secrets of the Father": J. CALVIN, *The Gospel According to St. John* (New York 1959) 26. St. Thomas considers κόλπος as the seat of divine secrets: Cf. THOMAS, *Evangelium S. Ioannis*, § 1804.

[55] It is implicit, because we do not see here a communication of the revelation which the Beloved Disciple receives from Jesus. Rather there is a lack of communication (cf.13,28). But in the context of the whole Gospel the Beloved Disciple is presented as one who enjoys a special revelatory role. Many scholars, considering the term κόλπος in the present text, attribute a special revelatory role to the Beloved Disciple: Cf. LORENZEN, *Der Lieblingsjünger*, 41; MINEAR, *The Beloved Disciple*, 114-117; ROLOFF, *Lieblingsjünger*, 138; J.N. SANDERS & B.A. MASTIN, *A Commentary on the Gospel according to St. John* (London 1968) 313, n.1; A. JAUBERT, *Approches de l'Evangile de Jean* (Paris 1976) 43-45.

[56] NEB translated the terms κόλπος (v.23) and στῆθος (v.25; 21,20) as *close to Jesus*.

[57] In Jn 13,23 κόλπος is used, whereas in v.25 and in 21,20 στῆθος is used.

[58] MINEAR, *The Beloved Disciple*, 114; cf. also BARRETT, *St. John*, 446; N.E. JOHNSON, "The Beloved Disciple and the Fourth Gospel", *CQR* 167 (1966) 281. In this connection Quast writes: "...even the physical proximity of the Beloved Disciple to Jesus is enough to enable one to discern the intended message of the Evangelist. It certainly is not reading too much into the description to conclude that the evangelist is here conveying the 'notion of tender relationship' by the use of this phrase as this is general metaphorical use of the phrase throughout the Biblical literature. The Beloved Disciple is in the closest relationship to Jesus": QUAST,

Beloved disciple as one *lying close to the breast (bosom) of Jesus* is a theologically rich expression which highlights the reciprocal dimension of their intimacy and friendship.

c. The disciple, who asks Jesus about His fate

" ἀναπεσὼν οὖν ἐκεῖνος οὕτως ἐπὶ τὸ στῆθος τοῦ Ἰησοῦ λέγει αὐτῷ· Κύριε, τίς ἐστιν" (v.25)

The question: Κύριε τίς ἐστιν; must be understood in the context of the entire pericope. In v.21 Jesus foretells His fate which is to be determined by one of his beloved ("his own": 13,1). It is all the disciples' interest (v.22) and Peter's beckoning (v.24)[59] which prompt the Beloved Disciple to put a very personal question to Jesus. In close intimacy illustrated in v.25 he asks Jesus: Κύριε, τίς ἐστιν;. The Beloved Disciple himself does not know who the

---

Beloved Disciple, 59.

[59] Regarding Peter's words to the Beloved Disciple (v.24) there are variant readings: 1)...πυθέσθαι τίς ἂν εἴη περὶ οὗ λέγει (A D W Γ Δ Θ and some Syriac versions); 2)...καὶ λέγει αὐτῷ, εἰπὲ τίς ἐστιν περὶ οὗ λέγει (B C L 068. 33. 892. *pc* (lat)...). Here εἰπέ is difficult to be translated. RSV translated it as "tell us..." (but not accurate in the context). Abbott translated it as "say" (to Jesus) or "ask" (Him): Cf. ABBOTT, *Johannine Vocabulary*, § 1359. Since the majority of the ancient textual witnesses support the first reading we consider it as superior and more original: Cf. METZGER, *Textual Commentary*, 240-241; BERNARD, *St. John*, Vol II, 472. Unlike in the Synoptic Gospels the Fourth Evangelist introduces a mediation to know of whom Jesus speaks. It seems to be relevant in the context of the present pericope where the Beloved Disciple is presented as one in close relationship with Jesus. For further details cf. BERNARD, *St. John*, Vol II, 472; QUAST, *Beloved Disciple*, 60.

betrayer is; rather he is very close to Jesus to enquire Him about an important matter. [60]

The position [61] of the Beloved Disciple presented in v.25 is quite convenient to converse with Jesus. In this context the Greek verb ἀναπίπτω means "to lean" or "to lean back" to speak with Jesus, sitting at the left side of the Beloved Disciple. [62] It need not indicate a physical touch or a state of rest on the chest of Jesus, but a turning back in a familiar way [63] to speak with Him. The physical closeness once again expresses the symbolic meaning of their interpersonal relationship. Roloff highlights the "co-relation" of love and knowledge in the Fourth Gospel, [64] evident in the relationship between Jesus and the Beloved Disciple in the Evangelist's presentation. In the pericope under consideration the Beloved Disciple is presented in close relationship with Jesus and hence he is entitled to share the innermost intimate knowledge of Jesus. The symbolic expression *lying close to the breast of Jesus* "suggests intimacy of vision and knowledge that qualifies a person to mediate divine grace and truth". [65]

---

[60] According to Hawkin the Beloved Disciple has not a special knowledge of Jesus, but he enjoys a special intimacy and relationship with Jesus: Cf. D.J. HAWKIN, "The Function of the Beloved Disciple Motif in the Johannine Redaction", *LavThéolPhil* 33 (1977) 143; cf. also QUAST, *Beloved Disciple*, 63.

[61] The position of the Beloved Disciple as one *lying close to the breast of Jesus* is repeated in v.25 with some terminological modification. Instead of κόλπος (bosom) στῆθος (breast) is used here.

[62] Cf. supra, pp. 257-258.

[63] Cf. D. MOLLATT & F.M. BRAUN, *L'évangile et les épitres de saint Jean* (2nd ed.) [La sainte Bible de Jerusalem] (Paris 1960) 151, n. b).

[64] Cf. ROLOFF, *Lieblingsjünger*, 137.

[65] MINEAR, *The Beloved Disciple*, 117, n.5.

In the Beloved Disciple's question regarding the identity of the traitor one can see his growing interest in the fate of his Master. In this respect the Beloved Disciple symbolizes "the ideal disciple".[66] The addressing of Jesus as Κύριε (Lord) [67] is noteworthy as it sheds light on the superiority of Jesus. So also through the question the Beloved Disciple indirectly admits Jesus' pre-knowledge regarding the traitor. Thus the superiority of Jesus is portrayed as an essential element in their interpersonal relationship.

In the dramatic scene of the Last Supper the Fourth Evangelist presents not only Jesus' love and friendship with the Beloved Disciple but also that disciple's intimacy and deep relationship with Jesus. The Beloved Disciple's intimacy was not something sentimental but based on deep love, trust and fidelity to his Master. This will be clearer in the light of the other Beloved Disciple texts.[68]

d. The disciple, to whom Jesus reveals His fate
ἀποκρίνεται ὁ Ἰησοῦς · ἐκεῖνός ἐστιν ...(v.26)

Revelation and sharing of knowledge are characteristics of friendship in the Johannine teaching (cf. Jn 15,15). In the context of the Last Supper, as an answer to the Beloved Disciple's

---

[66] LINDARS, *John*, 34.

[67] This Christological title need not be taken in this context as a post-resurrectional one. In the context of an expressed intimacy between Jesus and the Beloved Disciple this title shows the real nature of their friendship where there is always place for the superiority of Jesus.

[68] Cf. PANIMOLLE, *Giovanni*, Vol III, 196.

enthusiastic question Jesus reveals His betrayer's identity.[69] Jesus' revelation shows His predilection for the Beloved Disciple and the disciple's trustful nature,[70] verified in the course of the pericope (cf. v.28).[71] Jesus' revelation to the Beloved Disciple can be considered as a special privilege given to him and as a sign of their interpersonal relationship.

The Evangelist has a Christological motive when he puts into the mouth of Jesus the answer regarding His betrayal.[72] Jesus is the Lord of history, and as a divine person He knows future events. Therefore, in the interpersonal relationship between Jesus and the Beloved Disciple the superiority of Jesus is presupposed and highlighted. Judas' betrayal is foretold in the concrete context of an intimacy[73] which expresses the depth of the close relationship between Jesus and the Beloved Disciple. Thus even in Jesus' answer to the Beloved Disciple's question their intimacy and friendship are manifested.

So far we have been trying to understand the special characteristics of the expressions of friendship between Jesus and the Beloved Disciple in the Johannine Last Supper tradition. In the Evangelist's presentation of the Beloved Disciple's designation and position and in the dialogue between Jesus and the Beloved Disciple

---

[69] Cf. R. SCHNACKENBURG, "Der Jünger, den Jesus liebte", *EKK* 2 (1970) 100-102.

[70] Cf. PANIMOLLE, *Giovanni*, Vol. III, 190.

[71] The general expression οὐδεὶς ἔγνω in v.28 can be understood with an exception of the Beloved Disciple. The use of such expressions without a general connotation is Johannine style: Cf. supra, p. 55, n.59.

[72] Cf. SCHNACKENBURG, *St. John*, Vol III, 30.

[73] Dipping of the morsel in the common cup was a token of intimacy (Cf. Ruth 2,14) in the Middle-East: Cf. BERNARD, *St. John*, Vol II, 473.

one notices the depth and reciprocity of their friendship.[74] Moreover the whole context of the pericope is characterized by a strong dramatic tension between intimacy and hatred. Against such a background one can understand the real meaning of the disciple's friendship with Jesus.

B. Jn 19,25-27

The Beloved Disciple's second explicit appearance is in the central part of the crucifixion scene together with certain important persons in salvation history, viz. Jesus, His mother and a group of women who were His followers. Different from the Synoptic presentation (Mk 15,40f.; Mt 27,55f.; Lk 23,49) the Fourth Evangelist's presentation of the crucifixion scene is unique for certain theological motives.[75] The presentation of the Beloved Disciple in the pericope and the theological motive behind this presentation, expressed in the words and deeds of the characters, are

---

[74] Cf. GUNTHER, *The Beloved Disciple*, 129, where he writes: "The beloved disciple's location, designation and keeping secret the answer to a private question indicate that he was on particulary close terms with Jesus". Cf. also B. OLSSON, *Structure and Meaning in the Fourth Gospel* (Lund 1974) 273; ROLOFF, *Lieblingsjünger*, 138; LORENZEN, *Der Lieblingsjünger*, 83.87; DAUER, *Die Passionsgeschichte im Johannesevangelium*, 319.

[75] The characters mentioned in the Synoptic texts are not the same as in the Fourth Gospel. The mention of Mary as *mother of Jesus* and the presentation of the Beloved Disciple here are peculiar to the Fourth Gospel. While the Synoptics present the women as standing far away, the Fourth Evangelist presents them as standing by the cross of Jesus. Many authors find a theological and symbolic significance behind the Johannine account (vv.25-27). Cf. BULTMANN, *John*, 673ff.; LOISY, *Quatrième évangile*, 488. Brown writes: "A non-theological interpretation would make this episode a misfit amid the highly symbolic episodes that surround it in the crucifixion narrative": BROWN, *John*, Vol II, 923. For certain theological interpretations of the pericope cf. SCHNACKENBURG, *St. John*, Vol III, 279ff.

the points of our interest in view of extrapolating the nature and depth of the friendship between Jesus and the Beloved Disciple.

1. Delimitation of the Text

The text under consideration is a part of the pericope (19,16b-37)[76] which deals with Jesus' death on the cross. Within the context of the pericope, vv. 25-27 is an isolated episode which separates itself from the casting lots for Jesus' clothes (vv. 23-24) and Jesus' death on the cross (vv. 28-30).[77] The Greek construction μὲν ...δέ (vv. 24c and 25a) contrasts the actions of two groups of people and introduces a new scene, where there is a sudden *shift of the characters*, i.e. from the soldiers to the followers of Jesus. In v.25 there is the introduction of a group of pious women together with Jesus' mother and in v.26 the appearance of the Beloved Disciple.

In v.28, with the Greek expression μετὰ τοῦτο the Evangelist shows a *temporal shift* and calls back the readers' attention to the former scene of crucifixion. Here the scene separates itself from

---

[76] Mlakuzhyil proposes the end of this pericope in v.42 by considering the unity of the crucifixion, death and burial of the king of the Jews on Golgotha: Cf. MLAKUZHYIL, *The Christocentric Structure*, 234-235. But since one can consider the burial of Jesus as a separate scene in the light of the literary devices, we would like to delimit the pericope with v.37.

[77] About the isolated nature of the episode Dodd writes: "It is to be observed that this episode has two features which set it apart: it breaks the unities of time and place, since we are obliged for a moment to leave the scene of Golgotha on Good Friday afternoon and place ourselves at the home of the Beloved Disciple in the time following; and it shows an interest in the subsequent fortunes of subordinate characters": DODD, *Historical Tradition*, 127f.

v.27 and gives the preceding scene an isolated unity.[78] In vv. 28-
30 Jesus' last words and His death are narrated, denoting a *thematic
shift* from that of Jesus' last words to His mother and the Beloved
Disciple (vv. 25-27) to the theme of completing His salvific work by
giving up His spirit (vv. 28-30). In the light of the above mentioned
arguments we would like to deal with vv. 25-27 as an independent
literary unity.

2. The Literary Genre

The pericope under consideration is a part of the famous *passion
- death - and Resurrection* narrative of the Fourth Gospel. Such a
narrative is interwoven with monologues, dialogues and dramatic
scenes. The present text (vv.25-27) is a *narrative* in style, but to give
a dramatic effect to the scene the Evangelist employs *the form of a
direct speech* from Jesus' mouth. Here there is no dialogue because
one hears only the words of Jesus in direct speech, while the
response to Jesus' words is translated in deeds on the part of the
addressee. Such a literary style helps the reader to understand the
profound meaning of the text.[79]

---

[78] But Kügler finds a connection between vv. 25-27 and 28-30. He says that
μετὰ τοῦτο in v.28, in spite of indicating a new beginning, refers also back to the
preceding section. He notices a definite change of characters and place with v.31:
KÜGLER, *Der Jünger, den Jesus liebte*, 233.

[79] This literary style of the text helps the reader to understand the special nature
of divine - human friendship, where the superiority of Jesus is always respected.

3. **The Expressions of Friendship Between Jesus and the Beloved Disciple**

a. **The disciple, who is present at Calvary**

Ἰησοῦς οὖν ἰδὼν τὴν μητέρα καὶ τὸν μαθητὴν παρεστῶτα ὅν ἠγάπα (26a)

In the historical event of Jesus' crucifixion the Beloved Disciple is presented together with the mother of Jesus and a group of women, who were definite historical persons.[80] The Evangelist presents the mother of Jesus and the other women in the crucifixion scene as those *standing by the cross of Jesus* (Εἰστήκεισαν παρὰ τῷ σταυρῷ τοῦ Ἰησοῦ).[81] The Beloved Disciple is presented as one who stands together (παρεστῶτα) with Jesus' mother,[82] who stands by the cross of Jesus. Accordingly one can legitimately conclude that the Beloved Disciple's position was also nearby Jesus' cross. Such a position provides Jesus the possibility for addressing both His mother and the Beloved Disciple.

The position of standing *by the cross* (παρὰ τῷ σταυρῷ) and looking on at a discrete distance had a traditional connotation in the

---

[80] The appearance of the Beloved Disciple together with the historical figures affirms the historicity of that disciple. Some authors reduce him merely to a symbolic figure: Cf. supra, p. 249, n. 17. But, the anonymity of the Beloved Disciple and the mother of Jesus is deliberate in the Evangelists's programme as it highlights their representative role and the importance of their function: Cf. DE LA POTTERIE, *Il discepolo che Gesù amava*, 51.

[81] The Synoptic account is different where the women are presented as *looking from far away* (ἀπὸ μακρόθεν).

[82] The position of the Beloved Disciple as standing with Jesus' mother is, according to Bernard, to show his sympathy to her at the death of her Beloved Son: Cf. BERNARD, *St. John*, Vol II, 633. Apart from the synoptic tradition we see here the special interest of the Fourth Evangelist to present the Beloved Disciple in a very special way in an important moment of Jesus' life.

light of the passion psalms.[83] Against such a historical background the Beloved Disciple's position of *standing by the cross of Jesus* (with the mother of Jesus)[84] can be understood as an expression of his friendship with the crucified and as his participation in the paschal mystery of Jesus.[85] The personal presence of the Beloved Disciple at the crucifixion scene made him an authentic witness of Jesus' salvific death on the cross (19,35).[86] The Beloved Disciple's personal presence at the salvific death of Jesus and his witnessing of the same are genuine expressions of their friendship.

---

[83] DODD, *Historical Tradition*, 126, where Dodd writes: "The picture therefore, of the *friends* of the crucified standing at a distance is a part of the traditional presentation of the Passion of Christ in terms of the Righteous Sufferer of the Psalms". (Italics mine); cf. also LINDARS, *John*, 578.

[84] In the text under consideration the Beloved Disciple is not presented as one who stands by the cross of Jesus. But his presence near the mother of Jesus who stands by the cross logically denotes his nearness to the cross.

[85] The Beloved disciple's personal presence and participation in the important events are evident in the Beloved Disciple texts. The present text deals with Jesus' passion and salvific death on the cross where the Beloved Disciple is personally present.

[86] Some authors find it difficult to admit Jn 19,35 as a Beloved Disciple text. The difficulty arises in the context of the attempt to identify the Beloved Disciple as the author of the Fourth Gospel supposed to have been written much later. If one takes the testimony of the Beloved Disciple only as the source of the Fourth Gospel tradition, then there is no difficulty in identifying this witness with the Beloved Disciple, present at the crucifixion scene.

b. **The disciple, to whom Jesus entrusts His mother**
Ἰησοῦς λέγει· ἴδε ὁ υἱός σου ...ἴδε[87] ἡ μήτηρ σου (vv.26-27)

At the crucial moment of His death Jesus wishes to entrust His mother to one who can substitute Him in relation to His mother - "in lieu of Jesus himself".[88] Jesus finds this figure only in one beloved of Him and having the essential qualities necessary for substituting Him.[89] By entrusting His mother to the care of His Beloved Disciple Jesus shows His special and intimate relationship with that disciple.[90] Moreover, Jesus' trust in His Beloved Disciple is clearly manifested in this substitutive role. Such a deep trust is an essential element of friendship.

When Jesus says γύναι, ἴδε ὁ υἱός σου to His mother and ἴδε ἡ μήτηρ σου to His Beloved Disciple,[91] He assumes a special relationship between Mary and the Beloved Disciple, similar to the already existing relationship between Jesus and Mary. The words of Jesus heighten the stature of the Beloved Disciple to His

---

[87] With regard to this particle there are two different readings: ἴδε (ℵ B L N W Θ Ψ f¹³ 33 al); ἰδού (A Dˢ 054 f¹...). Since ἴδε is a favourite expression of the Fourth Evangelist, in the light of external and internal evidences we take the reading with ἴδε as the original. Cf. BERNARD, St. John, Vol II, 632.

[88] MINEAR, The Beloved Disciple, 119; cf. also J.F. O' GRADY, "The Role of the Beloved Disciple", BTB 9 (1979) 61.

[89] Cf. KÜGLER, Der Jünger, den Jesus liebte, 254.

[90] Dauer says, "Durch diesem Auftrag hat Jesus den Jünger wiederum vor allen anderen Jünger ausgezeichnet und ihm sein besonderes Vertrauen erwiesen": DAUER, Das Wort des Gekreuzigten, Teil II, 86.

[91] These words of Jesus can be understood as a double dimensional adoption-formula, because both, His mother and the Beloved Disciple are expected to accept mutually.

brother[92] In this context the Beloved Disciple is closely identified with Jesus so as to be, in effect, His "alter ego".[93]

The last words of Jesus from the cross to His Beloved Disciple must be understood as a responsibility entrusted to him rather than a favour which he obtains. The Beloved Disciple's designation as a son to Jesus' mother implies two levels of meaning. In the first level the Beloved Disciple was entrusted with all the duties of taking care of and giving protection to Jesus' mother. In the second level it has a meaning which surpasses the care-taking role of the Beloved Disciple and entrusts him with the duty of spiritual acceptance of Jesus' mother as his own mother.[94] The words of Jesus to His mother and to His Beloved Disciple have more the nature of a command rather than of a simple suggestion.[95] Such a command implies the superiority and Lordship of Jesus, essential aspects of Jesus' intimacy and friendship with His own.[96] The mother of Jesus and the Beloved Disciple have an identity in relation with Jesus in

---

[92] It is only after His resurrection Jesus calls the disciples as brethren (cf. Jn 20,17). But the Beloved Disciple is already given such a status. This status of the Beloved Disciple presupposes his deep faith in Jesus. For the Evangelist the friends and brethren of Jesus are those who believe in Him: Cf. DAUER, *Das Wort des Gekreuzigten*, Teil II, 82-83; cf. also LORENZEN, *Der Lieblingsjünger*, 84.

[93] E. L. TITUS, *The Message of the Fourth Gospel* (New York 1957) 230.

[94] The second level meaning is clear in the response of the Beloved Disciple in v.27b, which will be discussed later.

[95] Bernard writes: "The words "Woman, behold thy son ...behold thy mother" are more than a mere commendation or suggestion from a dying friend. They convey a command from Him who was, to Mary, as well as to John, Master and Lord": BERNARD, *St. John*, Vol II, 633.

[96] The superiority of Jesus is well expressed in the pericope even through the use of the verbs which denote mainly Jesus' words or deeds. The mother of Jesus and the Beloved Disciple seem to be passive recipients: Cf. KÜGLER, *Der Jünger, den Jesus liebte*, 245-246.

the sense that they are referred to as "Jesus' mother" and as "the disciple, whom Jesus loved".[97] Even in the expressions "the disciple, whom Jesus loved" and "behold your son" the interpersonal relationship and friendship between Jesus and the Beloved Disciple are literarily brought out. The stylistic presentation of these verses is structurally shown by De la Potterie [98] as follows:

V. 25 ἡ μήτηρ <u>αὐτοῦ</u> ... τῆς μητρὸς <u>αὐτοῦ</u>
V. 26 τὴν μητέρα ... τῇ μητρί ...
V. 27 ἡ μήτηρ <u>σου</u> ... αὐτὴν ...

This structure illustrates an inclusion between ἡ μήτηρ αὐτοῦ (v.25) and αὐτήν (v.27), both referring to the mother of Jesus. The Beloved Disciple's role of substituting Jesus is evident in the text as the Evangelist changes the possessive pronoun from αὐτοῦ (Jesus') in v.25 to σου (the Beloved Disciple's) in v.27a. Thus the Beloved Disciple is presented as the substitute of Jesus in his relation to His mother. In sum, the words of Jesus from the cross to His mother and to His Beloved Disciple in their ultimate analysis explicate the true nature of Jesus' friendship with that disciple.

In the pericope under consideration there is also the aspect of revelation, stylistically expressed by the Evangelist. In vv.26-27 one can see key expressions of the typical Johannine revelation formula: ἰδών (vision of a person) ... λέγει (an expression of saying) ... ἴδε

---

[97] Regarding this Chevallier writes: "qu'ils ne possèdent pas d'autre identité que leur relation personnelle à Jesus": M.A. CHEVALLIER, "La fondation de "l'Eglise" dans le quatrième évangile: Jn 19,25-30", *ÉTR* 58 (1983) 345.

[98] Cf. I. DE LA POTTERIE, "Das Wort Jesu, 'Siehe, deine Mutter' und die Annahme der Mutter durch den Jünger (Joh 19,27b)", *Neues Testament und Kirche* (Herausgegeben von Joachim Gnilka) (Freiburg 1974) 216.

(opening of the revelation with the particle 'behold').[99] The revelation of Jesus given to the Beloved Disciple as a representative of all Christian disciples regarding the universal motherhood of Mary is also an explicit expression of their friendship (cf. Jn 15,15).[100]

c. The disciple, who receives the mother of Jesus

ἀπ᾽ ἐκείνης τῆς ὥρας ἔλαβεν ὁ μαθητὴς αὐτὴν εἰς τὰ ἴδια (v.27b)

As we have already seen there is a tone of command or exhortation in Jesus' words from the cross. Accordingly it is legitimate to understand the action of the Beloved Disciple in v.27b as an exact execution of that command. If one understands Jesus' words only as the last wish of a dying friend, then also the Beloved Disciple's action can be seen as the fulfilment of that wish by his intimate friend. In the context of the present text the Greek expression: ἀπ᾽ ἐκείνης τῆς ὥρας is used only to express the Beloved Disciple's immediate and exact execution of Jesus'

---

[99] Cf. PANIMOLLE, *Giovanni*, Vol III, 409; M. DE GOEDT, "Un schème de révélation dans le quatrième évangile", *NTS* 8 (1962) 142-150; DAUER, *Das Wort des Gekreuzigten*, Teil I, 231. The examples of such revelation formula we see in Jn 1,29.35f.47. De La Potterie shows the aspect of revelation in this passage by making a comparison with the scheme of revelation in Jn 1,36: Cf. DE LA POTTERIE, *Il discepolo che Gesù amava*, 50-51.

[100] Through this revelation of Jesus to the Beloved Disciple Jesus stresses Mary's spiritual motherhood in relation to all Christian faithful. The representative role of the Beloved Disciple is clear in the designation of the Beloved Disciple as ὁ μαθητής in v.27. De La Potterie admits the interpretation of the spiritual motherhood of Mary on the basis of the representative role of the Beloved Disciple. Cf. DE LA POTTERIE, *Il discepolo che Gesù amava*, 51. By citing the encyclicals of Pope Leo XIII and Pius XI Unger shows the prevalent spiritual interpretation of Jn 19,25-27:Cf. D. UNGER, "A Note on John 19,25-27", *CBQ* 9 (1947) 111-112.

advice.[101] This positive response or obedience on the part of the Beloved Disciple is a vivid expression of his intimacy and friendship with Jesus.

Regarding the Beloved Disciple's action in v.27b there are different interpretations, both literal and theological. The Greek verb λαμβάνειν with the preposition εἰς in the semitic construction [102] has more a material or physical sense. The verb λαμβάνω has the etymological meaning "to grasp" or "to seize" which developed in two directions, viz. *an active one* in the sense of "taking" or "bringing under one's control on one's own initiative" and *a passive one* in the sense of "receiving" or "acquiring" (passively). [103] Such difference of meaning is clear in the various Johannine usage of the verb.[104] Depending on the objects which follow, λαμβάνειν has three different nuances in Fourth Gospel: a) an active sense of "taking" when the verb is followed by material objects (cf. 6,11; 12,3.13;13,4.26.30;18,3; 19,23.30.48;21,13) or a person treated as a thing (cf. 18,31; 19,1.6.40); b) a passive sense of "receiving" when the verb is followed by certain spiritual gifts (cf. 3,27; 5,44; 6,7; 7,23 etc.); c) a nuance special to John as "accepting", "admitting" or "taking up" when the object of the verb is a person (cf. 1,12; 5,43;

---

[101] In the wider context of the Fourth Gospel ὥρα (hour) has a deep theological meaning, viz. the hour of Jesus' salvific death. Dauer writes: "So wird der Evangelist nur sagen wollen, dass der Jünger *von dieser Zeit an* die Mutter Jesus sich nahm, d.h. den Auftrag des Meisters tatsächlich ausgeführt hat und zum Bruder Jesu wurde": DAUER, *Das Wort des Gekreuzigten*, Teil II, 85.

[102] This construction can be seen as a semitism in the text in question. The Hebrew equivalent ל לקח originally means *to take in marriage* (cf. 1 Sam 25,39.40; Ex 6,20). Later it acquires the meaning *to consider* (Cf. BLASS-DEBRUNNER, *Greek Grammar*, § 157 (3).

[103] Cf. G. DELLING, λαμβάνω, *TDNT* IV, 5-7.

[104] Cf. DE LA POTTERIE, *Siehe deine Mutter*, 214-216.

13,20) or his message (cf. 12,48; 17,8) or his witness (cf.3,11.32.33; 1 Jn 5,9). Considering the third nuance the object of the verb is always the person of Christ or His message except in Jn 19,27 and accordingly the verb λαμβάνειν is practically synonymous with πιστεύειν.[105] Taking into consideration the different nuances of the verb λαμβάνειν, its usage in Jn 19,27 can be understood in the third sense, viz. "accepting" or "admitting" ("annehmen" - "accogliere") the mother of Jesus as a person.[106] In the context of the present text the Beloved Disciple's acceptance of Jesus's mother is the same as his acceptance in faith of Jesus' revelation.

In the light of modern exegesis τὰ ἴδια is understood differently according to different contexts.[107] In Biblical and extra-biblical Greek literature the expression εἰς τὰ ἴδια or τὰ ἴδια is usually used with a verb of motion where it means "into the house". Still the expression τὰ ἴδια can have three different meanings, viz. one's own material or spiritual goods, one's private affairs (concerns) or one's house or country.[108] To understand the depth of meaning of this expression in Jn 19,27 one should understand it in the light of other Johannine texts where τὰ ἴδια is adopted by the Evangelist. In the Fourth Gospel the expressions ἴδιος (adjectival use) οἱ ἴδιοι, τὸ ἴδιον and τὰ ἴδια (substantival use) have different nuances according to their particular context. In the case of the adjectival use (7x in chapters 1-10) the meaning is clear since it is followed by a definite subject, whereas in the substantival use (6x in 1,11 (2x); 13,1;

---

[105] Cf. *Ibid.*, 215, esp. n.80.

[106] Cf. DE LA POTTERIE, *Il discepolo che Gesù amava*, 52.

[107] DE LA POTTERIE, *Siehe deine Mutter*, 204-214.

[108] Cf. *Ibid.*, 204-208. De La Potterie illustrates different instances where τὰ ἴδια is used in the Biblical and extra-biblical literature in its various nuances.

15,19; 16,32; 19,27) the meaning can be different. It can have a local, physical or spiritual connotation depending on the verb used in that connection. In Jn 1,11 it is Israel representing all mankind who signifies "his own" (τὰ ἴδια - οἱ ἴδιοι) to whom Jesus came. But in Jn 10,1-18 the general concept of "his own" (τὰ ἴδια) is applied to a selected group of Israel. In Jn 13,1 the expression "his own" (οἱ ἴδιοι) is further limited and applied to Jesus' disciples. In these three texts the Evangelist tries to underline the development of an idea of deep unity between Jesus and "His own". In Jn 16,32 τὰ ἴδια refers to the attitude of all disciples who have scattered due to the lack of deep faith in the revelation of Jesus. But in 19,27 this term refers to the mentality of the Beloved Disciple, representative of all disciples, in the sense of a unity due to a deep faith in the revelation of Jesus. Thus against the background of the theological development of the Fourth Gospel τὰ ἴδια in 19,27b is not the material goods (house) of the Beloved Disciple, but his spiritual goods (*spirtualia bona*) expressed in faith.[109]

The spiritual connotation of τὰ ἴδια in 19,27b is much more expressive in its connection with the verb λαμβάνειν followed by the preposition εἰς. In 19,27b the action of the Beloved Disciple has a spiritual meaning, i.e. his accepting or considering (annehmen) Jesus' mother as his own in deep faith.[110] The expression of the Beloved

---

[109] Cf. *Ibid.*, 214.

[110] The expression ἀπ' ἐκείνης τῆς ὥρας (from that hour) is an indication that it need not be taken as a physical lodging, since they did not seem to leave Calvary immediately. For details cf. DE LA POTTERIE, *Siehe deine Mutter*, 212ff. esp. 218, where De la Potterie shows the contrast between two attitudes in the light of two different uses of the expression τὰ ἴδια, viz. the attitude of the Old Israel as not accepting Jesus and His message (1,11) and the attitude of the New Israel represented by the Beloved Disciple as accepting the message of Jesus (19,27). In the case of Jn 1,11 there is no difficulty to consider the expression τὰ ἴδια in a spiritual sense. Thus in the presentation of the Fourth Gospel we see a theological

Disciple's deep faith in receiving the mother of Jesus as his own mother has an ecclesiological interpretation. Faithful disciples, represented by the Beloved Disciple, accept Jesus' revelation in the Church, represented by the mother of Jesus.[111] Acceptance of this revelation of Jesus, i.e. the spiritual motherhood of Jesus' mother, is the Beloved Disciple's positive response to the already established friendship by Jesus. Such an act of the Beloved Disciple elucidates the reciprocal dimension of their friendship.

Through a brief analysis we have been trying to understand the profound expressions of the intimate friendship between Jesus and the Beloved Disciple in the short but theologically rich account of Jn 19,25-27. Accordingly the Beloved Disciple's participation in the paschal mystery of Jesus, Jesus' last words from the cross and the Beloved Disciple's positive response to Jesus' advice are treated as supreme expressions of their intimacy. In the light of the analysis one can arrive at the conclusion that the intimacy between Jesus and an ideal disciple is a reciprocal friendship which entails privileges and responsibilities. [112]

---

development from a faithless community to a church founded in deep faith. Gunther understands this expression ἔλαβεν αὐτὴν εἰς τὰ ἴδια as receiving her in the Church, where the New Israel is gathered (cf. Jn 20,2.10.18;Acts 1,13-14): Cf. GUNTHER, *The Beloved Disciple*, 131; cf. also D.A. HUBBARD, "John 19:17-30", *Int* 43 (1989) 400.

[111] The Beloved Disciple has a representative role among the disciples of Jesus. So also, the mother of Jesus is a symbol of the Church. Therefore, the acceptance of the mother of Jesus is an acceptance of the Church itself in faith: Cf. DE LA POTTERIE, *Siehe deine Mutter*, 218; *Il discepolo che Gesù amava*, 52.

[112] The aspect of privileges and responsibilities as seen in the text will help one to understand the reciprocal dimension of friendship which is an essential element in Jesus-disciple relationship.

C. Jn 20,1-10

The third explicit reference to the Beloved Disciple is in Jn 20,1-10.[113] This pericope deals with Jesus' resurrection, the heart of the paschal mystery, culminated in the absolute faith of the Beloved Disciple. Peter and the Beloved Disciple play their representative roles in their own particular [114] but important manner. [115] Their functions represent not only the expression of their personal relationship with Jesus, but also an invitation to imitate their positive response, actualized in an exemplary faith in the Risen Lord. [116] Thus, the pericope under consideration has a theological thrust rather than a historical precision. In the present treatment of the text we evaluate the role of the Beloved Disciple in the theological perspective to elucidate the nature of friendship between Jesus and the Beloved Disciple.

---

[113] The Beloved Disciple is characterized here as ὁ ἄλλος μαθητής, ὃν ἐφίλει ὁ Ἰησοῦς (v.2). It is different from other Beloved Disciple texts since the Evangelist uses here φιλεῖν instead of ἀγαπᾶν. Because of such a change one need not find difficulty in identifying this disciple with the Beloved Disciple, since the Evangelist uses these two verbs interchangeably in different pericopes referring to the same person with certain theological motives: Cf. KÜGLER, Der Jünger, den Jesus liebte, 329; QUAST, Beloved Disciple, 109. The verbs ἀγαπᾶν and φιλεῖν are complementary and they explicate two aspects of love. The expression ὁ ἄλλος has a retrospective connotation in the sense that it refers back to the already mentioned Beloved Disciple.

[114] The repetition of the Greek preposition πρός before Peter and the Beloved Disciple shows their particular and important role: Cf. SCHNACKENBURG, St. John, Vol II, 307.

[115] Rather than the persons the functions of the disciples are noteworthy in the context. Mahoney writes: " ...not the persons but their functions are at the center of the Evangelist's interest": R. MAHONEY, Two Disciples at the Tomb, 278.

[116] Cf. Ibid., 282; cf. also SCHNACKENBURG, St. John, Vol III, 310.

1. Delimitation of the Text

In the context of the delimitation of the present text one cannot ignore the literary unity of John 20, 1-18, where there is a unity of time, place and persons.[117] The whole event takes place in the 'early morning on the first day of the week'[118] and only in v.19 there is a *shift of time* with the reference to 'the evening' of that day. The events narrated in vv.1-18 take place at the tomb of Jesus and with v.19 there is a *shift of place* to the cenacle. So also, there is a *change of the characters*[119] with the appearance of Mary Magdalene in v.1, the sudden appearance of Peter and the Beloved Disciple in v.2 and Mary's continuing presence till v.18. With v.19 there is an explicit change of the scene and characters.

In the light of the arguments mentioned above one finds the unity of the pericope from v.1 to v.18. According to some exegetes this pericope is interwoven with two traditions.[120] Against such a wide context we limit the present study to one tradition which extends from v.1(2) to v.10, where one can see the active role of the Beloved Disciple.[121] Hence, one sees the independent nature of the

---

[117] Cf. PANIMOLLE, *Giovanni*, Vol III, 436-437.

[118] This indication of time in Jn 20,1 marks a new opening in contrast with the temporal expression in 19,42. Also the Greek adversative particle δέ is an indication for such a change.

[119] In the preceding pericope we see Nicodemus and Joseph of Arimathea who are absent in the present pericope.

[120] Cf. BULTMANN, *John*, 681-683; W. WILKENS, *Die Entstehungsgeschichte des Vierten Evangeliums* (Zollikon 1958) 87.

[121] All the Evangelists speak of the empty tomb of Jesus but the Fourth Evangelist has his own particular way of presentation, connected with the Beloved Disciple tradition.

subsection: vv.1-10[122] which ends with the disappearance of Peter and the Beloved Disciple (v.10).[123]

2. The Literary Genre

The whole subsection (vv.1-10) is a narrative but very dramatic [124] in style, a drama without dialogue. Here the characters appear and disappear according to their proper role. Except Mary Magdalene, no one speaks in this episode. But the scene is full of action and dramatic climax.[125] The main actors in the scene are the Beloved Disciple and Peter. Their juxtaposed appearance and active role in the episode require a comparison of their characteristics which will help one to see the priority of the Beloved Disciple. Such a conclusion can be proved even stylistically, i.e. there are 9 actions referred to Peter, whereas 12 actions are referred to the Beloved Disciple.[126] In the Evangelist's presentation the Beloved Disciple has a special role regarding his relation with Jesus. In the present

---

[122] Bultmann considers Jn 20,1-10 as an independent unit in the Fourth Gospel since it has no direct effect on the content of the following pericope: Cf. BULTMANN, *John*, 681f.

[123] In v.11 there opens a new scene, where Mary Magdalene reappears and the Risen Lord appears to her. Thus we see a thematic change from the empty tomb tradition to the apparition tradition.

[124] Cf. PANIMOLLE, *Giovanni*, Vol III, 440, where the author writes about the Evangelist's dramatic presentation of chapter 20 as a whole.

[125] The frequent use of verbs of motion increases its dramatic quality.

[126] Cf. KÜGLER, *Der Jünger, den Jesus liebte*, 326; SEGALLA, *Il discepolo che Gesù amava*, 233.

pericope such a close relationship is even stylistically and literarily portrayed.

3. The Expressions of Friendship Between Jesus and the Beloved Disciple

a. The disciple, who listens to the gospel of resurrection

Μαρία ἡ Μαγδαληνὴ ... ἔρχεται ... καὶ πρὸς τὸν ἄλλον μαθητὴν ὃν ἐφίλει ὁ Ἰησοῦς καὶ λέγει αὐτοῖς· ...(v.2)

The Gospel tradition in general, both Synoptic and the Fourth Gospel speaks about the visit of the women [127] to the tomb of Jesus in the early morning of the first day of the week (cf. Mk 16,2; Mt 28,1; Lk 24,1; Jn 20,1). Together with Mk and Lk, the Fourth Evangelist describes the opened tomb of Jesus and the running of women towards Jesus' disciples. In the Johannine account it is Mary Magdalene, who runs towards Simon Peter and the disciple whom Jesus loved [128] with the surprising message of the empty tomb.

---

[127] The Fourth Evangelist names only Mary Magdalene as visiting the tomb of Jesus. But the plural οἴδαμεν in v.2 suggests that she was not alone. It is also unlikely that a woman alone goes outside the city wall before daylight.

[128] The repeated use of the Greek preposition πρός before Peter and the Beloved Disciple is noteworthy. It can indicate that these two disciples were not lodging in the same house and the woman had to visit them separately: Cf. BERNARD, *St. John*, Vol II, 658. But in the light of v.3 this argument of Bernard seems to be weak, since both of them came out of the house together to go to the tomb. In this context the repeated use of the preposition shows the particular importance of these two disciples in the Evangelist's presentation: Cf. supra, p. 278, n. 114.

In the Johannine theological presentation Mary's announcement to Peter and the Beloved Disciple has a special motive. In the early tradition of the Church Peter was the leading figure of the apostolic college. But in the particular historical context of the Fourth Gospel the special role of the Beloved Disciple has high esteem. Thus, what we see here is a Johannine presentation of the traditional material regarding the empty tomb. The announcement also to the Beloved Disciple shows his leading role in the community of the disciples and his intimate friendship with Jesus as well. For Mary Magdalene the empty tomb was not an occasion to believe in the resurrection of Jesus but prompted her to think that somebody had stolen Jesus' body. However, for the Beloved Disciple the empty tomb was a sign of Jesus' resurrection (v.9) and a means of his faith (v.8). Hence, the message which the Beloved Disciple received from Mary Magdalene was a gospel of resurrection. It was a special privilege to which he was entitled due to his intimacy with Jesus.

b. The disciple, who runs towards Jesus' tomb

ἤρχοντο εἰς τὸ μνημεῖον, ἔτρεχον ... ὁ ἄλλος μαθητὴς προέδραμεν τάχιον τοῦ Πέτρου (vv.3-4)

As an immediate positive reaction to the message of Mary Magdalene, the two representative disciples of Jesus run towards the tomb. However, in the episode the Beloved Disciple is presented in contrast with Peter, i.e. as one outrunning Peter. The exegetes interpret this act of the Beloved Disciple differently with natural, [129]

---

[129] Some authors interpret the outrunning of the Beloved Disciple on the basis of his age-difference with Peter: Cf. LAGRANGE, *Saint Jean*, 507; B. WEISS, *Das Johannesevangelium* (Göttingen 1893), 221. Such an interpretation cannot be definitely accepted since there is no reference at all about the age of the disciples.

polemic [130] and theological explanations. In the light of the whole Johannine theology, rather than a natural and polemic explanation, it requires a symbolic and theological interpretation.

In the theological framework of the Fourth Gospel the Beloved Disciple is presented as an ideal disciple and accordingly the outrunning by that disciple to the tomb of Jesus can be seen as an expression of his special love towards and faith in Jesus. [131] The outrunning explains not simply an emotional attachment, but a close relationship between them. [132] On the basis of this theologico-symbolical explanation the Beloved Disciple's outrunning and reaching the tomb first can be understood as a sublime expression of his friendship with Jesus. [133]

For further natural explanations cf. QUAST, *Beloved Disciple*, 111.

[130] This race to the tomb is envisaged by some authors as an occasion to emphasize the competitive relationship between Peter and the Beloved Disciple: Cf. GUNTHER, *The Beloved Disciple*, 132, where Gunther considers it even to explain the Beloved Disciple's primacy over Peter in love, devotion, faith etc.; cf. also LINDARS, *John*, 600.

[131] In this connection Brown writes, "...the writer is simply telling us that the disciple who was bound closest to Jesus in love was the quickest to look for him": BROWN, *John*, Vol II, 1007; cf. also D. MOLLAT, "La foi pascale selon le chapitre 20 de l'évangile de Saint Jean", in: E. DHANIS, *Resurrexit: Actes du Symposium international sur la résurrection de Jésus* (Città del Vaticano 1974) 321.

[132] Kügler says, "Sie übersieht nämlich, dass wir im Text nicht nur keine Information über die emotionale Beziehung des geliebten Jüngers zu Jesus erhalten, sondern dass das Verhältnis zwischen beiden grundsätzlich von Jesus her beschrieben wird": KÜGLER, *Der Jünger, den Jesus liebte*, 333.

[133] The arrival of the Beloved Disciple at the tomb first (v.4) can be explained as the primacy of the Beloved Disciple in love, devotion, expectant faith and hope, characteristics of a disciple's friendship with Jesus. Cf. GUNTHER, *The Beloved Disciple*, 132.

c. The disciple, who waits for Peter

ἦλθεν πρῶτος εἰς τὸ μνημεῖον...οὐ μέντοι εἰσῆλθεν (vv.4-5)

In the narrative the Beloved Disciple is presented as one who reaches the tomb first,[134] but he waits till the arrival of Peter and following him he enters the tomb. There is no unanimous interpretation among exegetes regarding the expectation of the Beloved Disciple.[135] Besides the scholarly opinions based on literary devices one can give a theological interpretation to this act of the Beloved Disciple. Accordingly one can understand the waiting of the Beloved Disciple as an act of acknowledging Peter's important role and primacy of honour.[136] Thus the Beloved Disciple's attitude of giving Peter his proper position is an expression of the Beloved Disciple's close relationship with Jesus. Even in the dramatic presentation of the episode the theological motive is manifested in the presentation of the characters with their proper actions. In the development of the story which reaches its climax in the Beloved

---

[134] The apparent precedence of the Beloved Disciple over Peter is expressed even phonetically with προέδραμεν and πρῶτος (vv.4.8):Cf. SCHNACKENBURG, *St. John*, Vol II, 310.

[135] The Beloved Disciple's waiting outside the tomb is considered by Lindars as a literary device of "John's delaying tactics so as to build the narrative to a climax": LINDARS, *John*, 601. According to Hoskyns "his entrance is delayed in order that his faith may form the climax of the narrative": HOSKYNS, *Fourth Gospel*, 541. Schonfield's explanation is quite different and according to him the Beloved Disciple being a priest did not want to take the risk of ritual contamination from a corpse. Only after Peter's affirmation that the tomb is empty, he enters into it: Cf. H. J. SCHONFIELD, *The Passover Plot* (Hutchinson 1965) 105. 175.; cf. also J.K. THORNECROFT, "The Redactor and the 'Beloved' in John", *ExpTim* 98 (1987) 137.

[136] Cf. QUAST, *Beloved Disciple*, 114-116; J. KREMER, *Die Osterbotschaft der vier Evangelien* (Stuttgart 1969) 90f.; SCHNACKENBURG, *Der Jünger, den Jesus liebte*, 104.

Disciple's absolute faith he appears as one who respects the related assignment given to Peter.[137]

d. The disciple, who went in, saw and believed
ὁ ἄλλος μαθητὴς εἰσῆλθεν καὶ εἶδεν καὶ ἐπίστευσεν ... (vv.8-9)

The expression in v.8b shows the climax of the whole pericope, both stylistically and theologically.[138] In the present pericope it is only in the case of the Beloved Disciple one finds a clear expression of faith.[139] "What" he believed is not mentioned in v.8, but the following verse (esp. ἀνίστημι) indirectly affirms the object of his

---

[137] Cf. DODD, *Historical Tradition*, 141; BROWN, *John*, Vol II, 1004-1007.

[138] **Stylistically** this expression is the climax in the sense that the Evangelist makes use of different vocabulary with different ranges of meaning which culminates in the expression of deep faith. The pericope opens with a situation of darkness (σκοτίας ἔτι οὔσης) (v.1), which can be seen in contrast with the faith of the Beloved Disciple (ἐπίστευσεν) (v.8). Unlike the Synoptics (cf. Mk 16,2; Mt 28,1; Lk 24,1) the Fourth Evangelist uses the expression in v.1 to stress the lack of understanding or spiritual blindness: Cf. BROWN, *John*, Vol II, 981; SCHNACKENBURG, *St. John*, Vol III, 308; QUAST, *Beloved Disciple*, 109. So also the growth towards a deep faith is stylistically brought out by using different verbs of seeing such as βλέπειν (vv.1-5), θεωρεῖν (v.6) and ἰδεῖν (v.8): Cf. SCHNACKENBURG, *St. John*, Vol III, 312. **Theologically** the expression under consideration is the climax since the whole story is striving towards the establishment of deep faith in the Resurrection of Jesus, verified in the Beloved Disciple's expression of faith.

[139] The faith of the Beloved Disciple seems to be absolute, clear from the absolute use of the verb πιστεύω (v.8): Cf. SCHNACKENBURG, *St. John*, Vol III, 312. In the light of the pericope one need not degrade the faith of Peter, since the Evangelist's scope of this episode is to highlight the exemplary, absolute faith of the Beloved Disciple: Cf. QUAST, *Beloved Disciple*, 120; KÜGLER, *Der Jünger, den Jesus liebte*, 327-328.

faith, i.e. the Resurrection of Jesus.[140] Jesus' Resurrection can be a matter of faith for the Beloved Disciple by means of certain "signs", viz. the linen cloths and the napkin in the tomb. For him there was no need of a personal appearance of Jesus as in the case of Thomas (cf. 20,24-28).[141] One can consider the meaning of πιστεύω in the present context as "absolute faith".[142]

The faith-response of the Beloved Disciple is dynamic and exemplary. The progressive movement towards deep faith is linguistically brought out in the pericope, viz. the Evangelist uses here three different Greek verbs for the act of "seeing".[143] In v.5 the verb βλέπειν is used to describe the Beloved Disciple's natural perception of the linen cloths in the tomb. In v.6 θεωρεῖν is used to illustrate the scrutinizing way of Peter's seeing with "an eye for detail". Finally in v.8 the Beloved Disciple's "spiritual seeing", connected with his faith, is described through the verb ὁράω in its

---

[140] St. Augustine considers ἐπίστευσεν in v.8 as a simple belief in the words of Mary Magdalene, that the body of Jesus is taken away: Cf. AUGUSTINUS, *Tractatus* CXX, 9; PL 35, 1955. But in the light of the deep meaning of εἶδεν and the absolute use of the verb ἐπίστευσεν one can transcend this primary level of meaning and consider it as a faith in the resurrection of Jesus: Cf. MAHONEY, *Two Disciples at the Tomb*, 262-263; BARRETT, *St. John*, 563-573; BROWN, *John*, Vol II, 1005. According to De la Potterie, the Beloved Disciple, being a man of faith, had an intuition of the mystery of resurrection and in that sense his faith is in the resurrection of Jesus: Cf. DE LA POTTERIE, *Il discepolo che Gesù amava*, 53.

[141] Cf. KÜGLER, *Der Jünger, den Jesus liebte*, 338-340, where Kügler speaks of the real nature of the Beloved Disciple's faith in Jesus' Resurrection. Matera considers the faith of the Beloved Disciple as an ideal disciple's response to the evidence of the resurrection which God provides: Cf. F.J. MATERA, "John 20:1-18", *Int* 43 (1989) 403.

[142] Cf. MAHONEY, *Two Disciples at the Tomb*, 263 ff.

[143] For the significance of the different verbs of "seeing" cf. G.L. PHILLIPS, "Faith and Vision in the Fourth Gospel", in: F.L. CROSS (ed.), *Studies in the Fourth Gospel* (London 1957) 83-96, esp. 86.

aorist form (εἶδεν).[144] A close analysis of these different verbs helps one to understand the depth of their meaning and their culmination in the absolute faith of the Beloved Disciple.[145]

The important qualification of a true Christian disciple is verified in the Beloved Disciple when it is said of him: "he went in, saw and believed"(v.8). One can see this expression against the background of the first calling to discipleship in the Fourth Gospel (cf. 1,39), where the first followers of Jesus were asked 'to come and see' and they 'came and saw'.[146] The same verbs are used in both texts (ἔρχομαι and ὁράω); in the first instance it was for a personal experience of Jesus, whereas in the present pericope it is the result of a personal experience which the Beloved Disciple experienced in the course of his interpersonal relationship with Jesus resulted in his absolute faith in the Resurrected Lord.[147]

In the presentation of the Beloved Disciple as one who came to deep faith in the Risen Lord one has to consider the role of the Scripture concerning the resurrection of Jesus (cf.v.9). It is not only the vision of the empty tomb but also the scriptural prophecy about

---

[144] Cf. J. CABA, *Cristo, mia speranza, è risorto: Studio esegetico dei "vangeli" pasquali* (Milano 1988) 252-258.

[145] For a detailed analysis of the different nuances of these verbs cf. MAHONEY, *Two Disciples at the Tomb*, 240ff.; SCHNACKENBURG, *St. John*, Vol III, 312; A.H. MAYNARD, "The Role of Peter in the Fourth Gospel", *NTS* 30 (1984) 540, where he writes, "These three words for seeing have been used with strict respect for their variant shades of meaning. Before he enters the tomb the other disciple 'sees' in a general sense. Peter when he enters only 'observes' the physical scene. But the Beloved Disciple upon entering 'sees with spiritual insight' and the result is faith".

[146] In the whole context of the Fourth Gospel this expression has a meaning of coming to faith in Jesus Christ, for which the disciples are ultimately called and the Gospel is written (cf. 20,31).

[147] There is a connection between *seeing* (ὁράω) and *believing* (πιστεύω) in the Fourth Gospel. In the combined occurrence it has a deep meaning.

Jesus' resurrection which arouse the Beloved Disciple's deep faith. The Greek particle γάρ in v.9 connects this verse with the preceding and brings out the interconnection between faith and Scripture. [148] The vision of the empty tomb provides an occasion for the Beloved Disciple to understand the Scripture. The plural verb ᾔδεισαν is applied to both the Beloved Disciple and Peter, in the sense that before going to the tomb they had not understood the significance of the scriptural prophecy regarding the resurrection of Jesus. But the absolute faith (ἐπίστευσεν) is explicitly attributed only to the Beloved Disciple which seems due to the Evangelist's interest of presenting the Beloved Disciple as a model believer. It is this deep faith which gives him the insight to recognize and proclaim the Risen Lord (cf.21,7). In the context of the narrative the Beloved Disciple's faith is presented as the highest form of faith. [149] Such a deep and absolute faith entitled the Beloved Disciple to be a true disciple of Jesus. [150] Thus, through a genuine faith in the Resurrected Lord the

---

[148] There is a real difficulty to explain the literary connection between these verses, since ἐπίστευσεν (v.8) in the singular refers only to the Beloved Disciple whereas ᾔδεισαν (v.9) in the plural refers also to Peter (according to some authors also to Mary Magdalene) whose faith is not at all mentioned in the pericope. However, in the immediate context the Evangelist affirms the exemplary faith of the Beloved Disciple. For details cf. CABA, *Cristo è risorto*, 256-257; E. L. BODE, *The First Easter Morning. The Gospel Accounts of the Women's Visit to the Tomb of Jesus* (AnBib 45) (Roma 1970) 80-81.

[149] Quast writes: "As an example of the ideal response of faith, the Beloved Disciple epitomizes the highest form of faith": QUAST, *Beloved Disciple*, 120; cf. also G.R. OSBORNE, *The Resurrection Narratives. A Redactional Study* (Grand Rapids 1984) 147; COLLINS, *The Representative Figures*, 128.130.

[150] QUAST, *Beloved Disciple*, 123, where he continues: "He exemplifies true discipleship and a close, loving relationship with Jesus. It would only be natural for him to run fast as humanly possible to the grave of the one who loved him....The function of the Beloved Disciple is to provide the example of a true disciple of Jesus. In this situation to be a true disciple is to come to a point of belief". Cf. also HARTIN, *The Role of Peter*, 56.

Beloved Disciple became a true disciple of Jesus, and being a true disciple, he verified in himself all the qualities of a true friend of Jesus.

By analyzing the episode of the empty tomb we have illustrated the depth and meaning of the interpersonal relationship between Jesus and the Beloved Disciple. The central theme of the pericope is the resurrection of Jesus and its affirmation by two of His disciples, representatives of all Christian disciples. In the dramatic presentation of the text the Evangelist portrays the exemplary response of an ideal disciple to a Master in a close interpersonal relationship. Rather than the identity of the Beloved Disciple, his exemplary faith is significant in this scene.[151] All the deeds of the Beloved Disciple can be seen as expressions of his absolute faith in the Lord. Accordingly, "the running", "going in", "seeing" and "believing" of the Beloved Disciple can be interpreted theologically since he was portrayed in the pericope as a model disciple.[152] Such an ideal discipleship of the Beloved Disciple is a proof for his friendship with Jesus.

D. Jn 21,1-14

Another pericope which requires our consideration is Jn 21,1 -14. It deals with Jesus' self-manifestation to His disciples through a miraculous catching of fish and the Beloved Disciple's recognition of the Risen Lord and the communication of his faith-experience to his fellow-disciples. In the text there are evident expressions of

---

[151] Cf. SCHNACKENBURG, *St. John*, Vol III, 314.

[152] Cf. KÜGLER, *Der Jünger, den Jesus liebte*, 333f.

friendship between Jesus and the Beloved Disciple which can be
interpreted in the general context of the Fourth Gospel and in the
particular context of the pericope itself.

1. Delimitation of the Text

Chapter 21 is generally considered as an epilogue [153] to the
Fourth Gospel with an editorial conclusion (vv.24-25). In such an
epilogue the present pericope (vv.1-14) can be treated as an
independent literary and thematic unity on the basis of different
literary devices. Jn 21,1 opens a new section with the Greek
expression, μετὰ ταῦτα. [154] Πάλιν introduces a new appearance of
the Risen Lord. Moreover, the beginning of a new pericope in v.1
is clear, since Jn 20,30-31 is considered as a formal conclusion of
the Fourth Gospel itself. There is also a *change of place* from the

---

[153] It is still an open question, how ch.xxi of the Fourth Gospel should be
considered. Some call it an *appendix* which is an inadequate term. An appendix is
something not related to the completeness of a work. Certainly ch.xxi is more
closely integrated into the Johannine thought and some of the themes of the Gospel
are developed in this chapter. Others call it a *post-script* or *supplement*, also not a
good designation for ch.xxi. A post-script or supplement often supplies information
acquired later, but in ch.xxi there is really nothing more to be said. Marrow and
Brown prefer the term *epilogue* which has the most exact English nuance for the
relationship of ch.xxi to the rest of the Fourth Gospel. Their position is justifiable
since the *epilogue* balances the presence of a prologue and leaves room for the
completion of some of the lines of thought left unfinished: Cf. BROWN, *John*, Vol
II, 1079; S.B. MARROW, *John 21 - An Essay in Johannine Ecclesiology* (Rome
1968) 43-44. Schnackenburg sees the inadequacy of the terms "appendix", "post-
script" and "epilogue" to designate ch.xxi of the Fourth Gospel. He considers Jn xxi
as an ultimate editorial chapter having an explanatory function, i.e. helping readers
in the Church of those days: Cf. SCHNACKENBURG, *St.John*, Vol III, 344.

[154] μετὰ ταῦτα is a general indicator of the past event and at the same time
it introduces something new. So it is a term of transition in a narrative (cf. Jn 3,22;
5,1; 6,1; 7,1; 19,38). For details cf. also supra p. 32.

preceding pericope, viz. in 20,26 the appearance of Jesus takes place in the house where the disciples were gathered, whereas in 21,1 Jesus appears by the sea of Tiberias.

In v.14 one sees a concluding remark of the Evangelist regarding the third appearance of Jesus which serves as a conclusion of the pericope itself. The theme announced in v.1 is concluded with v.14 and thus it forms a *thematic unity*. There is an *inclusion* between v.1 and v.14 with the verb φανερόω, which keeps the unity of the whole subsection. With v.15 there begins a new theme, i.e. the dialogue between Jesus and Peter. There is also a shift of time, viz. the end of breakfast. By considering all the above mentioned indications one can deal with Jn 21,1-14 as an independent literary unity.[155]

2. The Literary Genre

As all other preceding Beloved Disciple texts Jn 21,1-14 can also be considered as a narrative with highly dramatic elements. All the characters are in a way engaged in action but only the main characters lead the action in the mode of a dialogue. It seems to be the Evangelist's interest in the pericope to exalt the character of the Beloved Disciple who shares his revelatory knowledge with Peter. Such a knowledge and its sharing can be seen as the result of a deep and special interpersonal relationship between Jesus and the Beloved Disciple, well projected in the dramatic presentation of the pericope. The direct speech put into the mouth of the Beloved Disciple (v.7) makes the scene more lively and dramatic, and the central theme is

---

[155] For details cf. KÜGLER, *Der Jünger, den Jesus liebte*, 350f.; SCHNACKENBURG, *St. John*, Vol III, 351.

stylistically presented by placing the affirmation of Jesus' Lordship at the central part (v.7) of the text.

3. The Expressions of Friendship Between Jesus and the Beloved Disciple

a. The disciple, who recognizes the Risen Lord

ἔβαλον οὖν, καὶ οὐκέτι αὐτὸ ἑλκύσαι ...ἀπὸ τοῦ πλήθους τῶν ἰχθύων (v.6b)

In the beginning of the pericope (v.2) the Evangelist gives a list of certain disciples of Jesus in which the Beloved Disciple is also included. [156] In the attempt to explicate the expressions of friendship between Jesus and the Beloved Disciple, Jesus' addressing of His disciples as "children" (παιδία) is noteworthy. [157] The term παιδία in the present context shows Jesus' intimate relationship with His disciples which implies the superiority and authority of Jesus. [158] When the Evangelist states that the disciples did not know that it was Jesus (v.4), he means the incapability of all including the Beloved Disciple to recognize the physical appearance of Jesus. However, the miraculous catching of fish gives an intuitive knowledge *only* to the Beloved Disciple. None of the disciples other than the beloved one could experience the miraculous power of the

---

[156] This statement can be verified in the light of the clear mentioning of the Beloved Disciple in v.7. Lindars identifies the Beloved Disciple with one of the unnamed disciples of v.2: Cf. LINDARS, *John*, 625.

[157] The general term "children" includes also the Beloved Disciple.

[158] The NEB translated the Greek term παιδία here as "friends". According to Lindars, "as a familiar, diminutive form it implies the master/disciple relationship": LINDARS, *John*, 626.

Lord. This shows the nature of their personal relationship and ideal friendship.[159] The miracle is a means of Jesus' self-revelation (φανέρωσις).[160] The experience of divine power connected with the miracles is also a gratuitous gift of God to His selected ones.[161] Being a beloved of Jesus (ὅν ἠγάπα ὁ Ἰησοῦς), it is the Beloved Disciple who is the first to recognize the Risen Lord.[162] Hence, the intuitive knowledge of the Beloved Disciple is an expressive gift of his intimacy with Jesus.

b. The disciple, who communicates his Lord-experience

λέγει ...μαθητὴς ἐκεῖνος[163] ὅν ἠγάπα ὁ Ἰησοῦς τῷ Πέτρῳ· ὁ Κύριός ἐστιν(v.7a)

In v.7a one hears the public testimony of the Beloved Disciple's Christ-experience. It was the miraculous catch of the fish which

---

[159] Cf. LORENZEN, *Der Lieblingsjünger*, 85.

[160] The whole episode under consideration is presented as a self-revelation of the Risen Lord (cf. vv.1.4). Jesus mentions the revelation as the basis of His friendship with His disciples (cf.15,15). Thus, the context of revelation in the present text express the theme of friendship.

[161] The miracles of Jesus as narrated in the Synoptics were aimed at proving His divinity. However, everybody could not understand them as divine acts and accused Him of having demonic power.

[162] MINEAR, *The Beloved Disciple*, 115, where Minear writes: "It is fitting that the disciple loved by Jesus should be the first to recognize Jesus' presence as Lord. Love and insight are related".

[163] The demonstrative pronoun ἐκεῖνος gives an indication to the former references of the Beloved Disciple (cf.13,23b;19,26b;20,2d).

enables the Beloved Disciple to recognize his Lord.[164] His intimacy
with Jesus inspires him to communicate his Lord-experience to his
fellow disciple.[165] The Beloved Disciple's capacity to recognize the
Lord depends upon his theological insight rather than physical
vision.[166] His absolute faith in the Risen Lord (cf.20,8) provides him
such an insight.

The Beloved Disciple's recognition of the Lord and his
communication of the same to Peter change the course of the
narrative. The words of the Beloved Disciple prompt Peter to
respond positively to the Risen Lord (cf.v.7b) and provide an
occasion for the whole group of disciples to have a personal
encounter with the Lord and thereby to deepen their faith in the
Risen Lord (cf.12).[167] In the Johannine call to discipleship in the
first chapter of the Gospel the communication of one's Christ-
experience plays an important role (cf. 1,41.45.). Thus, the
communicating role of the Beloved Disciple is an expression of his
genuine discipleship, i.e. being a true disciple he is a real friend of
Jesus.

In the self-revelatory scene of the Risen Lord in Jn 21,1-14 one
sees the reciprocal dimension of friendship between Jesus and a true
Christian disciple, epitomized in the character of the Beloved

---

[164] Here the expression κύριος (Lord) is used as a designation for the Risen
Jesus (cf. also 20,18.20.25.28). According to Neirynck there is a correspondence
between the Beloved Disciple's recognition of the Lord as a direct reaction to the
miraculous catching of fish and Peter's confession after the miraculous fishing in Lk
5,8. Cf. F. NEIRYNCK, "John 21", *NTS* 36, 2 (1990) 326.

[165] About this communicating role of the Beloved Disciple Kügler writes: "Er
deutet richtig und gibt seine richtige Deutung auch weiter": KÜGLER, *Der Jünger,
den Jesus liebte*, 390; cf. also DE LA POTTERIE, *Il discepolo che Gesù amava*, 54.

[166] Cf. QUAST, *Beloved Disciple*, 150.

[167] Cf. S.M. SCHNEIDERS, "John 21:1-14", *Int* 43 (1989) 73.

Disciple. Jesus' self-manifestation is presented as a sign of His close relationship to His disciples.[168] A genuine response to such a friendly action on the part of the disciples is initiated and motivated by a disciple who was beloved to Jesus in Johannine the presentation. The Beloved Disciple is presented as one who recognizes the Risen Lord and communicates his intuitive knowledge to his fellow disciples. His recognition and communication are two explicit expressions of his friendship with Jesus.

E. Jn 21,20-24

The last appearance of the Beloved Disciple takes place at the concluding section of the Fourth Gospel, where he is portrayed in contrast with Peter.[169] In the pericope under consideration (Jn 21,20-24) he is presented as a true follower of Jesus, as one who is entitled to remain faithful till the parousia and as one who bears witness to the salvific deeds of Jesus even among the future generation through his Gospel. All such characteristics can be seen as expressions of the Beloved Disciple's intimate relationship and friendship with Jesus. The following analysis of the expressions of

---

[168] Jesus' appearance in a concrete life situation, the performance of a miracle in a disappointed situation of catching nothing (cf.v.3), His preparation of a meal with bread and fish, a Eucharistic connotation and a sign of His continued presence among them are all expressions of Jesus' friendship with "His own". Jesus' friendship is well expressed in a (Eucharistic) meal context and the meal referred to in the context of the present pericope is considered as "quasi-Eucharistic": Cf. LINDARS, *John*, 628.

[169] This way of presentation is not to degrade the figure of Peter, but to show another model of discipleship exemplified by the Beloved Disciple as a result of his constant relationship with Christ.

friendship will be done in the light of the Johannine theology of discipleship and friendship.

1. Delimitation of the Text

Chapter 21 of the Fourth Gospel consists of an epilogue (vv.1 -23) and an editorial conclusion (vv.24-25).[170] While some authors find three subdivisions (vv.1-14; 15-19; 20-23)[171] in the epilogue, others divide it into two (vv.1-14; 15-23).[172] For the completion of the investigation of the Beloved Disciple texts here we will treat only the last fragment regarding the Beloved Disciple (vv.20-24). Since one finds a thematic unity in the two preceding subunits (vv.1-14 and vv.15-19), the rest of the verses 20-24 can be considered separately as a unit where the Beloved Disciple is treated [173] as one who positively responds to his master. Such delimitation is conducive to portray the Beloved Disciple's characteristics by emphasizing his witnessing role, a concrete expression of his friendship with Jesus.

2. The Literary Genre

This small subsection (vv.20-24) is part of a narrative [174] where

---

[170] Cf. supra, p. 290, n. 153.

[171] Cf. MLAKUZHYIL, *The Christocentric Structure*, 235.

[172] Cf. PANIMOLLE, *Giovanni*, Vol III, 471ff.

[173] The demonstrative pronoun οὗτος connected with μαθητής in v.24 connects this verse to the preceding, where the Beloved Disciple is being treated.

[174] Schnackenburg considers Jn 21,1-23 as "a connected narrative complex with various individual elements": Cf. SCHNACKENBURG, *St. John*, Vol III, 341.

the Evangelist presents a dramatic scene with three characters, viz. Jesus, Peter and the Beloved Disciple. Even though the dialogue is centred on the fate of the Beloved Disciple, he seems to be silent on the stage. His important characteristics are brought out by the other actors on the scene and through the editorial comments of the Evangelist. The literary style of this pericope is different from that of the other Beloved Disciple texts where he himself is actively present on the stage. A close analysis of the text will help one to understand the nature of the intimate interpersonal relationship between Jesus and the Beloved Disciple.

3. The Expressions of Friendship Between Jesus and the Beloved Disciple

a. The disciple, who follows Jesus

ὁ Πέτρος βλέπει τὸν μαθητὴν ὃν ἠγάπα ὁ Ἰησοῦς ἀκολουθοῦντα[175] (v.20)

The Beloved Disciple seems to be a true follower of Jesus from the beginning till the end, not as an answer to a definite command, but in the manner of an assured obedience.[176] Unlike all other characters the Beloved Disciple is presented always with Jesus, as one who follows Him in all important moments of His paschal

---

[175] ἀκολουθοῦντα is omitted by some manuscripts: א* W ff². Since the majority of the important manuscripts adopt it and since it theologically fits in this context, we accept a reading with this term.

[176] Cf. HOSKYNS, Fourth Gospel, 558; R.H. LIGHTFOOT, St. John's Gospel, (Oxford 1983) 342; SANDERS & MASTIN, St. John, 456; KRAGERUD, Der Lieblingsjünger,38-40,where Kragerud argues for the Beloved Disciple's superiority over Peter in the light of this "following" of the Beloved Disciple. But Schnackenburg disagrees with this argument: Cf.SCHNACKENBURG, St.John,Vol II, 368.

mystery (cf. 13,23; 19,26; 20,2; 21,7; 21,20). In the present pericope he appears as an obedient disciple who follows Jesus willingly.[177] The term ἀκολουθεῖν in vv. 19 and 20 cannot be understood in the same range of meaning. In v. 19, connected with Peter's fate, the term ἀκολουθεῖν has the meaning of following Jesus by martyrdom, clear within its particular literary context in the form of an imperative. But in v. 20 referring to the Beloved Disciple ἀκολουθεῖν in its participle form is an already started but continuous act of following.

The verb ἀκολουθεῖν in the NT is strictly limited to the discipleship of Christ and is mainly found in the four Gospels. [178] Out of its 90 NT usages 79 are in the Gospels and among these 79 occurrences 73 refers to "following Jesus". The Fourth Evangelist uses it 19 times out of which 17 instances speak of "following Jesus". With the exception of a single usage all others refer to the following after Jesus by the disciples. The "following" can be accomplished in different ways, viz. by being faithful to Jesus and to His teachings, or by participating in the fate of Jesus even through a martyrdom, clear in the case of Peter and the Beloved Disciple (cf. 21, 19.20). The term ἀκολουθεῖν in both contexts has the meaning of following after Jesus, proper for the establishment of the master-disciple relationship. [179]

---

[177] BARRETT, St. John, 586, where he says: "The beloved disciple was already doing what Peter had just been bidden to do".

[178] Cf. G. KITTEL, ἀκολουθέω, TDNT I, 213; G. SCHNEIDER, ἀκολουθέω, in: H. BALZ & G. SCHNEIDER, Exegetische Wörterbuch zum Neuen Testament, Band I (Stuttgart 1980) 118-125.

[179] According to this explanation there is no question of the degradation of Peter's character in contrast with that of the Beloved Disciple. The ideal discipleship can be attributed to both. The only difference is that Peter was asked to follow Jesus, whereas the Beloved Disciple has already understood its meaning and began

In the present context the Beloved Disciple's following (ἀκολουθοῦντα) after Jesus and Peter is noteworthy.[180] The following here is absolute and the aim is not a place but a person, similar to the following of a true disciple after the master.[181] Since the Johannine use of ἀκολουθεῖν is closely connected with the concept of discipleship the following by the Beloved Disciple also must be understood in terms of discipleship.[182] Following Jesus and Peter, the Beloved Disciple functions as the "ideal follower, the epitome of what it means to be a believer".[183]

Against this background one has to consider the following (ἀκολουθεῖν) after Jesus by Peter and the other disciple (ἄλλος μαθητής)[184] into the high priest's palace (Jn 18,15). If one identifies

---

to follow Jesus: Cf. LINDARS, *John*, 638.

[180] Collins confirms the primacy and authority of Peter in this following of the Beloved Disciple after Jesus *and Peter*. Such an acknowledgement of the primacy and authority of Peter makes him an ideal disciple: Cf. COLLINS, *The Representative Figures*, 129; cf. also LINDARS, *John*, 622.

[181] Kügler writes, "Offensichtlich handelt es sich um ein Gehen im absoluten Sinn. Es legt sich deshalb nahe, im Nachlaufen der Jünger eine existentielle Ausrichtung auf Jesus im Sinne der Jüngernachfolge bezeichnet zu sehen. Objekt dieser Nachfolge ist immer Jesus": KÜGLER, *Der Jünger, den Jesus liebte*, 401.

[182] Cf. HARTIN, *The Role of Peter*, 57.

[183] O'GRADY, *Beloved Disciple*, 60. In this connection Collins writes, "The redactor who added chapter 21 to the Johannine Gospel reminds us that the Beloved Disciple was a disciple who followed after Jesus (and Peter). In this way he dramatized the notion that the Beloved Disciple continued to be a disciple of Jesus even after the Resurrection. By so doing, he continues and reinforces the earlier Johannine tradition which was consistent in describing the Beloved Disciple as *mathetes* (disciple)": COLLINS, *The Representative Figures*, 131.

[184] Regarding the identification of this *other disciple* in Jn 18,15 with the Beloved Disciple there are difference of opinion among the scholars. Those who identify him with the Beloved Disciple consider his appearance together with Peter (as in majority of the Beloved Disciple texts) and his designation ἄλλος μαθητής (cf. 20,2;21,2)

the *other disciple* with the Beloved Disciple this action of *following* can be understood as his characteristic action, i.e. to follow Jesus in all important moments of His paschal mystery. In Jn 18,15 it is not a following of Jesus' teaching but of the person of Jesus Himself, also an aspect of their master-disciple relationship. By following Jesus constantly the Beloved Disciple fulfils the essential quality of a Christian disciple (cf. Jn 1, 36.37.38.40.43).

The designation of the Beloved Disciple as one "whom Jesus loved", his trustful position as one "who had lain close to his (Jesus') breast at the supper" and whose personal enquiry of Jesus' fate as "Lord, who is it that is going to betray you?" etc. in Jn 21,10 are expressions of friendship between Jesus and the Beloved Disciple.[185] In the text in question when the Evangelist refers to the following of the Beloved Disciple, he refers back to the intimate relationship of the Beloved Disciple to Jesus in terms of his privileged position in the Last Supper scene.[186] The theological meaning of ἀκολουθεῖν can be better explained in the context of a friendship, verified in v.20. Hence, the "following" can be understood as a reciprocal expression of the Beloved Disciple's love for and friendship with Jesus.[187] In other words, in the Johannine presentation, the Beloved Disciple's following of Jesus is an expression of his discipleship and intimate friendship with Jesus.

---

as two main reasons for their argument.

[185] Cf. supra, pp. 255-263.

[186] According to Lindars, "the object of the full description at this point (contrast verse 7) is to remind the reader of the special place of intimacy with Jesus which the Disciple enjoyed": LINDARS, *John*, 638.

[187] Commenting on v.20 Agourides says: "The beloved disciple loves calmly, securely, without doubt or vacillation": AGOURIDES, *Peter and John*, 6.

b. The disciple, who is entitled to remain
ἐὰν αὐτὸν θέλω μένειν ἕως ἔρχομαι ...(v.22)

The Beloved Disciple, in Jesus' salvific plan (θέλω), is entitled to remain (μένειν) faithful as a true disciple of Jesus till His second coming.[188] The possibility of remaining faithful to Jesus is not simply due to one's merit, but is also a gift of God. In the strict grammatical construction of v.22 the particle ἐὰν does not stand for a hypothetical possibility,[189] but for the fact which Jesus relates. Hence, here the Evangelist means that it is Jesus' will (θέλω) that the Beloved Disciple should remain. In the context though v.22 seems to be a scolding of Peter,[190] emphasizing Jesus' love-relationship with the Beloved Disciple entitled to remain till Jesus' coming.

The term μένειν (remain) in the context of the narrative seems to mean 'remain alive'. But such a contextual meaning is denied by the comment of the Evangelist in v.23. In the Johannine corpus μένειν has a deep meaning of remaining true to Jesus and to His

---

[188] Schnackenburg uses the term 'parousia' for the expression "until I come" in v.22: Cf. SCHNACKENBURG, *St. John*, Vol III, 369.

[189] Cf. BLASS - DEBRUNNER, *Greek Grammar*, § 373 (1), where the author discusses with examples the use of ἐὰν in the sense of 'real' and he refers to Jn 21,22 not in the sense of "if", but as a fact. According to him ἐὰν indicates the fact that one should wait in a determined circumstance.

[190] The phrase, τί πρὸς σέ (what is that to you) reminds Peter that, being a true follower of Jesus, he has to accept the possibility of a true and intimate relationship between Jesus and another disciple. Jesus is free to execute His will as He wishes (cf. Mt 20,13-15).

teaching, whether in life or in death.[191] It can also be well understood in the light of Jn 11,25b, where Jesus speaks of a spiritually continued life of a believing disciple, even though he is physically dead. According to this interpretation of the term μένειν, one can assume that the Beloved Disciple is a true Christian disciple, a true believer of Jesus, entitled to have the eternal life.

"Following" and "remaining" are theologically connected. If one understands "following" as a moving forward along the footsteps of the master through an act of obedience, then "remaining" means the continuous enactment of the commandments of the master and an everlasting life based on obedience. Both are two phases of one and the same discipleship and they are profound expressions of one's intimacy with the master, Jesus. Thus, the close friendship between Jesus and the Beloved Disciple is highlighted in the pericope when the Beloved Disciple is presented as one who follows Jesus and is supposed to remain till the parousia.

c. The disciple, who bears witness to Jesus

Οὗτός ἐστιν ὁ μαθητὴς ὁ μαρτυρῶν περὶ τούτων καὶ ὁ γράψας ταῦτα (v.24)

In v.24 the Evangelist presents the Beloved Disciple as a genuine witness to Jesus and to His Gospel. The witnessing role of the Beloved Disciple has a continuous nature, illustrated by the

---

[191] μένειν in the present context and in the context of discipleship means *remaining in Jesus and in His Words* (cf. Jn 15,4ff.;8,31) which is different from the early Christians' apocalyptic understanding of it as *remaining in life* as Bultmann explains: Cf. BULTMANN, *John*, 715.

Evangelist attributing to him the authorship of the Gospel. [192] The use of the verb in its present participle form μαρτυρῶν together with the aorist participle γράψας denote the lasting nature of his testimony. [193] The witnessing of the Beloved Disciple is expressed as true, authentic (cf. also 19,35),[194] and being continued in the future generations in the form of the written Gospel, whose authorship is attributed to the same disciple.

The term μένειν (v.23) can be better understood in the light of the Beloved Disciple's continuous and lasting witnessing role. [195] By giving testimony to eternal truths the Beloved Disciple can have a continuous abiding in Jesus and in His teachings. Hence, the term

---

[192] Here we are not interested to make an investigation regarding the authorship of the Fourth Gospel. Behind this affirmation of the Evangelist one can see certain theological and apologetic motives. The Beloved Disciple could be a traditional witness to the words and deeds of Jesus and that might have given a value for the accounts of the Evangelist. One need not attempt to identify the authorship with the witnessing. The plural οἴδαμεν (we know) shows that this witnessing does not refer to the authorship of the Fourth Gospel. The Beloved Disciple's attributed authorship is a matter of dispute among the scholars, but about his function as a witness to Jesus' teaching for his community there is little doubt: Cf. QUAST, *Beloved Disciple*, 151; O'GRADY, *Beloved Disciple*, 61; OSBORNE, *The Resurrection Narrative*, 302; DAUER, *Das Wort des Gekreuzigten*, Teil II, 91. Schnackenburg, Brown and others give a causal interpretation for this authorship in the sense that the traditions and the essential thoughts come from the disciple whom Jesus loved: Cf. SCHNACKENBURG, *St. John*, Vol III, 373; BROWN, *John*, Vol II, 1123; ELLER, *The Beloved Disciple*, 43f.

[193] Cf. QUAST, *Beloved Disciple*, 151; DAUER, *Das Wort des Gekreuzigten*, Teil II, 90.

[194] The Beloved Disciple appears as a "dependable witness to all that had happened": MINEAR, *The Beloved Disciple*, 115.

[195] According to De la Potterie μένειν in v.23 must be understood in relation to the present participle ὁ μαρτυρῶν and accordingly μένειν is a remaining by way of an authentic written testimony of the Evangelist and of the tradition of the community: Cf. I. DE LA POTTERIE, "Le témoin qui demeure: le disciple que Jésus aimait", *Bib* 67 (1986) 453-454; *Il discepolo che Gesù amava*, 54; HARTIN, *The Role of Peter*, 57.

μένειν means continuity in the figurative sense as witnessing rather than the physical life being continued. [196] The Beloved Disciple's continuous witnessing to Jesus and to His Gospel, an expression of his intimacy with Jesus, provides him the status of an ideal Christian disciple. Thus, the continuous and authentic witnessing of the Beloved Disciple can be seen as a reciprocal response to Jesus' already established friendship with him.

We have been analyzing certain characteristic expressions concerning the friendship between the Beloved Disciple and Jesus in the concluding episode of the Fourth Gospel. The Beloved disciple's qualities, such as the continuous *following* of Jesus, the continuously *remaining* faithful to Jesus and to His Gospel, *a continuous witnessing* to Jesus' words and deeds through his Spirit-borne proclamation and Jesus' *divine will* to fulfil the above said qualities in the life of the Beloved Disciple are explicit expressions of the friendship between Jesus and His Beloved. The reciprocal dimension of the relationship between the master and the disciple is explicitly expressed in the pericope.

---

[196] Cf. QUAST, *Beloved Disciple*, 151; KÜGLER, *Der Jünger, den Jesus liebte*, 403; DE LA POTTERIE, *Il discepolo che Gesù amava*, 54-55. Regarding the figurative meaning of μένειν Schnackenburg writes: "Jesus desires that his disciple 'remains' yet not in an outward sense of 'remaining alive' but in another figurative way. That can then be understood as the continuing effect in the circle of his disciples and his Church, or as the continuance of his words, his Spirit-borne proclamation (as it is found in the gospel). Perhaps the writer who only wanted to defend against false interpretation, did not want to commit himself precisely. But this spiritual 'remaining' and continuing effect of the disciple is in line with what is also recognizable in v.24":SCHNACKENBURG, *St. John*, Vol III, 370; cf. also BROWN, *John*, Vol II, 1122.

II. Peter: a Model of True Friendship with Jesus (Jn 21,15-19)

The Fourth Evangelist presents Peter in a quite unique way from Peter's choice as a disciple, brought to Jesus by the testimony of his brother Andrew (cf.1,40-42).[197] Peter's role is well accepted in the Antiochean and Syrian Churches.[198] As in the case of the Synoptics Peter's leading role is duly respected in the Fourth Gospel. In the second part of the Gospel, especially in the Beloved Disciple texts, the Evangelist seems to present Peter's role subordinate to that of the Beloved Disciple.[199] In spite of apparent rivalry based on theological and apologetic reasons, one can see the representative and leading role of Peter in the Johannine presentation (cf. Jn 6,67-69; 13,36-37; 20,1-10; 21,7b. 15-19 etc.). In the present study we limit ourselves to an analysis of only one Petrine text (Jn 21,15-19), where one sees the explicit use of the two verbs ἀγαπάω and φιλέω

---

[197] According to the Synoptic and early Christian tradition Peter is listed as the first one among the disciples of Jesus, but the details of his call or process of his naming as Peter are not at all mentioned there (cf. Mk 3,16;Mt 10,2;Lk 6,14;Acts 1,13). It is the Fourth Evangelist who gives a short account of the election of Peter with the conferring of a new name as Κηφᾶς (Peter). The conferring of a new name and the name Κηφᾶς are to be interpreted theologically.

[198] Cf. LORENZEN, Der Lieblingsjünger, 91ff.

[199] Cf. Ibid., 94-96, where Lorenzen tries to explain the theological, ecclesiological and polemic motives behind such a presentation. Cf. also AGOURIDES, Peter and John, 3-7; GUNTHER, The Beloved Disciple, 138-140, where Gunther puts forward the opinions of different authors. Bultmann, in the light of such a presentation, finds Peter as a rivalry of the Beloved Disciple in the sense that Peter represents the Jewish Christian Church, whereas the Beloved Disciple represents the Hellenistic Christian Church: Cf. BULTMANN, John, 484-485. But Schnackenburg rejects this opinion of rivalry and symbolic interpretation: Cf. R. SCHNACKENBURG, "On the Origin of the Fourth Gospel", Perspective II (1970) 223-246. Roloff finds the influence of a double tradition, viz. the tradition of Peter as the head of the Apostles' circle and the tradition of the Beloved Disciple as one who enjoys a special position: Cf. ROLOFF, Lieblingsjünger, 140.

to express the interpersonal relationship between Jesus and Peter. In the context of this Petrine text he is called to manifest a unique expression of friendship, a sound idea in the Johannine theological understanding of the concept of friendship.

A. Delimitation of the Text

One can observe a literary and thematic unity in the small episode found in Jn 21, 15-19.[200] This section has a thematic unity, since it deals with Peter and his personal relationship with Christ. Peter is conferred pastoral care in the Church as the result of his undivided love for Christ and is asked to follow Him through martyrdom. But Bultmann denies the literary unity in this small pericope since he finds a close interconnection between vv. 18-19 and 20-23. For him the whole of vv. 18-23 is a later addition to a piece of early tradition in vv. 15-17 concerning Peter's commission for the leadership of the community.[201] However, in the light of the whole Johannine theology[202] we consider this small episode concerning Peter (vv. 15-19) as one unit.

---

[200] Cf. MLAKUZHYIL, *The Christocentric Structure*, 235-236. He sees these verses as a dialogue between Jesus and Peter concerning Peter's undivided love for Christ, his pastoral mission in the Church and his fate of martyrdom. All these themes are interconnected since they concern Peter, whereas the following section which begins with v. 20 deals with the fate of the Beloved Disciple. Schnackenburg treats this section as a thematic unity with the subtitle 'the Risen One and Simon Peter': Cf. SCHNACKENBURG, *St. John*, Vol III, 360.

[201] Cf. BULTMANN, *John*, 712-713

[202] The Johannine teaching on martyrdom, as the greatest expression of friendship (cf. Jn 15,13), and Jesus' choice of the disciples with a definite mission in the context of expressed friendship (cf. Jn 15, 16) are seen in direct application with Peter when we consider Jn 21,15-19 as one unit.

There are also certain literary devices which support such a delimitation. By referring to the *breakfast*, the pericope's setting is fixed. The context of the breakfast in which the preceding scene was staged on, is closed by v.15 and a new scene, i.e. Jesus' dialogue with Peter, is introduced. Thus there is a *shift of scene* in the opening verse of the pericope. The editorial comment in v. 14 concludes the preceding section and leaves room for the opening of a new section. The pericope closes with Jesus' exhortation to Peter to follow him (v.19). In the following section there is nothing new concerning Peter, only a repetition of the exhortation to follow Jesus (v.22). The expression ἐπιστραφείς (v.20) can be considered as a new editorial starting-point of a new section.[203] With the *introduction of a new character*, viz. the Disciple whom Jesus loved, the scene of the private dialogue between Jesus and Peter comes to an end. Now the theme of discussion concerns the fate of the Beloved Disciple. In the light of such arguments one can consider vv.15-19 as an independent unit in the context of the present study.

B. The Literary Genre

The pericope under consideration is a part of the "epilogue", narrative in style, but in the form of a *progressive dialogue*[204] between Jesus and Peter. Unlike the preceding section (vv.1-14) it lacks dramatic quality in the presentation, i.e. there is no shift of

---

[203] Cf. SCHNACKENBURG, *St. John*, Vol III, 360-361, where Schnackenburg justifies the position of considering vv.15-19 as a self-sufficient narrative unit and he even calls this pericope as the *Peter-fragment*.

[204] Cf. MLAKUZHYIL, *The Christocentric Structure*, 235, where the author denotes it a "moving dialogue". We prefer the term 'progressive dialogue' to emphasize the culminative nature of the narrative.

scene, change of characters and dramatic action. In the Evangelist's literary framework the dialogue between Jesus and Peter appears as an efficient device to express the close interpersonal relationship between Jesus and Peter. In the following analysis the important expressions in their dialogue will be treated in view of establishing the nature of the interpersonal relationship between Jesus and Peter.

C. The Expressions of Friendship Between Jesus and Peter

1. Peter, who confesses his supreme love towards Jesus

Σίμων Ἰωάννου, ἀγαπᾷς με πλέον τούτων; ναὶ κύριε, σὺ οἶδας ὅτι φιλῶ σε (vv.15.16), πάντα σὺ οἶδας, σὺ γινώσκεις (v.17)

The threefold questions to Peter by the Risen Lord and Peter's immediate, definite and positive answer to those questions are explicit expressions of their interpersonal relationship. Jesus' questions are not the result of a doubt about Peter's love towards Him,[205] but rather are symbolic and theological, parallel to the threefold denial of Peter.[206] Peter was asked to confess an undivided, self-giving love, a basic requirement for Christian discipleship and friendship with Jesus. Such a love confers responsibilities and demands martyrdom.

---

[205] In the other Petrine texts (Jn 6,67-69; 13,36-37; 20,1-10; 21,7b) Peter's genuine love towards Jesus is evident.

[206] Cf. supra, p. 246, n .6; cf. also SCHNACKENBURG, *St. John*, Vol III, 361; LINDARS, *John*, 635-636; KÜGLER, *Der Jünger, den Jesus liebte*, 396.

Jesus addresses Peter by using his father's name as Σίμων Ἰωάννου.[207] Jesus' addressing of Peter in a patronymic reference adds solemnity to the address.[208] It shows Jesus' superiority in naming Peter by referring to his physical origin. In the context of the style this expression can be seen as Jesus' attempt to treat Peter less familiarly and thus to challenge his friendship.[209]

Jesus' stereotyped question to Peter concerning his genuine love for Him and Peter's repeated answer by confessing his affectionate love towards Jesus are sublime expressions of their interpersonal relationship. In these questions and answers the Evangelist uses the two theologically pregnant verbs ἀγαπᾶν and φιλεῖν interchangeably. For many authors there is no distinction between these two verbs in Johannine account.[210] But, in the particular context, where the interpersonal love-relationship between a master and a disciple is well depicted, one can look for certain theological reasons behind the interchangeable use of ἀγαπᾶν and φιλεῖν.

Some modern authors differentiate ἀγαπᾶν and φιλεῖν as terms with different ranges of meaning. For them ἀγαπᾶν means a love

---

[207] Regarding this name there are two readings: Ἰωάννου (B ℵ[1] C* D L W Tat[pt] VL (except c) Vg cop.); Ἰωνᾶ (A C[2] Θ Ψ f.[13]...) The first reading is preferable, since it is confirmed by ancient manuscripts and is similar to Jn 1,42. The second reading is witnessed by later manuscripts which can be seen as an assimilation to Mt 16,17: Cf. BERNARD, St. John, Vol II, 701.

[208] Cf. LINDARS, John, 633.

[209] Cf. BROWN, John, Vol II, 1102.

[210] Cf. BROWN, John, Vol II, 1103; SCHNACKENBURG, St. John, Vol III, 363; LINDARS, John, 634; STÄHLIN, φιλέω, TDNT IX, 129-136; C.F.D. MOULE, An Idiom Book of the New Testament Greek (Cambridge 1953), 198; BERNARD, St. John, Vol II, 702; and many ancient Syriac, Greek and Latin Fathers.

of the will and not simply the affection of the heart.[211] They understand φιλεῖν as affection of the heart,[212] a human attachment or a "friendship love".[213] By taking into consideration the difference in nuances of these two verbs one can interpret their particular usage in the context of the present text.

In the formulation of the two questions of Jesus the Evangelist adopts ἀγαπᾶν, unlike the third formula, where φιλεῖν is used. Through the first two questions Jesus demands from Peter a special form of love, proper for a faithful Christian, rather than one of affection existing among friends. By listening to Peter's answer, confessing his affectionate love towards his Master, finally the Johannine Jesus changes the mode of His question by using the Greek verb φιλεῖν. Such a change from ἀγαπᾶν to φιλεῖν in the questions of Jesus shows the development of their interpersonal relationship from the level of a relationship between Jesus and a believer to that of close friends. It is noteworthy that in all three answers of Peter φιλεῖν is used and for him his love towards Jesus is always one of natural affection.[214] What Jesus asks from Peter is a form of love which involves rights and duties. Such a love is verified when Peter is immediately entrusted with the role of feeding and tending the sheep of Jesus. Peter seems to understand the

---

[211] Cf. WESTCOTT, *St. John*, 303; Gunther considers it as a love of "heavenly quality": Cf. GUNTHER, *The Beloved Disciple*, 133.

[212] Cf. SPICQ, *Agapè*, 234, where he defines φιλεῖν as "affection humaine". According to Evans φιλεῖν denotes the higher kind of love, for it is more inclusive, going beyond the notion of mere satisfaction which adheres to ἀγαπᾶν in the earlier classical usage: Cf. E. EVANS, "The Verb ΑΓΑΠΑΝ in the Fourth Gospel", in: F.L. CROSS (ed.), *Studies in the Fourth Gospel* (London 1957) 64-71.

[213] Cf. GUNTHER, *The Beloved Disciple*, 133.

[214] Cf. CABA, *Cristo è risorto*, 283.

depth of Jesus' question which is clear from his positive answer (ναὶ κύριε), but still he wants to go beyond the mere love of the will and express even his affectionate friendly love.[215] Peter's positive answer presupposes his awareness and readiness to fulfil the rights and duties proper to a friend of Jesus.[216]

The text ends with Jesus' invitation to Peter to follow Him by way of martyrdom, the greatest and a sublime expression of friendship. Such a following by Peter can be understood only on the basis of two other Johannine texts: Jn 13,37 and 15,13.[217] Accordingly, in the context of the present text Peter's love towards Jesus can be understood as one of close friendship to the extent of laying down his life for his friend (φίλος), Jesus. Hence, the choice

---

[215] In the present context the interchanged use of ἀγαπᾶν and φιλεῖν is noteworthy. When Peter answers Jesus through the term φιλεῖν he is emphasizing an aspect of love which is complementary to the love of a usual Christian believer expressed through ἀγαπᾶν. In the Johannine presentation the genuine love of a believer is a necessary requirement to enter into a friendship expressed through the affectionate love φιλεῖν. Love is the basis of friendship. Peter's love of friendship with Jesus expressed through φιλεῖν presupposes his love as a believer expressed through ἀγαπᾶν. Osborne tries to explain the use of the two verbs ἀγαπᾶν and φιλεῖν in the same context as an attempt of the Evangelist to show the universal aspect of love, "the love in its totality": Cf. G.R. OSBORNE, *John 21: Test Case for the History and Redaction in the Resurrection Narratives* (France/Wenham 1981) 308. One can agree with the explanation of Osborne when he considers ἀγαπᾶν and φιλεῖν as two different aspects of love. Cf. supra, p. 87, n. 1.

[216] Considering the nuance of the text Glombitza considers the figure of Peter as a "Freund im Hause des Herrn, des menschlichen Königs": O. GLOMBITZA, "Petrus - der Freund Jesu. Überlegungen zu Joh 21,15ff." *NT* 6 (1963) 279, n.1. He continues: "Diese Antwort läßt also erkennen, daß Petrus die Doppeldeutigkeit der Frage begriffen hat, er sagt mit seiner ändernden Formulierung: Du hast mich durch deine Gnadenwahl zum Freund in deinem Reiche und Hause gemacht; ich habe dadurch Rechte und Pflichten erworben, das Recht, mich auf deine Treue und Fürsorge verlassen zu dürfen, und die Pflicht, für die anvertrauten Menschen fürsorglich zu handeln": *Ibid.*, 279.

[217] Cf. LINDARS, *John*, 634-635.

of the verb φιλεῖν in the three answers of Peter and the change of
the verb from ἀγαπᾶν to φιλεῖν in the third question of Jesus can
be considered as theological [218] and in line with the Johannine
concept of friendship. [219]

The supreme nature of love, expected from Peter, is stylistically
brought out by the Evangelist by adding a comparative clause πλέον
τούτων to Jesus' first question. Since the exact reference of the
τούτων (these) is not mentioned in the text, different authors give
a variety of interpretations depending on the grammatical
construction. [220] In spite of the unresolved grammatical difficulties
πλέων with the genitive supports the popular interpretation: 'Do you
love me more than these men (who love me)?'. The possibility of
the variety of interpretations does not affect the crux of the question
regarding Peter's supreme love. [221] Through such a comparative
question the Evangelist depicts the uniqueness and sublimity of

---

[218] Cf. supra, pp. 309-311.

[219] It is also noteworthy that the verb φιλεῖν and the noun φίλος are from the
same root.

[220] Bernard and some others treat τούτων as the equivalent of an English
neuter object of the verb and understand the question as: 'Do you love me more
than you love these things (boats, nets and fishing)?': Cf. BERNARD, St. John, Vol
II, 705; QUAST, Beloved Disciple, 143-144. Fridrichsen understands τούτων as
the masculine object of the verb: 'Do you love me more than you love these other
disciples?': Cf. A. FRIDRICHSEN, "Älska, hata, förneka (försaka)", Svensk
Exegetisk Arsbok, 5 (1940) 152-162. Most scholars take this τούτων as the
masculine subject of an implied verb: 'Do you love me more than these other
disciples do?': Cf. SCHNACKENBURG, St. John, Vol III, 480, n.51; BROWN,
John, Vol II, 1104. Due to the grammatical difficulty Brown prefers the solution
proposed by Bultmann that the implications of the clause should not be considered
very seriously; it can be an editorial attempt to introduce the other disciples into the
scene and thus to connect the pericope with the preceding section.

[221] Cf. GLOMBITZA, Petrus - der Freund Jesu, 278.

Peter's love towards the Risen Lord, which makes him a prototype of Christian disciples and a true friend of Jesus.

In the special mode of Peter's answer to Jesus' repeated questions the sincerity and humility of Peter in acknowledging Jesus' superiority and divinity are evident.[222] The designation of Jesus as κύριος (Lord) in all three answers seems to be an acknowledgement of Jesus as the God of glory.[223] Instead of giving a direct answer to Jesus' question Peter expresses his love and loyalty to Him by referring to Jesus' divine knowledge which proves the authenticity of the answer. Through the repeated formula and a change of vocabulary the Evangelist tries to express the intimate relationship between Jesus and Peter. In the first two answers Peter acknowledges Jesus' knowledge of Peter's love, whereas in the third one Jesus' omniscience is illustrated by using the term πάντα (everything).

A progress in their interpersonal relationship is depicted even by the verbs selected to refer to Jesus' knowledge.[224] There is a change from the verb οἶδας, the knowing of a fact, to γινώσκεις, knowing something by feeling in an intimate way.[225] In this respect one has to understand the distinctive use of the two verbs of knowledge i.e. οἶδα and γινώσκω elsewhere in the Fourth Gospel.[226]

---

[222] Cf. PANIMOLLE, *Giovanni*, 480.

[223] Cf. *Ibid.*, 480. This Lordship of Jesus can be understood as a post-resurrectional title.

[224] Cf. CABA, *Cristo è risorto*, 283.

[225] Cf. LINDARS, *John*, 635.

[226] Cf. I. DE LA POTTERIE, " Οἶδα et γινώσκω : Les deux modes de la connaissance dans le quatrième évangile", *Bib* 40 (1959) 709-725. Unlike some authors like Barrett, Dodd and Schnackenburg, De la Potterie finds a clear

The Evangelist prefers οἶδα to γινώσκω (22 x 12) when he refers to Jesus' knowledge. Οἶδα is knowing absolutely, not a knowledge acquired through experience. Designating Jesus' knowledge by οἶδα indicates a divine and absolute quality, a sovereign knowledge.[227] However γινώσκω refers to the natural but acquired knowledge especially through experience; Jesus acquires such knowledge at a supernatural level (cf.Jn 2,25).[228] Against this background, the use of οἶδα in the first two answers of Peter can be seen as his appeal to the supernatural knowledge of Christ concerning his love towards his Master. In the third answer οἶδα is used to depict Jesus' omniscience, whereas γινώσκω refers to Jesus' *experiential knowledge* of Peter's love towards Him. Such an experience of Jesus regarding Peter's love towards Him can be understood as an expression of their friendship. By the choice of such vocabulary in the text, where the interpersonal relationship is depicted, the Evangelist highlights the nature of the friendship between Jesus and Peter.

---

distinction between the two Greek verbs οἶδα and γινώσκω in their usage of the Fourth Evangelist. We also find such a clear distinction of these two verbs in the present context.

[227] Cf. DE LA POTTERIE, *Οἶδα et γινώσκω*, 716-717.

[228] Cf. *Ibid.*, 713-715.

2. Peter, who is entrusted with pastoral ministry

ὁ Ἰησοῦς λέγει αὐτῷ· βόσκε τὰ ἀρνία μου (v.15c), ποίμαινε τὰ πρόβατά μου (v.16c), βόσκε τὰ πρόβατά μου (v.17c)

The solemn conferring [229] of the apostolic mission of feeding and tending the sheep of Jesus is the second explicit expression of the close interpersonal relationship between Jesus and Peter. It demands Peter's responsibility and confers special power upon him which are two aspects of Christian discipleship. Jesus grants him a position of trust and authority. [230] On the basis of this expressed love and entrusted authority Peter becomes "Jesus' friend by choice (cf. Jn 15,13-16)". [231] A close analysis of the terminology in Jesus' commission to Peter helps to understand the real nature of their friendship.

In vv.15 and 17 the verb βόσκειν [232] is used which has a limited meaning of feeding or provision of food. In v.16 the verb ποιμαίνειν [233] is adopted which has a wide range of meaning

---

[229] The threefold command can be seen as a solemn conferring of the shepherding role to Peter. Gaechter tries to analyze this threefold command in the light of ancient and modern Near-Eastern custom of saying something three times for the sake of solemnity: Cf. P. GAECHTER, "Das dreifache 'Weide meine Lämmer'", *ZKT* 69 (1947) 328-344.

[230] Cf. BROWN, *John*, Vol II, 1111.

[231] COLLINS, *The Representative Figures*, 129; cf. also GLOMBITZA, *Petrus - der Freund Jesu*, 277.

[232] In the Synoptics βόσκειν is always used of feeding swine, whereas in the LXX it denotes the feeding of sheep (cf. Gen 29,7; 37,12).

[233] Ποιμαίνειν is used by Luke and Paul in the literal sense of shepherding (cf. Lk 17,7; 1 Cor 9,7). In LXX it is used in the sense of feeding the sheep exactly as βόσκειν is used (cf. Gen 30,31; 37,2) and in both cases they are the translations of one Hebrew verb רעה. The Vulgata translated this verb in all three verses as *pasce*

covering all rights and duties of a shepherd (ποιμήν) in the sense of tending[234] or sovereign leading. Hence, Peter is entrusted with the role of a shepherd in the spiritual sense[235] with all the powers and duties of a shepherd evident in this connection from the use of the verbs βόσκειν and ποιμαίνειν.[236] Peter is asked to feed Jesus' flock with spiritual food and to tend them which comprises guarding them from enemies and leading them with authority to God's kingdom. It demands a service based on love and a total dedication for the flock even to the point of death.[237]

The shepherding for which Peter is appointed is also a substitutive role for Jesus. He was asked to represent Jesus, the Good Shepherd (Jn 10,11), who had the functions of feeding or finding pasture (vv.9-10), leading (vv.3ff.) and guarding or protecting (v.28). In the context of the text under consideration Peter's authority of shepherding is not absolute. He is asked to feed and tend the sheep which belong to Jesus,[238] clear from the expression

---

without any distinction from the Greek text.

[234] According to the OT understanding (cf. Chron 17,6; 2 Sam 5,2) and in the context of the Qumran community (cf. CD 13,9-10) "tending" has the sense of an authoritative mission.

[235] This spiritual sense of "shepherding" is found both in the OT (Ezek 34,2) and in the NT (Acts 20,28; 1 Pet 5,2; Rev 2,27; 7,17).

[236] According to Schnackenburg the interchanged use of these two verbs means here "all inclusive care of a shepherd with which Jesus invests Peter": SCHNACKENBURG, St. John, Vol III, 363.

[237] Cf. BROWN, John, Vol II, 1115.

[238] Cf. AUGUSTINUS, Tractatus, CXXIII, 5; PL 35, 1967, where commenting on this Johannine text he writes: "Tend my sheep as mine, and not as yours".

ἀρνία (πρόβατά) μου (vv.15-17).[239]   Peter is appointed as a substitute for Jesus, a shepherd for *all His flock*. Through the expression "my sheep" the proprietary right of Jesus is retained even when it is transferred to the care of Peter.[240] Jesus' commission to Peter can be seen as Peter's sharing in Jesus' work given by the Father, i.e. the task of protecting and leading of the faithful flock given to him (cf. 6,37-40; 10,27-30; 17,6.12). Thus, at two levels Peter is a substitute for Jesus, viz. at level of his person and at the level of his function. Such a substitutive role[241] can be seen as an explicit expression of their friendship.

---

[239] There are certain textual problems with regard to the different nouns used to describe the flock. In v.15 unlike the case of the majority of manuscripts instead of ἀρνία some manuscripts like C*, D etc. adopt a reading with πρόβατα. This may be an assimilation of the usage in v.15 to that of vv.16 and 17. In v. 16 προβάτια is read by B and C as against πρόβατα which is found in ℵ A D N Γ Δ. In v.17 πρόβατα is supported by ℵ D N Γ Δ instead of the witnessing of A B C, which read προβάτια. Considering the external evidence it is difficult to determine the original reading of v.16. But one has to take into account the progressive style of the whole pericope, where there is a tendency of using different terminology (ἀγαπᾶν - φιλεῖν and βόσκειν - ποιμαίνειν) to show a progressive comprehensive thought. In this respect a due consideration of the Syriac versions, which adopt three different words equivalent to lambs, young sheep and flock, is also necessary. On the basis of such considerations we are inclined to adopt the reading: ἀρνία ... προβάτια ... πρόβατα in vv.15. 16. 17 respectively. For more details cf. BERNARD, *St. John*, Vol II, 706. But for Schnackenburg it is difficult to defend such a position: Cf. SCHNACKENBURG, *St. John*, Vol III, 363.

[240] Cf. SCHNACKENBURG, *St. John*, Vol III, 363.

[241] In Jn 19,26-27 we have seen that Jesus' Beloved Disciple was made his substitute as a son to Jesus' mother.

3. Peter, who is asked to follow Jesus
καὶ τοῦτο εἰπὼν λέγει αὐτῷ· ἀκολούθει μοι (vv. 19b. 22b)

In the context of the love and loyalty professed by Peter, Jesus invites him to glorify God by means of martyrdom, which is closely connected with the pastoral ministry to which Peter is appointed. As the Good Shepherd, Jesus laid down His life for His sheep, for His own (cf.Jn 10,11; 13,1); therefore Peter, who was the substitute for Jesus, the Good Shepherd had to follow Him through martyrdom. Peter's martyrdom was foretold by Jesus metaphorically (vv.18-19), a martyrdom which was parallel to Jesus' death on the cross.[242] The gloss of the Evangelist in v.19 clarifies the metaphor found in v.18, concerning Peter's martyrdom. Peter's foretold martyrdom can be understood as the highest expression of His love and friendship with Jesus (cf. Jn 15,13).

Jesus' prediction of Peter's destiny prepares him to become a true disciple of Jesus here and now. Therefore, He says to Peter: "Follow me" (ἀκολούθει μοι).[243] The "following" in v. 19b must be understood in the light of Peter's readiness to follow Jesus even by laying down his life for Him which was postponed by Jesus (cf. Jn 13,36-38). True discipleship demands one's following after the master even to death. The destiny of a genuine Christian disciple

---

[242] Cf. KÜGLER, Der Jünger, den Jesus liebte, 397-398; SCHNACKENBURG, St. John, Vol III, 367; BERNARD, St. John, Vol II, 708ff., where Bernard analyses the terminology in the metaphor to interpret the prophecy of Peter's martyrdom as a crucifixion. Lindars proposes a parallelism between Jesus' crucifixion and the foretold martyrdom of Peter as a crucifixion by analyzing the expression "stretching out of hands" in early Christian literature: Cf. LINDARS, John, 636-637.

[243] ἀκολουθεῖν is theologically connected with discipleship: Cf. LINDARS, John, 636. Following Christ can be interpreted in different ways such as a call to a mission, to follow Christ's teaching etc.: Cf. SCHNACKENBURG, St. John, Vol III, 360.

can be one of martyrdom. In the context of the prophesied death of Peter (vv. 18-19a) Jesus' invitation to follow Him can be understood as an invitation for the 'imitation of the Lord' by a martyr's death. [244] Hence, Peter's call to share the same destiny of the Lord can be interpreted as a high estimation of Peter and an explicit expression of their friendship.

The portrait of Peter in the Fourth Gospel is quite unique. It presents him as a representative figure[245] and a true model of Christian discipleship, although perhaps different from that of the Beloved Disciple. Peter is depicted as a genuine disciple in the Johannine tradition, whose discipleship extends to the point of death (cf. Jn 21, 18-19).[246] The analysis of Jn 21,15-19 sheds light on the meaning of true Christian discipleship [247] in the context of a deep interpersonal relationship between Jesus and Peter. Hence, one can establish the correlation between discipleship and friendship in the context of a love-relationship expressed by the verbs φιλεῖν and ἀγαπᾶν.

---

[244] Cf. SCHNACKENBURG, *St. John*, Vol III, 348f.

[245] Cf. COLLINS, *The Representative Figures*, 127ff., where Collins tries to illustrate the uniqueness of Peter in the light of all Petrine texts in the Fourth Gospel.

[246] Cf. QUAST, *Beloved Disciple*, 164.

[247] According to Lindars the Evangelist's interest of introducing this scene (Jn 21, 15-19) transcends the idea of giving authority to Peter to a motive of bringing out the meaning of discipleship: Cf. LINDARS, *John*, 633.

III. The Theological Perspective

After the analysis of the important texts concerning the interpersonal relationship between Jesus and two of His model disciples, now we arrive at certain theological conclusions regarding the nature of Jesus-disciple relationship as friendship. What Jesus promised and said to all His disciples regarding friendship (cf. Jn 15,13-16) was already verified in the lives of the Beloved Disciple and Peter. In a genuine friendship between Jesus and a disciple the superiority of Jesus is always admitted. The real divine-human friendship is not unilateral but bilateral or reciprocal. Only a genuine Christian disciple can be a real friend of Jesus. Such friendship is the realization of a master-disciple relationship.

A. The Superiority of Jesus: An Essential Characteristic of Jesus-Disciple Friendship

One of the essential characteristics of the Jesus-disciple friendship is the fact of Jesus' superiority based on His divinity which is always acknowledged by the disciple.[248] The description of the Beloved Disciple as a *disciple* and as *one whom Jesus loved* presupposes a subordinated position of the disciple in relation to Jesus. In the Gospel narrative he has an existence only in connection with Jesus. In all the *Beloved Disciple texts* which we have analyzed, Jesus is the main actor either as a subject who is actively present in the episode or as an object of the active faith of the Beloved Disciple. In those pericopes Jesus appears as the one

---

[248] The analysis of certain Johannine texts in the former chapters of the dissertation also prove the same proposition.

who reveals, and the knowledge which the Beloved disciple shares is a revelatory one, gratuitous in nature.

In the context of the Last Supper Jesus' superiority is admitted by the Beloved Disciple in addressing Him as κύριε (13,25) and in asking the identity of the traitor (13,25; cf.13,11). In the second episode Jesus' superiority is evident in His words from the cross which He uttered in the form of a command.[249] The Beloved Disciple admits Jesus' superiority when he receives Jesus' mother as his own in accordance with His command (cf.19,27). So also in the empty tomb scene through a unique response of faith in the resurrection of Jesus, the beloved Disciple admits Jesus' superiority and divinity (cf.20,8). In the context of Jesus' self-manifestation the Beloved Disciple recognizes the divinity of the Risen Lord by referring to Him as ὁ κύριος (cf. 21,7). In the concluding scene of the Gospel the Beloved Disciple is presented as one following Jesus, a disciple entitled to remain faithful to Him by way of lasting and authentic witnessing (21,20-24). Here also Jesus' superiority is manifested and admitted by the disciple who was beloved to Him.

In the context of the already analyzed Petrine text also Jesus' superiority is expressively manifested which is admitted by Peter as well. As we have seen in Jn 21,15-17 Peter is made Jesus' disciple by choice[250] and is asked to confess his undivided love towards Jesus. As the reward for such a love Jesus confers His authority of pastoral ministry upon Peter. The repeated use of κύριος in the answer of Peter expresses his submissive will to his Master. Being a disciple of Jesus he was asked to follow Him even up to the point

---

[249] Cf. supra, p. 271, esp. n. 95.

[250] Cf. COLLINS, *The Representative Figures*, 129.

of martyrdom.   In such a master-disciple relationship Jesus'
superiority is well manifested.

Thus, our study of the interpersonal relationship between Jesus
and two of His model disciples sheds light on a theological principle,
viz. in a genuine friendship with Jesus one has to admit Jesus'
superiority and divinity. A real friendship between Jesus and a
believer does not reduce the dignity of Jesus who is Lord and
master.   It is not a friendship between two equals but between a
superior Jesus and a faithful Christian disciple.

B. The Reciprocal Dimension of Jesus-Disciple Friendship

The second theological conclusion which we derive from our
study of Jesus' friendship with the Beloved Disciple and Peter is that
a genuine Jesus-disciple friendship is always reciprocal. In the Last
Supper scene the Beloved Disciple appears as one who enjoys
special favour and love from Jesus, clear in his designation as *the
disciple, whom Jesus loved*, in his favoured position as *one lying close
to the breast of Jesus*, and in his privilege of being the only one to
whom Jesus reveals the identity of his traitor.   To Jesus who acts
as a friend the Beloved Disciple positively responds by addressing
Him as Lord and by enquiring about the details of Jesus' fate.

On Calvary also the reciprocal aspect of the friendship between
Jesus and the Beloved Disciple is made clear.   Out of His love for
and trust in the Beloved Disciple, Jesus entrusts His mother and His
friend to each other.   Thus Jesus makes His disciple His own
substitute, an expression of true friendship.   By an immediate
following of Jesus' words the Beloved Disciple fulfils the
characteristic of a reciprocal friendship.   In the empty tomb scene,
by running to Jesus' tomb and by believing in His resurrection the

Beloved Disciple expresses his friendship with Jesus. In the context of the miraculous catch it is only His Beloved Disciple to whom Jesus gives the spiritual enlightenment to recognize Him. By communicating this revelation to the other disciples the Beloved Disciple positively responds to his friend, Jesus. The reciprocal dimension of their friendship is very evident in the concluding scene of the Gospel, where Jesus, out of His divine will, entitles His Beloved to remain faithful to Him for ever. The Beloved Disciple's acts of "following" and "witnessing" can be understood as reciprocal expressions of his friendship with Jesus.

The reciprocity of friendship is clearer in the scene of Jesus' encounter with Peter (21,15-19). Parallel to Peter's profession of love and intimacy, Jesus also entrusts to him the power and responsibility of feeding His own sheep by being a substitute for Himself, the ideal shepherd. Moreover, Peter is asked to follow Jesus through martyrdom, the supreme expression of intimacy with Jesus (cf. 15,13) who sacrificed His life for the sake of His friends including Peter. In brief, the friendship between Jesus and a Christian disciple which the Evangelist envisages is not one-sided but reciprocal.

C. The Beloved Disciple and Peter: Two Prototypes of Christian Discipleship

The analysis of the *Beloved Disciple texts* and the one *Petrine text* in view of establishing the nature of their interpersonal relationship with Jesus prompts one to consider both the Beloved Disciple and Peter as prototypes of Christian discipleship. In their lives they enjoyed the essential characteristics of authentic Christian disciples which enabled them to become models. They are worthy to be called "paradigms for discipleship".[251]

There are many characteristics in the Beloved Disciple which make him a prototype of discipleship. His intimate and continuing relationship with Jesus can be considered as the first and foremost reason to qualify him as a prototype.[252] Such a close relationship enables him to share the knowledge about Jesus and His glorification (cf. 13,21-30) and to be present at Calvary where he is made a substitute for Jesus as a "son" to Jesus' mother (cf. 19,25-27).[253] It is his intimacy with Jesus which entitles him to be one of the first disciples who listen to the gospel of resurrection and to come to a deep faith in the Risen Lord (cf. 20,1-10), an example of a true disciple's response.[254] The Beloved Disciple's intimate relationship with Jesus helps him to obtain spiritual sensitivity and insight and thus to recognize the Risen Lord in the context of a "sign" of Jesus (cf. 21,1-14). Further, their friendship prompts the Beloved Disciple to follow Jesus[255] willingly and to remain faithful

---

[251] *Ibid.*, 153.

[252] According to Quast, "The Beloved Disciple also epitomizes the intimate and continuing relationship of a disciple to his Master. The Beloved Disciple abides (μένειν) with Jesus and is designated as the disciple whom Jesus loved": QUAST, *Beloved Disciple*, 160. Neirynck writes: "The evangelist has introduced the Beloved Disciple in the story of the Gospel at the dark moments of discipleship": NEIRYNCK, *John 21*, 336.

[253] In the light of the scene on Calvary Mahoney considers the Beloved Disciple as an ideal, the model of true discipleship: Cf. MAHONEY, *Two Disciples at the Tomb*, 107-109.

[254] Cf. QUAST, *Beloved Disciple*, 162; P. IAFOLLA, "Giovanni, Figlio di Zebedeo "il discepolo che amava" e il IV° Vangelo", *BeO* 28 (1986) 108.

[255] This following can be understood in the context of a master-disciple relationship. Being one who follows Jesus till the end the Beloved Disciple exemplifies in himself the necessary qualification of a prototype of discipleship.

to him through continued testimony (cf. 21,20-24). By considering the unique intimacy which the Beloved Disciple enjoys with Jesus, one can consider him as "the prototype of all others loved by Jesus Christ".[256]

Another characteristic of the Beloved Disciple which makes him a prototype is his mediatory and witnessing role. By being present in the context of the final discourse of Jesus (chs. 13-17) and by participating in His paschal mystery the Beloved Disciple becomes an authentic witness and interpreter of Jesus' words and deeds. In the Last Supper scene he is presented as a mediator [257] between Jesus and the other disciples, especially Peter, in obtaining divine knowledge regarding Jesus' fate, though there is no explicit mention of his communication of it to them(cf. 13, 24f.). The mediatory and witnessing role is evident in the scene of the appearance of the Risen Lord (cf. 21, 1-14) when he communicates his spiritual insight to Peter (v.7) and to other disciples (v.12). The Beloved Disciple is also given the privileged role of being the primary and ongoing witness. His bond of intimacy with Jesus qualifies him to be a true witness of Jesus, a role which is an essential characteristic of discipleship (cf. Jn 1,36-51).[258] The Beloved Disciple bears witness to the salvific meaning of the death of Jesus, since he is the only disciple present at the cross of Jesus (cf. 19,16f.; 34-35). The witnessing role of the Beloved Disciple has the characteristics of authenticity and continuity (cf. 21,24). Being an authentic witness to Jesus and to His Gospel "he typifies the disciple *par excellence*".[259]

---

[256] R. POTTER, "The Disciple whom Jesus Loved", *LifeSpir* 16 (1962) 297.

[257] Cf. MAHONEY, *Two Disciples at the Tomb*, 77.

[258] Cf. COLLINS, *The Representative Figures*, 131.

[259] *Ibid.*, 132.

Peter is also presented as a prototype of Christian discipleship. Peter's discipleship is evident from the moment of his choice (cf. 1,41-42), as one who is brought to Jesus by means of a testimony regarding the Messiah. The genuine qualities of his discipleship are very clear in the pericope which we have considered to establish his friendship with Jesus (21,15-19). There Peter appears as one who professes his deep love towards his Master. It is this supreme love which makes him a genuine disciple of Jesus.[260]

In Jesus' commissioning of Peter for the pastoral ministry, a ministry of Jesus, the Good Shepherd, Peter's discipleship qualities are presupposed. [261] Through this appointment Jesus grants him a position of trust and authority as a special favour to His disciple, Peter. Discipleship is expressive in martyrdom for which Jesus invites Peter by telling him to follow Him. As a genuine disciple Peter has to follow Jesus whose path is one of self-sacrifice. This following can be understood as a genuine disciple's following after his master, the prescription for discipleship (Mk 8,34 par.). The martyrdom of Peter is a traditionally accepted fact which can be understood as the exact fulfilment of Jesus' prophecy and invitation to Peter. Hence, Peter can be considered as a prototype of Christian discipleship in a unique way.

---

[260] Quast writes: "The theme of discipleship is basic to John's Gospel, and the primary criterion for discipleship is a relationship of love with Jesus": QUAST, *Beloved Disciple*, 154; cf. also BROWN, *John*, Vol II, 1111.

[261] The substitutive pastoral ministry is a characteristic of Jesus' disciples.

Conclusion

So far we have been studying the characteristics of two model disciples, the Beloved Disciple and Peter, in the perspective of their friendship with Jesus. In the light of the analysis we arrive at certain general conclusions regarding the nature of the divine-human friendship. Accordingly the friendship between Jesus and a faithful Christian disciple does not remain on the human and the psychological level, but transcends to a theological realm. Such a friendship is not between two equals, but between a Master (Jesus) and a disciple (faithful Christian). It is expressed in the greatest form of love, i.e. martyrdom, and in the disciple's obedience to his Master, who shares his revelatory knowledge (cf. Jn 15,13-15). Such a friendship is reciprocal and patterned after the close relationship between the Father and the Son, one of the main themes of the Fourth Gospel. All those who are in the status of "His own" can enter into a close friendship with Jesus.

CHAPTER SIX

FRIENDSHIP: JESUS - DISCIPLE RELATIONSHIP
(Synthetical Conclusions)

After the exegesis of the Johannine texts which employ φίλος and its derivatives to denote the interpersonal relationship between Jesus and others, a systematic presentation of the already derived conclusions of the former chapters is in order. Additionally general theological conclusions will be drawn to highlight the originality of the Johannine use of the term φίλος against the background of the non-Johannine use of the term. The reciprocity of the term φίλος, its usage as a term for the divine-human relationship and its special nuance in the Fourth Gospel denoting the master-disciple relationship will be duly considered as well to establish our argument.

I. Reciprocal Dimension of the Term φίλος

The term φίλος itself has a reciprocal connotation. The reciprocal aspect of the term can be understood in two levels, viz. the level of literary application and the level of theological content. The Fourth Evangelist never employs the term φίλος with reference to Jesus, rather he uses it as a designation for the Christian disciples in the context of their relationship with Jesus (cf. Jn 3,29; 11,11; 15,13-15).[1] Hence, the reciprocity of φίλος in the Fourth Gospel must be traced in its theological content rather than in its literary application.

---

[1] Luke employs the term φίλος as a designation both for Jesus (Lk 7,34; cf. also Mt 11,19) and for the disciples (Lk 12,4): Cf. supra, pp. 24-25.

The reciprocal relationship is inherent to real friendship. The examples of genuine friendship in the OT which we have already treated prove the reciprocal dimension of the term φίλος.[2] The expressions of friendship are on both sides even though the initiative is always on one side. In the context of divine-human friendship in the OT a total revelation on God's part and a reciprocal response on man's part are essential elements.

The reciprocity in the theological content of the term is more evident in the Fourth Evangelist's usage. In the context of the metaphor of "the friend of the bridegroom" the Evangelist clearly presents the reciprocal dimension of the term φίλος.[3] The friendship between the bridegroom and his friend at the level of the metaphor and between Jesus and John the Baptist at the level of its application involves an evident reciprocity in their interpersonal relationship. In the second occurrence of the term in Jn 11,11 the aspect of reciprocity is well depicted in the context of the entire pericope. The words and deeds of the main characters and the comments of the bystanders and of the Evangelist illustrate the different reciprocal expressions of the friendship between Jesus and the Bethany family.[4] The reciprocal dimension of the term φίλος is highlighted in the pericope (Jn 15,1-17) where Jesus teaches on the theme of unity and friendship. In vv.13.14.15 φίλος is repeatedly used in its double dimension. The reciprocal relationship is depicted through the imagery of the vine and branches. So also

---

[2] Cf. supra, pp. 15-21.

[3] Cf. supra, pp. 83-85.

[4] Cf. supra, pp. 97ff. Even though the term φίλος is used as a designation for Lazarus its meaning could be traced in the context of the entire pericope. Hence, the reciprocity of the term also must be extrapolated from the words and deeds of all characters.

the relationship between the Father and the Son is presented as the model and source of the reciprocal relationship between Jesus and His disciples. The friendship between Jesus and the believer is illustrated as a reciprocal "remaining in" which involves Jesus' initiative in the friendship through revelation and self-sacrifice and the believer's response through obedience, love, faith and trust.[5] Thus the term φίλος denotes a reciprocity in its theological content.

The intimacy between Jesus and the Beloved Disciple and between Jesus and Peter sheds light on the reciprocal dimension of the term φίλος.[6] The reciprocity is clear in the expressions of their friendship which we have already analyzed in chapter five. Hence, the friendship between Jesus and the two model disciples, viz. the Beloved Disciple and Peter, expressly manifested a reciprocal relationship.[7] In short, one can say that the friendship between Jesus and a Christian disciple which the Fourth Evangelist illustrates through the term φίλος and its derivatives is not unilateral, but reciprocal in its theological content.

---

[5] Cf. supra, pp. 238-239.

[6] Of course, φίλος is not used in those cases. But the verbs φιλεῖν and ἀγαπᾶν are employed to illustrate the intimate relationship between Jesus and those representative figures.

[7] Cf. supra, pp. 322-323.

II. Φίλος: A Term for the Divine-Human Relationship

The terms φίλος and φιλεῖν are generally understood as vocabulary depicting affectionate human relationship. [8] But their use in the course of history proves that they cannot be simply limited to explain affectionate love among human beings. From early time φίλος and its derivatives are used also to illustrate divine-human relationship.

A. Outside the Fourth Gospel

The idea of divine-human relationship depicted through the term φίλος and its derivatives is already seen in ancient Greek philosophy. The concept of the "friend of Gods" (φίλος θεῶν) was developed already by Plutarch. [9] In the OT the theological use of the term φίλος denoting divine-human friendship is clearer when it is employed to present Abraham and Moses as the friends of God. [10] In the Wisdom literature the term φίλος is used to bring out the divine-human relationship. [11]

The use of the term φίλος in the NT other than the Fourth Gospel confirms the fact that it is a term used for both the human relationship and the divine-human friendship. In the single occurrence of the term in Mt 11,19 it is used to present Jesus as the

---

[8] Cf. GÜNTHER & LINK, ἀγαπάω, DNTT II, 538.

[9] Cf. supra, p. 12.

[10] Cf. supra, pp. 15-21.

[11] Cf. supra, p. 21.

friend of the sinners and tax-collectors. In Lucan writings φίλος is used mainly to express human relationships with the exception of Lk 12,4 where the Evangelist highlights Jesus-disciple relationship. [12] But in the letter of St. James the aspect of divine-human friendship is verified when he presents Abraham as the friend of God. [13]

B. In the Fourth Gospel

Unlike Luke the Fourth Evangelist employs the term φίλος mainly to depict the divine-human friendship. Out of the six occurrence of the term in the Gospel of John with the exception of a single instance (19,12) all the five usages illustrate the intimacy between Jesus and others. In all such cases φίλος is used to explicate a relationship which surpasses human friendship based on psychological aspects. Therefore, one can legitimately say that the Fourth Evangelist adopts the term to portray the friendship between the divine Jesus and the genuine Christian followers.

III. Φίλος: A Term for the Master-Disciple Relationship

In the Fourth Gospel φίλος is used not to illustrate a relationship between two equals, but it expresses a friendship between Jesus who is superior and master and a believer who is an authentic Christian disciple. The superiority of Jesus can be understood from the point of view of His divinity, viz. His unique

---

[12] Cf. supra, pp. 24-25.

[13] Cf. supra, pp. 26-27.

revelatory role and His divine Sonship. So also, the Christian
discipleship of all those who enjoy a friendship with Jesus is stressed
in all texts where the Evangelist employs the term φίλος. As
authentic Christian disciples the friends of Jesus verify in their lives
the essential characteristics of Christian discipleship such as faith,
love, obedience and witnessing.

A. The Superiority of Jesus
1. Jesus: the Unique Revealer

In the context of the friendship between Jesus and others
explicated through the term φίλος the Fourth Evangelist presents
Jesus as the supreme revealer of the Father who gives testimony
concerning the divine realities. This revelatory role of Jesus is one
of the essential elements which shows the nature of Jesus' friendship.
As we have already seen the intimate relationship between Jesus and
John the Baptist highlights Jesus' supreme revelatory character. [14]
Jesus' figure as Messiah and bridegroom presupposes His revelatory
role in relation to the New Israel and the friend of the bridegroom.
The term φωνή in Jn 3,29 is interpreted as Jesus' authentic testimony
including His Father's precepts. [15] Moreover, within the context of
the metaphor of the friend of the bridegroom St. John emphasizes
Jesus' superiority in terms of His revelatory role (Jn 3,32.34). Thus
the Evangelist wants to stress the superiority of Jesus, an essential
characteristic of Jesus-disciple relationship, in the context of the
friendship between Jesus and the Baptist.

---

[14] Cf. supra, pp. 44-45; 70-75; 78.

[15] Cf. supra, p. 81-82.

The revelatory role of Jesus is an important element also in the friendship between Jesus and the Bethany family. The entire narrative of the Lazarus episode is a process of Jesus' divine revelation through words and deeds which culminates in the sign of Lazarus' raising.[16] Accordingly the intimacy between Jesus and the Bethany family finds expression in Jesus' superiority as a unique revealer of His Father. Further, in the context of the allegory of the vine and branches Jesus teaches about the fact and need of Jesus-disciple friendship. The Johannine Jesus presents His revelatory role as the fundamental reason for His calling the disciples friends (Jn 15,15).[17] In the context of Jn 15,15 the Evangelist presents Jesus as the master who shares His divine knowledge with His disciples in contrast with a master who does not share his plans with his servants. Hence, the friendship between Jesus and His disciples can be understood as a master-disciple relationship since Jesus' superiority as the unique revealer of the Father is highlighted.

Jesus' revelatory role is expressed also in the context of His intimate relationship with the Beloved Disciple and Peter. In the Last Supper scene Jesus shares His divine knowledge regarding His fate with the Beloved Disciple.[18] So also, Jesus' last words to His mother and to His Beloved Disciple have a revelatory nature which is clear even in the literary style of the verses, viz. in 19,26-27 the Evangelist employs His usual revelation formula.[19] The empty tomb

---

[16] Cf. supra, pp. 98ff. Jesus' comment on the sickness of Lazarus (v.4), His dialogue with His disciples (vv.7-16) and with Martha (vv.17-28a) and the performance of the sign etc. are expressions of His revelatory role. Jesus presents the raising of Lazarus as the manifestation of His Father's glory (cf. v.40).

[17] Cf. supra, pp. 219-221.

[18] Cf. supra, pp. 263-265.

[19] Cf. supra, pp. 272-273.

is a revelatory sign on the part of Jesus to bring the Beloved Disciple to a deep faith in Jesus' resurrection. The Fourth Evangelist presents the resurrection appearance as Jesus' self-manifestation (21,1-14).[20] The miraculous catching of the fish is a means of Jesus' self-revelation as it provides an intuitive knowledge to the Beloved Disciple enabling him to recognize the Risen Lord.[21] Further, the concluding pericope of the Fourth Gospel (21,20-24) portrays Jesus as a revealer since He reveals to Peter the destiny of the Beloved Disciple (v.22).

In Jn 21,15-19, a text which deals with the love-relationship between Jesus and Peter, Jesus' superiority is expressively manifested in the dialogue between them.[22] The revelatory knowledge of Jesus is depicted as an important aspect of His superiority. Peter affirms it when he refers to Jesus' divine knowledge regarding his love towards Jesus. Moreover, Jesus' prediction of Peter's destiny is a clear example of Jesus' revelatory knowledge in the context of their intimate relationship. In short, the friendship which Jesus establishes with His own is not merely human or psychological where the equality of relationship is respected, but it is theological since Jesus' superiority as a unique revealer is always acknowledged.

2. Jesus: the Son of God

Jesus' divine origin is another element of His superiority emphasized by the Evangelist in the context of the friendship

---

[20] Cf. supra, pp. 289ff.

[21] Cf. supra, pp. 292-293.

[22] Cf. supra, pp. 308ff.

between Jesus and the believers as expressed through the term φίλος. The Father-Son relationship is well developed to express the nature of Jesus-disciple relationship which sheds light on the theological content of the term φίλος. By referring to Jesus' divine Sonship in the context of the friendship between Jesus and the believer St. John illustrates the nature of that friendship as a master-disciple relationship.

The pericope concerning the intimate relationship between Jesus and the Baptist expressed through the term φίλος stresses the divinity of Jesus as one who came from heaven (v.31) and as the beloved of the Father (v.35).[23] So also, Jesus who is portrayed as the friend of the Bethany family appears as the Son of God with divine power. The expressions of Jesus' friendship with Martha, Mary and Lazarus have also divine characteristics. [24] Throughout the narrative there are references to Jesus' divinity (cf. vv. 4.40.41.42) which is more evident in the effective performance of the sign for the sake of Lazarus, Jesus' φίλος. Thus, the friendship between Jesus and the Bethany family has the divine characteristic which affirms Jesus' superiority as the Son of God.

Jesus' superiority based on His divine Sonship is more evident in the context of the *mashal* of the vine and branches, an imagery of interpersonal relationship against whose background we traced the theological meaning of the term φίλος (Jn 15,1-17). Jesus presents Himself as the vine cultivated by the Father (Jn 15,1). He portrays Himself as the beloved Son of the Father (vv.9-10). The answering of the disciples' prayer is also guaranteed on the basis of Jesus' divine Sonship (vv.7.16). It is the divine Sonship of Jesus which

---

[23] Cf. supra, pp. 77-78.

[24] Cf. supra, pp. 145-146.

enables Him to hear everything from His Father and to communicate the same to His disciples (v.15). Hence, the genuine friendship which the Johannine Jesus establishes with His followers has the divine quality since it denotes a master-disciple relationship involving Jesus' divinity and the qualities of believers as disciples.

Jesus' divinity is clear also in the expressions of His friendship with the Beloved Disciple and Peter which we have already analyzed above in chapter five. Jesus' divinity enables Him to foresee His fate which He communicates to the Beloved Disciple (Jn 13,21ff.).[25] Being the Son of God He rises from the dead which serves as the immediate occasion for the Beloved Disciple's absolute faith (Jn 20,9-10). The expression "ὁ κύριός ἐστιν", an expression of the Beloved Disciple's friendship with Jesus in Jn 21,7, sheds light on Jesus' Lordship and divinity. So also Jesus' divine will regarding the fate of the Beloved Disciple is expressed in the form of a divine revelation (Jn 21,22). Peter also acknowledges Jesus' Lordship and divine knowledge in the context of the confession of his love-relationship with Jesus (Jn 21,15-19).

In short one can say that the figure of Jesus which the Fourth Evangelist portrays in the context of Jesus' friendship with others is superior in nature. Such a superiority of Jesus is illustrated through His divine origin and His revelatory role. Thus, Jesus' intimacy with others depicted through the term φίλος surpasses human criteria for friendship since Jesus' superiority is well expressed in the Johannine presentation of Jesus-disciple friendship which is a master-disciple relationship.

---

[25] Cf. supra, p. 264.

B. The Characteristics of Jesus' Friends

The Fourth Evangelist presents the friendship between Jesus and believers in the context of certain pericopes where certain characters are portrayed as Jesus' friends. The analysis of such texts which we have done in our study substantiates the fact that the friendship explicated through the term φίλος is a master-disciple relationship. Those who are presented as friends of Jesus in the Fourth Gospel fulfill in themselves the following characteristics of Christian discipleship.

1. Faith

The theme of friendship which John develops by using the term φίλος expresses one's relationship with Christ based on faith in His person and teaching. John the Baptist who presents himself as the friend of Jesus, the bridegroom, was in possession of a deep faith in and knowledge of Christ. It is his faith in Christ which makes him an authentic witness of Jesus who leads many towards Him.[26] So also, the characteristics of faith and trust in Jesus, the essential qualities of genuine Christian disciples, are clearly manifested in the lives of the members of the Bethany family.[27] The words and deeds of Martha and Mary express their deep faith and trust in their divine Master as evident in the redactional level of the Gospel. The sending of the message (Jn 11,3), the words of grief uttered by Martha and Mary to Jesus (11,21.32), Martha's confession of her

---

[26] Cf. supra, pp. 78-79.

[27] Cf. supra, pp. 147-150.

supreme faith in Jesus (11,27) etc. are specific and concrete expressions of their deep faith and trust in Jesus Christ through words. Considering their deeds, the going of Martha and Mary to meet Jesus on the way to Bethany, Mary's prostration at Jesus' feet etc. are manifestations of their faith in their master. Lazarus who was raised from the dead can be considered as a symbol of every believer to whom Jesus promises a life after death (Jn 11,25-26).

Keeping of Jesus' commandments, a necessary requirement to enter into a friendship with Jesus, presupposes deep faith in Him who commands.[28] Hence, the disciples' friendship with Jesus on their part, is a relationship based on a life of faith. The Beloved Disciple and Peter appear as prototypes of Christian discipleship also on account of their deep faith in Christ.[29] The Beloved Disciple receives Jesus' mother in his deep faith,[30] comes to an absolute faith in the Risen Lord and becomes a genuine disciple of Jesus.[31] It is his deep faith in Jesus which provides the insight to recognize the Risen Lord and prompts him to communicate his experience of the Lord to his fellow disciples.[32] Inspired by his faith in Christ the Beloved Disciple follows Jesus and bears a continuous witness to Him. Likewise, Peter shows a deep faith in the divinity of Jesus when he admits Jesus' omniscience in the context of their love-relationship.[33] In short, the term φίλος in the Fourth Gospel

---

[28] Cf. supra, p. 207.

[29] Cf. supra, pp. 323-326.

[30] Cf. supra, pp. 274-277.

[31] Cf. supra, pp. 285-289.

[32] Cf. supra, pp. 293-295.

[33] Cf. supra, pp. 313-314.

includes the aspects of faith when it is used to depict the friendship between Jesus and a Christian disciple.

2. Love

In the Johannine presentation love is another quality of Jesus' friends which is a characteristic of Christian discipleship. John the Baptist's supreme love towards Jesus helps him to understand the great success of Jesus as a divine gift (Jn 3,27) and to rejoice in the spiritual marriage of the new people of God with Jesus, the bridegroom (3,29). The love-relationship between Jesus and the Bethany family is expressly manifested throughout the dramatic presentation of the pericope. The Evangelist's description of Mary's anointing of Jesus is interpreted as her love of and concern for Jesus. [34] The reference to Jesus' love towards the members of the Bethany family (Jn 11,3.5.36) presupposes a genuine reciprocal love on their part. Moreover, the words and deeds of Martha and Mary are expressions of their genuine love towards Jesus besides their faith response. [35]

In the context of the *mashal* of the vine and branches Jesus exhorts His disciples to remain in His love which has a double dimension, i.e. Jesus' love towards the disciples and the disciples' love towards Jesus. [36] The model and source of the love-relationship between Jesus and His disciples is that between the Father and the Son. The keeping of Jesus' commandments is the means to remain

---

[34] Cf. supra, p. 141.

[35] Cf. supra, pp. 122-134.

[36] Cf. supra, pp. 201-204.

in His love. It is possible by practicing fraternal mutual love which is the hallmark of Christian discipleship and the pre-requisite for the disciples' friendship with Jesus.

The characteristic of love is expressive in the relationship of the Beloved Disciple with Jesus which makes him a prototype of Christian discipleship.[37] The Beloved Disciple' love towards Jesus is manifested symbolically through their physical closeness in the Last Supper scene (Jn 13,21ff.). The same love motivates him to be present at Calvary, to accept Jesus' mother in his spiritual goods (19,25-27) and to run quickly to Jesus' tomb to experience the Risen Lord (20,1-10). The Beloved Disciple on account of his love constantly follows Jesus and becomes an authentic and continuous witness to his Lord. Peter also confessed his undivided and supreme love towards Jesus which is approved by Jesus by conferring His own pastoral ministry on Peter (21,15-19). The foretold martyrdom of Peter, the greatest expression of love, is verified in the life of Peter. Thus, through his love and obedience to his master Peter becomes a prototype of Christian discipleship who is entitled to be a friend of Jesus.[38]

3. Obedience

Obedience is another quality of discipleship considered as an essential requirement for the disciples' friendship with Jesus in the context of the Johannine use of the term φίλος. John the Baptist, taking the role of the friend of the bridegroom, fulfilled the

---

[37] Cf. supra, pp. 323-325.

[38] Cf. supra, p. 326.

characteristic of complete submission and obedience to Jesus, the bridegroom. The Evangelist presents the Baptist as one who stands (ὁ ἑστηκὼς) and hears (ἀκούων) Jesus' voice (φωνή) which express the Baptist's obedient nature. [39] Jesus' friendship with the Bethany family verified a response of obedience on the part of its members. [40] Since faith and obedience are interrelated elements in the Fourth Gospel the faith of the Bethany family highlighted in the Johannine presentation includes their response of obedience to Christ's words. Lazarus' coming out of the tomb with bandage is considered as the symbolic expression of his obedience to Jesus' voice. [41]

In the context of Jesus' teaching on the theme of friendship in Jn 15 obedience is characterized as the sole requirement to respond to Jesus' friendship (v.14). [42] The disciples are asked to keep Jesus' commandment of fraternal mutual love to become Jesus' friends. Jesus presents His obedience to His Father as the model and source of the believers' keeping of His commandments. Thus, the disciples become Jesus' friends only through a life of obedience.

The Beloved Disciple and Peter presented by John as two models of true friendship with Jesus, fulfilled the characteristic of obedience in their lives. The Beloved Disciple's execution of Jesus' command to receive Jesus' mother as his own mother is an explicit expression of his obedience to Jesus' words, [43] which have the nature

---

[39] Cf. supra, pp. 81-82.

[40] Cf. supra, p. 150.

[41] Cf. supra, pp. 135-136.

[42] Cf. supra, p. 241.

[43] Cf. supra, pp. 273ff.

of a command rather than a wish.[44] In the scene of the miraculous catching of fish Peter and the Beloved Disciple obey Jesus' advice (Jn 21,6). In the Petrine text which we have analyzed (Jn 21,15-19) Peter manifests his obedience to the divine commission for pastoral ministry which involves a great responsibility. Then Peter was exhorted to follow Jesus through martyrdom which is verified in his life. In short, the characteristic of obedience is essential to Christian discipleship and a necessary requirement for Jesus-disciple friendship.

4. Witnessing

Another characteristic of Christian discipleship which we see in the lives of those who enter into friendship with Jesus is their witnessing role (μαρτυρία). John the Baptist who identifies himself with the friend of the bridegroom, Jesus, fulfills the witnessing role in a profound manner. In the Johannine presentation John the Baptist is portrayed as Christ's authentic witness who was sent (ἀποστέλλω) before Him to give testimony to many about Jesus.[45] In the episode of the raising of Lazarus Jesus' friendship with the members of the Bethany family calls for a reciprocal response in terms of their witnessing role. Their total dependence on Jesus' divine power which leads to the performance of the sign of raising Lazarus has a witnessing aspect since many believed in Jesus on account of Lazarus (Jn 11,45; 12,11).

---

[44] Cf. supra, p. 271.

[45] Cf. supra, pp. 79ff.

The fraternal mutual love expected in the context of Jesus-disciple friendship has a witnessing quality since Jesus considers it as a distinguishing mark of Christian discipleship (cf Jn 13,35).[46] Martyrdom is an effective means of witnessing and is considered as the greatest expression of friendship (15,13). Even the bearing of lasting fruits is the fulfillment of the disciples' witnessing of intimate union with Christ (15,16). The witnessing role of genuine Christian discipleship is accomplished in the lives of the Beloved Disciple and Peter.[47] The representative role of the Beloved Disciple is evident in the Last Supper scene where he, appearing as the spokesman of other disciples, asks Jesus about His fate. Further, his mediatory and witnessing role is clear in Jn 21,7 where he communicates his intuitive knowledge to others. The authentic and continuous nature of the Beloved Disciple's witnessing role is portrayed by the Evangelist in the concluding section of the Fourth Gospel (21,24). Peter also is asked to follow Jesus through martyrdom which is the effective means of bearing witness to Jesus (Jn 21,19.22).

In short, one can conclude that the Fourth Evangelist's use of the term φίλος depicts a relationship between Jesus who enjoys superiority due to His divinity and a disciple who fulfills the essential characteristics of Christian discipleship. Accordingly φίλος designates a master-disciple relationship.

IV. Φίλος: A Designation for the Jesus-Disciple Relationship

The present research provides ample reasons to establish the

---

[46] Cf. supra, p. 241.

[47] Cf. supra, pp. 325-326.

argument that in the Fourth Gospel φίλος is a term for the Jesus-disciple relationship. [48] The Johannine originality in the use of φίλος however does not deny certain points of similarity with pre-Johannine use of the term. There are many points of convergence between the Fourth Evangelist and other biblical and non-biblical authors regarding the use of the term φίλος. The idea of revelation and sharing of knowledge is intrinsically connected with the theme of friendship from antiquity. The aspect of communication between the partners in friendship is already developed by the Greek philosophers. [49] In the OT, revelation and sharing of knowledge are considered as essential elements in human and divine-human friendship. [50] As we have already seen John further develops revelation as a characteristic element in the context of Jesus-disciple relationship. [51]

The reciprocal response on the part of the other partner in friendship is another aspect of similarity one sees both in Johannine and non-Johannine use of the term φίλος.[52] Divine initiative in friendship characterized by the term φίλος is a common element in the OT and in the Fourth Gospel. For example: Abraham was

---

[48] Since the use of the term φίλος in 19,12 is understood as an official title we arrive at such a conclusion in the light of other occurrences of the term in the Fourth Gospel.

[49] Cf. supra, p. 11.

[50] Cf. supra, pp. 13-21.

[51] Cf. supra, pp. 334-336.

[52] Cf. supra, pp. 329-331. In the context of divine-human friendship both in the OT and in John faith, trust, love and obedience are seen as main reciprocal responses.

called (ἐκλήθη)[53] the friend of God (Jas 3,23); Jesus calls His disciples and Lazarus as His own friends (Jn 11,11; 15,15).[54] Further, the connection between friendship and self-sacrifice is evident in ancient Greek literature [55] and in John (15,13).

In his conception of the term φίλος John has striking similarities with Luke. The term illustrates a connection between friendship and table fellowship, noteworthy both in Luke and in John (cf. Lk 15,6.9.29;Jn 3,29; 11,11 with 12,1-8; 13,21-30). In the Fourth Gospel and in Luke one finds the correlation between friendship and joy (cf. Lk 15,6.9.29;Jn 3,29; 15,11). The connection between friendship and martyrdom can be seen as another point of similarity between Lucan and Johannine thought (cf. Lk 12,4; Jn 15,13; 21,18-19). Moreover, both the Lucan and Johannine Jesus calls His disciples φίλοι (Lk 12,4; Jn 15,15).

Yet, besides all the above mentioned similarities, one finds certain originality in the Johannine understanding of the term φίλος in the Fourth Gospel. For John φίλος is a highly theological term since it is used to depict a master-disciple relationship. Only a genuine Christian disciple is eligible to be called Jesus' φίλος. Thus in the Fourth Gospel the term φίλος is a designation par excellence for the Jesus-disciple relationship.

---

[53] The theological passive shows the divine initiative. The aorist suggests that it is related to certain specific events in Abraham's life (cf. Gen 15,1-6; 22,9f.).

[54] Cf. STÄHLIN, φίλος, TDNT IX, 169.

[55] Cf. ARISTOTLE, Ethica Nicomachea, IX,8, p.1169a, 18-20.

BIBLIOGRAPHY

After the first citation as given in the bibliography, a shortened title of the books and articles are employed throughout the thesis.

1. Texts and Versions

ALAND, K., BLACK, M., MARTINI, C.M., METZGER, B.M., WIRKGREN, A., *The Greek New Testament* (New York 1975^3).

ELLIGER, K. & RUDOLF, W., *Biblia Hebraica Stuttgartensia* (Stuttgart 1967/77).

NESTLE, E. - ALAND, K., (ed.), *Novum Testamentum Graece* (Stuttgart 1979^{26}).

RAHLFS, A., (ed.), *Septuaginta*, editio minor (Stuttgart 1979).

The Holy Bible. Revised Standard Version Containing the Old and New Testaments. Catholic Edition (London 1966).

2. Reference Works

ABRAMS, M.H., *A Glossary of Literary Terms* (New York 1981).

ARNDT, W.F. & GINGRICH, F.W., (eds.), *A Greek-English Lexicon of the New Testament and the Other Early Christian Literature*, A Translation and adaptation of W. Bauer's Griechisch-Deutsches Wörterbuch zu den Schriften des Neuen Testaments und der übrigen urchristlichen Literatur (Chicago 979).

BAUER, L., *Wörterbuch des palästinischen Arabisch. Deutsch-Arabisch* (Leipzig/ Jerusalem 1933) 419.

BLASS, F.- DEBRUNNER, A., *A Greek Grammar of the New Testament*, R.W. FUNK (trs. & ed.) (Chicago 1961).

BROWN, C., (ed.), *The New International Dictionary of New Testament Theology*, 3 Vols, (Exeter 1975-1978).

BUTTRICK, G.A., *Interpreters Dictionary of the Bible* (Abingdon 1962).

DEIMEL, A., *Sumerisches Lexikon*, II, 4 (Romae 1933).

DELITZCH, F., *Assyrisches Handwörterbuch* (Leipzig 1986).

DENZINGER, H., & BANNWART, C., (eds.), *Enchiridion Symbolorum, definitionum et declarationum de rebus fidei et morum* (Freiburg 1928³¹).

HATCH, E. & REDPATH, H.A., *A Concordance to the Septuagint and Other Greek Versions of the Old Testament*, 2 Vols (Graz 1975).

KITTEL, G., & FRIEDRICH, G., (eds.), *Theological Dictionary of the New Testament*, 10 Vols (Grand Rapids 1964-1976).

LEVY, J., *Chaldäisches Wörterbuch über die Targumim*, Vol ll (Leipzig 1881).

------------, *Wörterbuch über die Talmudim und Midraschim*, Vol IV (Berlin 1924).

LIDDEL, H.G. & SCOTT, R., *A Greek-English Lexicon*, New Edition Revised and Augmented by H.S. Jones (Oxford 1940).

MEISSNER, B., *Akkadisches Handwörterbuch* (Weisbaden 1965).

METZGER, B.M., *A Textual Commentary on the Greek New Testament* (London 1975).

MORGENTHALER, R., *Statistik des Neutestamentlichen Wortschatzes* (Zürich 1982).

MOULE, C.F.D., *An Idiom Book of the New Testament Greek* (Cambridge 1953).

MOULTON, W.F. & GEDEN, A.S.,(eds.), *A Concordance to the Greek Testament* (Edinburgh 1963).

SHIPLEY, J.T., *Dictionary of the World Literary Terms* (London 1970).

STRACK, H.L., BILLERBECK, P., *Kommentar zum Neuen Testament aus Talmud und Midrasch*, 6 Vols (München 1922/1961).

ZERWICK, M., *Biblical Greek*, J. SMITH (trs & ed.) (Rome 1963).

ZERWICK, M. & GROSVENOR, M., *A Grammatical Analysis of the Greek New Testament* (Rome 1981).

3. Other Literature

ABBOTT, E.A., *Johannine Vocabulary* (Diatessarica V) (London 1905).

------------, *Johannine Grammar* (London 1906).

ABRAHAMS, I., *Studies in Pharisaism and the Gospel* (New York 1967).

AGOURIDES, S.,"Peter and John in the Fourth Gospel", in: F.L. CROSS (ed.), *SE* 4 (Berlin 1968) 3-7.

ALBRIGHT, W.F., *The Archeology of Palestine* (London 1960).

ANDERSON, B.W., "Abraham, the friend of God", *Int* 42 (1988) 353-366.

ARENILLAS, P.,"El discípulo amado, modelo perfecto del discípulo de Jesús, según el IV Evangelio", *CiTom* 89 (1962) 3-68.

ASMUSSEN, H., *Theologie und Kirchenleitung. Joh 15,3* (München 1935).

AUGUSTINUS HIPPONENSIS, "Tractatus in Evangelium Ioannis", in: J.P. MIGNE, *PL* 35, 1379-1970.

BAIRD, W., "Abraham in the New Testament, Tradition and the New Identity", *Int* 42 (1988) 367-379.

BALAGUÉ, M., "La resurrección de Lázaro (jn 11,1-57). Confirmación solemne del poder de Jesús sobre la vida", *CB* 19 (1962) 16-29.

BAMMEL, E., Φίλος τοῦ Καίσαρος, *TLZ* 77 (1952) 205-210.

----------,"The Baptist in Early Christian Tradition", *NTS* 18 (1971) 95-128.

BARRETT, C.K., *The New Testament Background: Selected Documents* (London 1957).

----------, *The Gospel According to St.John* (London 1987).

BARROSSE, T.,"The Relationship of Love to Faith in St.John", *TS* 18,4 (1957) 538-559.

----------, *Christianity: Mystery of Love: An Essay in Biblical Theology* (Notre Dame, Indiana 1964).

BARTLETT, D.L.,"John 13:21-30",*Int* 43 (1989) 393-397.

BAUER, W., *Das Johannesevangelium* (HNT 6) (Leipzig 1933).

BEASLEY-MURRAY, G.R., *Baptism in the New Testament* (London 1962).

----------, *The Word Biblical Commentary: John*, Vol 36 (Waco, Texas 1987).

BECKER, H., *Die Reden des Johannesevangeliums und der Stil der gnostischen Offenbarungsrede* (Göttingen 1956) 109-113.

BECKER, J., "Die Abschiedsreden Jesu in Johannesevangelium", *ZNW* 61 (1970) 215-246.

------------, *Johannes der Täufer und Jesus von Nazareth* (Neukirchen-Vluyn 1972).

-----------, *Das Evangelium nach Johannes*, 2 Vols (Würzburg 1979. 1981).

BEHLER, G.M., *Die Abschiedsworte des Herrn* (Wien 1962) 161-190.

BERNARD, J.H., *A Critical and Exegetical Commentary on the Gospel according to St.John* (ICC) A.H. McNEILE (ed.) 2 Vols (Edinburgh 1985).

BERROUARD, M.F., "[Jn 15,3] Le Tractatus 80,3 in Iohannis Euangelium de saint AUGUSTIN, la parole, le sacrement et la foi": *RéAug* 33 (1987) 235-254.

BEUTLER, J., *Martyria:Traditionsgeschichtliche Untersuchungen zum Zeugnisthema bei Johannes* (Frankfurt 1972).

BEVAN, E., "Note on Mark 1,41 and John 11,33.38", *JTS* 33 (1932) 186-188.

BIETENHARD, H., "Name",in: C. BROWN (ed.) *Dictionary of the New Testament Theology*, Vol II (Michigan 1986) 648-688.

-----------, ὄνομα ..., in: *TDNT* V, 242-283.

BLACK, M., *An Aramaic Approach to the Gospels and Acts* (2.ed.) (Oxford 1954).

BLOCH, A.P., *The Biblical and Historical Background of Jewish Customs and Ceremonies* (New York 1980).

BODE, E.L., *The First Easter Morning. The Gospel Accounts of the Women's Visit to the Tomb of Jesus* (AnBib 45) (Roma 1970).

BOGART, J., *Orthodox and Heretical Perfectionism in the Johannine Community* (Missoula, Mont. 1977).

BÖHLIG, A., *Mysterion und Wahrheit. Gesammelte Beiträge zur spätantiken Religionsgeschichte* (Leiden 1968).

BOISMARD, M.-E., "L'ami de l'époux (Jo 3, 29)", in: A. BARUCQ & J. DUPLACY et al. (ed.) *A la rencontre de Dieu - Mémorial A.Gelin* (Paris 1961) 289-295.

-----------,"Les traditions johanniques concernant le Baptiste", *RB* 70 (1963) 5-42.

BOISMARD, M.-E. & LAMOUILLE, A., *L' Évangile de Jean: Synopse des quatre Évangiles en français*, III (Paris 1977).

BORIG, R., *Der wahre Weinstock, Untersuchungen zu Jo 15,1-10* (SANT 16) (München 1967).

BORNKAMM, G., *Geschichte und Glaube*, Vol II (München 1971).

BRAUN, F.M., *Jean le Théologien*, 3 Vols (Paris 1966).

BRAUN, H., "Qumran und das Neue Testament", *ThR* 28 (1962) 192-234.

BROWN, R.E., "The Qumran Scrolls and the Johannine Gospel and Epistles", *CBQ* 17 (1955) 403-419; 559-574. Reprinted in K. STENDAHL (ed.), *The Scrolls and the New Testament* (New York 1957) 183-207.

------------, *New Testament Essays* (Milwaukee 1965).

-----------, *The Gospel according to John*, 2 Vols (New York 1970).

-----------, *The Community of the Beloved Disciple* (New York 1979).

BRUCE, F.F., *The Gospel of John* (Michigan 1984).

BRUNS, J.E., "Ananda : The Fourth Evangelist's Model for 'the Disciple whom Jesus Loved'", *SR* 3 (1973) 236-24.

BUBY, B., "The Commitment of Faith and Love in the Fourth Gospel", *RR* 40 (1981) 561-567.

BULTMANN, R., *The Gospel of John. A Commentary*, G.R. BEASLEY-MURRAY (trs.) (Philadelphia 1971).

------------, γινώσκω κτλ, in: *TDNT* I, 689-719.

BURGER, T., "Der wahre Weinstock", *BK* 9 (1954) 113-116.

BURROWS, M., *The Basis of Israelite Marriage* (New Aaven 1938).

BYRNE, B., *Lazarus. A contemporary Reading of John 11:1-46* (Zacchaeus Studies: New Testament) (Collegeville 1991).

CABA, J., *La Oración de Petición: Estudio exegético sobre los evangelios sinópticos y los escritos joaneos* (AnBib 62) (Rome 1974).

------------, *Cristo, mia Speranza, è risorto: Studio esegetico dei "vangeli" pasquali* (Milano 1988).

CADMAN, W.H., "The Raising of Lazarus (Jn 10,40-11,53)", *SE* (TU 73, 1959) 423-434.

CAIRD, G.B., *Language and Imagery of the Bible* (London 1980).

CALVIN, J., *The Gospel According to St. John* (New York 1959).

CARSON, D.A., *Jesus and His Friends: His Farewell Message and Prayer in Jn 14-17* (Living Word) (Leicester 1986).

------------, ἑταῖρος, in: *DNTT* I, 259-260.

CHAPAL, R., "Jean 20,1-10", *ÉTR* 30, 4 (1955) 63-65.

CHEVALLIER, M. A., "La fondation de "l' Eglise" dans le quatrième évangile: Jn 19,25-30", *ÉTR* 58 (1983).

CLEMENS ALEXANDRINUS, "Commentariorum in Joannem", in: J.P. MIGNE, *PG* 73-74.

COLLINS, R.F., "The Representative Figures of the Fourth Gospel", *DownRev* 94 (1976) 118-132.

CONRAD, J., *Das Geheimnis von Jo 15* (Neukirchen 1957).

----------, *Er der Weinstock - wir die Reben. Eine biblische Studie über Jo 15* (Berlin 1961).

CROSS, F.L.,(ed.), *Studies in the Fourth Gospel* (London 1957).

CULLMANN, O., *Urchristentum und Gottesdienst* (ATANT 3) (Zürich 1950).

-----------, *The Johannine Circle. A Study in the Origin of the Gospel of John*, J. BOWDEN (trs.) (London 1976).

CULPEPPER, R.A., *An Anatomy of the Fourth Gospel: A Study in Literary Design* (Philadelphia; Fortres 1983).

DAUER, A.,"Das Wort des Gekreuzigten an seine Mutter und den 'Jünger, den er liebte' : Eine Traditionsgeschichte und theologische Untersuchung zu Joh. 19, 25-27", *BZ* 11 (Teil I) (1967) 222-239; 12 (Teil II) (1968) 80-93.

-----------, *Die Passionsgeschichte im Johannesevangelium. Eine traditiongeschichtliche und theologische Untersuchung zu Joh 18,1-19,30* (München 1972).

DAVIES, W.D., *The Sermon on the Mount* (Cambridge 1966).

DE BOOR, W., *Das Evangelium des Johannes*, 2 Vols (Wuppertal 1970).

DEDEK, J.F.,"Friendship with God", in: *New Catholic Encyclopedia*, Vol VI (Washington) 207-208.

DE DINECHIN, O., " καθώς: La Similitude dans L'évangile selon Saint Jean", *RechScienRel* 58 (1970) 195-236.

DE GOEDT, M., "Un Schème de Révélation dans le quatrième évangile", *NTS* 8 (1962) 142-150.

DEISSMANN, A., (rev. ed.), *Light from the Ancient East* (New York 1927).

DE LA POTTERIE, I., " Οἶδα et γινώσκω: Les deux modes de la connaissance dans le quatrième évangile", *Bib* 40 (1959) 709-725.

------------, *Gesù Verità: Studi di Cristologia Giovannea*, A. MILANOLI et al. (trs.) (Torino 1973).

------------,"Das Wort Jesu 'Siehe, deine Mutter' und die Annahme der Mutter durch den Jünger (Joh 19,27b)",*Neues Testament und Kirche* (Herausgegeben von Joachim Gnilka) (Freiburg 1974) 191-219.

------------,"Le témoin qui demeure: le disciple que Jésus aimait", *Bib* 67 (1986) 343-359.

------------,"Le nozze messianiche e il matrimonio Cristiano", *PSV* 13 (1986) 87-104.

-----------,"Il discepolo che Gesù amava", in: L. PADOVESE (ed.), *Atti del I Simposio di Efeso su Giovanni Apostolo* (Roma 1991) 33-55.

DELEBECQUE, É.,"Lazare est mort (note sur Jean 11,14-15)",*Bib* 67 (1986) 89-97.

DELLAGIACOMA, V., "Il Matrimonio presso gli Ebrei", *RivB* 7 (1959) 230-241.

DENNEY, J., *The death of Christ* (London 1956).

DERRETT, J.D.M., "Water into Wine", *BZ* 7 (1963) 80-97.

DESCAMPS, A.L., "Une lecture historico-critique", *Genèse et Structure d'un texte du Nouveau Testament (Jn 11)* (Paris 1981) 35-80.

DE SMIDT, J.C., "A Perspective on John 15,1-8",*Neot* 25,2 (1991) 251-272.

DIBELIUS, M., *Die Urchristliche Überlieferung von Johannes dem Täufer* (FRLANT 15) (Göttingen 1911).

------------, "Joh 15,13. eine Studie zum Traditionsproblem des Johannesevangeliums", in *Festgabe für Adolf Deissmann zum 60. Geburtstag* (Tübingen: Mohr 1927) 168-186. Reprinted in Dibelius' *Botschaft und Geschichte* 1 (Tübingen 1953) 204-220.

DIMMLER, H., *Die Auferweckung des Lazarus. Dem Evangelisten Johannes nacherzählt* (München 1926).

DODD, C.H., "Eucharistic Symbolism in the Fourth Gospel", *The Expositor*, 8. Series, Vol II (1911) 530-546.

------------, *The Interpretation of the Fourth Gospel* (Cambridge 1953).

-----------, *Historical Tradition in the Fourth Gospel* (Cambridge 1963).

DOLTO, F. & SÉVÉRIN, G., "Résurrection de Lazare", *L' Évangile au risque de la Psychanalyse* 1 (1977) 125-140.

DRAPER, H.M., "The Disciple Whom Jesus Loved", *ExpTim* 32 (1920-21) 428-429.

DUBLIN, J., "Continue Ye in my love (Jn 15,9)", *ExpTim* 47 (1935-36) 91-92.

DUNKERLEY, R., "Lazarus", *NTS* 5 (1958-59) 321-327.

EERNSTMAN, P.A., *Οἰκεῖος, ἑταῖρος, ἐπιτήδειος, φίλος*, Diss. (Utrecht 1932).

EICHLER, A., "Zu Evang. Johannis 11,25-26", *N Sächs. Kirchenbl.* 39 (1932) 309-314.

EISLER, R., "Das Rätsel des Johannesevangeliums", *ErJb* 3 (1935) 323-511.

------------,"Der Jünger, den Jesus liebte", *ErJb* 3 (1935) 371-390.

ELLER, V., *The Beloved Disciple, his Name, his Story, his Thought. Two Studies from the Gospel of John* (Grand rapids 1987).

ENGEL, F., "The Ways of Vines Jn 15,1", *ExpTim* 60 (1949) 84.

ENSLIN, M.S.,"John and Jesus", *ZNW* 66 (1975) 1-18.

EPSTEIN, L.M., *The Jewish Marriage Contract* (New York 1927).

EUSEBIUS, *Onomasticon*, in: E. KLOSTERMANN & H. GRESSMANN (eds.), *GCS* (Leipzig 1904).

EVANS, E., "The verb ΑΓΑΠΑΝ in the Fourth Gospel", in: F.L. CROSS (ed.), *Studies in the Fourth Gospel* (London 1957) 64-71.

FILSON, F.V.,"Who was the Beloved Disciple ?", *JBL* 68 (1949) 83-88.

FORTH, T.F.,"The Tomb of Lazarus and the Text of John (Jn 11)", *TLond* 4 (1922) 232-234.

FORTNA, R.T., *The Gospel of Signs* (Cambridge 1970).

-----------, *The Fourth Gospel and its Predecessor* (Edinburgh 1989).

FRIDRICHSEN, A., " Älska, hata, förneka (försaka)", *Svensk Exegetisk Arsbok*, 5 (1940) 152-162.

FURNISH, V.P., *The Love Command in the New Testament* (1972) 139-143.

GAECHTER, P., "Das dreifache 'Weide meine Lämmer'" *ZKT* 69 (1947) 328-344.

GAETA, G., "Battesimo come Testimonianza. Le Pericopi sul Battista nell' evangelo di Giovanni", *CristStor* 1 (1980) 279-314.

GANDER, G., "Jean III, 22 á IV, 3 Parle-t-il d'un baptême administré par Jésus?, *RThPhil N.S.* (1948) 133-137.

GAROFALO, S., *Con il Battista incontro a Cristo* (Milano 1981).

GENUYT, F., "Ressusciter pour apprendre à vivre et à mourir. La résurrection de Lazare selon l'évangile de Jean (11,1-44)", *LumVie* 35 (1986) 63-74.

GEORGE, A., "Gesù la Vite Vera : Giov. 15,1-17", *BibOr* 3 (1961) 121-125.

GIBLIN, C.H., "Suggestion, Negative Response, and Positive Action in St. John's Portrayal of Jesus (Jn ii, 1-11; iv,46-54;vii,2-14;xi,1-44)", *NTS* 26 (1980) 197-211.

GIBSON, G.S., "Joy", *ExpTim* 94 (1983) 244-245.

GLASSON, T.F., "John the Baptist in the Fourth Gospel", *ExpTim* 67 (1955-56) 245-246.

GLOMBITZA, O., "Petrus - der Freund Jesu. Überlegungen zu Joh 21,15ff.", *NT* 6 (1963) 277-285.

GODET, F., *Commentaire sur l'évangile de saint Jean*, 3 tom. (Neuchatel 1903).

GRANQVIST, H., *Marriage conditions in a Palestinian Village* (Helsingfors 1935).

GRASSI, J.A., *The Secret Identity of the Beloved Disciple* (New York/Mahwah 1992).

GRAY, G.B., *A Critical and Exegetical Commentary on Numbers* (I.C.C.) (Freiburg 1903).

GRIFFITH, B.G., "The Disciple Whom Jesus Loved", *ExpTim* 32 (1920-21) 379-381.

GROSSOUW, W., *Revelation and Redemption. A Sketch of the Theology of St.John* (Westminster 1955).

GRUNDMANN, W., "Das Wort von Jesu Freunden (Jn 15, 13-16) und des Herrenmahl", *NT* 3 (1959) 62-69.

----------, *Der Zeuge der Wahrheit: Grundzüge der Christologie des Johannesevangeliums* (Berlin 1985).

GÜNTHER, W., Φιλέω, in: *DNTT* II, 547-551.

GÜNTHER, W., & LINK, H.G., ἀγαπάω, in: *DNTT* II, 538-547.

GUNTHER, J.J., "The Relation of the Beloved Disciple to the Twelve", *TZ* 37 (1981) 129-148.

HÄNCHEN, E., *John, a Commentary on the Gospel of John*, R.W. FUNK (trs.), 2 Vols (Philadelphia 1984).

HANSON, A.T., "The Old Testament Background to the Raising of Lazarus", *SE* 6 (1973) 252-255.

HARRIS, R., "A note on John XI,25", *BulBezanClub* 5 (1928) 5-8.

HARTIN, P.J., "The Role of Peter in the Fourth Gospel", *Neot* 24,1 (1990) 49-61.

----------, "Remain in me (John 15:5). The Foundation of the Ethical and its Consequences in the Farewell Discourses", *Neot* 25,2 (1991) 341-356.

HAWKIN, D.J., "The Function of the Beloved Disciple Motif in the Johannine Redaction", *LavThéolPhil* 33 (1977) 135-150.

HEISE, J., *Bleiben. Μένειν in den Johanneischen Schriften* (Tübingen 1967).

HEMRAJ, S., "The Verb 'To Do' in St.John", *SE* 7 (1982) 241-245.

HENDERSON, A., "Notes on John.11", *ExpTim* 32 (1920-1921) 123-126.

HENDRIKSEN, W., *The Gospel of John* (London 1969).

HINRICHS, B., *'Ich bin'; die Konsistenz des Johannes-evangeliums in der Konzentration auf das Wort Jesu* (SBB 133) (Stuttgart 1988).

HIRSCH, E., *Das Vierte Evangelium in seiner ursprünglichen Gestalt verdeutscht und erklärt* (Tübingen: Mohrsiebeck 1936).

HOH, J., "Omnis qui vivit et credit in me non morietur in aeternum (Ioh. 11,26)", *VD* 2 (1922) 333-335.

HÖLZEL, J., *Der tägliche Umgang mit Jesu: (Joh 15,1-16)* (Schwerin 1927).

HOSKYNS, E.C., *The Fourth Gospel*, F.N. DAVEY (ed.) (London 1947).

HUBBARD, D.A., "John 19:17-30", *Int* 43 (1989) 397-401.

HUBER, H.H., *Der Begriff der Offenbarung im Johannesevangelium* (Göttingen 1934).

HUBY, P.J., *Le discours de Jésus après la Cène* (Paris 1942).

HUMBERT, A., "L'observance des Commandments dans le écrits Johanniques (Gospel and First Epistle)", *Studia Moralia* 1 (Academia Alfonsiana) (Roma 1963) 187-219.

HUNTER, W.B., "Contextual and Genre Implications for the Historicity of John 11,41b-42", *JETS* 28 (1985) 53-70.

IAFOLLA, P.,"Giovanni, Figlio di Zebedeo "Il discipolo che amava" e il IV° Vangelo", *BeO* 28 (1986) 95-110.

IBUKI, Y., *Die Wahrheit im Johannesevangelium* (Bonn 1972).

INFANTE, L., *L'amico dello Sposo, Figura del Ministero di Giovanni Battista nel Vangelo di Giovanni* (Roma 1982).

JACOBS, L., "Greater Love Hath No Man … The Jewish Point of View of Self-Sacrifice", *Judaism* 6 (1957) 41-47.

JAUBERT, A., "L'image de la Vigne (Jean 15)", *Oikonomia* (F.S. O. CULLMANN) (Hamburg 1967) 93-99.

-----------,*Approches de l'Evangile de Jean* (Paris 1976).

JEREMIAS, J., νύμφη νυμφίος, in: *TDNT* IV, 1099-1106.

JOHANNES CHRYSOSTOMUS, "Homiliae in Ioannem", in: J.P. MIGNE, *PG* 59, 23-482.

JOHNSON, N.E., "The Beloved Disciple and the Fourth Gospel", *CQR* 167 (1966) 281.

JOHNSON, L.,"Who was the Beloved Disciple?", *ExpTim* 77 (1965-66) 157-158.

JOHNSTON, G., "The Allegory of the Vine: An Exposition of John 15, 1-17", *CJT* 3 (1957) 150-158.

JONES, J.R., *Narrative Structures and Meaning in John 11,1-54* (Ann Arbor: University Microfilms 1982).

JONGHE, M., "De Resurrectione Lazari", *CollBrug* 28 (1928) 41-45.

KÄSEMANN, E., "Ketzer und Zeuge: Zum johannischen Verfasserproblem", *ZTK* 48 (1951) 292-311.

KEPPLER, P.M., *Unseres Herrn Trost* 2-3 (Freiburg 1914).

KILPATRICK, G.D., "Some Notes on Johannine Usage (ἀληθής and ἀληθινός)", *BT* 11 (1960) 173-177.

KLAIBER, W., "Der irdische und der himmlische Zeuge: Eine Auslegung von Joh 3. 22-36", *NTS* 36,2 (1990) 205-233.

KRAELING, C.H., *John the Baptist* (New York 1951).

KRAGERUD, A., *Der Lieblingsjünger im Johannesevangelium. Ein exegetischer Versuch* (Oslo 1959).

KREMER, J., *Die Osterbotschaft der vier Evangelien* (Stuttgart 1969)

------------, "Der arme Lazarus. Lazarus, der Freund Jesu. Beobachtungen zur Beziehung zwischen Lk 16,19-31 und Jn 11,1-46", in: *À Cause de l'Évangile*, FS. J. Dupont (Cerf 1985) 571-584.

------------, "Die Lazarusgeschichte. Ein Beispiel urkirchlicher Christusverkündigung", *GeistLeb* 58 (1985) 244-258.

------------, *Lazarus: Die Geschichte einer Auferstehung: Text, Wirkungsgeschichte und Botschaft von Joh 11,1-46* (Stuttgart 1985).

KRIEGER, N., "Fiktive Orte der Johannestaufe", *ZNW* 45 (1954) 121-123.

KÜGLER, J., *Der Jünger, den Jesus liebte* (SBB 16) (Stuttgart 1988)

LAGRANGE, M.J., *Évangile selon saint Jean* (EB) (Paris 1948).

LANDFESTER, M., *Das griechische Nomen "Philos" und seine Ableitungen* (Spudasmata 11) (Hildesheim 1966).

LARSEN, I., "Walking in the Light: A comment on Jn 11,9-10", *BT* 37 (1986) 432-436.

LATTKE, M., *Einheit im Wort. Die Spezifische Bedeutung von Agape, Agapan und philein im Johannesevangelium* (SANT 41) (München 1975).

LEAL, J., "De amore Jesu erga amicum Lazarum (Jo 11)", *VD* 21 (1941) 59-64.

LEE, G.M., "John 21,20-23", *JTS* 1 (1950) 62-63.

------------, "John 15,14 : 'Ye are my Friends'", *NT* 15 (1973) 260.

LÉON-DUFOUR, X., *Lecture de l'évangile selon Jean*, 2 Vols (Paris 1988.1990).

LEROY, H., *Rätsel und Mißverständnis. Ein Beitrag zur Formgeschichte des Johannesevangeliums* (BBB 30) (Bonn 1968).

LEWIS, F.W., "The Disciple Whom Jesus Loved", *ExpTim* 33 (1921-22) 42.

LIGHTFOOT, R.H., *St. John's Gospel*, C.F. EVANS (ed.) (Oxford 1983).

LINDARS, B., "Two Parables in John", *NTS* 16 (1969-70) 318-329.

-----------, *The Gospel of John* (New Century Bible) (London 1972).

LINNEMANN, E., "Jesus und der Täufer", in: G. EBELING, E. JÜNGEL & G. SCHUNACK (eds.), *Festschrift für Ernst Fuchs* (Tübingen 1973) 219-236.

LOFTHOUSE, W.F., *The Disciple Whom Jesus Loved. Lectures on the Fourth Gospel* (London 1936).

LOISY, A., *Le Quatrième évangile* (2. ed.) (Paris 1921).

LORENZEN, T., *Der Lieblingsjünger im Johannesevangelium* (Stuttgart 1971).

MACE, D.R., *Hebrew Marriage:A Sociological Study* (London 1953).

MACGREGOR, G.H.C., *The Gospel of John* (Moffatt Commentaries) (London 1959).

MACRAE, G.W., "The Ego Proclamations in Gnostic Sources", in: E. BAMMEL (ed.), *The Trial of Jesus* (SBT II,13) (London 1970) 124-125.

MAHONEY, R., *Two Disciples at the Tomb. The Background and Message of John 20,1-10* (Theologie und Wirklichkeit, 6) (Bern 1974).

MALATESTA, E., *Interiority and Covenant: A Study of εἶναι ἐν and μένειν ἐν in the First Letter of Saint John* (AnBib 69) (Rome 1978).

MARROW, S.B., *John 21 - An Essay in Johannine Ecclesiology* (Rome 1968).

MARSH, J., *The Gospel of St. John* (London 1968).

MARTIN, J.P., "History and Eschatology in the Lazarus Narrative, Joh 11,1-44", *SJT* 17 (1964) 332-343.

MATEOS, J. & BARRETO, J., *Il Vangelo di Giovanni* (Assisi 1982).

MATERA, F.J., "John 20:1-18", *Int* 43 (1989) 402-406.

MAYNARD, J.A., "Who was the Beloved Disciple?", *JSOR* 13 (1929) 155-159.

MCNEIL, B., "The Raising of Lazarus", *DownRev* 92 (1974) 269-275.

MEALAND, D.L., "The Language of Mystical Union in the Johannine Writings", *DownRev* 95 (1977) 19-34.

MERLI, D., "La scopo della risurrezione di Lazaro in Giov 11,1-44", *BibOr* 12 (1970) 59-82.

MEYER, R., κόλπος, in: *TDNT* III, 824-826.

MIELGO, G.S., "Aspectos eclesiales en San Juan. Estudio exegético-teológico de Jn 15,7-17", *Escritos del Vedat* 1 (1971) 9-58.

MINEAR, P.S., "The Beloved Disciple in the Gospel of John, Some Clues and Conjectures", *NT* 19 (1977) 105-123.

MLAKUZHYIL, G., *The Christocentric Literary Structure of the Fourth Gospel* (AnBib 117) (Roma 1987).

MODERSOHN, E., "Die letzten Worte Jesu (Joh 19,25-30)", *Heilig dem Herrn* 30 (1939) 497-500.

MOLLAT, D., *La révélation de l'Esprit-Saint chez saint Jean* (Roma 1971).

----------, "La foi pascale selon le chapitre 20 de l'évangile de Saint Jean", in: E. DHANIS, *Resurrexit: Actes du Symposium international sur le résurrection de Jésus* (Città del Vaticano 1974) 316-339.

MOLLAT, D. & BRAUN, F.M., *L'évangile et les épitres de Saint Jean* [La sainte Bible de Jerusalem] (Paris 1960).

MOLONEY, F.J., "Jn 1,18: 'In the Bosom of' or 'Turned towards' the Father?" *AusBR* 31 (1983) 66f.

----------, "The Structure and Message of John 15:1-16,3", *AusBR* 35 (1987) 35-49.

MORENO, J.F., "El discípulo de Jesucristo, Según el evangelio de S. Juan", *EstBíb* 30 (1971) 269-311.

MORETON, M.B., "The Beloved Disciple Again", *Studia Biblica* 11 (1978); Papers on the Gospels (en Collab.) (1979) 99-114.

MORLET, M., "Le dernier signe de la glorification de Jésus. Jn 11,1-45", *5 e Dimanche de Carême. AssembSeign* 2/18 (1971) 11-25.

MORRIS, L., *The Gospel According to John* (Michigan 1971).

MOULE, C.F.D.,"The meaning of 'Life' in the Gospels and Epistles of St. John. A study in the story of Lazarus, John 11:1-44", *Theology* 78 (1975) 114-125.

MOURLON BEERNAERT, P., "Parallélisme entre Jean 11 et 12. Étude de structure litéraire et théologique", *Genèse et structure d'un texte du Nouveau Testament (Jn 11)* (1981) 128-149.

MUÑOZ LEÓN, D., "¿Es El Apostol Juan el discípulo amado?" *EstBíb* 45 (1987) 403-492.

NEIRYNCK, F., "The Anonymous Disciple in John 1", *ETL* (April 1990) 5-38.

----------,"John 21", *NTS* 36,3 (1990) 321-336.

NEUBAUER, J., *Beiträge zur Geschichte des Biblisch-Talmudische Eheschliessungsrechts* (Mitteilungen der Vorderasiastischen Gesselschaft) (Leipzig 1920).

NEUFELD, E., *Ancient Hebrew Marriage Laws* (London 1944).

NEWMAN, B.M., & NIDA, E.A., *A Translator's Handbook on the Gospel of John* (New York 1979).

NICCACCI, A., "Esame letterario di Gv 15-16", *Anton* 56 (1981) 43-71.

NICOLL, W.R., *The Expositor's Greek Testament*, Vol I (London 1907).

NOIR, L., *Le chapitre 21 de Jean, étude critique et exegetique* (Geneva 1967).

O'GRADY, J.F., "Johannine Ecclesiology : A Critical Evaluation", *BTB* 7 (1977) 36-44.

------------, "The Good Shepherd and the Vine and the Branches", *BTB* 8 (1978) 86-89.

------------, "The Role of the Beloved Disciple", *BTB* 9 (1979) 58-65.

OLSSON, B., *Structure and Meaning in the Fourth Gospel* (Lund 1974).

ORIGEN, *Commentaria in Evangelium Joannis*, E. PREUSCHEN (ed.) *GCS*, Origenes, IV; *PG* 14, 21-830 (Berlin 1903).

OSBORNE, G.R., *John 21: A Test Case for the History and Redaction in the Resurrection Narratives* (France/Wenham 1981) 293-328.

------------, *The Resurrection Narratives. A Redactional Study* (Grand Rapids 1984).

PAESLACK, M., "Zur Bedeutungsgeschichte der Wörter φιλεῖν, φιλία, φίλος in der LXX und im Neuen Testament unter Brücksichtigung ihrer Beziehungen zu ἀγαπᾶν, ἀγάπη, ἀγαπητός", *ThV* 5 (1953-54) 51-142.

PAJOT, C., L'interprétation johannique du ministere de Jean Baptiste (Jean I), *FoiVie* 63, 3 = *CahBib* 7 (1969) 21-37.

PAMMENT, M., "The Fourth Gospel's Beloved Disciple", *ExpTim* 94 (1983) 363-367.

PANACKEL, C., *ΙΔΟΥ Ο ΑΝΘΡΩΠΟΣ (Jn 19,5b) : An Exegetico-Theological Study of the Text in the Light of the Use of the Term ἄνθρωπος Designating Jesus in the Fourth Gospel* (AnGre 251) (Roma 1988).

PANIMOLLE, S.A., *Lettura Pastorale del Vangelo di Giovanni*, 3 Vols (Bologna 1978-1980).

PEARCE, K., "The Lucan Origins of the Raising of Lazarus", *ExpTim* 96 (1984-85) 359-361.

PERKINS, P., "Johannine Tradition in Ap.James", *JBL* 101 (1982) 403-414.

PETERSON, E., "Der Gottesfreund. Beiträge zur Geschichte eines religiösen Terminus", *ZKG* 42 (NF V) 2 (1923) 161-202.

PHILLIPS, G.L., "Faith and Vision in the Fourth Gospel", in: F.L. CROSS (ed.), *Studies in the Fourth Gospel* (London 1957) 83-96.

PIROT, J., *Paraboles et allégories évangeliques, La pensée de Jésus - Les Commentaires patristiques* (Paris 1949) 452-464.

POLLARD, T.E., "The Raising of Lazarus (John XI)", *SE* 6 (T.U.112) (1973) 435-443.

POPKES, W., *Christus Traditus* (Zürich/Stuttgart 1967).

PORTER, J.R., & ROGERS, D.G., "Who was the Beloved Disciple?", *ExpTim* 77 (1965-66) 213-214.

POTAMIUS, "Tractatus de Lazaro", in: J.P.Migne, *PL* 8 (1844) col.1411-1415.

POTTER, R., "The Disciple Whom Jesus Loved", *LifeSpir* 16 (1962) 293-297.

PRAZYWARA, E., *Christentum gamäss Johannes* (Nürenberg 1954).

QUAST, K., *Peter and the Beloved Disciple* (Sheffield 1989).

RADERMAKERS, J., "Je suis la vraie vigne. Jn 15,1-8", *AssembSeign* 26 (1973) 46-58.

RALPH, M., *"And God Said What?"* (New York 1986).

RAU, C., *Struktur und Rhythmus im Johannesevangelium* (Stuttgart 1972).

REGENSTORF, K.H., κλαίω κλαυθμός, in: *TDNT* III, 722-726

RICHARDSON, A., *The Gospel according to St. John* (Torch Commentaries) (London 1960).

RICHTER, G., *Die Fusswaschung im Johannesevangelium. Geschichte ihrer Deutung* (Regensburg 1967).

RIGG, H., "Was Lazarus 'the Beloved Disciple'?", *ExpTim* 33 (1921-22) 232-234.

RIGOPOULOS, G., "Jesus Christ 'the True Vine' (Jn 15,1-17)", *DeltBiblMelet* 4 (1976) 161-180.

RINALDI, G., "Amore e Odio (Giov 15, 1-16,4a)", *BibOr* 22 (1980) 97-106.

RITTELMEYER, F., "Ich bin der Weinstock, ihr seid die Reben", *Christengem.* 17 (1940-41) 69-71; 87-89.

----------, *Ich bin; Reden und Aufsätze über die sieben 'Ich bin'-Worte des Johannesevangeliums* (Stuttgart 1986).

ROLOFF, J., "Der Johannische 'Lieblingsjünger' und der Lehrer der Gerechtikeit", *NTS* 15 (1968) 129-151.

ROMANIUK, K., διδάσκαλος, in: *TDNT* II, 148-159.

-----------, "Je suis la Résurection et la Vie (Jean 11,25)", *Concilium* 60 (1970) 63-70.

RUCKSTUHL, E., "Der Jünger, den Jesus Liebte", *SUNT* 11 (1986) 131-167.

----------, *Die Literarische Einheit des Johannesevangelium* (Freiburg 1987).

RUSSEL, R., "The Beloved Disciple and the Resurrection", *Scr* 8 (1956) 57-62.

SABOURIN, L., "Resurrectio Lazari (Jo 11,1-44)", *VD* 46 (1968) 339-350.

SANDERS, J.N. & MASTIN, B.A., "Those whom Jesus Loved (Jn XI,5)", *NTS* 1 (1954-55) 29-41.

------------, "Who was the Disciple whom Jesus Loved?", in: F.L. CROSS (ed.), *Studies in the Fourth Gospel* (London 1957) 72-78.
-----------, *A Commentary on the Gospel according to St.John* (London 1968).

SANDWIK, B., "Joh.15 als Abendmahlstext", *TZ* 23 (1967) 323-328.

SASS, G., *Die Auferweckung des Lazarus : Eine Auslegung von Johannes 11* (Neukirchen-Vluyn 1967).

SCHNACKENBURG, R., "Offenbarung und Glaube im Johannesevangelium", *BibLeb* 7 (1966) 165-180.

------------, "Der Jünger, den Jesus liebte", *EKK* 2 (1970) 97-117.

------------, "On the Origin of the Fourth Gospel", *Perspective* II (1970).

------------, "Aufbau und Sinn von Johannes 15", in: L. ALVAREZ VERDES Y E.J. ALONSO HERNANDEZ (eds.), *Homenaje a juan Prado* (Madrid 1975) 405-420.

-----------, *The Gospel according to St. John*, K. SMYTH (trs.) 3 Vols (London 1980).

SCHNEID, H., *Marriage* (Jerusalem 1973).

SCHNEIDERS, S.M., "Death in the Community of Eternal Life. History, Theology and Spirituality in Jn 11", *Int* 41 (1987) 44-56.

------------,"John 21:1-14", *Int* 43 (1989) 70-75.

SCHONFIELD, H.J., *The Passover Plot* (Hutchinson 1965).

SCHRENK, G., ἐντέλλομαι, ἐντολή, in: *TDNT* II, 544-556.

SCHULZ, S., *Komposition und Herkunft der Johannischen Reden* (BWANT LXXXI) (Stuttgart 1960).

------------, *Das Evangelium nach Johannes* (NTD 4) (Göttingen 1972) 194.

SCHÜTZ, R., *Johannes der Täufer* (Zürich 1967).

SCHWANK, B., "Ich bin der 'wahre Weinstock': Joh 15,1-17", *Sein und Sendung* 28,6 (1963) 244-258.

-----------,"Christi Stellvertreter: Joh 21,15-25", *Sein und Sendung* 29 (1964) 531-542.

SCHWARTZ, E., "Aporien im vierten Evangelium", *NGG* 3 (1908) 149-188.

SCHWEIZER, E., *Die religionsgeschichtliche Herrkunft und theologische Bedeutung der Johannischen Bildreden, zugleich ein Beitrag zum Quellenfrage des vierten Evangeliums* (FRLANT NF 38) (Göttingen 1939).

------------, *Ego Eimi* (Göttingen 1939).

------------, *Gemeinde nach dem Neuen Testament* (Th St [B] 26) (Zürich 1949).

------------, *Gemeinde und Gemeindeordnung im Neuen Testament* (ATANT 35) (Zürich 1959).

SCOBIE, H.H., *John the Baptist* (London 1964).

SCOGNAMIGLIO, R., "La Vite e i Tralci; rilevanze sacramentali di Gv. 15,1-7 nella primitiva tradizione cristiana", *Nicolaus* 9 (1981) 399-413.

SCOTT, E.F., *The Fourth Gospel: Its Purpose and Theology* (Edinburgh 1906).

SEGALLA, G., "La Struttura Chiastica di Giov. 15,1-8", *BeO* 12 (1970) 129-131.

------------,*Giovanni* (Roma 1976).

------------,"Il discepolo che Gesù amava e la tradizione Giovannea", *Teologia* 14 (1989) 217-244.

SEGOVIA, F.F.,"The Theology and Provenance of John 15,1-17", *JBL* 101 (1982) 115-128.

------------, *Love Relationships in the Johannine Tradition* (SBLDS 58) (Chico 1982).

SHADIN, H., *Die Typologie des Johannesevangeliums* (Uppsala 1950).

SMITH, C.R.,"The Unfruitful Branches in Jo 15", *Grace Journal* 9 (1968) 3-22.

SPICQ, C., *Agapè dans le Nouveau Testament. Analyse des Textes* , Vol III (Paris 1959).

STÄHLIN, G., φιλέω, κτλ,in: *TDNT* IX, 113-171.

STÄLHIN, H., θρηνέω, θρῆνος, in: *TDNT* III, 148-155.

STANLEY, D.M.,"I am the Genuine Vine (Jn 15,1)", *BiTod* 1,8 (1963) 484-491.

STEELE, F.R.,"The Code of Lipit-Ishtar", *AJA* (1948) 425-450.

STENGER, W., "Die Auferweckung des Lazarus (Joh 11,1-45) - Vorlage und johanneische Redaktion", *TTZ* 83 (1974) 17-37.

STEVENS, C.T., "The 'I am' Formula in the Gospel of John", SBT 7, 2 (1977) 19-30.

STIMPFLE, A., *Blinde Sehen: Die Eschatologie im Traditiongeschichtlichen Prozess des Johannesevangeliums* (Berlin 1990).

STRATHMANN, H., *Il Vangelo Secondo Giovanni*, G. CECCHI (trs.) (Brescia 1973).

STRÖGER, A., "Die Lazaruserzählung - neu gesehen", *BLit* 59 (1986) 121-124.

SUGGIT, J.N., "The Raising of Lazarus", *ExpTim* 95 (1984) 106-108.

SWETE, H.B., "The Disciple whom Jesus Loved", *JTS* 17 (1916) 371-374.

SZLAGA, J., "Die literarische Struktur der Pericope über die Lazarus Auferweckung [Joh 11,1-44] und ihre theologische Funktion", *RoczTK* 27 (1980) 81-91.

TEEPLE, D.M., "Qumran and the Origin of the Fourth Gospel", *NT* 4 (1960) 6-25.

----------, *The Literary Origin of the Gospel of John* (Evaston 1974).

TEMPLE, S., *The Core of the Fourth Gospel* (London-Oxford 1975).

THILS, G., "De interpretatione Evangelii Sancti Johannis 13,18-30", *ColctMech* 28 (1939) 624-626.

THOMAS AQUINATIS, *Super Evangelium S. Ioannis Lectura*, P. RAPHAELIS CAI (ed.) (Roma 1952).

THORNECROFT, J.K., "The Redactor and the 'Beloved' in John", *ExpTim* 98 (1987) 135-139.

THUESING, W., *Die Erhöhung und Verherrlichung Jesu im Johannesevangelium* (Münster 1970).

THYEN, H., "Niemand hat grössere Liebe als die, dass er sein Leben für seine Freunde hingibt (Joh 15,13)", in: C. Andersen & G. Klein (eds.), *Theologia Crucis Signum Crucis*, Festschrift für Erich Dinkler zum 70. Geburtstag, (Tübingen 1979) 476-481.

THUREAU-DANGIN, F., *Die sumerischen und akkadischen Königsschriften* (Urukagina 1907).

TITUS, E.L., "The Dignity of the Beloved Disciple", *JBL* 69 (1950) 323-328.

------------, "The Identity of the Beloved Disciple", *JBL* 69 (1950) 325-328.

------------, *The Message of the Fourth Gospel* (New York 1957).

TOSATO, A., *Il Matrimonio nel Giudaismo antico e nel Nuovo Testamento* (Roma 1976).

-----------, *Il Matrimonio Israelitico* (Roma 1982).

TRUDINGER, L.P., "A 'Lazarus Motif' in primitive Christian Preaching", *AndNewtQuart* 7 (1966) 29-32.

------------, "The meaning of 'Life' in St. John. Some Further Reflections", *BTB* 6 (1976) 258-263.

-----------, "The Raising of Lazarus - A Brief Response", *DownRev* 94 (1976) 287-290.

TURNER, N., "Syntax", in: J.H. MOULTON, *A Grammar of New Testament Greek*, III (Edinburgh 1963).

UNGER, D., "A Note on John 19,25-27", *CBQ* 9 (1947) 111-112.

UNTERHASSMAIR, F.G., *Im Namen Jesu: Der Namensbegriff im Johannesevangelium* (Stuttgart 1973).

VAN DEN BUSSCHE, H., "La Vigne et ses fruits", *BVC* 26 (1959) 12-18.

-----------, "Le paroles de Dieu, Jean 3, 22-36", *BVC* 55 (1964) 23-28.

-----------, *Jean* (Bruges 1967).

VAN KASTEREN, R.P., "Jo 3, 29: Vox Sponsi", *RB* 3 (1894) 63-66.

VAN PRAAG, A., *Droit Matrimonial Assyro-Babylonien* (Amsterdam 1945).

VAN SELMS, A., "The Best Man and the Bride. From Sumer to St.John", *JNES* 9 (1950) 65-75.

VELLANICKAL, M., "'Discipleship' according to the Gospel of John", *Jeevadhara* 10 (1980) 131-147.

-----------, *Studies in the Gospel of John* (Bangalore 1982).
VON RAD, G., *Genesis: A Commentary* (Old Testament Library) (London 1985).

-----------, οὐρανός, in: *TDNT* V, 504-507.

VOUGA, F., "'Aimez-vous les uns les autres'. Une étude sur l'église de Jean", *BCPE* 26 (1974) 5-31.

-----------, *Le cadre historique et l'intention théologique de Jean* (Paris 1977).

WAEKER, A.J., "St.John's Gospel 3, 22-26", *ExpTim* 46 (1934-35) 380-381.

WAKEFIELD, G.S., *The Liturgy of St.John* (London 1985).

WALLACE, W.A.,"Friendship", *New Catholic Encyclopedia*, Vol VI (Washington 1967) 203-205.

WEISS, B., *Das Johannesevangelium* (Göttingen 1893).

WELLHAUSEN, J., *Das Evangelium Johannis* (Berlin 1908).

WENDLAND, P., *Die Urchristlichen Literaturformen* (HNT 1,3) (Tübingen 1912).

WENZ, H., "Sehen und Glauben bei Johannes", *TZ* 17 (1961) 17-25.

WESTCOTT, B.F., *The Gospel according to St.John*, A. Fox (ed.) (London 1958).

WESTERMANN, C., *Genesis 12-36: A Commentary*, J.J. SCULLION (tr.) (Minneapolis 1985).

WIKENHAUSER, A., *Das Evangelium nach Johannes* (Regensburg 1961).

WILCOX, M., "The 'Prayer' of Jesus in John XI. 41b-42", *NTS* 24 (1977) 128-132.

WILKENS, W., *Die Entstehungsgeschichte des vierten Evangeliums* (Zollikon 1958).

-----------,"Die Erweckung des Lazarus", *TZ* 15 (1959) 22-39.

WILSON, J., "The Integrity of John 3, 22-36", *JSNT* 10 (1981) 34-41.

WINK, W., *John the Baptist in the Gospel Tradition* (Cambridge 1968).

ZEVINI, G., "Gesù lo Sposo della Communita messianica (Jn 3, 29)", *PSV* 13 (1986) 105-117.

ZIENER, G., "Weisheitsbuch und Johannesevangelium", *Bib* 38 (1957) 396-418; 39 (1958) 37-60.

ZIMMERMANN, H., "Das Absolute Ego eimi als die neutestamentliche Offenbarungsformel", *BZ* 4 (1960) 266-276.

William Loader

The Christology of the Fourth Gospel
Structure and Issues
2nd, revised edition

Frankfurt/M., Berlin, Bern, New York, Paris, Wien, 1992. 314 pp.
Beiträge zur biblischen Exegese und Theologie – BET.
Edited by Jürgen Becker and Henning Graf Reventlow. Vol. 23
ISBN 3-631-44943-7   pb. DM 78.--

Christology is at the heart of the theology of the fourth gospel. Since Bultmann's impressive synthesis much has been written about its individual themes and motifs, its sources and history. The present study sets out to identify the basic structure of Johannine christology and to show how it underlies and integrates the various motifs and themes which surface in the transmitted text of the gospel. From the perspective gained through this analysis it re-examines the major issues of Johannine christology and their significance for understanding the gospel, both in its setting and in our own.

Contents: Identifying the Central Structure – Christological Issues: the Death of Jesus – Glorification and Exaltation – Salvation as Revelation? – 'Divine' Sonship – 'Human' Jesus – Gospel and History

From Reviews of the First Edition:
"... a thorough and full presentation ... a mine of information ..."
P. O'Brien in *Reformed Theological Review*
"... eine respektable Leistung ..."
R. Schnackenburg in *Biblische Zeitschrift*
"Voilà une étude magistrale ..."
X. Léon-Dufour in *Recherches de Science Religieuse*

Verlag Peter Lang Frankfurt a.M. · Berlin · Bern · New York · Paris · Wien
Auslieferung: Verlag Peter Lang AG, Jupiterstr. 15, CH-3000 Bern 15
Telefon (004131) 9411122, Telefax (004131) 9411131
– Preisänderungen vorbehalten –